Béla's Letters

Béla's Letters

by Jeff Ingber

Copyrighted Material

Béla's Letters

Copyright © 2016 by Jeff Ingber. All Rights Reserved.

No part of this publication may be reproduced, stored in a retrieval system or transmitted, in any form or by any means — electronic, mechanical, photocopying, recording or otherwise — without prior written permission from the publisher, except for the inclusion of brief quotations in a review.

For information about this title or to order other books and/or electronic media, contact the publisher:

Jeff Ingber
www.jeffingber.com
jingber@gmail.com

ISBN: 978-0-9854100-2-5
Printed in the United States of America

Cover design: Arielle Morris

*For Aunt Libu, Uncle Joe, Uncle Miki, Uncle Oli,
and all our family members who perished in the Holocaust.*

CONTENTS

Family Tree xii

Preface xvii

Chapter 1   *Magda Futo: December 12, 2010* 1

Chapter 2   *The Schnorer: 1928* 7

Chapter 3   *The Book of Job* 21

Chapter 4   *Jabotinsky: July 1934* 30

Chapter 5   *Jenő Ingber: August 17, 1936 (Prague)* 46

Chapter 6   *Ágnes Lőwie: December 9, 1937 (Kibbutz Degania Alef)* 49

Chapter 7   *Ágnes Lőwie: March 10, 1938 (Netanya)* 51

Chapter 8   *Feri's Bris: March 20, 1938* 52

Chapter 9   *The Newspaper Office* 68

Chapter 10 *The Csillag* 72

Chapter 11 *A Walk to the Shtiebel* 84

Chapter 12 *The Shivah: September 18, 1938* 90

Chapter 13 *November 1938: The Hungarians Return* 95

Chapter 14 Adolph Ingber: September 3, 1939 (Tel Aviv) . . . 101
Chapter 15 Jóska Ingber: October 4, 1940 (New York) 103
Chapter 16 Passover: April 22, 1941. 107
Chapter 17 The Walnut Tree 114
Chapter 18 The Sadist's Passions 124
Chapter 19 Home: September 1941 130
Chapter 20 The Hanging 145
Chapter 21 Miki Ingber: February 17, 1942 (Oroszvég) . . . 151
Chapter 22 The Colonel: Spring 1942 153
Chapter 23 Tetzi: October 17, 1942 166
Chapter 24 Marika 182
Chapter 25 Ferencz Ingber: October 26, 1942 (Southern Russia) . 188
Chapter 26 Libu Ingber: May 20, 1943 (Oroszvég). 189
Chapter 27 Sister Zsuzsa: June 1943 191
Chapter 28 Eszter Mermelstein Ingber: August 22, 1943 (Oroszvég) 208
Chapter 29 Picnic in Buda: September 3, 1943 210
Chapter 30 Cluj: October 1944 218
Chapter 31 Horthy's Speech 225
Chapter 32 The German Occupation 231
Chapter 33 The Destruction of Budapest Jewry 239
Chapter 34 Jóska Ingber: September 20, 1944 (Paris) 248
Chapter 35 Adolph Ingber: September 30, 1944 (Caen) 251
Chapter 36 Marika Leiner: March 7, 1945 (Budapest) 253

Chapter 37	*Return: March 1945*	256
Chapter 38	*Ecclesiastes*	266
Chapter 39	*My House*	271
Chapter 40	*Marriage: June 1945*	281
Chapter 41	*Dachau*	288
Chapter 42	*The Red Triangle: Summer 1945*	290
Chapter 43	*Bergen-Belsen*	301
Chapter 44	*Jóska Ingber: September 10, 1945*	303
Chapter 45	*Libu Ingber: September 22, 1945 (Helsingborg, Sweden)*	304
Chapter 46	*The Rape: September 1945*	306
Chapter 47	*Escape: October 1945*	319
Chapter 48	*Jóska Ingber: November 27, 1945 (New York)*	327
Chapter 49	*Libu Ingber: December 15, 1945 (Motor Ship Stig Gorthon)*	329
Chapter 50	*Italy: 1945–46*	331
Chapter 51	*Miki Ingber: October 12, 1946 (New York)*	346
Chapter 52	*The Bells of St. Mary's (October 1946)*	349
Chapter 53	*Libu Ingber: November 1, 1946 (New York)*	354
Chapter 54	*Miki Ingber: November 4, 1946 (New York)*	357
Chapter 55	*Jóska Ingber: December 7, 1946 (New York)*	359
Chapter 56	*Miki Ingber: January 27, 1947 (New York)*	361
Chapter 57	*Esther Malka*	363
Chapter 58	*Jóska Ingber: March 5, 1947 (New York)*	365
Chapter 59	*Oli Ingber: March 25, 1947 (London)*	367

Chapter 60	*Jóska Ingber: April 17, 1947 (New York)*	369
Chapter 61	*The Saturnia: May 1947*	371
Chapter 62	*Assimilation*	384
Chapter 63	*Oli Ingber: April 12, 1948 (London)*	393
Chapter 64	*Elmhurst*	395
Chapter 65	*Karpatalja Balls*	398
Chapter 66	*The Butcher Shop: November 1953*	401
Chapter 67	*Fleischmanns: Summer 1954*	413
Chapter 68	*Bingo Night*	425
Chapter 69	*A Son!*	435
Chapter 70	*Klari Nosti: 1956 (Budapest)*	438
Chapter 71	*The Trial: July 1961*	441
Chapter 72	*Eugene Schachter*	447
Chapter 73	*Uncle Joe Visits: June 1963*	452
Chapter 74	*Flushing Meadow: August 26, 1965*	457
Chapter 75	*Oli Arrives: September 1, 1966*	464
Chapter 76	*Mamaleh*	473
Chapter 77	*The New York Public Library: April 1969*	479
Chapter 78	*Yad Vashem: December 1977*	484
Chapter 79	*The Dream: May 20, 1979*	488
Chapter 80	*Eulogy: May 1981*	492
Chapter 81	*Aviva's Letter: August 12, 1986*	494
Chapter 82	*Clement Clarke Moore Homestead Park: June 1989*	498

Chapter 83	*Oli Ingber: April 30, 1990 (London)*	503
Chapter 84	*The Bar Mitzvah: October 4, 1997*	505
Chapter 85	*A Passionate Life: January 1998*	513
Chapter 86	*Final Letter: December 2002*	516
Chapter 87	*Bookend*	519
Acknowledgments		524
Selective Timeline		529
Bibliography		557

Descendants of KÁLMÁN and ESZTER INGBER

KÁLMÁN INGBER
B: 1882–Kielce, Poland
D: May 1944–Auschwitz

ESZTER MERMELSTEIN
B: 1884–Gdansk, Poland
D: May 1944–Auschwitz

ILONA INGBER
B: 1905–Munkács
D: May 1944–Auschwitz

JOSEPH HAUPT
B: Sept 1899–Chust
D: Circa 1970–Israel

FERENCZ INGBER
B: Dec 21 1908–Munkács
D: Unknown

ROSA FEUERSTEIN
B: Unknown
D: May 1944–Auschwitz

JENŐ INGBER
B: Sept 10, 1906–Munkács
D: Jan 1942–Mauthausen

JÓSKA INGBER
B: Dec 12, 1910–Munkács
D: May 29, 1989–New York

SUZANNE MILLER
B: April 27, 1919 –Skierniewice, Poland
D: Nov 5, 2002–New York

FERI HAUPT
B: March, 1938–Munkács
D: May 1944–Auschwitz

ANDRÁS INGBER
B: 1941–Munkács
D: May 1944–Auschwitz

KENNETH ALBERT INGBER
B: Sep 8, 1947–New York

MARCEL HAUPT
B: Jan 1943–Munkács
D: May 1944–Auschwitz

DEBORAH LEA INGBER
B: June 20, 1959–New York

KÁLMÁN INGBER
B: 1882–Kielce, Poland
D: May 1944–Auschwitz

ESZTER MERMELSTEIN
B: 1884–Gdansk, Poland
D: May 1944–Auschwitz

ADOLPH ("OLI") INGBER
B: Mar 21, 1915–Munkács
D: Jan 7, 1998–London

MARY MCVADY
B: Mar 26, 1921–London
D: August 25, 1989–London

ERZSÉBET ("LIBU") INGBER
B: Jan 12, 1925–Munkács
D: Oct 2012–Florida

MIKLÓS HERMEL
B: Oct 24, 1916–Beregszaz, Hungary
D: May 2013–Florida

BÉLA INGBER
B: Feb 15 1913–Munkács
D: Nov 6 2003–New York

MARIKA LEINER
B: Dec 27, 1925–Budapest

MIKI INGBER
B: Aug 23, 1922–Munkács
D: May 6, 1981–New York

INGE MITCHELL
B: Dec 25, 1924–Berlin
D: Feb 10, 2004–New York

ESTHER MALKA INGBER
B: Feb 11, 1947–Rome

ILONA INGBER
B: Oct 13, 1947–London

BARBARA ELLEN INGBER
B: Jan 28, 1954–New York

JEROME JOEL HERMEL
B: Sept 15, 1950–New York

JEFFREY FRED INGBER
B: Sep 26, 1954–New York

SUSAN INGBER
B: Aug 8, 1956–London

RONALD COLMAN INGBER
B: Nov 1, 1957–New York

EVELYN LEAH HERMEL
B: May 27, 1956–New York

Ingber family, circa 1928
Back row (from left): Adolph, Béla, Ilona, and Ferencz
Front row (from left): Jenő, Eszter, Libu, Miki, Kálmán, and Jóska

PREFACE

*There are stars whose radiance is visible
on Earth though they have long been extinct.
There are people whose brilliance continues to light
the world even though they are no longer among the living.
These lights are particularly bright when the night is dark.
They light the way for humankind.*
—Hannah Szenes

At first, I envied my father's proficiency in languages, appreciating only later that his mastery of tongues had been crucial to our existence. Béla Ingber conversed in Hungarian with my mother, discoursed in Yiddish with fellow congregants, grumbled in German when complaining of a late reparations payment, passed the time in Russian or Czech with landsmen during summers in the Catskills, and gossiped in Italian and Polish with coworkers at a sheet metal factory in Long Island City. Not to mention the daily prayers in Hebrew. Being linguistically challenged, I whined when he spoke in any language but English, particularly when I sensed that I was the subject of the conversation.

Dad was born in Oroszvég, a suburb of Munkács (pronounced "Moon-Katch"), a centuries-old city nestled in a lush valley split by a lazy river that curls from the jagged Carpathian Mountains to the Danube. Now a part of Ukraine, Munkács is an easy drive from four other nations—Hungary, Poland, Romania, and Slovakia—in a locale that has long been an ethnic hodgepodge.

For most of its recorded history, Munkács belonged to the Kingdom of Hungary and remained profoundly Hungarian in nationalist tradition, a binding tie that would reach its inglorious zenith during my father's lifetime—and then shatter. Although Dad technically was born in Hungary, he proudly considered himself a Czech. In 1919, when he was six years old, following World War I and the breakup of the Austro-Hungarian Empire, the region surrounding Munkács (known as Ruthenia—because one of its major ethnic groups was the Rusyns, also called Ruthenians—or the "Rus") was encased within the newly established Republic of Czechoslovakia. Hence the joke about the man who was born in the Austro-Hungarian Empire, grew up in Czechoslovakia, married in Hungary, raised a family in the Soviet Union, and died in Ukraine, all without leaving his village.

As I grew up in Queens in the 1960s, my father regaled me with stories of his childhood. Lacking running water, several families shared a communal well and hand pump, requiring the relentless lugging of pails of water using a plank fitted with a special neck device. They had no electricity or appliances, not even an icebox. My grandmother sewed on a foot-cranked machine illuminated by a kerosene lamp. Most food was home grown, with milk fresh from its source. Clothes were handed down until threadbare. In the warm months, children were bathed in wooden tubs in the Latorica River. Horses and wagons were critical, as were skis. For half the year, bitter cold permeated the house. Blanket-wrapped family members retired to bed early while logs still fed the fireplace's flames. And though education was prized, scant money was available for books or school supplies.

Preface

Ensconced in our apartment and surrounded by modern comforts, I asked for details about the Old Country. "Dad, did you have to go outside to pee even when it was really cold?" "Dad, how did you cook your food?" No matter what the answer, its remembrance was cloaked in reverence, recited with compassion for my misfortune in not having been nurtured by those unknowable times.

These reminiscences were recounted with a vividness that belied the decades that had passed. All his days, my father embraced a love, frozen in time, of a world vanished yet ever present. Essential to his yearning was a spirituality based on worship not of G-d but of family, and of the timeless traditions that guided their lives.

Munkács and Judaism were intertwined. Jews had flourished there for ages, and the Munkács Jewish community, known for its religious fervor, was the largest one in the Rus. The city's municipal library offered a section overloaded with Yiddish and Hebrew manuscripts. On the Sabbath and Jewish holidays, most stores were closed. After services, the narrow streets and courtyards of the city center were filled with the observant in their prayer shawls and traditional garb.

By the beginning of World War II, Munkács' Jewish population neared 14,000, close to half of the city's total residents (an extraordinarily high percentage for a European city). They fought, derided, condemned, gossiped, and cursed each other, while forming a vibrant society that allowed for varying approaches to devoutness and fulfillment. Gradually, their differences were eroded, then erased.

When the end arrived, the community was bound in anguish. Some of the clan would survive, cheating death repeatedly to do so. For each of them, the comforting rituals of a traditional Jewish household had unraveled. Amid the world's betrayal, trust lay only with blood. One's brother would remain one's brother. Not even G-d, who appeared to have looked away, was as certain.

Béla's Letters

The letters and postcards that the family members wrote to each other, undeterred by the feasibility of delivery, were their lifeline. Those documents, evidence of a resilient family dynamic that the Holocaust could not fracture, remained of such sustenance to my father that he preserved many and carried them to the New World. Following his death, I discovered this treasure and was compelled to uncover these buried voices.

Most of the Ingber correspondence was in a longhand I would have found undecipherable in any language, resembling a doctor's script growing smaller at the edges to fill every inch of yellowed and crumbling paper. Fortunately, I found Magda, the one whose talents and intuition would unlock all secrets.

CHAPTER 1
Magda Futo: December 12, 2010

G-d employs several translators; some pieces are translated by age, some by sickness, some by war, some by justice; but G-d's hand is in every translation...

—John Donne

The sadness is not that I will have lost my profession. I am too old for this concern. Rather, I worry about the disappearance of the personal letter, ever rich with detail and nuance, and the prospect of words that the writer would not dare speak in person. Its fading will diminish the capacities to convey the fullness of our lives and to meaningfully preserve our histories.

My own story is mundane. I was born in Veszprém, a medieval town not far from Budapest, where I moved to as a child. At university, I received degrees in chemistry and physics, and was employed in various research labs for years. But gnawing at me was an unfulfilled love for English literature, which drove me to learn to appreciate novels in the language in which they were written.

Opportunity arose in 1992, when an American company purchased my husband's, transferring us to the United States with our two children. I suffered from troubles with my hip and was seeking to work from home. My husband suggested I try translation, an esteemed profession in Hungary, whose insular language is spoken only by a tiny percentage of the world's population. Some of our greatest writers, like Vörösmarty and Petőfi, were translators of Shakespeare and others.

My son, a computer engineer, created a Web site and set up dual monitors, allowing me to simultaneously review text and translate. Actually, while I call myself a "translator," that is a touch imprecise, as every translation should be acknowledged as an interpretation. (Thus, I use "translator" and "interpreter" interchangeably.) What is integral is the ability to transform expressions and concepts created in one language into another while preserving the integrity of the context and shades of intent.

As a Lutheran, I accept that the Father Almighty chose this path for me. That I am to do my good works by serving as a voice for others—although on many days, while laboring on tedious matters such as legal documents, I am less assured of this. But then there arise magical moments when handwritten family letters are presented to me. To be let into their inner circle, and serve as the magnifying echo of these distant lives, is humbling.

I've been told that the Talmud teaches, "A dream not interpreted is like a letter not read." I am no expert at understanding dreams, but letters can require a similar level of analysis and explanation. And often I face my task with fewer clues than can be obtained from oral communication, where one has the benefit of tone and facial expression. When someone speaks, one also has the advantage of knowing which words they've stressed.

I drifted into my line of work too late, cursed by the imperatives of the modern era of ubiquitous social media outlets. In an era before

Chapter 1

copy machines, letters received would be copied by hand and forwarded to other family members and friends. Correspondence was so vital that those struggling with separation obsessed about the act of writing itself. "I did write." "I will write." "I just received your letter...." To this day, Hungarians, if they craft a letter, may end it with "Now I am finishing my lines." As though apologizing for not writing more.

We must interpret the written word to know the past and to complete our identities. In that sense, all human knowledge and experience arises from translation.

The first interpreters were the prophets, who revealed divinely given messages to their people and understood that there are as many ways of interpreting the word of G-d as there are sparks in a raging fire, with each version representing one facet of the entire truth. It may be argued that the Jewish people, cast into the Diaspora for two thousand years, would not have been able to maintain their religion if not for the translation of the holy books from Hebrew into whatever was the language of their adopted country.

Martin Luther, the first to convert the New Testament to German, and a patron saint of translators, taught that every passage of Scripture has one straightforward meaning: that the Bible is the Word of G-d and to be taken literally. I must admit that this approach runs contrary to my belief that interpretation is an art and that there is no absolute rendition of a writing. The subtleties are significant and the choices diverse. The selection of a single word over another can influence the context of an entire writing. Nor can one ignore the sound of the language. When I interpret, I don't only decide on words—often I speak them aloud. They need to be logical to the tongue as well as to the mind.

And, as with any art form, the performer's own essence influences his work. So the writer must be deciphered along with his language. I'm obligated to search beyond the words and past the connection that the author seeks to make with the reader, to the nuances created by her own personality. And you, as the ultimate reader, should judge my psyche, as I can understand others only through my own limited perceptions. So interpretation adds its own layer of opaqueness. An exasperating notion, no?

The ancient scriptural interpreters assumed that the texts they worked on were cryptic. That remains a safe supposition for those in my profession. To interpret a letter properly, one must first amass and assess various facts. I take into account the time period, the local dialect, the background of the reader and writer, and the level and depth of their relationship. And I approach handwritten documents differently from typed ones. Scripting a letter forces the writer to focus more, because your hand tires, and you don't want to keep erasing or crossing out. You are writing less but portraying more.

The interpreter's talent as a detective is not as challenged for diaries, where the writer is prone to introspection and revelation. But letter writers are more manipulative and inhibited, and the apparent message can obscure truths. For example, a document may appear to be composed by the husband. It's even signed with his name. But there are clues that indicate it's his wife who is responsible for the text.

And the correspondence may have been censored, in which case you had to stick to mundane matters. When reading the postcards sent from Munkács by Béla's mother and siblings in 1943, I was mindful that the authors needed to be careful not to cross a certain line.

When I convert a letter to English, I do so as a native Hungarian would. Hungarian is such an expressive language. For example, "siblings" in Hungarian is "testvérek," which literally means "body-bloods" (from the same body and blood). This is a much more beautiful word than the English equivalent. Another example is that no one, especially in the old days, would say, "My health is fine." They would say, "Thanks be to the good G-d that my health is fine." And they

Chapter 1

would abbreviate that to "H. I.," which is short for "hála istennek," meaning "thanks be to G-d." "H. I." came to be used for giving thanks for other positive developments, such as "My business is doing fine" or "We had a healthy baby."

We have varied ways of addressing each other, based on the nature of the relationship and level of politeness and familiarity required. When you meet someone you esteem, the traditional greeting is "Kezét csókolom," which means "I kiss your hand." Nowadays, it is simply "Csókolom," or "I kiss you."

The arrival of the Ingber letters was rejuvenating. At first, I was a voyeur, uncomfortable with their frankness. Over time, I became an acquaintance, enriched and absorbed by their stories. In their correspondence, particularly after the war, the family members habitually meddled, complained, and questioned motives, to the point of insult. But there was never a scent of the cardinal sin of indifference. Each letter's end reaffirmed eternal devotion.

Six months were required to complete the translations. I would concentrate on a letter for a while, become frustrated, set it aside, and come back to it days later. The difficulties were innumerable, the advances often incremental. Certain letters had pages from one mixed up with others, which was not surprising, given similarities in script and paper quality. Many lacked dates. Some pages were torn or contained holes. Others had their last page missing, leaving the writer's identity a mystery to be solved. Because of space limitations, ends of sentences at times were crammed into the corners of a page. I fought through wet spots that had left blotches and faded ink. So intense was the concentration needed, that one day, after finding myself irritated that I could not understand certain Hungarian words, I let out a laugh upon realizing that they were in English.

Poor handwriting was my greatest challenge. One brother, Adolph, had penmanship so terrible—as if a goose had tiptoed around the page after traipsing in the mud—that I threatened to charge more for translating his letters. But that was offset by Erzsébet, the baby of the family, who suffered so. The short version of her name is Erzsi, but her parents called her "Libuka," which transformed into "Libu." She had a gorgeous script, with consistent slopes and spacing. It is perhaps childish of me, but I am tempted to attribute inner beauty to a person merely as a reflection of her handwriting. And there was a splendor to her words, which made literal translation readily faithful to the meaning.

The survivors lost both parents, their mother country, their youth, their health, and their innocence. Each coped distinctively, but none wallowed in hatred or bitterness. I identified with them all, but, by the end of my work, one was most special to me. Béla. Even though his own letters were not available, I had followed the road map to his heart. His pain was palpable. He clung to the correspondence as his salve. And thus I was let into his life—a life that now will be told in his words.

CHAPTER 2
The Schnorer: 1928

*It's not G-d that I do not accept, you understand;
it is this world of G-d's, created by G-d, that
I do not accept and cannot agree to accept.*

—Fyodor Dostoyevsky

My Papa, Kálmán, made a living trading in horses and cattle, often buying the latter from local ranches for shipment to slaughterhouses. Each of my brothers inherited his gift of entrepreneurship. I, Béla, did not.

Setting the pattern was Jenő, the oldest. Taking advantage of Czechoslovakia's freedom of the press, Jenő had earned respect throughout Eastern Europe as a reporter and writer of a weekly editorial that was sold to various newspapers.

But the supreme businessman in our family was Ferencz, the second-oldest brother, who earned commercial success in the face of significant challenge. The Carpathian Mountains stretch 1,500 kilometers across the breadth of Central and Eastern Europe. Although not as lofty as the neighboring Alps, they're dense with the vitality of dark forests, sparkling lakes, rushing rivers, lush vegetation, and diverse wildlife. In my youth, only a limited number of passes crossed through the Rus's white-capped peaks. In this isolated region, the harsh daily life was dictated by the seasons. Heavy rains and snowmelt turned the unpaved streets into thick rivers of mud that would suck into their maw pedestrians, horses, and vehicles. And World War I ravaged the Munkács region. Representatives of the American Jewish Joint Distribution Committee (known as the "Joint") who visited the Rus in 1919 encountered widespread starvation, disease, and poor sanitation and medical facilities, expressing life there as "lamentable beyond description."

Not that my hometown was a *shtetl*. By the early twentieth century, Munkács had restaurants, theaters, publishing houses, and hotels. Other modern facilities, including a movie house where a piano player accompanied the picture, soon would follow. Most of the town's shopkeepers were Jewish. The well-to-do owned lumber, textile, or brick factories, although much of the local population labored long hours at low-paying, physically demanding jobs such as sheep herding and woodcutting.

Ferencz, while still young, had initiated several ventures, one of which was a travel agency. "Entrepreneurship," he insisted, "is all about grasping life's overtures, which often appear only in a flash." One of Ferencz's fruitful forays was joining forces with Yaakov Pollack.

Pollack, an adherent of the local Vizhnitzer rebbe, operated a general-goods store on Bereksas Street. Flour, beans, fabric, boots, pots and pans, hardware, toiletries, soft drinks, tobacco products, newspapers—all could be found in his shop. Over the years, he expanded the size of his establishment and the variety and quality of merchandise offered. Originally he was a seller only of dry goods; by the 1920s local farmers were peddling their animals and perishable

Chapter 2

produce at Pollack's for cash or bartering them for shovels, picks, harnesses, and the like.

My brother and Pollack developed an anomalous partnership. Pollack was burdened with a family of eight, including his submissive wife, whereas my brother was unattached when they began their affiliation. Pollack, a creature of habit and comfort, departed from Munkács only reluctantly, while Ferencz suffered from wanderlust. Pollack memorized his accounts receivable (many regular customers were farmers who settled their bills only after harvesting their crops) and kept meticulous track of all purchases made on credit, while Ferencz delighted in ambiguity, freely delegating. Ferencz would draw to an inside straight, while Pollack would fold with two pair. Each enjoyed the pursuit of money, although, with Ferencz, the lust was in his head more than his heart.

When I was fifteen, at the request of my brother, Pollack interviewed me for a job, squeezing in a couple of minutes between servicing customers.

"Ferencz tells me that you're a good boy, and a hard worker."

"Yes, sir, I am."

His cow eyes sized me up, while his face displayed an exaggerated frown. "Are you clever like your brother?"

"No, sir. But smart enough, I think."

Pollack nodded. "So, you're cocky like your brother. Well, at least he has reason to be. Did you know that, when Ferencz wasn't much older than you are now, he would travel as far away as Prague to *hondel* (bargain) with manufacturers to ship their goods to Munkács for resale? He convinced a Prague bank to ensure my creditworthiness. Yes, a business *gaon* (genius) he is."

"I'm not surprised to hear that, sir."

"Béla, are you *frum* (religious)?"

How best to answer this? I told the truth. "Yes, sir, but not like you are."

Pollack burst into laughter. "Good, because I can't afford to have someone working here who's too observant."

I was hired, although being Ferencz's brother didn't elevate my status. We clerks were expected to be docile quarter horses that would trot in any direction Pollack pointed us toward.

Pollack also had in his employ a "*Shabbos* Goy," who on Saturdays and holidays cleared snow, lit fires to heat the store, and kept watch. Tóni Endre was a husky, everlastingly cheerful simpleton several years older than me, who lived diagonally across the street from the store and was a chanter in the local Russian Orthodox Church. Pollack valued Tóni's loyalty and continually cemented their bond with favors.

On a languid Friday afternoon in early November, Pollack and I were in the back of the store. Amid empty produce boxes and piles of lined books containing inked tax records and customers' accounts, we were unloading cartons of German cigarettes known as "Engelhardts." Manning the front counter was my classmate, Ágnes Lőwie, who, in place of precise manners and expertise, offered customers a contagious smile wrapped in innocence.

Also working for Pollack was Tetzi Judka, one year my junior, who lived at the bottom of our curved road. Her family and mine were part of a community whose homes were open to all, no invitation needed. Long-limbed, with protruding front teeth that would later remind me of Eleanor Roosevelt, Tetzi was a gazelle on cross-country skis, faster than the boys her age and many of the older ones. She worked mostly in the snowy months to deliver goods, when the store's tarpaulin-covered horse-drawn wagon became immobilized, or to make collections from customers.

Winter had chased away the fall early that year, the weather characterized by a perpetual, penetrating chill that brutalized one's equilibrium on the brightest of days. Flurries were floating down from a pewter nimbus layer, heartlessly adding to the half-foot eiderdown

Chapter 2

of shimmering snow numbing the world we had awakened to. Tetzi grabbed bamboo poles with faded leather hand straps and slipped into her wooden skis, her feet mounted to them only at the toe. She sped off for a final delivery of canned goods to an elderly couple.

Each Friday, Pollack wore an open-faced gold Omega pocket watch on a chain looped over his buttoned vest. When he wasn't winding the watch meticulously, as if testing the combination to a safe, Pollack would glance at its hands obsessively, as it was his custom to squeeze in time for a stop at the *mikveh* (ritual bath) for spiritual cleansing after closing the store early and before returning home.

Ágnes emerged from the front. "Mr. Pollack, there's a *schnorer* here to see you."

"Tell him I'm not here," Pollack boomed.

With a frozen stare, Ágnes replied, "But I told him you were."

Pollack grimaced, maintaining his composure to ward off hysteria from Ágnes. He commanded, "Help Béla," and stomped out.

The appearance of a *schnorer*, who these days would be called a "beggar," although that scarcely conveys the sophistication of the profession, was unusual only in that they normally visited residences. *Schnorers* were common in Munkács, familiar figures who had, in effect, been assigned households to visit. Many were orthodox men who hawked copies of their religious commentaries. The most gifted among them exuded a sense of entitlement and privilege, assuming an air of respectability that broadcast his deliberate choice of that lifestyle, much as one would resolve to become a tailor or a dentist. Whether asking only for a one-*pengő* silver coin for a meal or cajoling for a large sum of money for a daughter's engagement, a *schnorer* would negotiate with the donor and might chide him condescendingly, to the point of calling his benefactor a *gonif* (thief) for shaming him with too meager a gift.

Motioning to Ágnes to keep quiet, I snuck into an alcove that afforded a view of the front. Ágnes tiptoed behind me, peering around my neck as though snipers might be in the distance. In front of the counter, by a carbon-black kitchen scale with chrome weights, stood a middle-aged man, shoulders slumped, wearing a dark wool suit, a tie, and boots, a soiled, soaked overcoat draped over his arm. Faded flakes of snow clung to the tip of his nose. His worn skis were leaning near the entrance.

"Good afternoon, Mr. Pollack," he said.

"Do I know you?"

"We met once before. I'm Tetzi's father, László. László Judka."

"Tetzi isn't here," Pollack grumbled.

"I know. I saw her leave." Judka slouched lower, head hung forward, his body collapsing in on itself.

"I'm a busy man, Mr. Judka. What can I do for you?"

"Mr. Pollack, I wouldn't come to you if I had any other choice. I've been to the Chevra Tzedakah Vachesed (the Society for Charity and Kindness), but...."

"It isn't sufficient that I hired your daughter?"

Raising his fatigued eyes to meet Pollack's, Judka responded, "I am very grateful for that, Mr. Pollack. And I don't want to take advantage. It's just that *Shabbos* is here, and we have little to eat. I am no longer employed at the brickyard."

"Why don't you use Tetzi's money?"

"You are a good man to have hired my daughter, Mr. Pollack. Her money helps but doesn't go far enough. We recently sold our animals. If you could spare some food, I will pay you back as soon as I can."

Pollack's upstretched eyebrows translated to, "How might you be able to repay me?"

Judka clarified. "I would be pleased to help in your store to satisfy my debt."

Pollack cocked his head sideways and then pulled it back. "Maybe you should run the store, Mr. Judka. And I can borrow what I need from you."

Chapter 2

Judka hesitated. "I will not rest until I've found a job. I'm a good worker."

Only the back of Pollack's head was visible to me (obesity had eliminated his neck), which glowed crimson, with his few remaining hairs standing upright. In the seconds of stillness that followed, as if we were in a camera shot, Pollack vacillated between dark shadows and enlightenment until his heart rebalanced. He reached for an empty cardboard box underneath the counter. Controlling his speech as if responding to a business offer, he said, "Mr. Judka, please help yourself to those canned goods and vegetables you will need for a proper *Shabbos* meal."

Tetzi's father grasped the carton and mechanically gathered a few items from a nearby shelf, his rigidity a denial of any pleasure in the act. He placed the box on the chipped counter while buttoning his coat and tucked the box under his arm, clutching his skis with his free, winter-blistered hand. As Judka left, he murmured over his shoulder, "I'm truly sorry to have bothered you, Mr. Pollack. I am very appreciative. Please don't tell Tetzi that I was here. *Gut Shabbos.*"

"*Gut Shabbos* to you, Mr. Judka."

When the front door closed, Pollack slammed his fist on the counter. "I have my own mouths to feed and keep warm." Ágnes and I shot to our posts. Pollack stormed in and scowled at her. "You don't recognize Tetzi's father?"

"I never met him."

"Why did you tell me he was a *schnorer*?"

"I thought…he was," she stammered.

"Idiot! You should have given him some money from the *pishka* (charity box) and not involved me." He jabbed his plump forefinger in her direction. "Get back to the counter."

Ágnes fled, sobbing, leaving Pollack and me to recommence stacking cigarettes. Spewing out a curse (his standard one, to the effect of, "Why

13

bother getting up alive?"), Pollack tore open one of the cartons. With yellow-tinted fingers, he jammed the wrong end of a cigarette into his mouth before correcting it. Pollack pulled an adjacent chair beneath him, the curve of his hips parenthesizing narrow legs, drew deeply on the cigarette, and glared as though contemplating a physical attack.

"Béla, what do you wish for?" He threw his arms out theatrically. "You want to be a prosperous businessman? You want a store like this? How about a house with indoor plumbing? A good bank account? A wife? Many children?" His volume undulated as he emphasized the last word of each question.

Pollack blew a stream of smoke through his nostrils, stinging my eyes. He leaned closer, near his toppling point.

"Maybe a close relationship with the rebbe? A seat up front on the High Holidays? I'll throw in acknowledgment as a Hebrew scholar. Respect from family and friends. And from the entire Vizhnitzer community. Would that be enough?"

I had asked my father whether Chassids were better Jews than we were because they understood the Torah as a divine revelation, complete and immutable, and were committed to living by it. Chuckling, Papa explained that the devout find His divine spirit even in the most common occurrences. They regard every morning sky, whether threatening or endlessly clear, as His gift. They remain humble, questioning to understand, not to challenge. But, he had added, many Chassids had lost their way, not accepting that Judaism requires constant transformation and renewal.

Without stopping the cigarette stacking, I replied, "My father told me that you are a successful and distinguished man, Mr. Pollack."

He wrinkled his boxer's nose and pulled down his bushy eyebrows. "Your father knows nothing. NOTHING." With his index finger, he flung the extinguished butt across the room, landing it under a poster, taped crookedly to the wall, of a silhouetted man in a tuxedo, lighting

Chapter 2

up. "Some days, I would trade what I have, all that I've worked for, just to sleep late. In an empty house, with no one to wake me." Pollack, in the grip of his fantasy, halted and glanced upward. "Relax in bed in my underwear with a newspaper. Suck down a cigar or two. And a bottle of apricot *Pálinka*. Lie outside if it's warm. Sit and take a shit, for as long as I want. Do all that again the next day. And the next. Without speaking to a single person."

Pollack softly exhaled more smoke, this time uncurling from his mouth; then he cooed, "That's all I want, Béla. You can have the rest." He smirked, "Would your father still think I'm distinguished?" Standing to don his fur-lined coat, he turned up the black lamb collar and headed for the back door. "*Boychik*, please close shop for me. And be sure to wish your papa a *Gut Shabbos* from me."

I joined Ágnes behind the counter, her lustrous eyes now red and glossy.

"Is he going to fire me, Béla?"

"Of course not."

"What did he say about me?"

"Nothing, Ágnes. Honest. He just went on and on complaining about how tired and unhappy he is."

"And you told him to keep it to himself, right?" she winked.

Although a touch zaftig, Ágnes was alluring, with midnight-black hair that fell past her shoulders, pillowy lips, arching eyebrows, and hazel eyes that changed color with the surrounding light (she and I shared that attribute, which later would help convince her that we were soul mates). I fantasized about telling her that she was the most beautiful woman in Munkács.

I had never been alone with her in the store and felt lightheaded, as I had months ago while attempting to smoke an entire cigarette. "Ágnes, do you want to switch places? You can work in the back until you're less upset. I'll watch the front."

She arched her back and crossed her arms beneath the swell of her breasts. "Who made you the boss?" she playfully responded.

Her smile was inviting. I reached for her hand, the first time I had ever touched her on purpose. My intention was to hold onto it. Instead, I merely brushed the top skin, our hands two blossoms quivering in the wind.

Ágnes observed me as though I were a child in her care, innocently exploring a world brand new. Sensing my hammering heart, she planted a kiss on my cheek, letting its moisture slowly bleed from her lips and bewitching me with a thirst that would take years to be quenched.

Not long after, before the steam whistle of the communal *mikveh* announced the coming of the Sabbath, Ágnes left, and I locked up, shuttering the windows and slipping a wood bar over the back door. Racing to Oroszvég, first on skis and then on foot, I burst into the house to find Mama by the dining room table, with three-year-old Libu and six-year-old Miki at her sides. Papa and my brothers had left for *shul* (synagogue).

Wearing an apron over her traditional cotton ankle-length dress, her head and shoulders were covered by an ivory hand-crocheted shawl. Two loaves of *challah*, each braided, sprinkled with poppy seeds, and brushed with egg yolk prior to baking to provide sheen, sat on a table, covered with an embroidered cloth. A *pishka* was perched on a side table. Mama would add a few *fillér* (Hungarian pennies) to it before the start of each Sabbath. Next to the charity box was a rusted tray upon which she would drop spent matches.

Mama's candle-lighting ritual, required to be completed before sundown, is a childhood memory that, despite my fading power of recall, I can readily summon. Libu's birth had added a tenth candle to the squat silver holder that lay on the side table. After lighting the final one, Mama would stretch her hands out over the red-orange

Chapter 2

edges of the flames and slowly move them inward three times in a circular motion. Then she would cover her eyes with her palms and recite the blessing. Silent prayer would follow, as she gently rocked from side to side, moving her lips, often weeping. During each of the countless times I observed her conduct this rite, as she drew in the glow, it enveloped me, like a warm bath.

"Béla, you're late," Mama said, laying down her unstruck match. "Hurry and get dressed for *shul*."

"Mama, I need to tell you something."

Under the vanishing light, vacillating as though the day and night were struggling to co-exist, I recounted the tale of Pollack and Judka, leaving aside Pollack's diatribe. Mama listened without comment, snatched an oil lamp, and pulled me and my siblings to the cellar. We found an empty container and, working together, filled the bottom with eggs, cushioned by layers of straw. Climbing back upstairs, we came into a room dark enough for a single lit match to make it glow.

"Mama, the candles!"

While picking up the match box, Mama instructed me, "Leave the eggs in front of their house. Do not knock on the door. Try to be as quiet as possible and not let anyone see you."

Oroszvég had no outside lights then, only candle lanterns dangling from trees, but I benefited from a luminous moon that hung like a spotlight adrift, its reflection bouncing off the glazed snow drifts. During my shuffle down the street, which ended where the sky began, I passed a three-ball snowman with arm branches standing guard, whose coal eyes followed me. Several neighbors on their way to *shul* beheld me with furrowed eyebrows but asked no questions, merely conveying good wishes. I dropped off the box and headed home. Overtaking a family on a horse-drawn sleigh whose oiled runners marked gentle paths, Tetzi bounded up on her skis. I waved to her but kept trudging.

"Hey, slowpoke, looking for me?" she shouted.

"See you on Sunday," I yelled back.

Back inside my house, candlewax drippings had formed finger-like white roots on a table where my clothes had been laid out. I hurriedly changed, tucking my pants inside scuffed leather boots.

During the High Holidays, we would attend the Gross Beis Midrash, one of the two great synagogues of Munkács—so massive that white storks with pointed red beaks nested in its towers—where I would stand among hundreds, overstimulated and unseen. But on most mornings and weekends, particularly in the colder months, Papa preferred the nearby *shtiebel*, an expanded house with rooms set aside by the homeowner for prayer. Men congregated in the main living room, with a makeshift altar up front surrounded by metal folding chairs and wood benches. Women were designated to an adjoining foyer.

Papa bowed and swayed in prayer every morning, insisting that to do otherwise is to invite apathy and feelings of entitlement. Intoning melancholy *Shacharit* psalms while wearing his multicolored *tallis* (fringed shawl) and leather *tefillin* (phylacteries), each kept in a cabinet, he would begin his daily spiritual ascension.

On Fridays, he returned to the *shtiebel* at night. During every Sabbath eve service, the congregation would chant the Kabbalistic hymn *Lekha Dodi* (Come, My Beloved), its tender melody a seamless vehicle for transitioning to the upcoming day of rest. With their heads wrapped in shawls and eyes shut, each word was sung as if it were an ingredient of a miracle. Upon reaching the last verse, the tune slows as the entire congregation rises and turns to the open door to greet the "Shabbos Queen." Which is precisely when I arrived.

Kálmán Ingber stood in his usual spot near the front. Stocky and taut, he was forty-six years of age. His beard, which he meticulously trimmed each day with a pair of thinning scissors, was now specked with touches of silver. His hairline had receded in a manner that I would inherit.

Chapter 2

Papa was sandwiched between Jóska and Adolph, my brothers closest in age to me. Each one flashed me a wicked grin. As I stood before a nearby seat, Papa burned me with his gunmetal eyes. I leaned toward him to explain, but he held up his palm and returned to his *siddur* (prayer book).

I rehearsed my defense during the hour-long service, which I lip-synched through while in an underwater chamber of my thoughts, and the serenade of *Gut Shabbos* greetings among the congregants that concluded it. Outside, I rushed to Papa and, again, he cut me off with a raised hand.

"How dare you come late to the service."

"But Papa, there was a reason…."

"You've embarrassed me. In front of the entire congregation."

Papa strode away from me, stone-faced. I hustled to remain at his side and persisted in reciting my tale. Babbling without reflection, I failed to notice my father's shift in demeanor. He signaled for my brothers to walk ahead, then draped his arm around me.

"All right, Béla, I understand now. I'm sorry I didn't let you explain."

"You're not mad at me?"

He sighed. "You're still so young. No, I'm proud of you. We do not honor G-d by mindlessly following His laws. Sometimes they conflict, and we must understand which take priority."

"But they told us in *cheder* that every commandment is to be strictly obeyed," I responded. When I turned six years old, I had begun two years of study at a school, run by the Munkáczer rebbe, that taught Hebrew prayers, the *Chumash* (the five books of Moses), and the Talmud. Starting every morning at 6 a.m., in a spartan room, up to thirty boys sat on benches surrounding a long table ringed by oil lanterns. The teacher, a rabbi, sat at the head of the table, demanding and armed with a bamboo switch. Asking a question that bordered on doubting or was insufficiently respectful of G-d would be met with a swift slap.

Papa had long warned me that Judaism offers few absolute truths. Its secrets were revealed through lifelong personal learning and introspection. "Whoever told you that is a fool. Piousness requires deep understanding. The commandments are best viewed as a framework. Their aim is to point us to a higher moral code." He squeezed my shoulder, the pressure of his fingers lingering. "The proper action for every situation cannot be prescribed. And Jewish law makes concessions for human weaknesses and errors, so long as we strive to live righteously."

"So following each of the commandments precisely can lead to its own errors?"

"Exactly, Béla. Judaism allows for choices, because that is the essence of what makes us human. And often the worst choice is to do nothing."

"I doubt the rabbi would agree."

Papa glared, while maintaining the semblance of a smile, appearing not displeased but, rather, disappointed that manifest truths are not inherent in one's genes. He kissed the top of my head. *"Gutskeit iz besser fun frumkeit"* (Kindness is better than piety).

Spotting a pinch of condescension on Adolph's face, I raced ahead, snow creaking under my boots, to tackle him before he reached our front door. All was well. I may have offended G-d, but upsetting father was more significant.

CHAPTER 3
The Book of Job

*What's the point of life when it doesn't make sense,
when G-d blocks all the roads to meaning?*

—Book of Job

Through his inherent clairvoyance (or perhaps word slipped from Mama), Ferencz learned of Mr. Judka's plight. He arranged for Tetzi to make deliveries for additional store owners, including Ágnes's father, Oskar, who maintained a tailor shop burrowed into one of the crevices of an alleyway, where he and an apprentice spent long hours basting and sewing on a treadle machine.

Pollack revisited the incident with me cryptically. "You buy yourself an enemy when you give a man charity," he said, expelling a gush of breath. When I asked him to explain, Pollack countered, "Wisdom you don't learn in *cheder*." I informed him that my father wholeheartedly agreed.

Weeks later, Ferencz, a mirror image of our father facially and in body type, sauntered into the shop as I was preparing to close. I was alone. Pollack had left early to light Hanukkah candles and play games with his children. Ferencz threw coins into a drawer underneath the counter and ambled to the back, reappearing with three green bottles of ale. "Don't tell Mama or Papa," he said.

As we sat on stools behind the counter, I straightened my back, reaching my head toward the ceiling to mask my immaturity. In contrast to my worn clothes, Ferencz wore cuffed slacks (before he pulled them on, he would turn the cuffs inside-out to brush out every speck of dust) and a custom-made dress shirt with gold-plated cufflinks. He shared with Jenő a precision regarding his appearance, although Jenő's goal was professionalism while Ferencz veered toward ostentation. He was one of the few people I knew, male or female, who had his nails manicured.

The alcohol was welcome to diffuse Ferencz's intensity. Expecting it to taste medicinal or acidic, I found the dark amber beer sweet and palatable. Ferencz recounted his attendance months earlier at the Summer Olympics.

"Jenő and I arrived in Amsterdam as the opening ceremony began. I didn't miss a day of the competitions." He closed his eyes, appearing to be reminiscing over a religious experience. "Or a night in the *Rossebuurt* (red-light neighborhood)."

"I read in Jenő's column about the parade of nations in the opening ceremony."

"Yes, Greece was first. The games are a spectacle that must be experienced. I'll take you to the next one."

I wanted this prospect to be as concrete as possible. "Where will they be?"

"I've no idea. But wherever they choose, I'm going. And it might be close by. Not many people know that Budapest was the original choice for the 1920 Olympics. But because of the Hungarians' stupid decision to ally with Germany during the war, the games

Chapter 3

were shifted to Antwerp. And both countries were banned from competing."

"Which events in Amsterdam did you see?

"I mostly followed the Czech athletes. We did well in gymnastics. But I loved the boxing best. I had a seat so close to the ring that, after one of the matches, a boxer spat out his gum shield and it landed on me. I tell you it's an inhumane sport. But mesmerizing." For emphasis, he punched me in the shoulder, spilling some beer. "Then we went to Berlin."

Ferencz pulled from his back pocket a postcard displaying an ornate structure that I guessed was a cathedral. "The Theatre am Schiffbauerdamm," he said, pointing his finger at the building. "I just saw *The Threepenny Opera* there." He allowed me to admire the image before pushing the postcard back in his pocket. "Berlin is the center of culture in this world, Béla. The best writers, painters, and filmmakers flock to it. You can stay up all night at a café, spending just a few *koruna* and having the most sophisticated of conversations."

He eyed me as though I had shown ill intentions toward him. "And there's one more thing."

"What?"

"The Jews there are mostly Reform, and not obsessive about religious practices."

"They're Zionists?"

"No, just the opposite. They pray in German, not Hebrew, and they actually listen to their prayers. And they don't scream all day about restoring Palestine as the Jewish homeland. So forget Paris. Or Vienna. Or Budapest. Berlin is where I will make my home one day."

I wanted to be Ferencz's best friend. To know him as no one else did. To make him laugh. But, in the shadow of my brother's breadth of experiences, I could only respond, "I like Munkács."

23

"Munkács is boring. At least move to Prague." I had been told that residents of our capital city, Jews included, considered people from the Rus akin to cavemen. Ferencz was oblivious to this slur on us Munkáczers. He winked at me. "They have such beautiful women there. Who wear sleeveless, low-cut dresses that don't even cover their knees. All of them slim, with makeup, painted nails, and high heels. You should see how they walk, and dance."

In religious study, they taught that even staring at dresses strung on a clothesline could bring on impure thoughts. "Do you know any of these women?"

"Of course. I'm courting one now. I met her in the Deutsche Haus casino, when I was with my buddies celebrating a football club victory."

"Do Mama and Papa know?"

"They will, if the time ever is right." Ferencz gazed upward to the God of Loveliness. "Her name is Rozsa. My beautiful rose petal."

"Do you love her?"

"Could be."

"Will you marry her?"

"Maybe. But there are many more delightful flowers in the garden. I want to sample them all. The lovely ones, as well as the ones who wish they were. They all want the same thing—sin under the pretense of virtue."

I waited for him to go on, to reveal to me the mysteries of sex. But Ferencz was content to wash his mouth with beer, savoring it.

"What's Prague like, Ferencz?"

"Magical. Its main square is the most magnificent in Europe. Some are put off by all the churches, but I find the place inspiring. I listened to Masaryk speak there, commemorating the tenth anniversary of Czech independence. A great orator, although his speeches last forever. He's such an idealist, going on and on about right and justice."

Chapter 3

With that reference, and emboldened by the intimacy that flows from alcohol, I could refrain no longer. "How can you be in business with Pollack?"

Ferencz clutched his chest, feigning shock. "Why shouldn't I be in business with him?"

"No one likes him."

The corners of his mouth quirked upward. "I like him."

"How could you? He's mean."

"Maybe. But he's smart also. *Mit a nar tor men nit handlen* (Don't do business with a fool). And he's honest. He'll swindle you gladly, but he won't do it by stealing."

"Is he your friend?"

"I suppose." Ferencz spread his hands, palms up. "In that sense, I have hundreds of friends."

"So anyone can be your friend. Even a bad person."

Ferencz pressed a fist to his mouth, then released it. I regretted my comment.

"Béla, someone who behaves poorly may also do good things. I admit that Pollack is an insensitive, arrogant lout, but he works hard and provides for a large family. He contributes to his temple, he supports the yeshiva boys who study all day, he gives other *tzedakah* ["righteousness," a phrase referring to giving to the less fortunate]—"

"He does that for show," I interrupted. "Not out of goodness."

"I see. You have the remarkable ability to read others' hearts. That will certainly serve you well with the ladies. How about that cute girl who works with you?" He placed a hand over his chest again. "Has she secret desires for you? I bet she does." He wagged his finger at me. "But I couldn't be sure as I don't have your gift."

I mused incessantly about Ágnes and her feelings for me, hoping to be permitted to listen to the echoes of her cravings, even ones outworn. "I'm not reading his heart. I'm watching what he does. I saw

Pollack humiliate Mr. Judka, who only wanted some food. Who was already embarrassed."

"Did he also help him?"

"Yes, but that doesn't make up for his shaming him."

"Well, that's Pollack." After using it as an ashtray, Ferencz placed an empty beer bottle on the ground and spun it around several times. I would have done the same, but mine was half full. "Béla, I'm not defending his behavior. In fact, I'll bet that my friend Yaakov gets no sense of fulfillment from his supposed charitable acts. All I'm saying is that it's a waste of time to judge the goodness or evil in people, or to try to assess someone's motives. You know why?"

He lingered over the last word, challenging me. "Because all our motives ultimately are selfish, aren't they? Even love arises from selfishness." With a cannon-loud belch, Ferencz finished his second beer and wiped foam from his mouth with a forearm. "Focus on actions. Watch what a person does, or doesn't do. Especially when he thinks that no one is watching. Leave it to G-d to reward goodness and punish wickedness."

"I'm not looking to reward or punish. I'm just saying that I don't like Pollack. And I can't ignore his lack of compassion for others."

Ferencz shook his head, not in direct response but in exasperation. "Béla, do you remember the story of Job? Who feared G-d and rejected evil. And what happened to him?"

I knew the legend well. G-d and Satan disputed over whether Job's piety was real. To test him, they brought fire, wind, lightning, and bandits to destroy his animals and wealth and to kill his ten children. And they caused him all sorts of personal afflictions, like boils and sores from head to toe. His miseries became so monumental that friends and admirers decided that Job must be a wicked person who had sinned, or else G-d would not have allowed such suffering. "After he lost everything, his wife told him to curse G-d. But he remained faithful."

Chapter 3

"Right. He told her, 'We take the good days from G-d, why not also the difficult ones?' And so his fortunes were restored, he had ten more children, and he lived a long life." Ferencz narrowed his eyes. "So, what do you think the lesson of the Book of Job is?"

"That the good are rewarded in the end?"

His face soured. "No, how can that be? Job grieved for the deaths of ten children. Having ten more doesn't make up for that. Every life is precious."

Damn, I'm such a simpleton. "So the lesson is that nothing is certain in this life, however good you are?"

"That's the obvious one. But it also teaches us that goodness can be difficult to recognize. That it can seem to be bad." Ferencz wagged his finger. "Maybe Pollack did Judka a favor, by pushing him to find a way to provide for his family on his own. In the end, Judka may thank Pollack."

While I pondered this, my brother gripped each of my shoulders. "I'll tell you something else. Something I want you to remember. Forever."

His breath stank, but I resisted the urge to lean back. Insights were forthcoming from my brother, ones that were unlike the teachings I received from Papa.

"I make a lot of money from my friends. And for them."

"But are they real friends? Or just business friends? Because—"

Ferencz cut me off with a dismissive wave. "And I have fun with them. Lots of laughs. And you know what, Béla? Let me tell you how important all these friendships are."

Ferencz scrunched his eyes. "They are...." He paused to create an effect, like that of a conductor who raps on a music stand and holds his arms high for a few seconds. "*So* important that I wouldn't trade my little brother for the whole lot of them." He stood. "And now I have to pee."

I grabbed my jacket and locked up, joining my brother in a game of imprinting our names in yellow in a nearby snow bank, undeterred by children on a nearby slope sitting on a chain of sleds. (Since I drank only half a can, it helped that my name is shorter.) Enclosed in a sharp cold masked by the brightness of the sun, Ferencz leisurely lit a hand-rolled cigarette, twisted at both ends, while studying the view as though he were considering offering the nearest alpine peaks for sale.

"Ágnes kissed me," I blurted out.

Ferencz grinned. "Where?"

"In the store."

He let out a snorting laugh, with wisps of smoke steaming out of his nostrils and billowing into nothing. "That's not what I meant. Did she kiss you on the lips?"

"No, on my cheek."

"Well, that's a start."

"Do you think she wants me to be her boyfriend?"

Ferencz flung a butt in a parabolic arc onto a patch of pee-stained snow, after using it to light another cigarette. "I wouldn't assume that much yet. Only that she likes you."

"Should I ask her if she wants a boyfriend?"

"No," he said. "That likely will have the opposite effect of what you want to have happen."

"Why?"

Ferencz chuckled. "If there's one thing I've learned over the years, it's that the woman controls the relationship. She decides whether you have one, when you have it, how intense it is, and when it ends. Your role is to play along. To think otherwise is to fool yourself."

"So what should I do?"

"That's my point, Béla. You don't have to do anything. Until she gives you your cue."

"But how will I know when she does?"

Chapter 3

"Trust me. You'll know. Just don't ever appear desperate."

One butt later, we skied toward Oroszvég. Ordinarily, the trip was a chore, with its undulations and abrupt icy patches along an all-too-dreary uphill path. But I shadowed my brother with a smooth effortlessness, past ghostly snow drifts and snapping branches, matching his speed and serenity, determined to follow him forever.

Nearing home, we passed Tetzi's house, caked with snow that pressed its weight against the slate roof. Through open curtains and the calm glow of blue and white Hanukkah candles against a windowpane splashed with needles of frost, I imagined I glimpsed her father. Honoring us with the slightest bow.

CHAPTER 4
Jabotinsky: July 1934

Eliminate the Diaspora, or the Diaspora will surely eliminate you.

—Ze'ev Jabotinsky

My father was observant, but he accepted the secular world, sending his children as they grew older to a local school that taught in Russian. His religious intensity fell along the median of the extraordinarily diverse Jewish experiences that Munkács offered.

The heart of Jewish life was Latorica Street, in the "Jewish Quarter." Branching off Latorica were claustrophobic streets and dank alleys laden with houses of worship of all ilk. At the edge of the city lay a neighborhood of Gypsies, who lived in brick huts and whose talents and familiarity with Jewish life led them to be among the best Klezmer musicians.

The city was a Chassidic center, the Munkáczer sect headed by Rebbe Hayim Elazar Shapira, the son and grandson of Munkáczer rebbes, each of whom was said to have never walked a single step without thinking of G-d. Shapira was a famed scholar who wrote numerous books on Jewish law, philosophy, and customs. His three-building courtyard served as his home, a study hall, and the eminent Darkei Teshuva yeshiva, which attracted students from all corners of Eastern Europe. Challenging the dominant Munkáczer faction were the Belzer, Spinka, and Vizhnitzer Chassidic courts. Rivalries among the groups were passionate (as was the case among Zionist groups of differing religious, political, and ideological bents).

In 1933, Shapira's only child, Chaya Frima Rivka, a plain woman with a hunched back, was married. (The rebbe had divorced his first wife after twenty years of marriage because she was unable to conceive. Papa maintained that this was understandable, but Mama observed that the rebbe had thousands of children and need not have insisted on one of his own blood.) The nuptials and attendant festivities carried on for a week and were celebrated by more than twenty thousand devotees, many of whom had traveled for days. During the ceremony, hundreds of well-wishers encircled the wedding party as they made their way through the courtyard and stood under the *chuppah*. The rebbe roused the multitude with a fiery sermon. Focusing his fears for the future on the assimilative power of the New World rather than the destructive forces amassing in his backyard, his speech included a message to Jews in America on the importance of keeping the Sabbath.

Although Munkács was a stronghold of ultra-Orthodoxy, for which any change in tradition was anathema, the Zionist movement that developed at the turn of the century had gained a substantial presence, aided by the Czech government's express recognition of Jews as a national minority—and not merely a religious one. The epicenter of the bad blood between the Zionists and Chassids was education and, in particular, the Hebrew Reform Real Gymnasium (High School) of Munkács. Established in 1924, the Gymnasium, with its emphasis on academics, became for non-Chassidic Jews an attractive alternative to yeshiva instruction.

The Gymnasium (pronounced "Gimnazium," with a hard G) was committed to Zionist idealism and the promotion of Hebrew as a modern Jewish language. Shapira, legendary for both his Torah genius and obsessive anti-Zionism, condemned the school for not reserving Hebrew exclusively for the study of the holy texts, insisting that the Gymnasium issued "heresy and atheism." Shapira, who is said to have spat every time he passed the school building, warned his disciples that it was off limits and anyone participating in its activities would be an outcast to be mourned for, "just as is done for the deceased."

Within this simmering cauldron, a romance blossomed. I had realized my teen-aged daydreams, although whether they were achieved from my following Ferencz's wooing advice, I doubt. After the incident with Tetzi's father, six years earlier, Ágnes and I began a routine of passing each other notes during work, often ones making fun of Pollack. I agonized over the significance of each of her motions, modulations, and expressions. One day, emboldened by beer, I blurted out how beautiful I thought she was. I began to walk Ágnes home from work; then came hand holding, followed by kisses that she succumbed to.

During the summer of 1934, Ágnes and I were inseparable. On weekends, we took rides on a tandem bike to nearby villages, day-long hikes to secluded spots where we would picnic and lie together enraptured, and swimming and rafting excursions in the Latorica. Having turned twenty-one, I was scheduled to report for military training in the Czech Army in September, when Ágnes would leave for university in Prague. Every day counted.

Late afternoons would find us by the bridge connecting Munkács and Oroszvég, from whose stone arches my brothers and I, as children, would leap into the river. Now, Ágnes and I crafted new rituals, as

Chapter 4

the lightness and freedom of summer allows. A contest of skipping rocks, with a frustrated Ágnes insisting that I throw only with my left hand. Drinking dark crimson Bull's Blood wine from the bottle while gnawing soft Trappista cheese out of the red plastic foil. Or lying in a curtain of shade with the rusted underside of the bridge replacing sky. Cushioned by a thicket of crushed blades of grass and unkempt dandelions, one of us would use the other's lap as a pillow, with our shallow pontifications on life enhanced by the nourishment of sunflower seeds. Which could lead to a hull-spitting contest. Occasionally we were joined by others, and if Adolph ambled down, a card game was likely to break out.

One Sunday, Ágnes and I expected to cycle to a nearby farm to pick blueberries. She had schooled me in the ideal method of collecting the berries: holding a bucket under them with one hand and with the other cupping a bunch and gently rubbing them between my fingers before letting the ripened ones drop into the bucket. Yet another exhibition of her sensuality. But the sky took on a bruised, purplish color and fell back on us in slants of rain, forestalling the trip.

Without planning it, and much to Ágnes's annoyance, I spent the afternoon at Pollack's store. As with my pay, my responsibilities had expanded to include dealing with the authorities over licenses and taxes, bartering with local farmers for produce to sell, and taking inventory, which was that day's agenda.

At twilight, the skies cleared. Carrying a couple of Pilsen Lagerbier bestowed on me by Pollack, I met Ágnes near the bridge, underneath intertwining weeping willow boughs bent further from the weight of water. (Did Pollack know that I was with Ágnes? Few secrets survived in Munkács. They were too delicious to be kept long.) She was a glorious vision, barefoot on a blanket with her hands clutching her knees. She wore a vanilla blouse that had molded itself to her breasts.

And light blue shorts sculpted onto her that revealed lines of tanned thighs and smooth calves that were heaven's workmanship, ones that I imagined seeing with my dancing fingers. Unlike other women, whose beauty appeared meaningless to them, Ágnes embraced hers and unshackled it, displaying a banquet of pleasures.

Regrettably, she wasn't alone. The two nearby figures were familiar. Adolph and Tetzi. As I approached, all three stood. Ágnes rolled up the blanket.

"Hey, I just got here."

Adolph skimmed a flat rock across the river, counting the skips. It splash landed near a brown-and-white shepherd dog, disturbing its pursuit of a speckled trout, which were so plentiful that one could catch them by lifting a rock and dipping a net loosely near it. "You must be the only one in Munkács not to know what's happening tonight," he said.

"Is the rebbe throwing another wedding? I doubt we're invited."

The women giggled. "Jabotinsky is speaking at the Gymnasium," Adolph said, while reaching for one of my beers.

"Not like his photo isn't plastered on every tree trunk in town," I responded.

"Finally, a celebrity in our town," Adolph said. "Let's go see what all the fuss is about. If he's boring, we'll come back and play pinochle."

I winked at Ágnes. "Sure, Adolph. I'll even let you win."

"You play cards even worse than you do football," he snapped.

Ágnes slipped into her hobnailed sandals. I expected that she'd be the most eager of us to listen to Jabotinsky. Her sister, Dora, had moved to Palestine last year, after Dora's husband, David, lost his job as an architect. Years earlier, the two had honeymooned in the Holy Land and, before returning, had impulsively bought, using money David had inherited, a piece of property in Netanya, a new settlement south of Haifa. The last I gleaned from Ágnes, Dora and David had

Chapter 4

joined others in building the first hotel on the Mediterranean, named the Metropol.

As we walked, Ágnes and I picked raspberries from bushes spread along the river and fed each other, while Adolph and Tetzi grasped hands. I hadn't understood them to be a couple before that. Once over the bridge, the buzz of a crowd grew louder.

Turning the corner onto Rákóczi Püspök Street, we were forced to slow our pace. The school entrance was obscured by the throng gathered in front of it. Much of the commotion arose from the Betar members, chanting slogans praising settlement in Palestine. Some carried firearms and wore coffee-brown uniforms with a belt strap that ran diagonally from the shoulder to the waist, making them appear uncomfortably similar to Nazi Brownshirts. Their idol was Jabotinsky, and it was at their fawning invitation that he had consented to make the trip to Munkács.

The auditorium could not accommodate all the attendees, and, in a last-second decision, the school authorities shifted the event to the school's sizable backyard, where a crude podium had been erected. Rows of slat-back chairs were filled by the time we filed in. Before we settled on a patch of weeds and grass, I spotted Jenő seated near the front, a pocket notepad and Leica Rangefinder camera resting on his lap.

Surrounding us were mostly Zionists affiliated with the school, but also secular and orthodox Jews. Several Chassids stood near us toward the back, veiled in their traditional garb—black slippers, silk socks, white shirt with strings instead of buttons, sash girding the waist of their pants, a round, fur-lined *shtreimel* hat, and side hair locks dangling like tendrils in front of their ears. Despite the season, they also wore long black caftan coats that reached to their ankles and wrists, appearing as penguins amid a sea of short-sleeved shirts, shorts, and sandals. I made eye contact with the Chassid closest to me, whose hands were rhythmically clenching and unclenching.

After the crowd settled, the Betar members marched toward the stage as if stomping on drums, lining both sides of it. Chaim Kugel stepped onto the podium, to fervent applause. The director of the Gymnasium was a familiar figure in his three-piece brown gabardine suit and trademark owlish glasses. Born in Minsk, he had moved to Prague to obtain a doctorate and remained in Czechoslovakia, becoming a member of Parliament. He was now the best-known Jew in the country—beloved by the Zionists and reviled by the Chassids.

Kugel motioned for those seated to rise, then began to sing sotto voce in Hebrew, caressing each word, the opening lines of *Hatikvah*. The crowd joined in, providing an unharmonious, off-key recital that, given the somber tune, was nonetheless moving.

Kugel spoke in Yiddish, the most commonly understood language in the Jewish community. "For those who don't know me…." Laughter and clapping broke out. "For those who don't know me, I'm Doctor Chaim Kugel." More applause.

"My friends, thank you for joining us. Soon, we will celebrate the tenth anniversary of this distinguished place of learning." I glanced at the Chassids, lone trees straining against the winds of adulation.

"Our institution is based on a love for our people and for our ancient land. We are fortunate to have with us tonight a person who exemplifies these values."

Kugel pointed to the black-lacquered sky stretched above us and, raising his voice, said, "Unless Theodore Herzl was still alive, we could not have found a greater spokesman for Jews and Zionism than our guest of honor." Those in seats rose again and cheered. Kugel took his time before motioning for them to settle down.

"I could spend hours speaking of his accomplishments. Let me try to summarize them quickly. Our speaker was born in 1880 in Odessa. At the age of eighteen, he commenced a study of law but before long

Chapter 4

turned to follow his true passion: journalism. His reports and articles in several Russian newspapers were widely read. In 1903, he traveled to Kishinev to cover the aftermath of its pogrom, a barbaric massacre of men, women, and children, prompted by the ancient blood libel. In the face of Jewish passivity, he organized a Jewish self-defense unit. That same year, he was a delegate at the Sixth Zionist Congress in Basel, the last one in which the great Theodor Herzl participated."

I peeked at Ágnes. She was scanning the crowd for familiar faces. Catching her eye, I mouthed, "Soon," as I inclined my head toward the exit.

"Over the next decade," Kugel continued, "our speaker was active in spreading the Hebrew language and culture throughout Russia. His vision helped lead to the establishment of the Hebrew University in Jerusalem. And during World War I, he was instrumental in persuading the British to agree to the formation of three Jewish battalions, in one of which he himself fought. My friends, this was the first time in modern history that Jews have fought under their own insignia and flag."

Tetzi whispered to Ágnes that the introduction would be longer than the speech, leading to snickering and invoking glares from those in front of us.

"After the 1921 Jaffa riots, he convinced the Palestine leadership to create the Haganah to protect Jewish farms and kibbutzim. For his efforts, he was arrested and condemned by the British to fifteen years of hard labor. After receiving amnesty and being released from Acre Prison, and distrusting the British assurances of a Jewish homeland, he went on to establish the Revisionist Party and its youth movement, Betar—"

Kugel halted as dozens of young men and women interrupted with violent hooting and screaming.

"For years now, he has been denied reentry to Palestine. Still, he devotes his life to the protection of Jews and to the Zionist cause."

Kugel paused, building to a crescendo. "Without further delay, it is my great honor and privilege to ask to the podium…Ze'ev Jabotinsky."

Howling (Ze'ev means "wolf") erupted from the Betar enthusiasts, their heads thrown back with noses pointed at a sickle moon still climbing the sky, staining it with white. A man similar to Kugel, with jug ears and a receding hairline, and wearing gold-rimmed glasses, rose from the front row and bounded to the spartan, pinewood platform. Amid drums of applause, he and Kugel hugged. Flashbulbs popped, and the two men, arms around each other, stood smiling in the grip of the cameras. Kugel stepped off to give Jabotinsky center stage.

Jabotinsky exuded a ferocious vitality that belied his slight build. Not counting interruptions, he would speak for close to an hour, his voice rising to become our sky.

Jabotinsky began with a review of the political situation in Europe. He labeled Adolf Hitler the most dangerous anti-Semite since Haman. "If Hitler's regime is destined to stay, world Jewry is doomed." Jabotinsky cautioned that Polish Jews in particular were "living on the edge of a volcano."

Railing against the historic scattering of Jews to countries outside the Holy Land, Jabotinsky insisted that the Diaspora itself was the source of Jewish suffering, because it caused Jews everywhere to be a minority. I anticipated Jabotinsky would reference the curse of Cain, which condemned Jews to be perpetual wanderers, but instead he invoked the eternal hatred between Jacob and Esau.

The remedy to these lurking dangers was, of course, emigration to Palestine, through either legal or illegal means. "The problem is, above all," Jabotinsky explained, "the inherent xenophobia of the body social or the body economic under which we suffer." He predicted that those escaping from the impending catastrophe would live to see "the exalted moment of the rebirth and rise of a Jewish state." A frenzied roar erupted from the throng when Jabotinsky shouted, "Those Jews

Chapter 4

who do not remove the rust of exile from themselves and who refuse to shave their beard and side locks will be second-class citizens."

The Munkáczer rebbe preached that a person who cuts his side locks or facial hair has removed the semblance of G-d's image. I pictured my father, frowning.

As I reflected on this, an egg splashed against the podium. And another. One more flew by the left ear of Jabotinsky, who stood resolute. The three Chassids closest to me reached into their coats for more eggs. Before they could unleash a second round, Adolph barreled into the one nearest him, knocking him flat, as Tetzi let out a shriek. Adolph was joined by Betar members standing near the back, who collectively pummeled the Chassids. I rushed over and managed to pull Adolph away, but not before his elbow hammered the bridge of my nose. Ágnes helped me staunch the flow of blood with a lace handkerchief.

Meanwhile, Kugel regained the stage and implored several policemen in the yard to restore order. The Chassids, bloodied and gashed about the face, their clothes littered with egg shells and comically rearranged, were lifted and dragged out of the yard. A Betar leader crouched to wipe off yolk dripping down the platform.

Jabotinsky wiggled his eyebrows and half-smiled before resuming his normal demeanor. He continued to tear away at the crowd, his voice the flute of a snake charmer. I imagined his oratory, which carved up the air's stillness, akin to that heard by the rebels on Masada, when Elazar ben Yair pleaded with them to die as free men rather than submit to Roman conquest.

Jabotinsky warned of the ongoing struggle in Palestine with the British and the Arabs, and declared, pointing to the heavens, the right of Jews to their own homeland. Pounding the lectern, to the point where I was certain it would break, he proclaimed, "We are a people. A people as all other peoples."

A young woman sitting near Jenő, whom I recognized as a former schoolmate, shouted out, "We are with you, Ze'ev." Jabotinsky acknowledged her and called on all the women to stand. Appearing to make eye contact with each one of them, he praised the female soul as "woven from strings of steel and silk." Sweeping his arm across the plaza, he said, "I hold the woman's place over that of men in every fundamental aspect of public and private life. Except for brute labor, which demands physical prowess, there is no position or profession that I would not prefer handing to a woman." Carried away on the feminine tide of emotion, Tetzi clapped fiercely, while Ágnes screamed her approval.

At the close of his speech, Jabotinsky proclaimed, "I devote my life to the rebirth of the Jewish State, with a Jewish majority, on both sides of the Jordan." A thunderous standing ovation followed, energizing our speaker further. Forging the will of the crowd one final time with his internal furnace, he raised two clenched fists and shouted over the rising din, "I call on each of you to join me and your brethren in emigrating to Palestine."

A mob of admirers, as bees to a honey pot, engulfed him. The four of us stood in place, as you would when the ending credits slowly roll on after a movie that had enthralled you. As the crowd filtered out, we wove our way toward the platform in an attempt to greet Jabotinsky. But the crush of devotees was as dense as concrete.

Reversing course, I smacked into Jenő, who was furiously scribbling notes on a pad before heading to the newspaper office to file his story. Jenő stabbed his pen toward the podium. "That's a man who understands the truth and has the courage to state it," he shouted. "He doesn't parse words, nor does he debate endlessly each side of an issue."

On the street outside, we were met with a scene of Betar members faced off against a group of the rebbe's adherents. Each faction

Chapter 4

had armed itself with rocks, bottles, and tree branches. Separating them were a dozen local policemen waving truncheons. The police chief stood in the middle of the street, refereeing a vehement argument between the yolk-cleaning Betar leader and one of the elder Chassids. The standoff was broken with the arrival of Rebbe Shapira's emissary, who, along with the chief, persuaded the assemblage to disperse.

Adolph and I stood under luminous electric lights, shielding the girls behind us. The shiner under Adolph's left eye had turned glossy. "I bet the other guy looks worse," I said.

He laughed, pointing to my nose, which was caked in dried blood; then he fumbled in his pocket. "Even you look worse. Sorry."

"Next time, I'll let you kill the guy."

"Next time, you should join in." Adolph pressed in my hand a crumpled cotton hanky with a faded paisley pattern. "You know what one of them said to me before I hit him?"

"He asked you for more eggs?"

"He said, 'Unless the Lord builds a house, its builders toil in vain.' Then he called me a blasphemer and spit at me."

A bias against Chassids had developed on my part, although I was unable to reconcile this with the respect I had for Pollack, the only one I truly knew. "In the old days, Adolph, we apostates all would have been stoned to death."

"Or at least excommunicated."

Staring at the retreating Chassids, Tetzi said, "I've seen them sing and dance with such joy. Why do they hate us?"

"Because we dress better than they do," Adolph teased. He bent forward to plant a peck on her cheek, but Tetzi backed away, causing him to stumble.

"And why do you have to look for fights all the time?"

"What did you expect me to do? Stand still and do nothing?"

"How about letting the constables maintain order?"

Tetzi stomped away, with Adolph in servile pursuit. After apologizing, Adolph escorted her to the nearby Csillag, a popular, inexpensive coffee shop that welcomed local musicians and singers.

Ágnes and I strolled, hand in hand, back to Oroszvég under a raven canopy painted with pinpricks of light each vying for attention. Not far from the Gymnasium, the echoes of the crowd having faded, tree crickets swelled the air with a sweet staccato music.

When I was a child, I would sit in the evenings on the lap of Mama's mother. As we gazed at the arching Milky Way, she would stroke my head while pointing out, in words that were lullabies, clusters of stars hanging low in the sky that were shaped in the form of Hebrew letters. On an evening filled with the calling song of crickets, she whispered to me that one could calculate the temperature by counting the number of chirps per minute. When I later asked my mother if this were true, she smiled and said, "I wouldn't know. But I do know that all G-d's creations are wonderful." Reaching to hug me, she added, "And there is no greater evidence of this than you, my beautiful boy." I believe to this day that Mama said this only to me. That I was her favorite child.

Ágnes interrupted my musings. "Still think we should have stayed by the bridge?"

"No, it was a night not to be missed. I should have told you that Pollack had warned me there would be trouble with the Munkáczer Chassids."

"So how does your delightful boss explain their behavior?"

"They're convinced that the Zionists are sinning by believing that the salvation of the Jewish people and our passage to the Holy Land is not dependent first upon the coming of the *Mashiach* (Messiah)."

Ágnes's delicate nostrils flared. "I don't know what's worse. Their blindness or their hypocrisy."

Chapter 4

"You should know that Pollack believes that violence against a fellow man is unacceptable, even in order to prevent sinning against G-d. Because the purpose of Judaism is the hallowing of life, not the salvation of the soul. Otherwise, he says, we all might as well be Christians."

"What exactly does he mean by the 'hallowing of life'?"

"That we should respect each other above all."

"What are you talking about? He doesn't respect anyone."

Her coral cheekbones were taut with an anger that radiated vitality, enhancing her beauty. "In any event, I'm glad I went, Ágnes."

"We should learn more about Jabotinsky's views, shouldn't we?"

"He made them clear. If we stay in Europe, we're doomed. All Jews must pack up and leave for Palestine."

"No, Béla, there was more. So much more. Weren't you inspired by all he said?"

Whether admiring a butterfly, critiquing a movie, or complaining about a classmate, Ágnes was incapable of merely offering her views. Her blunt opinion invariably would end with a question, requiring me either to agree with her or to argue the point.

"I liked how he insisted that we take pride in being Jewish. That we must defend ourselves. That we take our place among the peoples of the world. That each of us is capable of greatness."

"You only liked it? Weren't you moved by his words?"

"I'm not you. I don't get overemotional about things." I kept glancing at Ágnes's blouse, which was clinging to her form and placing pressure both on her top buttons and my restraint. I coaxed her forward, but she pushed me away.

"That's belittling! All I'm asking is for you to tell me how you feel."

"I heard him. Loud and clear. But what do you want me to do now? Run out and join Betar and spend my days parading around like a monkey in a silly brown uniform and going on camping trips where we learn to fire rifles? I'll get enough military training from the Czech Army." I risked a step forward. She followed, and we resumed our meandering pace.

"I'm sorry, Ágnes. Jabotinsky is brilliant. And inspirational. Maybe the most important Jew in the world. But he's fallible."

She squeezed my hand, her warmth flowing into me as if I were cold-blooded. "But you admit that his words have merit?"

"Sure," I blurted out. "But frankly, I'm tired of being told how to think and what to do. By rabbis, teachers, and preachers." I was tempted to add, "And girlfriends." "I want to figure out life on my own terms. Thankfully, we live in a country that allows us that privilege."

"I've never liked those Betar zealots, either. Or Kugel and his sycophants. But Jabotinsky didn't come across as preachy to me. He was empowering."

"Seems to me, Ágnes, that he demands a lot from us."

"But what if he's right, Béla? What if those 'super-pogroms' he talked about are coming? What then? Will you, or anyone, be able to protect me and my family?"

"The Czech Army is one of the strongest in Europe, Ágnes. Bigger and better equipped than most others—even the United States Army. And we have many Allies as well." Did I believe that myself?

She hooked her arm through mine. "He scared me. What he said makes sense."

"Jabotinsky's also a man with an agenda. And not all of that is what I want for myself."

She poked my side with her free hand. "So what is it that you want, Béla?"

We were nearing the bridge. I stopped, drew her to me, and pressed the heat of my mouth and body against hers. Only when I sensed Ágnes yielding to a more urgent inner voice did I pull back.

Chapter 4

Slipping my arm around her waist, we veered onto the soggy dirt path leading to the bridge's underside.

*

Many of those in the audience, including Adolph, Tetzi, and Ágnes, would later describe that evening as a defining moment in their lives. But not I. I fought the orator's spell, as if struggling not to sneeze while in mid-prayer.

Why? Jabotinsky had come to Munkács to seduce us into being his echoes. He wanted to capture my heart cheaply, without knowing me, and I would not allow that. Because I understood that the verses of a stranger must be listened to cautiously.

I do return to that night often. While I know that I should avoid playing the "what if" game, which imprisons one in the past, I admit pondering ceaselessly what might have been if Jabotinsky had not journeyed to Munkács and shuffled the deck of our lives. If so, the alternate fates for each of us were countless.

Béla Ingber in his Czech Army uniform, 1935

But we were destined to be among the many who, on a calm summer evening turned turbulent in my remote hometown, listened raptly to the song of a great man. One whose melody reflected our own longings. And, after that, nothing was the same.

CHAPTER 5

Jenő Ingber: August 17, 1936 (Prague)

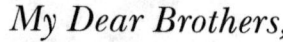

My Dear Brothers,

Ferencz and I have just arrived in Prague, after more than two weeks in Berlin. I am sorry to not have written earlier, but I could not safely post to you from Germany.

The Germans built a vast limestone stadium for the Olympic events, one with magnificent pillared curves, which was jammed constantly with screaming Germans. Above it, monopolizing the sky, drifted an airship with swastika markings on its tailfins, one so immense that it could hold much of the population of Munkács.

Berlin is now a ballast of evil, papered with swastika flags that form the harsh edges of its beauty. They flutter like cancerous butterflies over the Unter den Linden. Hitler, dressed in military uniform, attended every day, his hand raised as if blessing the crowd, adulated like he was Moses bringing the tablets from Mount Sinai. This stiff,

Chapter 5

expressionless, unexceptional man is a modern-day Chmielnicki. An acrid wind carries the smell of his savagery.

I admit to my heart pounding and muscles tightening whenever he entered the stadium and the crowd rose as one. Their roar was deafening, followed by shrieks of "Heil Hitler," which go on like the tide until the Führer motions for silence. The men near me wore crazed expressions, while the women swooned. The evident power of their solidarity heightened my insignificance.

The world appeased the Nazis by participating. During the opening ceremony, after a torch relay reminiscent of ancient Greece, each country's team paraded into the stadium. Were you able to find a wireless to listen to it?

You should be proud of the Jewish athletes. A female Hungarian Jewish fencer won the gold medal. And there even was a half-Jewess competing on the German team. Although the best athlete of them all was an American Negro.

Our hosts ply us reporters with fine food and accommodations. Most of my colleagues were content to cover only the competitions. I had limited interest in them. Often, I roamed out of the stadium to the great bell tower, observing the sights and attempting to speak to the locals, whose fear of being perceived as in any way anti-Nazi was profound.

The air reeked of anti-Semitism, now a natural part of the world order. You cannot imagine the torment of being a German Jew. The eternal outsider within a society that tolerates only conformance. Unable to hide and, thus, unable to work, eat properly, or even live except as a trapped animal. Caught in a vise. Knowing that the Nazi bonfires are there to light his path to the underworld.

Though the Nazis were careful to remove all the anti-Jewish posters, there were plenty of "Zur Neuen Welt" ("Into the New World") signs, which belie the German media fiction that Hitler has peaceful intentions. He means to remake German society into an Aryan hell.

Béla's Letters

Do you recognize the name Harold Abrahams? He is a Brit who was born a Jew but converted to Catholicism. Abrahams is a former Olympic champion who now is a BBC commentator. He appeared to know everyone of importance in Berlin and perversely was on speaking terms with a few of the Nazis.

Fortunately, Abrahams speaks German well, as my English is quite poor. It was he who whispered to me of all the efforts to conceal the mistreatment of Jews. And he warned me not to write of any of this until I left Germany.

Please do not share this letter with our parents or sisters.

I will be home soon, once I finish my article.

I kiss you all a million times. Your loving brother,

Jenő Ingber

CHAPTER 6

Ágnes Lőwie: November 10, 1937
(Kibbutz Degania Alef)

My Dearest Béla,

I'm sorry that I haven't written in a while. I just returned to the kibbutz from visiting Dora, her husband and their new baby, Rachel, in Tel Aviv, on the Mediterranean Sea coast. Rachel is such a darling and pretty little girl. I couldn't stop talking about her, and finally Dora said to me, "You'll have to marry and make a Rachel of your own."

Speaking of babies, I received your latest letter and was so happy to hear that your big sister is going to have one. You will be Uncle Béla! And a wonderful uncle you will be.

In your letter, you asked me to describe Degania. As you can imagine, it's so very different from Munkács. A burning sun that takes over the arc of the sky. Pastel, lifeless hills in every direction. Even with a huge lake in view, water is the most precious commodity, which must be passed through a sieve to filter out the worms. Fields plowed by braying donkeys. Black hawks and eagles so large that they can pick up and kill chickens. Violent storms that come upon you in an instant. Swarms of flies, and mosquitoes as thick as pudding that carry malaria. Outside the barbed wire, the area is barren except for the occasional olive tree.

I'm ashamed to admit that I didn't realize what hard work farming is. The physical strain, plus a heat that hung over us like a shawl, was more than I could bear at first. For a while, they switched me to indoor work, like milking the sheep. That was easier, but they teased me because the sheep kept pooping in my milk pot. Or I'd kick over the pot. Or get kicked by the sheep. But it's so rewarding to see the miracles that your hard work helps to generate.

I may try to come back to Munkács for a visit sometime early next year. I will write to you more about this.

Promise you'll write to me more often, as I want to know everything going on with you and your family. Are you and Adolph still in the Army? How are your parents? Your brothers and Libu?

I think about you all the time. Please write to me soon, or I shall believe that you have forgotten me.

I shower you with kisses from a faraway world.

With all my love,

CHAPTER 7

Ágnes Lőwie: March 10, 1938 (Netanya)

TELEGRAM

MY DARLING BÉLA

I AM ABOUT TO LEAVE FOR TEL AVIV TO BOARD A SHIP BOUND FOR ODESSA. I HOPE TO BE IN YOUR ARMS SOON. ALL MY LOVE,

CHAPTER 8
Feri's Bris: March 20, 1938

Your children are not your children.
They are the sons and daughters of Life's longing for itself.
—Kahlil Gibran

Rabbi Mordechai Gonzvi, the *mohel* (circumciser) for my new nephew Feri, was renowned in the community for his intimate knowledge of the ancient Gemara scholars, on which he lectured interminably. But I remember him most for his putrid breath. His exhalations had cast a constant stench on the front row of the *cheder* I attended, in a time when I believed that answers were clear and further questions unnecessary. Two decades later, his hygiene hadn't improved much. Mama attributed it to ill-fitting dentures.

More than forty people were in our house that afternoon, crammed together so tightly that one could not easily avoid eye contact and small talk. Built at the turn of the century from blocks of mud, with a thatched roof, the house was now fortified with brick and stone and

Chapter 8

painted on the outside in a pastel yellow. Seven tables had been placed in the living room, in the corner of which Papa housed his precious gold-embossed scriptures and tomes of Jewish history and scholarship in an overflowing credenza. Each was lit with a braided candle, set with floral white lace, decorated with a vase of bright fuchsia primrose picked from the backyard, and cluttered with bottles of homemade sour cherry wine, raspberry juice, and plum slivovitz sitting on embroidered doilies. Every tabletop also displayed a loaf of *challah*, which meant that Mama had risen before the night had let go of the sky to knead dough. (Papa often joked that no one in our family benefited more than Mama from the commandment to do no work on the Sabbath.)

In the center of a room electric with anticipation sat my parents, my older sister, Ilona, who had endured childbirth and five days of prescribed bed rest, and her husband, Józsi Haupt, and his parents. The rest of the attendees were either Ingbers or Haupts, along with a few neighbors.

Ilona had not married until she was thirty. My parents were desperate, and close to hiring a *shadchan* (matchmaker) for her, when she met Józsi, six years her elder, at the nuptials of my father's business partner's daughter. They wed within a year.

Rabbi Gonzvi, who had taken off his wide-brimmed, felt fedora with a gentle crease down the middle to reveal a high, graphite-black yarmulke, was privileged with a seat at my parents' table. For other of the town's circumcisions, the new Munkáczer rebbe often would preside, but my family's negligible social standing and lack of ultra-orthodoxy did not warrant his presence. This did not trouble my father, who insisted that Judaism is a religion of the people. "We have no need," he would say, "for our beliefs to be supervised by men who think they are superior and wiser."

Nonetheless, Papa and Rabbi Gonzvi were close, and my father would seek Gonzvi's guidance and blessing on significant personal and business decisions. As a child, I would play with Gonzvi's son, Shmuel, who had curly earlocks touching his shoulders and a head shorn by the *mikveh* barber to make room for a yarmulke.

The ceremony had begun in Libu's room, one crowded with apprehension, where Feri lay wrapped in a slate gray towel atop a pillow on which prayers were sewn in silver. With shaking hands, Ilona passed her pink-skinned, eight-day-old baby to her husband's sister, Marta. Needing heels to reach five feet, Marta's burnt-orange hair, which cascaded down like fire, clashed with her pink dress. With a cherub's face, she appeared more like a perpetual child than a woman married for more than three years.

Marta was the *kvatterin* (godmother) and had been given the honor of carrying Feri into the room where the service would take place, out of belief that this would enhance her own chance of conceiving. As Marta cuddled the baby, who slept with his fists in his eyes, Ilona shrank to the back of the living room, where she could hear but not observe the proceedings. She armed herself with a glass of plum brandy, a family specialty made in wooden vats out back. We chanted "Blessed be he who comes," in Hebrew.

Marta gingerly handed the baby to her husband, Pinchas, the *kvatter*, who paled and without hesitation passed him to my beaming mother. Mama, wearing a sky blue *tichel* (headscarf) tied in the back, positioned her first grandchild on another pillow, which rested on a red velvet chair covered in ornaments and reserved for the prophet Elijah, the guardian of newborn boys. After a blessing by the *mohel*, Feri was scooped up by my father, honored to be the *sandek*. When the cutting commenced, he placed the baby on a table and pinned his chicken-bone legs.

The rabbi, whose tangled beard and flowing side curls had turned ashen since I last met him and who also seemed half a foot shorter, asked for the father's permission to perform the circumcision, invoking

Chapter 8

a snicker from my teenage brother, Miki. In a lilting, nasal voice, Gonzvi discoursed on the genesis of the ritual, explaining that G-d had appeared to Abraham when Abraham was ninety-nine years old and commanded him to circumcise himself, his thirteen-year-old son Ishmael, and all the other men in the community as a sign of their bond with Him. Upon hearing this revelation, Miki only half stifled a laugh, eliciting a glare from Papa and a gentle kick in the shin from me.

With our guests crowded around him, awaiting a performance, the rabbi proclaimed the importance of the *bris milah* (circumcision ceremony), declaring that the Talmud compares its importance to that of all other 612 mitzvoth combined. "G-d said to Abraham," he thundered, "A male who will not circumcise the flesh of his foreskin, that soul shall be cut off from its people, for he has invalidated my covenant."

Would a fair and just G-d reject a man because of his lack of circumcision, a sin far less grave than so many others? In my teenage years, I might have enjoyed debating this. But I don't stir the pot anymore, having come to understand that logic not only was irrelevant to the rabbi's teaching, but anathema to it.

"Praised are you, Adonai our G-d, King of the Universe, who has sanctified us with your commandments and instructed us in the ritual of circumcision," he recited over Feri. He drew from a weathered black leather bag a sharp clip blade and a suction cup, as well as cotton pads.

Feri, now wearing a navy blue conical wool hat that Mama had knitted and placed on him, had been in a serene sleep. Yet upon the placement of the knife on the table where he lay, Feri began to whimper, as if he comprehended its significance. A slight wave of nausea rolled over me. Though an Army veteran and a witness to bloody fights, bayonet mishaps, and accidental shootings during live-fire exercises, I could not bring myself to watch.

As the rabbi chanted and Feri's cries grew louder, I edged away from the table and worked my way to the back door. Passing the kitchen, where milky sunlight seeped in through a lace-covered window, I breathed in the nectar scent of soup made from chickens that Mama had scalded in a basin of hot water, plucked the feathers off, and salted. A group of women were fussing with the food preparations.

Ilona, clad in a long-sleeve knit sweater, was sitting on a folding chair, in surrender to any pretense of enjoyment of the ceremony. Behind her were the pickets of a white fence to which arms of vines had woven themselves like serpents. The shrill voices of gander resonated from their netted pen. Melting snow slid off the roof onto frail spikes of spongy yellow grass that had forced their way to the surface.

A difficult childbirth had not diminished Ilona's radiance. A decade older than me, she always was too grown-up to be a close friend, but she had never imposed herself on me as a second mother. My sister resembled our mother, each blessed with petite figures, deep-set eyes, and high cheekbones that melted into aquiline noses. Unlike Mama and many other married women of our village, Ilona did not wear a *sheytl* (wig). A breeze played with her thick brunette hair, worn loosely with a pearl clip on one side, which flowed to her shoulders.

"Why are you out here? Waiting for Elijah to emerge from the heavens?"

Clutching a half-empty glass of schnapps, she responded without looking at me, "I wish I had given birth to a girl. Gonzvi is as old as time. Can he even see the foreskin?"

"Gonzvi performed my circumcision. And I can assure you it turned out fine."

Ilona let out the briefest laugh. "I remember how horrified I was years ago, the first time I went to a bris, and Mama explained to me what was taking place."

Chapter 8

"Me, too, when Papa told me what would happen at Miki's bris."

"I had believed that nature is wise and creates nothing in a human that is superfluous. That our imperfections are man-made."

"And now?"

"Now I know that everything is flawed. And everyone."

"So that's why you're so gloomy."

She adjusted the collar of her lavender-scented blouse, as if it were chafing her. "Something important has happened." She pointed to my shirt pocket, where Ágnes's telegram had peeked through, a paper that I felt as if it were aflame. "Is that a telegram? Is there more news about Austria?"

"No, it's from Ágnes." I could sense my face flushing. "I expect her back any day now."

Ilona flashed a grin and then wiped her expression clean. "I know that trouble is coming to our world. But no one will talk to me about it. Will there be a war?"

"There's no war coming. What happened was a peaceful annexation by Germany of Austria."

"Peaceful?" she said, licking her lips.

"Completely. The Austrians invited Hitler in. He's one of them. It's nothing that we Czechs would do."

"How do you know? There are millions of Germans in this mongrel country of ours."

"Nevertheless," I said, "the Czech Army is strong, with a million and a half well-equipped soldiers." It occurred to me that, four years ago, I had given another woman similar assurances.

"Are they a match for Germany and its allies? Even steel melts in the sun's grip."

"We also have allies—France, Britain, and Russia. And do you think, after all the horrors of the Great War, that the world would allow another one?"

"My sweet brother, even you are trying to shield me."

"I've never known you to care about world events, Ilona."

She raised her chin toward the house. "Now I have reason to care."

I let my fingertips touch Ilona's shoulder. "One day you'll be here at Ferike's son's bris, assuring his wife there is nothing to fear." She gripped my hand and squeezed it. "Ilona, I wish you much *nachas* (bliss) from your new family." Ilona stood and kissed me on the forehead and then led me toward the house. Stopping by the vase-shaped umbrella stand outside the door to allow a neighbor to exit with her bawling child, she said, "You know how you can tell that G-d has a sense of humor?"

"Sure. He bothered to give every male a foreskin, only to demand that it be cut off soon after birth."

She chuckled. "I've got another one. G-d bestowed most of the good looks on the Ingber men. You guys are gorgeous, and we girls look like you." I was taken by surprise, as my sister rarely revealed her vulnerabilities.

"I think you are a beautiful woman, Ilona."

She sighed. "A candle cannot replace the sun." Her eyes widened, glassy pupils sparkling in the cool light. "But thank you, my charming young brother. I know that Józsi truly feels that way."

I risked a question. "Is Józsi your first love?"

She lurched back, feigning having been affronted. "Of course not. I've loved some, and some have loved me. But, cruelly, it was never mutual." I had imagined that even unrequited love had its joys. Our internal pilot ignited. But I knew little of that, for I had lost my only love to the promise of Palestine. She chose to travel alone, over twenty-five hundred dangerous kilometers, rather than stay with me. And now the wait for her return pained me more than her leaving.

Ilona, shivering in the breeze, stepped one foot over the threshold. "There was one man," she whispered, "who I gave my heart to. He promised he would love me forever, and then he met someone else."

Chapter 8

I shifted my eyes, discomforted by the hint of my sister's sexuality.

"Thankfully, I finally met a most wonderful man, who thinks me wonderful as well. But before that, I suffered."

A neighbor rushed up toward Ilona, yanked her toward the door, and said to me, "I was told to bring you in also." As I passed through the doorway, Ilona gripped my elbow. "Béla," she again whispered, "you have the prospect of great, lasting love in your grasp. With all its joys and blessings. Don't let it slip from you."

I followed Ilona into the kitchen, where a couple of women rushed over to hug and comfort her, while another continued to methodically comb Libu's cascade of long amber hair with her fingernails. My mother was hovering over the wood-burning iron stove, arranging on a platter carps that not long ago had enjoyed their last swim in a bucket of water behind the house. Following culinary traditions generations old, Mama earlier had placed the carps on a flat stone positioned on our wood tabletop, deboning and grinding them to make gefilte fish.

"Can I help, Mama?" I said. She declined. Glancing at Ilona, Mama said, "I was also nervous at my Jenő's bris. After that, the rest were easy." Smiling, she cast her gaze toward a tanned, slim figure who had walked through the front door.

My pulse quickened, as though I were a child let out to touch the season's first snowfall, one pure as milk. Ágnes's eyes bored through the crowd at me as I pushed toward her. I shouted her name, the din of the house swallowing my voice. My kiss landed more on her upturned nose than cheek. Not an elegant start, although her smile, which I could not catch without being transfixed, announced it to be magically placed.

She stroked my cheek, while I raked my fingers through ringlets of her hair. We pulled back, feeling eyes upon us. Finding an empty corner of the house, I cradled her face in my hands, sensing the slight tremble it caused. We cuddled. Her familiarity, unblemished by absence, was comforting.

"Ágnes, I don't have the words… When did you arrive?"

"Yesterday. It was a long voyage. I needed a day to sleep. Meanwhile, my mother ran into yours and told her that I was back. They decided that I should come to the bris and surprise you." She pressed against me, letting me feel the delicate pressure of her breasts, and kissed me with our former precision, her top and bottom honey lips captured between mine as her eager tongue flickered teasingly. I was the frog-prince, and my savior had arrived. With her caress, we now would dissolve into one.

"I've wanted to do that for a long time, Béla."

"I've waited even longer."

"You didn't respond to some of my letters." She affected a leer. "Were you too busy with all your other girlfriends?"

I shook my head, addressing only the suggestion of not having had sufficient time. It was true that I had written to her sporadically, and my correspondence, out of resentment for her leaving, was guarded. But, also, I could not connect with Ágnes through the mail. Her vivaciousness, which I dreamt of often, was not absorbable through the written word. When I read her letters, it seemed as though someone else were writing to me, making me miss her even more.

"All those months…there were so many times I fantasized having you by my side, holding me," Ágnes said.

I took her hand, feeling the once-glossy skin that had become callused, and rubbed my thumb up and down its back, ensuring her presence and calming me. "I wasn't there, Ágnes, but trust me, I was with you." She answered with a tight hug.

A burst of laughter from a group nearby broke the spell. "Béla, your family looks well. Libu is becoming a beautiful young woman. Is she in Gymnasium now?"

"A year away. She's doing quite well in school."

Chapter 8

"And you? How are you faring? I want to hear everything."

How much to tell her? I had been discharged from the Army for five months, yet was unable to establish a career or leave my parents' home. With growing German influence in Czechoslovakia, being Jewish handicapped my options. "I'm working at the *Yiddishe Shtime* (the *Jewish Voice*)," I offered. Starting as a gopher for Jenő, who was the senior reporter, I now wrote routine articles, badgered merchants for advertisements, edited, and proofread.

I anticipated that this news would please her, as the paper followed a Zionist ideology. But she nodded without expression. "What else is new, Béla?"

Should I tell her of the innumerable football matches, card games, and brandy toasts? Perhaps drone on, like a tree full of cicadas, about the details of all the family events and holiday celebrations? Surely she'd enjoy details of my visits to the *Kuplieri* (the Munkács brothel, a legal establishment). "You're the one with all the adventures. Tell me about Dora and her family. Are they well?"

"Yes. But I didn't spend much time with them. I stayed mostly in Degania." Degania, the first kibbutz, located on the banks of the Jordan River at the southwestern end of the Sea of Galilee in a spot where the Garden of Eden was said to have once stood, was legendary among Zionists. One of them predicted to me that water from the Galilee would, one day, turn the wrinkled desert green.

"A group of us now want to form our own kibbutz. Rothschild is buying land."

So she is rooting herself there. Ágnes was inches from me, yet still out of reach. "I hear the Arabs are causing trouble."

Ágnes's head sunk. "They raid kibbutzim sometimes, and steal or burn crops." She added in a whisper, "Or worse."

"Meaning what?"

"It's complicated. They also fight against the British. And the Grand Mufti kills his own people, although now he's fled to Baghdad. Please don't mention any of this to my parents."

I stroked her hand. "I also worry about you. Is it worth the risk?"

Ágnes tilted her head, as if a different angle of me would obscure my cynicism. "It's not like Jews are beloved in this polluted continent of ours."

"True, but in this country, we enjoy the rule of law." Preventing her from arguing the point, I digressed. "Have you adjusted to kibbutz life?"

She frowned. "Somewhat. But it demands such physical and mental strength. It will take more time." I thought of Papa, who knew much about life in Palestine from the Bible, but only as an abstraction. "Béla, did I tell you what happened the very first day I picked tomatoes in the midday sun?" She snickered and rubbed the bridge of her nose, as though the memory pained her. "I fainted and had to be carried to the shade of a cowshed."

The image of a strapping boyfriend carrying her from the field, nursing her to health and comforting her, cut deep. "If you stay here, I'll look after you."

"And if you come with me, you can look out for me there," Ágnes retorted. "Béla, you can't imagine how it feels watching new miracles occur each season. And I was part of that."

I fought the brewing sensation in my gut that tempted me to disparage her. Ágnes reached into the pocket of her blouse to remove a tattered photo, which she slid toward me. In it, she stood smiling in a work shirt and trousers, her arm around another woman in similar attire. In the background, sheets of flame silhouetted the women's lower halves. "Dancing around the campfire every night until the embers burn out and you fall down in a dead faint. Isn't that what you all do there?"

She paused, considering a rebuke, and then forgave me my weakness. "Not exactly. Most nights I collapse into bed after some talk of

Chapter 8

politics or news over dinner. But there's a sense of belonging that I've never experienced before."

Could I say the same about Munkács? "That part does sound wonderful. Ágnes, I admit I resented that you left. But I want you to know that I admire you for it, too." With that, her hand grasped the back of my neck, causing a shiver. She pulled me toward her, gently but firmly, with a confidence born of long association. Her kiss lingered, allowing me to savor her.

In the background, Józsi was reciting the blessing thanking G-d for bringing the child into the covenant of Abraham. The circumcision ceremony was ending.

"I should join my family for the *Kiddush* (special blessing). Can you stay?"

"Sorry, I need to get back home. My mother's birthday is today, and some of my cousins and others are coming to celebrate."

Nodding, I gripped her biceps, holding her in place. "Ágnes, please. When can I see you?"

"I'm not going anywhere for now."

"I'll come to your house tonight. Is that okay? Will your parents mind?"

"Of course, come. They adore you."

I pictured her house, filled with relatives, many of whom I'd met. The hellos, introductions, and goodbyes, each a pretended intimacy, would be an endless loop. "Listen, I don't want to be a burden. Let's meet instead at the coffee shop. Around eight?"

"I can't wait! And surely I will have had enough of family by then."

She hugged me, her suppleness replaced by muscle whose strength was oddly comforting. I kissed the delicate hairs on the underside of her pulsing neck, letting the warmth of my breath weave its way into her pores, and walked her to the door.

Ágnes's fading image was a mirage taunting me. I slipped into the living room, where Józsi and Ilona, their postures now relaxed, were accepting congratulations.

I sat down next to Adolph and Jóska, a Prague newspaper spread tautly between them underneath the table. During gaps in the activities, however brief, they pored through the coverage of Germany's annexation of Austria (called the *Anschluss*, meaning "union"), which had occurred a week ago. The Republic of Austria had ceased to exist as an independent state.

Across from me was Miki, who bore watching. An expert at tying a prayer shawl to a chair without notice, he was eyeing the rabbi and his yellowed *tallis*, with faded blue and silver embroidery, which had earlier been draped around his head and upper torso but whose *tzitzit* (knotted fringes) on one side now crawled along the floor.

"Don't even think about it, Miki."

"It would be so easy. He'd stand up and his *tallis* would fall right into his soup."

"You'd embarrass your entire family. The penalty for which would be a repeat circumcision." Miki shrugged, the pleasure of his achievement largely having been in its conception.

My father, presiding at the head table with the rabbi and Józsi, recited the blessing over the wine and placed a drop into the baby's mouth. An entreaty for his well-being was chanted, followed by a longer prayer that bestowed his Hebrew name, Osher ben Isaac. Papa loudly repeated the appellation, explaining that "Osher means happiness, which he has already brought, and will continue to bless us with for a long time." Never missing an opportunity to teach, he added, "We Jews have been able to retain our identity as a people for thousands of years because each child's name is a connection to previous generations."

Mama, Ilona, and Libu paraded from the kitchen with bowls of chicken broth flavored with carrots and parsnip preserved by freezing

Chapter 8

last year's harvest. Half-hearing the rabbi blessing G-d and requesting His permission to proceed with grace, I planned for my get-together with Ágnes. How much time did we have before she left again? Could I convince her not to leave again?

A graceful hand pressed on my back. Mama's. "Béla, please tell your brothers to come to the table. The soup is getting cold."

As agnostic as they had become, it was out of character for Jenő and Ferencz to neglect a family gathering. I wound my way into the next room, one in which I had lived for most of my life with various combinations of my brothers. How could six boys have managed in this space, living like a litter of cats?

I found them wrapped in a haze of tobacco smoke that wafted toward an opened window. Jenő was slumped on the lone chair, chewing on his ornate meerschaum pipe, while Ferencz lounged on one of the bunk beds, an overflowing glass ashtray on his lap. Under the bed sat a porcelain chamber pot, used for peeing during cold nights, which sometimes would freeze over. Typically, the two would be cynically dissecting the latest fanatical pronouncement of the grand rebbe. Now, neither was laughing. Curious about any conversation sufficiently distracting to risk incurring our father's ire, I forgot my mission.

"The Allies have a commitment to uphold," insisted Jenő. "The Treaty of Versailles prohibits the union of Austria and Germany. But no one has the stomach to confront Hitler."

"So what's the value of the treaty then?" complained Ferencz. "The trouble is that the English and French public believe all Hitler wants is German-speaking lands. But the bastard will take all he can get, starting with the Sudetenland, where they'll give him a rousing welcome." Ferencz, given his journeys, claimed paramount knowledge of nationalistic intentions.

Although intimidated by my brothers' worldliness, my confidence had grown over the months of newspaper apprenticeship. "So you think we are next," I declared. "Maybe you're right. The difference is that the rest of Czechoslovakia won't be throwing flowers at the Nazis like the boot-licking Austrians did."

Their eyebrows raised, either in response to my comment or because they hadn't noticed me in the doorway.

Jenő said, for my benefit, "Anyone who thinks we Czechs alone can fight off the Nazi tide is deluding himself. We need help. The French and the Soviets are committed by treaty to assisting Czechoslovakia."

"You expect France to send troops to help us?" Ferencz responded.

I cut in. "Why not? After all, their Prime Minister is Jewish. Beneš may be able to persuade the British to help us also."

Jenő snickered. "I bet Chamberlain can't even find Czechoslovakia on a map."

"And," I added, "there are other ways. The German military despises Hitler. We can provide incentives for them to overthrow him. Maybe put the Kaiser back into power."

Ferencz's rebuttal was interrupted when Mama appeared behind me. "You men, with your constant talk of war and politics. We have a houseful of guests, food on the table, and you're in here arguing. Be respectful and come out now."

In the living room, we were greeted by Feri's whimpering from the cradle. His tone displayed a knowing quality, as though his subconscious grasped G-d's plan for us to begin life in pain, before we are even cognizant of its meaning. To prepare us.

Amid a clinking of glasses, Ilona crept to the center of the room, leading Józsi by the hand. Glancing at a sheet of paper she held at her waist, my sister addressed us, her pastel voice ensuring the stillness of the surrounding ensemble. "Thank you so much, my dear family and friends, for being here, and for your good wishes. Józsi and I are exhausted, yet exhilarated. Nervous, yet confident. And overwhelmed with gratitude." The baby squirmed and passed gas, initiating a

Chapter 8

welcome ripple of laughter. "For so long, I did not believe that this day would come. What my heart ached for had appeared as a distant mountaintop. Mysterious and unattainable."

She pursed her mouth to contain the bubbling sentiment. Ferencz hurriedly poured a swallow of brandy into a tumbler and quick-stepped to Ilona with it. She smiled and kissed his cheek, then waived him off.

"I'm so blessed to be surrounded by love. And now to have someone to pass that love on to. My dearest little boy...." Ilona glanced at Feri, ensconced now in his grandma's arms, sleeping with a softened expression. And then the struggle for composure ended, as she burst into a sobbing that racked her body. Józsi wrapped his arms around her, and Ilona buried her face in his chest. He took the paper from her, scanned it, and whispered, "I thank you as well." With a chortle, he added, "And all of you are, of course, invited to the bar mitzvah."

After the applause died down, discussions resumed at other tables, with men discoursing on the significance of yesterday's Torah portion, and women chattering about preparations for *Pesach* (the Passover holiday), a month away. My brothers and I continued the political debate, although in a more cursory way. Jenő moved to Ilona's table, where he engaged Józsi and my sister in an intense conversation. Their expressions belied the joy of the occasion.

One day you'll be here, at Ferike's son's bris, assuring his wife there is nothing to fear. Why did I offer Ilona that vacuous prophecy of peace? Instead of protecting her from worry, I should have prepared her for action. I failed her, and she was not the last person who could have said that of me.

CHAPTER 9
The Newspaper Office

It is a press, certainly, but a press from which shall flow inexhaustible streams. Through it, G-d will spread His Word. A spring of truth shall flow from it: like a new star it shall scatter the darkness of ignorance, and cause a light heretofore unknown to shine amongst men.

—Johannes Gutenberg

As the bris celebration continued, strands of dialogue wafted around me, melding into a singular hum. Józsi Haupt's father, a secular Jew from nearby Chust, fled from the Talmudic rhetoric of his table and took Jenő's seat at ours. As he caught up on my brothers' lives, I wolfed down the carp and potatoes, mumbled an apology and rose, deeming there no place left for me in my own house.

Dancing around others to make my way through the room, I offered the obligatory goodbyes. My standard line was that I was expected at the newspaper office to help prepare for the next morning's edition. After kissing Ilona and my parents and pounding Józsi's back in congratulations, I sought to escape the rabbi with a simple nod. But he

Chapter 9

extended his hand and we shook, although I maintained a distance. "*A guten tag, rebbe.*" He stared at me through watery, cobalt-blue irises set in yellowed sclera. "*A bi gezunt*, Béla."

Impressive that he remembered my name. The rabbi wasn't as senile as I suspected. If his faculties were intact, I might take the time to speak with him of my concerns about the Nazis. To gain assurance that our covenant with G-d surely meant His protection.

*

Crossing over the bridge, which I viewed as the property of Ágnes and myself, I reached the empty newspaper office on *Zsidó Utca* (Jewish Street). An old, squat brick building that reeked of lithographic ink, it was riddled with cracks and stingy radiators that kept it colder inside than out. The press operator, a man with perpetually purple-blotched fingers, would not arrive until dawn. I proofed several pieces and spent the next couple of hours absorbed in the recent news coverage.

As I was preparing to depart, Jenő arrived. "Are we set for tomorrow, Béla?"

"I've checked all the articles."

Jenő began scanning the proofs and then stopped to blow onto laced fingers. "It's freezing in here. How are you able to concentrate?"

In the Army, they had taught that the trick to coping with long periods in the cold was to wrap yourself in it and believe that it was revitalizing you. "I'm a soldier. When we trained during the winter, we lived for days outside, building our shelters and killing to eat. This is easy."

Jenő nodded, as much to himself as to me. This was, for him, high praise.

"I've got to go," I told him.

"Why?"

I smirked. "Ágnes…."

"Ah, I thought I saw her earlier. Listen, give me a minute."

He stepped closer to me and lowered his voice, as if the furniture might eavesdrop. "I'm leaving for Prague tomorrow. I'll be there for a while, I'm not sure for how long. To work on some editorials for *Prager Tagblatt*. Anti-Nazi pieces."

"I'll come with you."

"No, I need you here, to help keep this paper going. Pick up some of my work while I'm gone."

My first opportunity to perform meaningful work would come at a time when the local news was increasingly irrelevant. "Be careful, Jenő. I hear that Prague is filled with German agents."

"Exactly. We've got limited time to raise awareness."

"What do you want me to do?"

"I think you're ready to draft editorials. But write them like a mature newspaperman, not a hothead. Do your homework and check all your facts. Or they won't pass muster with our illustrious editor-in-chief."

"I'm not a kid anymore, Jenő. Believe it or not, you're not the only one capable of writing for this paper."

Ignoring me, he added, "And one more thing." Jenő moved even closer and stared me down. His eyes were midnight-black opals, opaque as storm clouds. "Nothing appears in your name. Use a pen name if you have to. It's unfair, but this is not up for debate. I do not ever want to see the name 'Béla Ingber' in print."

Was he protecting me from the world, or from myself? "Understood."

He gave me a playful shove. "Now go to your paramour. I'm jealous."

"Why? You're a far better ladies' man than I am." Over the years, Jenő had collected many friends of prominence. His qualities didn't leave him lacking for female attention either, although he hadn't married. Following tradition, Jenő had waited for Ilona to wed, which had cost him at least one serious girlfriend.

Chapter 9

He wagged his head as though my compliment had wounded him. "Don't sell yourself short. I may have more practiced charm. But a good woman wants to be with the kind of man you are. Not the self-absorbed egotist I've apparently become."

"You're the most generous person I know, Jenő. And the wisest."

His eyes reddened. "Time will tell, Béla."

I walked to the door, and then pivoted on my heels. "Hey, don't be a hothead yourself. And thanks." He was seated, reviewing a new story. Jenő waved without glancing up. Within the week, the article was published in Prague and copies were circulated widely. Forty years would pass before I would have the opportunity to read it.

CHAPTER 10
The Csillag

*The courage to wait is greater
than the courage to pour out one's heart.
One may attract people once one is in
pain, but it is different if one is waiting.*

—Nathan Zach

    I hustled from the newspaper building to the Csillag, only blocks away. Adjoining it was a hotel of the same name considered the best in town, with a dim, boisterous bar where earlier that week I had escaped to play five-card stud.

    At the front of the shop was a hand-cranked gramophone, its needle dropping to play jazz on scratchy records. Single men and couples sat on Bentwood chairs and sofas, smoking, reading, and playing chess, oblivious to the chill that rushed inside with every door opening. Ágnes had settled in the back, near the fieldstone fireplace. I forced my way through the haphazard arrangement of tables and chairs, drew her out of her seat, and squeezed her to me, harder than was gentlemanly. She pushed me away. "Béla!"

Chapter 10

"Sorry." I launched into my prepared remarks. "And I apologize for not writing more often. To set the record straight, it wasn't for lack of caring."

"So why didn't you?"

"Honestly, I tried. But most of what I might have written seemed so trivial compared to your escapades."

"But I'm interested in everything you have to say. You should know that."

A half-empty tea cup sat in front of Ágnes. In the past, she would never have ordered before I did. "How were the birthday festivities?" I said. My mama refused to allow any fuss over her own birthday, insisting that it was best not to remember one's age.

"Not good. My mother cried much of the time."

"Why?"

"Because Dora wasn't there. Because she didn't expect me to make it back here in time. Because my father is sick. I'm not sure which reason. Probably all of them."

"What's wrong with your father?" Oskar Lőwie was an unassuming man who in these times would be labeled a workaholic. He carried an intensity that had been inherited by his daughter. For a modest fee, Mr. Lőwie had sewn the only suit I ever owned.

"They're not sure. He's suffered with a persistent cough for months, which, of course, he chose to ignore. Now Papa sometimes is too weak to open shop. We're taking him to a hospital in Prague for some tests."

"I'm so sorry, Ágnes. He's a good man. I wish him health."

The waitress approached. I ordered a demitasse and a custard slice. Ágnes waived her off, in a gesture suggesting that all the nourishment Ágnes needed lay deep within her. "I still have such strong feelings for you," I blurted out.

She wove her fingers through mine. "And you must know how I feel for you, also."

"Then we can get back together. Pick up where we left off."

"Is that your way of asking me if I plan to stay in Munkács? Everyone seems to believe that."

"No, because I intend to put a ball and chain around your ankles."

She scrunched her nose. In our early courtship days, I possessed a ready ability to bend Ágnes's mood and focus it to my will. To make her laugh, or to distract her from pursuing a particular topic. No more. "Will you come to Palestine with me?"

Her question was one I still had no ready answer for, because I never seriously considered leaving. But how to convince her to stay? Ágnes's passion was the Holy Land, while mine was Ágnes. Only in her presence was I fully conscious.

"I don't know. What would I do in Palestine? My two careers have been training as a soldier and learning the newspaper business."

"You can do both there. We need everyone's talents."

"I'm not sure I'm truly the literary type."

"But you definitely are a man of action, good with his hands." She squeezed my fingers, gently, as if clutching an egg. "I've come to value that more. And the Haganah will also."

"I don't have to schlep over two thousand kilometers for a combat opportunity."

She shook her head. "In Palestine, there's plenty of raw land to buy or share and build on. And you wouldn't go there just to plant tomatoes, either. We'd be building a future. To ensure that we actually have one."

"We can make a good life here as well. At least I want to believe that."

"How can you be so naïve?" Ágnes pleaded. "You're a newspaperman. You know all about the approaching madness."

What was naïve was my hope that I could keep her from leaving again. That she could be loved by me and not feel trapped. "It may not last long."

Chapter 10

"Why are Jews so content to sit around and wait for the next pogrom to end? Don't you see that the pattern of hatred of us in this continent is timeless? It will never be broken!" She snatched her hand away. "And even if it were to end, my mind wouldn't change. Because I've come from a place where being Jewish has purpose." The last word burst from her mouth like a gunshot.

"And why don't the Jews here have purpose?"

"Because in Palestine, we are creating a homeland for our children, and theirs. While here you have a perpetual caste system, with gray-bearded rebbes on top, spouting supposed wisdom from the ages and demanding that we accept their interpretation of all things. Asking us to wait for a Messiah to lead us to a place that we already can go to. Well, I'm not willing to sacrifice my life for the sake of loyalty to them or their dead ancestors."

"Ágnes, no one's asking you to pay heed to them."

"But you are, by asking me to stay. In the kibbutz, everything seems so rational. All that we do—growing crops, building houses, guarding against trouble, welcoming the harvest—goes toward rebirth. And we do all that together. Women included."

"Just don't let your idealism blind you."

"I think it's the other way around. It's you who is blinded. By your trust that all can be good and safe here. Despite all the evidence to the contrary."

In the Army, we learned how wars are won. By strategy, application of superior resources, and deception. She had all three of these advantages over me. "Ágnes, what are you really angry about? That the rebbes don't want change? Or is it about feeling dominated by men?"

"I don't care what these old men think. I care that they don't want me to live fully. I am not Vashti, and I will not submit to any pretend king!" Ágnes squeezed her brows together. "Did you listen to Gonzvi? That covenant with G-d. It's only for those with a penis

75

to cut some skin from. How can you worship a god who shuns half of the Jewish community?"

Ágnes had listened closely to the rabbi. But she couldn't hear me. Or was it that she saw through me? "The covenant is with all of Abraham's seed. All women are created in the image of G-d, as men are."

"No, the Bible teaches that Eve came from Adam's rib. She was submissive to him, and we've been subservient to men since. Until now!"

The last time that Ágnes and I had attended temple services together, more than a year ago, she was content to sit upstairs behind the lattice and gossip with the other women, oblivious to the men praying below with the intensity of the possessed. I nodded in sympathy, but not vigorously enough to satisfy Ágnes, as she absentmindedly brushed her hair back with her fingers.

"Béla, think of how you'd feel if, for seven days a month, you were considered unclean. G-d gives women this incredible gift of fertility, and we're made to feel dirty about it. And the men in our lives are given an excuse to run to the *Kuplieri*."

"I can't change these old-fashioned views. But I'm telling you that, because the Czechs allow us freedom, you and I can make whatever life here we choose. And I promise that I'll do everything I can to make you happy."

"Those are just words, Béla. As pretty as they sound, I can't feel them. They have no meaning to me."

No, Ágnes, my words are like a deathbed promise—sacred. "Give me a chance to make them meaningful. Stay here with me."

"Why don't you answer my question? Why won't you give Palestine a chance? You can't be a Zionist outside of Palestine. I don't want to talk about it—I want to live it."

She believed herself to be an organ grinder, bringing sweet music to a bitter land. Was I to be her monkey? I raised my hands, palms facing her. "The last thing I wanted to happen tonight is for us to fight."

Chapter 10

She blew out her cheeks, as if preparing to pop them for a child's entertainment. "You joked about nights around the campfire in Degania. Well, they did happen, and each time I felt so alive that it scared me. As if every moment was worth remembering for a lifetime." Ágnes choked off a cry and then let it surface, to be dissolved in the air. "I want more of those moments. To feel the fire like I did then. And I want to do it with you." She pouted. "Why is that so hard for you to understand?"

I pictured her swaying to music. Aflame with licentious dance. "It isn't. Trust me on that."

"I'm not so sure. And listen to yourself. They 'allow us freedom.' In Palestine, we fight for it. How happy will you be when Czechoslovakia is occupied?"

"That's not going to happen. Because men like me will fight."

"So you admit that it's dangerous to stay here."

"Yes. So I worry about that. I also worry about you leaving for another dangerous place. And I honestly don't know what's best. But I believe I can protect you if you stay. As irrational as that may sound."

"You're right. It's irrational. No one will be safe here if there's war."

"And G-d forbid," I continued, "that were to happen, how can I abandon my parents? Even though my brothers—"

"Béla," she interrupted, "think about who you're saying this to." Her tone was venomous, and I could not help but wonder if she had made a conscious decision to hate me, making it more tolerable for her to leave. "My parents have two children, and Dora isn't coming back. My father is ill, and now we have the latest version of the Cossacks at our door."

I reached for her hand again, but she pulled away. "I can respect that you don't want to leave your family. But I'm wondering if that's the true reason." She drank me in with searing eyes, her gaze too intense for me to meet. "Maybe, with all your soldiering, deep down you're just a coward. You consider yourself to be heroic by remaining here, but isn't it that you're really afraid to follow a different path?"

I couldn't breach her defenses. Instead, I had inadvertently rubbed open the milky sap of the sumac, and her streaks of rage were brushing my skin. I downed the remainder of the chicory coffee, so thick that it felt chewable. But what I needed was a beer. "You can't understand that I'm reluctant to leave the place where I was born and grew up. Where my family is. And my job, however modest that is. In a beautiful city that's half Jewish. In a democratic country that protects our rights as a minority. You can't understand that I might not be thrilled to live among a bunch of communists with nothing to call my own, slaving daily in the brutal heat, eating strange foods, forced to learn yet another language, catching malaria and other exotic diseases, and surrounded by hostiles?"

Ágnes kept her calm, drumming on the table's edge methodically with her fingernails, as if I were falling asleep. "You're judging a place that you know *bubkes* (nothing) about."

Ágnes's love now came and left like waves. Part of me yearned to tell her that I would accept every speck of her venom if only she would look at me as she once did, with the eyes of a bride. "I know what you've told me and written to me."

"Sure, it isn't paradise. But at least if you fight there, you're doing it for a people whose loyalty you can trust." I envisioned Ágnes and Jenő debating. The master of facts, deductive reasoning, and rhetoric versus Hera, the dazzling goddess of simmering rage and vengeance. "And there's one more thing, Béla."

"What's that?"

The coquette in her surfaced, as she covered my foot with hers. "It's quite simple. If you come to Palestine, you'll have me."

Faced with her alternating ice and fire, I imagined the intensity of being with her every day. To capitulate would be sedative. Did I

Chapter 10

have another life in me, an alternate one that I hadn't yet recognized? "Give me more time to consider it," I appealed. "You've had time to adapt to the idea of where you belong. I haven't."

She studied me. "You can't adapt from afar. And, anyway, if you haven't been able to decide by now to come back with me, you won't change your mind. You're too much of a Mama's boy."

I slammed an open palm on the table. The couple sitting next to us, vaguely familiar, halted their conversation, the man's fork paused halfway to his mouth. "Don't you dare call me that! Not running off with you doesn't make me a Mama's boy. Or a coward."

"So stay here," Ágnes spat out. "In a place run by a rebbe who wants us to live in the Dark Ages. With no good jobs. No universities that accept Jews anymore. Winters six months long and so cold that the only thing on the ground not frozen is a fresh pile of dung. With a maniac marching toward us. Stay here, and wait for a savior who isn't coming!"

A chill overcame me, brought on by the realization that I was in love with a woman who no longer existed. Yet I couldn't let go. I would remain in everlasting orbit, unable to land. "Ágnes, a few weeks to consider this is all I'm asking for."

Without expression, she said, "There's a handsome and educated man in the kibbutz who's passionate about me. Waiting for me. He would marry me in an instant."

I felt a tinge of sorrow for this man unknown to me, for believing that a butterfly would linger on his hand forever. "If he's so wonderful, why are you here with me?"

"Because I'm a fool. Obviously."

Blood rushed to my head. "No, that's not it." I pointed at her. "You're just being selfish. If you loved me enough, more than you love an idea, you would stay with me."

"That's not fair, Béla. I could say the same thing to you. That if you loved me enough, you wouldn't want me to give up my dream. You would want to share it with me."

I wanted life to go back to the way it was before she left, when I knew Ágnes intimately. Each thought. All feelings. No secrets. "Ágnes, I can't view the world exactly as you do. I want to remain rooted in a place that I know, with people I love. Even losing myself in you won't change how I feel."

Ágnes began a response and then gazed wordlessly to her right and down. As she arose from the chair, I grabbed her sleeve and gently pulled her back. "Please, this isn't how I want the evening to end. Can't you see? I've never stopped thinking about you. Or wanting you."

She allowed that appeal to sink in, softening her expression. "You're a good man, Béla. Outside of my family, you're my only reason for schlepping back to Munkács. But I won't stay here. Not even for you."

Tearing up again, she stood abruptly and gathered her topcoat. "I've got to get home."

A part of me could not swallow another drop of Ágnes, yet still I was thirsty. I jumped up and threw a few *pengős* on the table. "I'll take you back. Let's go the long way."

We ambled, arm in arm, in seamless cadence along the wide, spruce-lined *Korzo*. The boulevard was empty, its stillness broken by stray cats and flocks of starlings flipping over leaves, searching for worms. The sky was awash in stars that appeared remarkably close, as though we were watching them through black water. Although I admit that this recollection may be illusory, as false memories are often the loveliest.

In the face of the night's breath, Ágnes lifted the collar of her coat to cover her ears. A breeze blew strands of hair across her face, even more sensuous now than it had been at the beginning of the evening. Trembling, she leaned against me.

Chapter 10

"I'm not used to the cold anymore."

I stretched to pull off my jacket. "No," she said, lifting my arm, which I dutifully placed over her shoulder, drawing her closer. "So often in the kibbutz," she continued, as if talking to herself, "I felt…lonely."

We live so much of our lives in a cocoon of our own creation. "What about your boyfriend there?"

"He's no more than a good friend to me. Better than all the lugs who just try to grope me. But he isn't you."

"Of course. Who else has my outstanding looks?"

"If I missed your face, I could have taken out a photo." She stroked my biceps with the top of her hand. "You are my Dov, my protector."

Dov, my Hebrew name, means "bear." Her pet name for me. I would call her Aviva, which means "springtime," because, I had told her, she reawakened me each time I was with her.

"I am. I would do anything for you."

"Almost anything," she corrected. Ágnes's smile was on the border of a pout. "I'm sorry for being such a bitch. It's not an excuse, but I'm worried about my father."

"I know. You love him."

"I'm not so sure. Under these circumstances, would a caring daughter consider leaving again?"

I would have walked with her for as long as it took to reach the horizon. But Ágnes's pace slowed. Up ahead was a gated park, with barren flowerbeds marked with cracked pine borders and scattered garden benches whose backrests were missing half their paint. I led her to one, careful to avoid spots that offered us splinters. We sat, and I rubbed her back.

"Béla, you said that you never stopped thinking of me."

"That's true."

She drew a line along my jaw with her index finger. "Why?" Her tone was wistful, an unfamiliar quality for Ágnes.

81

Warmth rushed to my cheeks. I had waited for many months to utter these next words. Now I feared they might be frail and shabby. "Because I love you. You must know that. I've loved you since we were kids. Before I understood that I did."

"But I'm so difficult. I know I am. Why am I lovable to you?"

An answer arose, scripted by a voice from the hidden part within me. Lifted from hundreds of petty moments that had been silently but ever loudly speaking to me. "Because you see me."

"How do you mean?"

"With my family, I am a son, a brother, an uncle. I am who they expect me to be, constantly spouting all the standard banalities. Never being asked to reveal more than what they want to see. Does this make sense?"

"Of course."

"But I don't want to be an extra in their movie. I want to be the star of my own."

"And you shouldn't feel bad for wanting that."

I let out a breath that whistled through my nostrils. "When I'm with you, I'm Béla. Flaws and all."

"Yes." Ágnes rested her head on my chest, her hair tickling her face as she melded into me. "And I love the person you are."

I inhaled her scent. "Now that you're back, Ágnes, everything is clearer. I know who I am."

She hugged me, her knees pressing against my legs. "I want to hear you say that you love me, in Hebrew, as we lie by the shores of the Sea of Galilee at sunset, as we used to at the bridge. Is that so unreasonable?"

"No," I smiled. "Not at all."

Ágnes stroked my cheek with her hand. "Béla, please tell me why you won't come to Palestine with me. Whatever you say, I promise that I won't get angry, and I won't argue with you. I just need to know."

Chapter 10

There are two of me. Which one would emerge? I kissed her palm and returned it to my cheek. "It's not because I'm not willing to make a change in my life. And it's not because I don't want to contribute to building a Jewish homeland. And it's not because I'm scared of anything there. And it certainly isn't because I don't want to be with you."

"Then what is the reason?"

"I can't go because...." Why couldn't I tell her that my heart was not small enough that only she could fill it? Because I was afraid of hurting her? I had already done that. "It's the same reason your love for me isn't enough to hold you here. If either I left with you or you stayed with me, one of us would be a lost soul. Once a person is torn in half, he can't be put back together."

Ágnes's reply was a tender breath against my face. She whispered, "Will we ever be able to make a life together?"

Whom was I more willing to deceive—her, or me? I longed to tell Ágnes that she was mine and it would never be otherwise. But now I understood that she had taken the long journey back to Munkács to say goodbye.

I lifted Ágnes's chin and kissed her parted lips, tasting the sadness. Longing for her more than I had ever wanted anyone, or anything. Yearning to tell her that I want to die before she stops loving me.

We continued for the longest while until, despite pressing our bodies together, her shivering resumed. We rose and ambled to her door. As Ágnes passed through it, a sudden current of wind, warmed by my passion, whistled toward her a final embrace.

CHAPTER 11
A Walk to the Shtiebel

The real loneliness is living among all these kind of people who only ask one to pretend.

—Edith Wharton

Early the following morning, still in my dress clothes and sleepless, I raced from my bed to the front door upon hearing Papa preparing to leave for the *shtiebel*.

"Papa, can I walk with you?"

He eyed my disheveled appearance. "Are you all right?"

I nodded. Choosing not to pry, Papa pointed his head, covered with a tattered ebony fedora decorated with a single silver plume, toward the door. "Come, it wouldn't hurt you to pray with me once in a while."

We donned coats and stepped into the dawn chill, purified by the rapid serenade of yellowhammers and the gurgling of a beetling brook across a road flecked with bronze light.

Chapter 11

"It was a wonderful celebration yesterday, *nu?*" Papa said.

"Yes, it was."

"So, to what do I owe the honor of your company?"

"I wanted to talk to you about something."

He slowed down. "Then let's not rush."

"Last night, I was with Ágnes."

"Yes, I was glad to see her back home. She comes from a good family."

"I like her, Papa. Very much. Actually…I'm in love with her."

"She's a beautiful woman. Does she have a good heart, like your Mama?"

"Yes, she does. But it's more than that, Papa. She has such strength, and passion."

"Are you two thinking of marriage?"

"I wish it were that simple. Ágnes plans to return to Palestine. For good. She wants me to join her."

Papa came to a stop on a miserly patch of weeds. He leaned forward to make close eye contact with me, sharing his understanding that a lover's desires could be both prized and feared. "What did you tell her?"

"That I want to be with her, and protect her, but that I wasn't ready to leave here…and my family."

"She always was a headstrong girl. Nice, but a little *meshuga* (crazy). A woman who doesn't understand that she must follow her man, not the other way around."

How could I tell my father that I needed Ágnes? That my life didn't work without her? I could not show my tears to him, as I might with Mama. "Did I make the right decision, Papa? If I don't go with her now, I'll lose her."

"So you are seriously considering this?" A fellow congregant strolled by. Papa acknowledged him and then asked, "She would force you to choose between her and your family? Is that what a woman who loves you would do?"

I don't care what these old men think. I care that they don't want me to live fully.

Papa, doesn't love often demand difficult choices, ones where you can't make a right decision without also making a wrong one? "I tried to convince Ágnes to stay, but she says that she feels alive only in Palestine." I looked away. "Apparently, I don't make her feel alive. But I can't bear the thought of her leaving again."

He draped his arm around me, and we resumed a slow walk. "What does your heart tell you to do, Béla?"

Sometimes hearts touch. Other times, they wander and cannot be reined in. "That's the problem. It isn't giving me a clear answer. Jenő says that the *Anschluss* is just the beginning and that Czechoslovakia is next. That we may be at war soon, and fall under the Nazis' thumb."

"No one knows for sure what will happen, including my oldest son."

"I think that Jenő is right."

Papa frowned. "And what does this have to do with you and Ágnes?"

"It has to do with Palestine. Shouldn't we all be thinking of leaving here? Of making *aliyah* (return) to the Holy Land?"

He shook his head. "I hear all sorts of things about what's going on in Palestine. Can you be certain that it's safer there than here?"

"No," I admitted. "But wouldn't it be better to fight for our own land and nation rather than fight for a country where we're only tolerated?"

"This is our land. And your Mama and I have made a home and a good life here for all of us."

"Yes, you have, Papa. But—"

"Maybe you're confusing your yearning for Ágnes with your desire for us all to emigrate?" he said, in a tone cold enough to freeze us into stillness. But I could not allow that.

"Papa, leaving my family in harm's way is the heaviest of anchors. If we would all settle somewhere safe, maybe America with Uncle

Chapter 11

Lou's help, then after some time I may be able to join Ágnes. I would visit you as often as possible."

Papa long considered America to be *trefe medinah* (an unkosher land). "Do you know the full story of your mama's time in America?" My mother had lived in the United States as a child. She emigrated from Kraków with her mother and brothers around the turn of the century, after her father, who had come to New York first, sent money for their passage. Her family stayed there for only a few years. All returned to Europe except for her oldest brother, Ludko, who was engaged by then to an American woman.

"Mama told me how difficult life was there." I had confused feelings about the United States and whether it was right for us. Maybe I would be less hesitant if I had gone there myself. Ferencz had wanted to take me with him to the 1932 Olympics in Los Angeles, where he planned to set up a partnership with an agency specializing in travel to Europe. But that had been a Depression year, one difficult for both Papa's and Ferencz's businesses, and the money for my trip was needed elsewhere. Ferencz regaled us with tales of a vast city drunk with beauty, although he complained of the heat and lack of culture.

"'Difficult' is not the right word to describe it. Mama and her family lived in a crowded, filthy tenement with no bathrooms or even outhouses. They used chamber pots and emptied them into the streets. They had to share an apartment with another family to make the rent. The water was rancid and the air stifling from lack of ventilation. They sweltered in the summer and froze in the winter. And there was a lot of crime and disease."

"That must have been awful."

"They all found jobs for little pay. Mama worked in a garment factory. Twelve hours a day, six days a week, in slave conditions and for beggar's wages."

I shook my head at the image. "Papa, I don't expect to find streets paved with gold there. Only safety."

Papa took a long breath, water vapor steaming out of his nose as if a ghost were emerging. "It would be a long, hard journey. There are a dozen of us now, counting the baby. Would everyone be willing to rearrange their lives? Could we pay for everyone's transit? Obtain the necessary visas for all of us? And what about Mama's mother? She's too frail for such a long trip, and Mama would never leave her behind."

"I understand how tough it would be to arrange, but couldn't we at least have a family gathering to discuss this?"

"And how would we live when we got there? I'd have to learn a new trade. I'm not young anymore."

"We'd all contribute."

"And what if it became impossible for you to get to Palestine from America? You'll be miserable without Ágnes. I wouldn't want that. Palestine isn't as far from here, *nu*?"

"Then it will be my problem to deal with."

"Béla, I know that you're telling me all this out of love. But you must have faith also."

All my life, I had remained confused about the boundary, for People of the Book who prized education and learning, between reason and faith, as if I were playing checkers on a board with no squares. "Faith in G-d?"

"Yes. I don't agree with Rebbe Shapira that it's sinful to want to make *aliyah* to Palestine. But I do believe in the Bible. Which teaches us that there is a time for everything. It tells us that, before the time of the Messiah, there shall be war and sorrow. The Anointed One will come when he is most needed. When the world is sinful. And then we all will be renewed and reunited in the Holy Land."

I remembered being told that, during World War I, the Munkáczer rebbe had compared that conflict to the battle of Gog and Magog,

Chapter 11

stating it to be an unequivocal harbinger of the Messiah. And in 1933, when Hitler ascended to power, the rebbe described that event as the "unmistakable birth pangs of the Mashiach."

"Maybe the Mashiach will come too late for us, Papa."

Papa kissed me on the forehead. "Béla, take comfort in the stories of Purim and Hanukkah."

"Because they teach us that goodness prevails over evil?"

"Yes. And because of their other lesson."

I knew what Papa was about to say. He had told me this many times before. But I could not speak those words myself. I no longer accepted them.

Papa pointed to the *shtiebel*. "Our people have survived for thousands of years. We are eternal!"

CHAPTER 12
The Shivah: September 18, 1938

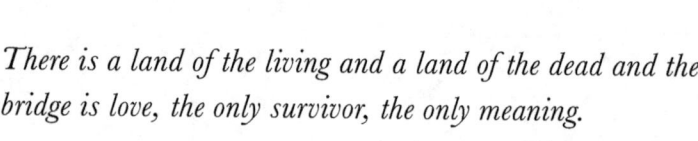

There is a land of the living and a land of the dead and the bridge is love, the only survivor, the only meaning.
—Thornton Wilder

Tetzi stood at the open front door of her house, the collar of her blouse torn in mourning, her face a prism of sorrow. As I hugged her and kissed her high forehead, she burst into a rhythmic sobbing bubbling up from a limitless well. I tugged at her wrist to lead her into a living room drenched with the somber hum of condolence, but she pulled me out toward her front step, where we sat pressed together.

"I came as soon as I heard. I'm sorry for not bringing any food."

"Your mother was here earlier with a basket of hard-boiled eggs and bread. Which is so helpful because the entire village is in my house now."

I clasped her shoulder. "I'm so sorry."

Chapter 12

"Thank you." Tetzi clenched her fists. "If I hear one more time, 'Everything happens for a reason.'"

"How about, 'He's in a better place'?"

"The worst one is, 'Time will heal.' But time doesn't always heal. I think that sometimes it only masks the pain."

"My favorite is, 'You must be strong.'"

She shook her head. "But I'm not strong. And Mama, she's really in bad shape."

Tetzi had no siblings. Her younger brother had died of tuberculosis as a child. "What happened?"

"Two days ago, Papa was struck by a train at the station." I shook my head as I closed my eyes. She added, "We don't know any reason for him to have been there."

The murmur of prayer, like a trickling waterfall in late summer, drifted past us. "Last night, I lay in bed with his voice in my ears." More whimpers. "But I couldn't make out the words. Only the pain in them."

"It's good that you slept a bit."

She covered her face with lean, fragile hands. "He didn't say goodbye to me."

"Because he wasn't intending to leave."

"Yes, he was." Her tears leaked unchecked, though she tried to catch them with her fingertips. "He was hurting, and I ignored him. My own father."

"You didn't know...."

"But I did!" Tetzi bowed her head. "I pretended not to, because I couldn't bear seeing him that way. So I looked away. So selfish."

Twilight approached, blushing with pastel colors one could grow old watching. With the sky an ocean of stars impatient to take the stage. "If there's one thing I know about you, Tetzi, it's that you're not selfish."

She reached for my hand. "Having you here helps. And Adolph. He's been here all day."

"Is there a card game inside?"

Tetzi punched me playfully. "You're the only one who talks to me normally. Listen, I've got to go back to Mama. They're about to recite *Kaddish* (the mourner's prayer). Join me."

"I'll be there in time for the prayer. Can you tell your boyfriend to come outside for a minute?"

"Ex-boyfriend." Tetzi stood, kissed the top of my head, and stepped inside. Across the road, a brown otter with distinctive white streaks chased prey at the edge of a stream, poking its nose into the ripples of water. An elderly couple came out of the house, the woman sniffling while the man finished unwinding the leather straps of his phylacteries. They were replaced by a couple who, after kissing the *mezuzah* (a small case containing a parchment scroll) on the doorpost, entered the house, carrying a box of *Yahrtzeit* (memorial) candles. Soon Adolph was slumped down, bruising the grass beside me, his arms behind his head.

"I thought you might need a break."

"Thanks. I couldn't take another minute."

"What's this about you being an 'ex-boyfriend'?"

Adolph shook his head. "It wasn't my choice. Tetzi said that she needed a break from relationships."

"Don't feel too bad. I'm now an ex-boyfriend also."

"Sorry to hear that, Béla. I guess we're both lousy with women."

"No, your situation is different. Tetzi is just going through a rough time. I think that she'll come around."

"Everyone inside is whispering that it was a suicide."

"Tetzi believes that, too."

Adolph picked up a rock and pitched it toward the otter, who had been staring at the water's reflection as if admiring himself. He eyed

Chapter 12

us with the surprise of a homeowner encountering a trespasser in his backyard. "Her father may end up being the lucky one."

"Meaning what?"

In late May, in response to concentrations of German soldiers massing near the Sudeten region of Czechoslovakia, which lay on a jagged border with Germany and was inhabited largely by ethnic Germans, Adolph and I had been called up along with all other Czech Army reservists. The Czechs manned bunker fortifications, stretching hundreds of kilometers, which our army had built over a period of years. That "May Crisis" was averted. "He doesn't have to face whatever is coming. You know that we're going to be called up again."

"I heard that Chamberlain is in Germany now, meeting with Hitler."

Adolph rose and stretched. "I think that we're days from a war with the Nazis. Who knows? Our family might be sitting *shivah* for us next week."

"Or there might just be a lot of dead Germans. Stop being so morbid."

The roar of a stag, a cross between a chainsaw and a belch, echoed. Red-deer mating season had begun. "I've made a decision," Adolph said.

"Even more gambling and booze over the next few days?"

"Of course. But it's more than that. I know that you and I have to stay and fight. But if by some miracle war is avoided, or if I do somehow survive it, I'm leaving Czechoslovakia."

"Why the need to leave?"

Adolph leaned down and with his index finger drew a triangle in the dirt. Then another overlapping one upside down.

"Palestine. So first Ágnes, and now you."

"I don't feel I've decided to leave. More like I'm finally not going to force myself to stay."

"When will you tell Mama and Papa?"

Adolph grabbed another rock and flung it at the otter, which scampered across a nearby log, dragging along marks of newfound fear. "I already told Papa. He said that I'm a grown man who can make his own choices. But that he had hoped the family would stay together."

"Papa is Old World. With Old World ideas."

"He's also worried about how upset Mama will be. He wants to tell her first."

"I envy you, my little brother. You know what you want."

"Why envy me? Come with me."

Again I was being asked to emigrate. Why couldn't I say, "Yes"? I longed to be with Ágnes. Maybe my method of coping with impossible choices was to remain unconscious to them. "I won't leave our parents."

"So you think I'm wrong to want to go?"

"No, Adolph, it's right for you. When Ágnes first spoke to me about building a Jewish homeland for future generations, it seemed fanciful. And needless. But now I understand better."

"So, you might follow me one day."

"If I can convince Mama and Papa." I stood. Time to say *Kaddish*. "The only thing I know for sure is that, for now, my place is here."

Adolph grasped my arm. "I can't help but think that one of us will be making a terrible mistake."

CHAPTER 13
November 1938: The Hungarians Return

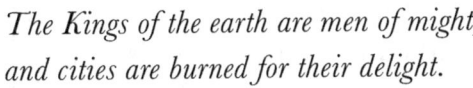

*The Kings of the earth are men of might,
and cities are burned for their delight.*

—Joyce Kilmer

By 1938, interspersed with substantial German, Magyar, Ukrainian, Polish, and Slovak minorities, Czechoslovakia remained, alone among the countries of Eastern Europe, a democratic, tolerant nation. A "little America," we later called it. The Czech government granted Jews citizenship rights and protected them from persecution—unlike Hungary, which had legitimized anti-Semitism well before Hitler came to power.

Czechoslovakia between the wars was led by two admirable men, Tomáš Masaryk and Edvard Beneš, each a liberal humanist opposed to the rising fascist tide. (Masaryk, whose wife was Brooklyn-born and an American citizen, publicly opposed anti-Semitism and even traveled to the Holy Land to visit Jewish agricultural settlements.)

Until World War II, our country remained relatively immune from the contagion infusing itself across the continent.

The Jews of Munkács were spared widespread acts of violence, although not the softer anti-Semitism pervasive in Europe. Jews bore a heavier share of taxes, had difficulty attaining senior civil-service positions, and were required to achieve higher school grades to be admitted into a university. As a child, I feared Christian holidays, especially Christmas and Easter, when parishioners, as they left church, would spit, strike, or throw stones at any Jews who passed.

I had been trained for years to fight and was impatient to do so. The radio had broadcast Hitler's labeling of our country as "the open ulcer of Central Europe," and Göring calling Czechs a "miserable pygmy race without culture" who were being manipulated by Moscow and the "Jew devil" to oppress ethnic Germans.

Days after the *shivah*, the Czech Army was mobilized, and again Adolph and I were called to join our garrisons. War appeared inevitable but was avoided, although on Satan's terms. As we had feared, England and France, to appease Hitler, signed the Munich Agreement (and pressured Beneš to acquiesce to it), providing for the partition of our country. Our Army reluctantly withdrew from the Sudetenland, with its key defensive frontiers and fortifications, whose population welcomed the oncoming Germans. As Churchill stated, "The German dictator, instead of snatching the victuals from the table, has been content to have them served to him course by course."

By early November 1938, having tasted our blood, Germany, along with Italy, came back for more. They granted Czechoslovakian territories in southern Slovakia and the southwest Subcarpathian Rus (including our city) to Hungary, a country that had never known democracy and that openly sympathized with the Axis powers. Hitler was now in our lives. By the following March, in an adult version of

Chapter 13

the street game "I Declare War," the remainder of Czechoslovakia was gobbled up by Germany and it, like Austria, lost its independence. A cloud of bile had smothered the sun.

Hungary's armed forces were an embarrassing fragment of Czechoslovakia's. Nevertheless, on November 10, in the icy chill of a premature winter that muted nature's green morsels, flag-carrying Hungarian cavalry soldiers entered our city unopposed. Clad in ill-fitting uniforms, they made futile attempts to stay in formation as they marched into the town square accompanied by a military band. Jóska and I stood silently among a cheering crowd of villagers of mixed ethnicity who were exulting over the resurrection of the motherland. Before us, an elderly Jewish lawyer greeted the Army commander, as his granddaughter presented a bouquet of chrysanthemums to him in the name of the city.

"The fool," said Jóska, "He thinks he can buy the Hungarians' goodwill cheaply."

"Most of the older generation believes that," I said. "They remember too fondly the days before the Great War, when the Austro-Hungarian monarchs were good to Jews."

"What they forget," Jóska replied, "is that Hungary always returns to anti-Semitism. After the war, Germany wasn't the first country to pass anti-Jewish laws. It was Hungary."

"Jóska," I said, "isn't it at least better that we're being occupied by Hungary, not Germany?"

"Maybe. Maybe not."

On the night of their entry into my town, Hungarian soldiers beat and whipped Jews they encountered on the street. Legal persecution followed. Hungary's existing laws, now enforced in Munkács, already limited the number of Jews in a wide range of professions to twenty percent, on the grounds that excessive Jewish influence was harmful to the nation's economy. These restrictions compounded the longstanding reality throughout Hungary that many occupations had long been closed to Jews. By year's end, many local government officials were summarily fired, without severance pay or pension.

The economic noose was pulled tighter the following May, when a law was passed, similar to a Hungarian statute that had briefly existed after World War I, further limiting Jews to six percent in the professions and in business activities generally. (Why six percent? Because that was allegedly the proportion of Jews in the total population.) Drastic reductions were made in the number of licenses issued to Jewish lawyers, doctors, pharmacists, and engineers. Tens of thousands lost their jobs. Jews were compelled to sell or lease their land to non-Jews and lost their voting rights. The law also permitted retroactive withdrawal of citizenship, which provided a basis for expelling Jewish refugees who had fled to the Rus from fascist oppression elsewhere.

In Munkács, among the first to suffer were the owners of small businesses, when the government cancelled authorizations for the sale of items such as tobacco, alcohol, and gunpowder. Most of the stores in the city were owned by Jews, and a large number of them closed. Those stores allowed to remain in Jewish hands had to change the lettering on their signs from Hebrew to Hungarian.

Yaakov Pollack found another option. He took on a non-Jewish *strohmann* (straw man), who eventually took full ownership of the store. When I visited Pollack, he'd rail against the "Mongol descendants of Attila the Hun" who had taken control and the injustice they had brought. My old boss believed that G-d was an approachable entity ("Why else should we pray?") and would challenge Him directly to remedy the situation. Before we were occupied, witnessing these confrontations amused me. Later, I came to adopt Pollack's approach.

Miki and Libu's access to education, along with all other young Jews, became more restricted. Popular schools that taught in Czech

Chapter 13

were closed. After a brief shutdown, Munkács' Gymnasium reopened, but was a shell of its former self. Chaim Kugel and many of its professors had fled (Kugel would make his way to Palestine and become mayor of Holon, a suburb of Tel Aviv), and Hungarian became the school's new primary language. Worse, the quota system that had been in place for university attendance was expanded into a total exclusion of the People of the Book.

After the German invasion of Poland in September 1939, many Polish Jews, including former Polish Army soldiers, escaped through the mountains to the Rus, as my ancestors had done in the last century. Families arrived with their bundled possessions on foot, on the back of trucks, or on bicycles. They were sprinkled throughout the streets of Munkács. My father, along with others, brought them spare clothing and food. He inquired of his relatives from Kielce, to no avail. These refugees conveyed disturbing stories of the brutalization and massacre of their countrymen by the Nazis. As was the case with most of us, I could not bring myself to fully accept their accounts.

I reflected on Ágnes, happy that she was safe, and wondering if I still was in love with her only because we were apart. And did I still walk inside her dreams?

Limited emigration of families continued, with the help of Zionist groups. But, by 1940, the Hungarian authorities persecuted Zionist leaders, many of whom had joined underground movements. The Munkács mayor was forced to publish a list of those Jewish and Zionist organizations whose activities were banned. The *Jewish Voice* closed.

The Royal Hungarian Gendarmerie, whose training emphasized militant anticommunism—and xenophobia—had been granted oversight of anti-Jewish activities. In contrast to the local police, the gendarmes were harsh and feared. Known for their hard, black Beau Brummel top hats, into which were tucked brightly colored cock feathers, they set up their Bereg county headquarters in Munkács.

Jews passing them in the street had to remove their caps and salute smartly. Many local Jews, in particular ones associated with communist and socialist movements, were interrogated on suspicion of illegal political activity. The wealthy also were a regular target, grilled and tortured for information on their assets and properties.

Ethnic Germans from Swabia, notorious for their anti-Semitism, arrived in Munkács. Recognized by their German military shirts, they attacked Jews while the police turned a blind eye. For traditional, observant men such as my father, who maintained beards and wore hats or other identifying clothing, it was difficult to appear in the town without incurring some form of humiliation or physical abuse. And in schools, Miki, Libu, and other Jewish students, including the youngest ones, were subjected to taunts and violence from classmates and teachers. Nor did we feel safe in our own home. Neighbors told us of gendarmes breaking into houses, under the pretext of conducting military exercises or searching for concealed weapons. They would ransack rooms in a quest for valuables.

Papa was less able to ply his trade, one that was perilous even in good times because of the constant danger of being attacked by locals intent on stealing cattle. Our family survived by depleting our savings and with the assistance of money earned by my brothers and me. Jenő moved to Prague to work at a Czech paper, publishing articles under an assumed name. I was conscripted into the Hungarian Army, Ferencz directly into the Hungarian labor system. For as long as we received pay, we sent money to our parents.

As the war ground on, the increasingly oppressive physical environment, the gradual elimination from public, economic, and cultural life, and the impoverishment that befell many imposed a harsh toll on the Jews of Munkács. Yet with it all, for the longest while, we were among the lucky ones.

CHAPTER 14

Adolph Ingber: September 3, 1939 (Tel Aviv)

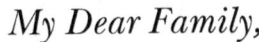

My Dear Family,

I am sorry for not writing sooner. You are all always in my thoughts and prayers.

Can you imagine living in a place built totally by Jews? It was difficult to find an apartment at first, but I managed, T.G. I live in the first floor flat of a stucco apartment building that sits on stilts. The best part is that I'm near an endless gleaming beach in a city that appears as white as Mama's bed sheets. Yet it saturates the senses. Sights and smells and tastes so different from those of Munkács. To arrive here is to be reborn.

As I wrote previously, to make ends meet, I am apprenticing as a dental technician. What I haven't yet told you is that I am also making a bit of extra money by playing football. I've joined the Hapoel Tel-Aviv team. We train on the sand, which makes running on grass seem easy.

Béla's Letters

All the talk here is of the war. And the situation with the Arabs remains difficult. But please don't worry about me. I am flourishing in the Holy Land, in a young city filled with romantics, whose whispered passions shout in my ears. I am sure to make a good life for myself here. H.I. And Mama, there are so many shayner maidel. I will write more of that another time.

I dreamt last night that I was back home with you. But our home was here.

Please take care of yourselves. I am sorry, truly sorry, for not being in a position to help. I have registered for military service with His Majesty's forces. We are hopeful that the British will form a Jewish Legion, as they did during the last war. We may need another Jabotinsky to make that happen.

I kiss you all a million times.

Your loving son and brother,

Adolph Ingber (far right) in Herzliya, Palestine, 1939

CHAPTER 15

Jóska Ingber: October 4, 1940 (New York)

My Dear Beloved Brother,

I am writing to you directly because these words must remain between the two of us.

As you know, I've told Mama and Papa of my decision to stay in the United States, and to enlist in its Army. They assure me they understand, but I imagine they have mixed feelings at best. I've lost touch with Jenő and Ferencz, who I know would be supportive. I hope you are also. And I want you to know the background, in case something happens to me.

But, first, let me tell you about what they call "the Wonder City." It is so vast, and such a Jewish place. Here we are a majority because there is no majority. The shops, the stores, the streets, the newspapers, the politicians, the radio programs, the entertainers, they all have a Jewish flavor. Even the public schools are closed on the High Holidays.

Yesterday, during a long walk in Manhattan, I must have passed at least a dozen shuls filled with Rosh Hashanah worshippers. The city appears to shut down on the High Holidays, as it was in Munkács. There's even a Betar camp nearby, where they teach self-defense. You remember Jabotinsky? He died at that camp a couple of months ago.

You can be Jewish openly in New York. Without fear. No one bothers you. No one cares. There is apathy to religious differences, if not clear acceptance. Americans are all about commerce. They only care whether you can help them make a buck.

The World's Fair is remarkable. And to think that, a few years ago, the area it's in was a big garbage dump.

I wish I had Jenő's gift of description. In the Fair, I saw a time capsule with writings by Einstein and others, and an assortment of everyday items preserved for history. You can find a copy of the Magna Carta. There are performing elephants, camel rides, and exotic birds. A model future city that you watch from a moving walkway high above floor level.

Best of all are the inventions. An amplifying radio with a photo tube, called "television." It's like watching a movie on a small screen. Photographs that are in color. Electric lights so bright that they turn night into day. An electric typewriter. A robot that walks and talks. And something called "air conditioning" that makes a room feel like you're sitting between ice cubes no matter how hot or humid it is outside.

Many countries have pavilions here, although the Czechoslovakia one is now closed. I've been to most of them. And best of all, there is a Palestine Pavilion. Einstein came here last year to dedicate it. Our people have their own building!

It was at the Palestine Pavilion, a small building far apart from those of the other nations, where it all happened. I was with cousin Milan, Uncle Lou's son, who I'm staying with. We were speaking in Hungarian as we passed by a booth manned by U.S. military personnel. A fellow standing there interrupted and asked if he could chat with us.

Chapter 15

I cannot put his name in a letter, but he is a Jew who's a major in the U.S. Army, assigned to the Military Intelligence Division. Milan left to meet up with a friend, but I stayed and continued speaking with the Major, initially in English, but that was too difficult for me, so we switched to Yiddish. We went to get coffee.

The conversation was casual at first. We exchanged histories, and the Major told me that his parents were Polish Jews. I mentioned that we were trying to find word of our Polish relatives and he replied, "You likely won't be able to locate them."

Much of our conversation I can't repeat, but the Major had specific information on the herding of Jews into ghettos and forced labor camps, where they live under horrid conditions. He had some photos as well, which I'm sorry I saw.

He asked me when my visa expired, and made me an offer. Instead of returning to Europe, he proposed that I stay in America and join the Intelligence Unit that he is a part of, to contribute to the British and Free French efforts to fight the Nazis. The Americans are seeking men and women with an Eastern European background who know the local cultures and languages. And they trust Jews most of all not to be enemy agents.

The Major also said to me, "If you stay in the Army for at least two years, you will be eligible to become a U.S. citizen."

I declined his offer, but I found myself thinking of nothing else. Days later, just before my visa would expire, I returned and found the Major still there. I confessed my uncertainty. He whispered to me, "We believe that it is inevitable that the Nazis will begin to kill the Jews under their domain. And Hungary is likely to join the Axis alliance and fall under Nazi domination. Jóska, isn't it best for you to stay here and work against them?"

Is it wrong for me not to rejoin my family? I have agonized over this choice but, in the end, I envisioned what Jenő would advise me to do. Also, the Major assured me that, after I become a U.S. citizen, I will be able to sponsor my family members to immigrate to the U.S. Those were the deciding factors.

Please understand that I am doing this not for myself. And forgive me if I've made a mistake.

Béla, please try to take care of yourself. Hopefully, the war will be short, and America will stay out of it, so I can continue to write and to send money and goods.

Have you heard from Adolph? My last letter to him was returned.

Did I tell you that it was Ferencz who was scheduled to come here and see the World's Fair? But Rozsa's sister became engaged, and he would have had to miss her wedding. Because I speak some English, Ferencz offered me the tickets and visa. To ascribe this chain of events to arbitrariness would be blasphemy. They must be part of a heavenly plan.

I pray that my cherished family, and our people, will survive this latest Pharaoh.

I hug and kiss you a million times.

Your loving older brother,

CHAPTER 16
Passover: April 22, 1941

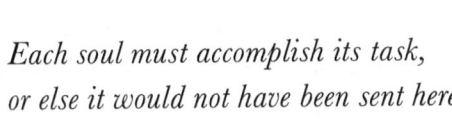

*Each soul must accomplish its task,
or else it would not have been sent here.*
— Isaac Bashevis Singer

    My recollections of the war years have blended into vignettes that crisscross in time. No longer a complete narrative, they appear of their own volition. Pressed against them are the experiences of my new life, flush with joys from those who are unaware. Those unblemished memories require less effort, being solidified by thousands of photos and videos that can be summoned on the computer (although not by me) at a moment's notice.

    My earliest Passover memory, one that I believe is more than fantasy, is of my father placing me on his lap and explaining, "Every Jew must identify with our ancestors. This is one of the ways we remain as a people." Only years later did I appreciate how our spirits were intertwined with the Israelites. And how futile it was to expect that we might escape the suffering imposed upon each generation of His chosen ones.

The 1941 Seder was the final one I attended in our Munkács home. Ordinarily, our ceremonial Passover items would have been displayed on an ornate pewter plate that had been passed down through the generations. Its smooth surface depicted scenes of a father reclining at the Seder table, the Paschal sacrifice, and the four sons, while its edges were decorated with signs of the zodiac.

"Mama," I overheard Libu say, "where is your mama's Seder platter?"

"This year, let's keep it safe in the attic."

In those vanishing days of Eden, there were twelve of us, including Ilona, Józsi, three-year-old Feri, Ferencz, and his pregnant wife, Rozsa. Adolph and Jóska were missing, although the lack of chairs and settings for them did not inhibit their presence.

After the men returned from *shul*, Mama took her accustomed place in front of our polished silver candlesticks and lit the holiday candles. With a cup in hand and reclining on a pillow placed on his chair, my father, who had donned a *kittel* (a white linen robe decorated with lace), began the service by softly chanting the *Kiddush*, proclaiming the holiness of the holiday. We drank sweet Passover wine that had been bartered for in the black market in the absence of local kosher vineyards. Each of us finished the Cup of Sanctification except for Mama. She took a sip, then handed her glass to Ferencz, who teased, "Mama, you can't possibly be a good Jew if you don't drink wine."

Papa washed his hands with lye soap at a porcelain washbasin in the bedroom. Mama, sitting closest to the kitchen, passed to each of us a boiled potato that we dipped into saltwater, the tears of our ancestors whom we had now become, another generation to be mourned by successive ones. While we collectively recited the blessing over vegetables, Feri shoved a potato toward his mouth and gnawed at it before flinging the spud half across the table. Miki and Libu, sitting together, guffawed. Józsi reached for the bruised potato and gobbled

Chapter 16

it down. He motioned for Feri to sit on his lap, where the boy would grab at József's grizzled mustache and pop his father's blown-out cheeks. They would entertain each other for most of the evening, the high point arriving when József thrust his finger into the lower lick of flame above a candle's hollow, causing Feri to shriek, his face an open stare.

Papa broke a thin, round *shmura* matzoh in half, one of a meager few that we were able to obtain. He wrapped the larger piece in a linen cloth and hid it in the kitchen for a later game with Feri of "find the *afikomen*." A second cup of wine was poured. Papa reached for his *Haggadah*, bound in cedar and adorned with mosaics. Ours—plain and worn, in Hebrew with Yiddish translations—were handed out, and we recalled the exodus from Egypt. As Papa, at appropriate points, sang the refrain, we all expertly joined in to provide the harmony.

We came to the four questions. In past years, Papa had explained that questions are essential to the Seder, to spark understanding and absorption of the Passover narrative. Miki recited them begrudgingly, having argued that, after more than a decade, it should be someone else's turn. But he still was the youngest male who could read, although, by that time in the war, none of us were young anymore.

The dialogue of the four sons was my least favorite portion of the service, for I was the fourth of my father's male children and thus eternally designated to be the one without the capacity to inquire, to whom it must be explained all that the Lord did for us when we fled Egypt. As if silence meant ignorance, when it is the door to contemplation. I played my character well. However, the youngest son was not still.

"Are we not again slaves?" whispered Miki to no one in particular. He asked again, more loudly.

My parents traded alarmed glances. "These are difficult times, Miki," responded Papa. "Which makes our *Haggadah* reading all the more meaningful."

"Why, Papa? We're reciting a story centuries old. It's no longer relevant."

"It is quite relevant. The Pharaoh persecuted us, but we triumphed. And we will do so again."

Miki persisted. "The Israelites prevailed only after hundreds of years of bondage, tortures, and killings. Is that what we must accept?"

Jenő, his face a feverish red, began poking his index finger rapid-fire on the table, sending Feri to the refuge of Ilona's lap, his hands around her neck. "Look how bad it's gotten in our own backyard," Jenő said. "And it's worse elsewhere in Europe. Let me tell you what is happening in Poland…."

"You're scaring your family, Jenő," Papa said, as spittle flew from his mouth. Raising his voice, he added, "Isn't it bad enough that two of your brothers aren't here with us?"

I had been following the debate by ping-ponging my head toward each speaker. Now it was my turn. "I'm glad Adolph and Jóska are far from here." Ferencz and Jenő nodded in support as I continued, "And deep down I know that you and Mama are, too."

Papa lifted his *Haggadah* into an air that had lost its oxygen, and shook it. "Is it a sin that I want our family to be together on this holy day? Together and not arguing."

Jenő flung his tie over his shoulder and removed a newspaper article from a jacket pocket. "Just let me read a few sentences…."

"No," Papa said, through gritted teeth.

Jenő faced Mama, his eyes pleading like those of a boxer hit below the belt. Mama, who had been sitting with hands pressed against her blue-veined temples, tenderly addressed Papa. "We should hear more from Jenő. He is so knowledgeable." She reached across Ferencz to place her hand on Jenő's. "But this is not the best time, Jenő. We will find a better one."

Chapter 16

Jenő spoke more calmly. "No, now is the best time to discuss this, Mama. We may not have another chance while we're all together." He glanced at Miki. "Miki is right. There's no Moses to lead us. Isn't it obvious after all these years of our people's suffering that the covenant is lost? Now, we must save ourselves."

The skin on Papa's cheeks tightened. "No more of this talk during the Seder!" He reopened his *Haggadah* and returned to melodically reciting the liturgy, which told of the miracles performed by the Almighty for the redemption of His people. Papa had drawn the shades, allowing only edges of light, marching us by rote toward an unsatisfying climax.

Talk was muted during the meal. Mirth too, except when Mama found a wishbone in her piece of chicken. She passed it to Ferencz. "You grab one end, and let Rozsa hold the other end; then each of you pull," Mama said, her face sparkling for the first time all night.

Feri, now wearing a shirt darkened with saliva and food residue, said in a high-pitched voice, "Why, *Bubbe*?"

"To find out if they will have a boy or a girl, *Tataleh*."

Feri's eyes were as wide as billiard balls. He moved closer to the wishbone to observe the contest.

"I have a better method," Ilona said. She grabbed Rozsa's free hand and inspected it. "Your hand is so smooth, Rozsa. You will definitely have a girl."

"No," chimed in Libu. "You can tell by looking at Rozsa's face. It's getting thinner. That means she's carrying a boy."

"You two know nothing," insisted Józsi. "You can best tell by touching her feet. If they're cold, it's a boy."

Ferencz and Rozsa broke the wishbone, with Rozsa left holding the larger end. "It's a girl," shrieked Mama. Rozsa smiled at Feri, and they both began clapping, a sound that remains too loud to ever be erased.

As we neared the end of the service, Ferencz withdrew a flask from his jacket, uncapped it, and drank. He rose unsteadily. "A toast, my beloveds." Each adult raised a glass, anticipating a tribute likely to range from the heartwarming to the embarrassing.

"Let us celebrate the love that we have for one another. And let it sustain us through this difficult time, and for all eternity."

A chorus of "Amens" followed. Ferencz headed for Miki's room, to sleep it off, I assumed. Papa recited the blessing over the last cup of wine and poured for everyone. He signaled for Ilona and Libu to have the honor of opening the front door to welcome Elijah to join the Seder. As was customary, we would implore Elijah to save us from peril and to beseech G-d to discharge His wrath upon our oppressors.

I was savoring the remnants of my wine when a high-pitched scream emanated from the front door, then strangled itself. Jumping up, I frantically calculated which implement on the table could double as a weapon. Papa caught my eye, winking at me as Mama frowned. Moments later, Ilona and Libu crept back in, faces flush. There followed Ferencz, wearing a red-and-black mask festooned with gilding and gold-leaf work, with a pronounced jaw that jutted to a point. How befitting that Elijah the Redeemer had at last revealed himself.

As Ferencz reentered the room, Feri erupted into a frenzied wailing that neither parent could remedy, even after my brother ripped off the mask. Perhaps the child subconsciously understood that one could not wear a hideous mask without, in due course, transforming into the creature it represented.

With Ilona's nod, I hoisted Feri on my shoulders for a ride through the house that ended with a discovery of the *afikomen* and an award of ten fillér. Returning to the dining room, I tickled his palms while singing a favorite nursery rhyme: "*Boci, boci, tarka, Se füle, se farka...* (Spotted, spotted, cow, cow. Has no ears and no tail)." I chanted it again, the second time for me.

Chapter 16

I don't pretend to remember much else of that year's service, or perhaps I choose not to, because remembrance cannot save the lost ones but only allow me to lose them over and over again. No doubt, Ilona, with a tremulous voice, led the family's slapstick rendition of the best of the holiday folk songs, *Chad Gadya*, which tells of a little goat that is eaten by a cat, which is bitten by a dog, which is beaten by a stick, which is burned by fire, etcetera, etcetera. Only the Master of the Universe survives unscathed.

As tradition demands, the Seder ended with our proclaiming, "Next year in Jerusalem." A testament to our faith that the Messiah will have reappeared by then and established his kingdom in the Holy Land. Would that only have been so.

CHAPTER 17
The Walnut Tree

Row, brothers, row, the stream runs fast,
the rapids are near, and the daylight's past.

—Thomas Moore

I stepped into our backyard, awash in a silver glow from a pockmarked moon tempered by a softer light angling out from the kitchen. The days had turned warm enough to dry the winter's mud, but the nights retained their cold cruelty. I stood in place in rolled-up shirtsleeves, adjusting to the chill, taking it on. Near the first of the surfacing vegetables were several plum trees, whose fragrant pink blossoms were awakening.

Towering above them all, standing out like a bride on her wedding day, was a lone black walnut tree, awaiting bloom. Its furrowed bark was arranged in diamond patterns. A favorite pastime for us boys had been to climb its limitless expanse barefoot, challenging each other to reach ever-higher branches. In the height of summer, after a day of play, we would lie on the membranes of tree roots or on folding cots

Chapter 17

and gaze at the night sky's portrait. Sensing the vast open distances above and around us. Fighting the sleep that wanted us. And in the fall, after the first frost, we would gather the walnuts that showered down on us and crack their shells with a hammer; then we'd eat the kernel with honey.

I found Jenő under the tree, sitting cross-legged on the edge of a thick log, idly sucking on a pipe. The halo from the bowl and its sweet tobacco scent were familiar. Ilona and her family had departed. Ferencz had escorted his wife home and then likely ambled to the bar in the Csillag, which was open on the holiday to the dismay of the observant, for some gambling. I claimed a spot on the other end of the log.

Jenő acknowledged my presence as if we had made an appointment to meet.

"How are you, Béla?"

"Ate too much." I hungered for the rapture of a cigarette. I could never master the art of pipe smoking. Invariably, I would puff too hard or pack the tobacco improperly.

"How Mama is able to serve a traditional Seder meal these days is a mystery."

"'G-d will provide,' she still tells us. But I think Mama was particularly determined this year."

Jenő, who had limited capacity for polite conversation, tamped the tobacco and relit his pipe. "So you are back in the Hungarian Army. How's the retraining?"

"It's not the Czech Army, that's for sure. We would have slaughtered them in battle."

"I don't doubt that. Did you know that the Hungarians, in all their long, glorious history, have never won a war?"

"Yet the country still exists," I complained.

"Have they shifted you to labor camp service?"

115

"I suppose, although no one has explained it quite that way."

"What do you mean?"

I succumbed to the reporter's questioning. "Everything had been fine until a month ago. Some of the troops were anti-Semites with big mouths, but our commander, Colonel Lauder, was a decent sort, or so I believed. Our unit had been stationed near Szolyva. One Monday, as soon as we got back from furlough, they ordered all two hundred of us in the unit to line up. The colonel yelled, 'All Jews step forward.' We did."

Jenő gazed ahead of him, listening as if memorizing my story for future use.

"He shouted, 'Jews, lay down your guns.'" My mouth stayed opened, but it became useless, as if my lungs had filled with water. I dug in the dirt with my heel.

Jenő finished for me. "And you did."

I exhaled deeply, clearing the smoke encircling me. "He shouted, 'Because your tribe have proved to be untrustworthy for the protection of our country, henceforth you will have only a pick and spade in your hands.' Then he yelled to the others, 'And you must guard these unreliables with the utmost rigor. If anyone attempts to escape, shoot him in the head.'"

"I'm sorry. You're a better soldier than any of them. They are no more than a bunch of hooligans."

"I swear to you, Jenő, if I had known what would happen, I never would have dropped my gun. They would have had to take it from me!"

"The world is filled with dead heroes. Why be another one, for the sake of some misguided sense of honor? What would that have accomplished, except to break your family's heart?"

Opening my palms and raising them, I choked out, "I feel so helpless. How can I protect myself, much less my family, with a shovel?"

Jenő reached to squeeze my open hand. "What do you do now?"

"We lay railroad tracks. Clear forests. Clean barracks. Unload military freight. Dredge rivers. And the like. All the crap work."

Chapter 17

Cupping the pipe in his hand, he raised it to his mouth. "Béla, just do as they ask. You're better off anyway being out of the regular Army. The war will spread. I suspect Russia is the next battle scene. And the Hungarian Army may be sent off to fight against the Allies. You don't want any part of that ugliness."

I changed the subject. "Jenő, did you hear that Mama and Papa received a letter from Adolph?"

"No."

"He mentioned that he met a woman. Who grew up in Palestine. He wants to marry her."

Jenő drew deeply from the pipe. "So that's why Mama's been upset."

"Yes, she wrote back to Adolph asking that he wait."

"For what?"

"Until she and Papa can meet the woman."

Jenő rolled his eyes. "Our mother, bless her, will not gladly relinquish her role. I realized that too late."

Years ago, Jenő had been engaged to a fellow reporter from Prague, a woman so vivacious as to quickly fill up a lover's memory. But who was out of place in the confines of Munkács. "I thought Mama and Papa weren't opposed to your marrying Judit, but wanted you to wait until after Ilona married. Judit wasn't willing to wait?"

"It was more complicated than that. I've learned that when you're in love with someone, sometimes there's someone else close to you who tries to diminish that love. In my case, it was our parents."

"Be honest. Was it Mama and Papa's fault, or your own inability to commit?"

"Both perhaps. Judit wasn't convinced that my parents' request was my sole reason for delaying the wedding. Our relationship soured." Jenő knocked the top of the pipe bowl against the tree trunk and relit.

"Perhaps it was a blessing after all. Judit was a free spirit. Marriage might have changed what I loved about her."

Even now, any sign of my oldest brother's lack of invincibility disturbed me. "Jenő, will you follow Adolph? If anyone can arrange the journey, it's you. I hear that Romania still allows refugees to embark from Sulina."

He cleared his throat, accentuating the dissonant sound as though the act were a language of its own. "Not yet. I still have things to attend to here."

"Like what?"

"I'd rather not get into it now."

We lapsed into a meditative silence, two mimes burrowing inside ourselves to come up with a new act, until Jenő chuckled. "Béla, do you know how Adolph arrived in Palestine?"

After Adolph's most recent letter arrived, Mama read it out loud once the Sabbath meal had ended, her finger moving across the page as she spoke. "Sure. Betar helped him obtain a forged Liberian transit visa. He traveled over the Black Sea and through Turkey. Then he bribed his way onto a coal ship. Near Haifa harbor, a Haganah boat brought him in."

Jenő shook his head. "It's *bubbameisse* (a made-up tale). If you're going to be a good reporter, you've got to be able to spot that." Jenő had commented that he envied my trusting nature, but it hindered developing a reporter's instinct, fundamental to which is understanding the many different people every one of us is. In turn, my brother was cursed by his ability to "see" things so well. "There were no Haganah boats. The British would have sunk them in a minute. Adolph made that up so Mama and Papa wouldn't worry."

"I thought his story sounded too good."

"The British Navy stopped his ship over a mile from shore. They demanded that it return to Turkey. So Adolph jumped overboard

Chapter 17

in the middle of the night and swam ashore. He must have been in tremendous shape from all the years of playing football."

"My G-d, he could have drowned. Or been shot. How do you know all this, Jenő?"

"Adolph wrote to me separately."

I peered down as I shoved my hands further into my pants pockets, imagining Adolph's feat.

"Béla, Adolph's story reminds me of the true meaning of Passover. You know what I mean?"

"Let me guess. The celebration of human freedom?" Any answer I proffered would be wrong, but the fun was in the game.

"Hardly. We've never attained freedom for any length of time."

"The triumph of good over evil?"

"Only in fairy tales."

"Rebirth. Renewal. That's why the holiday occurs in the spring."

"Hogwash."

Jenő once had told me that the answer to most questions lies within them. "So tell me."

I sensed him staring at me as if my skin were transparent. He enunciated his words precisely. "It's simple. That we should remember our suffering."

"In order to fortify conscience. Papa told us that."

Jenő's thick eyebrows rose in concert, providing a unibrow look, his incredulity a searing reminder of our differences. "The hell with conscience. Suffering is a call to action. The anguish of the Israelites reminds us of the wisdom of fleeing. That's why it's called the Book of Exodus."

"But we Jews always are running from one place to another. That can't be the holiday's significance."

"But it is! Béla, don't get too enamored with ritual, or overanalyze but then miss the larger context. Each generation must find its own truths. We need to interpret the *Haggadah* in the context of our lives, or why bother reading it? And escape is the important lesson for this year. The Jews of that time fled from the Egyptians. We need to run from this Nazi maniac."

"Try to convince Papa of that!"

My brother sucked so hard on his pipe I thought he'd gulp down the tobacco. "Papa and his generation believe this is just another pogrom and that the Nazis are just a bunch of Cossacks with better guns. They imagine that if they keep their heads down until the war ends, they won't be among the small number of unfortunate Jews killed."

"I think that Mama and Papa are as worried as the rest of us." All the war news was disheartening. Rommel was marching through North Africa, on a path that would lead him to Palestine. Yugoslavia had surrendered, with Greece next. A pro-Nazi Vichy government ruled southern France. London was being pummeled with air raids. "Jenő, how bad do you think things will get?"

"Recently, I read *Mein Kampf.* How I got through that tedious, horribly written rant I don't know. Hitler speaks of a decisive fight with France, which has happened, after which comes Russia. But at the heart of his fury are the Jews. He is obsessed with us."

Spinning through my mind was Jabotinsky's apocalyptic prophecy of more than a half-decade ago. "Does he write of killing us?"

"He describes Jews as bacilli and parasites. What does one do with those?"

The night's darkness could not hide my newly hatched fears. Its freeze leeched into me. I rolled down my shirtsleeves. "I hear that the Americans, and the British in Palestine, now have imposed a zero quota on immigration."

"It doesn't have to be either of those places. People have found sanctuary in Switzerland. And there are other neutral countries, such

Chapter 17

as Portugal and Turkey. Some have made it all the way to Shanghai. And to South America, through Lisbon."

A gray owl made his presence known with fugitive screeches that cut through the air. Jenő continued. "It's rather ironic that I'm a widely read journalist, yet no one in my own family will listen to me. They think I'm a self-important know-it-all." He laughed as one would curse. "And I probably am. But it doesn't make me wrong."

"You're not a know-it-all, Jenő. You're just too smart for the rest of us." The kerosene lamp in the kitchen, whose glass chimney had to be washed of soot every morning, was put out, heightening the glow of my brother's pipe and our seclusion. "I saw you speaking with Ilona and Józsi earlier."

"I have hope of getting through to them. They're like most people, who only accept what they want to hear. But now the thunder drums louder, and they feel more vulnerable. It hurts to imagine Feri's life if the war comes here. Or if the Germans occupy us."

"But no luck with our parents?"

"No. They remain with their blinders on. I tried to appeal to our father's respect for scholarship, by quoting Rabbi Akiva, who said that man is master of his own destiny. That man needs G-d's grace to triumph over evil but that such triumph depends on his own efforts. But Papa responded that we need only fear G-d."

"I think that Papa's just trying to reassure us. And himself."

Jenő slapped his knee, the sound cutting through the air. "He's given up. And we can't allow that. Béla, maybe they'll listen to you. Speak to them about emigrating."

"I've tried also, but I'll talk again to Papa."

"The *Haggadah* says that the Lord brought us out of Egypt. Not an angel or some other emissary of his, but G-d Himself. That's a message."

"Of what? That we can expect G-d to lead us out of this mess?"

"No! The mistake we're all making is waiting for someone else to handle our difficulties. Have you read Spinoza?"

Rabbi Gonzvi had warned against our reading Spinoza, declaring him to be an *apikoyres* (heretic). "I'm uneducated. Barely literate, apparently."

"We have to stop believing that there's a wise man looking down on us from some lofty perch in the heavens, who has complete control of a universe separate from Him. It's our own body that houses the spirit."

"Sure. That's why we go to the *mikveh*."

"Yes, because G-d is us. In our soul's reflection is Him. That's Revelation! And that's what the rabbinical fools never tell you. Yet it's what seers and fortune-tellers know." My brother's erudition knew no bounds. He continued, "They learn to subdue their self-conscious ego, to become a passive instrument of the deity emanating from them."

Certain seminal times in one's life are obvious—the birth of a child, your wedding day, a parent's death. Other such moments conceal themselves yet cling to you and brew incessantly in the heart's cauldron. They require a more sophisticated judgment to recognize, one not available to the fourth son who, true to form, only nodded in understanding. With his tobacco spent, Jenő rose, bent to kiss me on the forehead, moseyed back inside to say his goodbyes, and left for Prague.

*

Writing anonymous anti-Nazi articles from the capital, Jenő was betrayed, then arrested by the Gestapo. Years later, I learned that he died in the middle of the following winter in Mauthausen, a barbaric concentration camp near Linz, where Hitler spent his childhood. Mauthausen housed the intelligentsia and members of the higher social classes deemed "incorrigible political enemies of the Reich," who were exterminated through hard labor. In that perdition, where

Chapter 17

time lingered like a layer of filth, law was established by a commandant who indulged his eleven-year-old son's amusement in shooting inmates and whose guards trained bloodhounds to tear apart captives who had committed a "disciplinary offense."

Jenő, I have returned to our walnut tree countless times. Feeling again the chill in the darkness. Basking in the radiance of your passion. Inhaling your sweet cherry aroma. Listening to the unblinking owl mock us. Explaining why I failed to find the right words, or to craft a thoughtful plan, sufficient to convince our family members to leave.

My dearest brother, if only I could reconstruct the end of our conversation. In my revised version, I stood and kissed you back. I hugged you. I told you that I loved you. I thanked you for always watching out for me. And I acknowledged that you were right.

CHAPTER 18
The Sadist's Passions

Yet another sad topic, the Jewish companies. 20,000 to 30,000 men are at the mercy of the sadist's passions. Is it possible to take them home to work there? Otherwise, in spring, only a few will be alive.

—István Horthy, son of Regent Horthy,
at the Russian front in 1942

I spent most of the war's dog years in the 108/26 *Királyi Munka Század* (Royal Labor Company) battalion of the *Munkaszolgálat* (the labor camp system). Although Jews were deemed unfit to carry arms, the Hungarian government, unlike other Axis countries, did want the benefit of our toils for military purposes.

We and our Army guards, many of whom had a far more meager Hungarian lineage than the average Jewish serviceman, traveled endlessly. When I refer to our travel, that must be understood as walking, because horses and motorized transportation were for soldiers. Often we marched 30 kilometers or more a day, stopping only when the horses were rested, mostly throughout Hungary although at times we

Chapter 18

crossed into Poland, Romania, and Ukraine, hiking the Carpathians, the Bihor mountains, and the Transylvanian Alps.

Near Gyertyánliget, we camped for weeks in the summer of 1941 on the eastern branch of the Sopurka River, which splits a verdant valley sprayed with wildflowers that lies within a panorama of peaks shaped like soft breasts and stretching to the sun. The Romans had considered that location sufficiently breathtaking to have constructed an enormous spa there. We repaired the remnants of a later spa with cement, lime, and bricks that we lugged in canvas bags along a winding road from a railway terminal. Labor servicemen also built roads, much as the Romans did two millennia earlier, when they ruled the northern frontier of the world and battled the Goths in the depths of the Carpathians.

We removed rocks, fallen tree trunks, and other debris ahead of those who compacted the ground and laid the stone, sand, and limited supply of asphalt. Although an assortment of rusted axes, shovels, and picks were available, the work of clearing the path was largely accomplished with brute strength, blistered hands, and conveyor-belt-precision teamwork. Our shoulders stood tall as our bodies turned robotic, concealing the pain that counseled normal men's actions. Slackers were beaten with a cavalry stick (often while tied to a tree) or kicked until they fell.

During daytime breaks, often occasioned when our guards had obtained alcohol, I forced myself to walk to nearby fields or valleys boiling with life. My illuminated skin absorbing the restorative, cleansing power of the sylvan landscape. Letting nature's animation burn my senses. Searching for tangles of glossy purple blackberries and sweet raspberries. Lying on the blinking grass and crushing torn-up blades between my fingers for their musty smell. Slowing my breathing in tune with the earth's, allowing me to hear euphonious sounds that had woven together and repeated since primeval times. Reminding myself what remained in this world to live for.

Béla's Letters

The "Musz" began in July 1939 when the Hungarian Parliament enacted a law deeming all "unreliables" 21 or older fit for national defense work. Pursuant to that statute, Defense Minister Károly Bartha ordered the creation of an "auxiliary" workforce comprised mostly of Jews but also others, including Gypsies, Jehovah's Witnesses, and communists, a pool whose ranks would swell to over 100,000 men. This forced-labor system, designed to ensure that we had no access to sensitive military information and wielded no positions of authority, was subject to a chain of military command, although concentrating Jews into special units afforded their commanding officers enormous discretion regarding their treatment.

Within two years, all Hungarian men of military age had been drafted into the armed forces, except for those studying in university or essential to the military industry. Jewish men could avoid labor service by paying a sufficient bribe. I knew a fellow whose parents' prosperity delayed his entry into the labor system for a year. Once he joined us and was no longer able to suck from his family's breast, he sank into depression and died within months.

On a typical day, we were roused at 5 a.m. by a bugle blast and screams for us "Jewish bastards" to get to work. Time was allowed for an icy-water washing, a trip to the latrine, and a breakfast of coffee that tasted like pencil shavings and one piece of hard-crusted bread. Many of the junior officers I served under were ignorant, superstitious, and sadistic to varying degrees. One sergeant, Desző Valler, often would order, after a long day's exertion, that we perform hundreds of push-ups in the mud before being allowed supper. Or he had us line up for a march up a mountain and back.

Many of their seniors though, each distinguished by an arm braid with a gold center stripe on his tunic, were decent military men who followed protocol. During the early years, we received lousy pay, clothing, and rations equivalent to those in the armed forces, and we

Chapter 18

were allowed to send letters and packages, although our receipt of a reply was uncertain because our address was a field post-office number. We often were able to travel home on furlough, were permitted to pray and hold services, and could visit with local Jews, who would invite us to their homes for kosher meals.

However, after Hungary officially joined the Axis coalition in November 1940, and particularly after it declared war against the Soviet Union in June 1941, our treatment deteriorated. Because of the offensiveness of seeing Jews in uniform, our military garb, except for our caps but including boots, were confiscated, compelling us to provide our own. The emblem we had worn that contained stripes in the Hungarian national colors was replaced with armbands marred by a yellow star. (Converts were entitled to wear a white band and served in separate battalions that were marginally better treated, including having Sunday mornings off to attend Mass. Many of these "non-Jewish Jews" themselves exuded anti-Semitism, as if they had been made to suffer for our sins. But the different armband was fool's gold, yet another example of how so many of us wallowed in delusion during the war years.)

The guards began to steal the food sent to us, which we replaced by slipping out of camp at night to take the harvest from nearby farms and gardens, competing with the wildlife. I remembered how Mama had taught me to find edible mushrooms under a cover of leaves after a cleansing rain, and to nibble on white acacia flowers. Beets, turnips, dandelion stalks, and ripe grain could be found in fields, and we fought rodents for sunflower seeds. We would stand on each other's shoulders to gather apples and pears, even those unripe ones that would cause bloating and diarrhea. Many times I gratefully chewed on potatoes encrusted in dirt, wolfed down cucumbers with the toughest skin, or slurped down a raw egg or two. Occasionally, we caught fish on a string or stole swill from a pig sty. And when the hunger pangs could not be quenched, we washed down tea made from grass. Or we rolled dried flower petals, lit them with the help of the lens from a pair of thick glasses, and smoked them.

In September 1942, Miklós Horthy, Regent of Hungary since 1920—soon after he led a revolution that drove out the short-lived, brutish communist government established by Béla Kun (a half-Jewish intellectual whose background linked Jews with communists in the minds of many Hungarians)—appointed General Vilmos Nagy de Nagybaczon as Minister of Defense. This general sought to curb the military's culture of anti-Semitism and the inhumane treatment of the forced laborers, and issued numerous orders for the improvement of their conditions. For his efforts, he was accused of being a "Jewish lackey" and by the following June was forced by the extreme political right to resign.

Prior to Nagybaczon's appointment, about 50,000 Jewish men, many from the Rus, had been sent to the Eastern Front as forced laborers. Ferencz's unit was assigned to accompany the Hungarian Second Army, which joined in the invasion of Russia and was annihilated in the savage winter of 1942-43.

When and how Ferencz's rapturous song ended, I never learned. Over the years, accounts surfaced from those who survived. One fellow told me of Jews forced to climb trees, crow like roosters, and shout, "I am a dirty Jew." Jewish servicemen replaced horses, pulling heavily laden wagons. Many froze solid. Some were doused with water until they became ice sculptures. Infirmaries housing sick Jews were set aflame. The officers commanding the labor companies whose units had been liquidated were allowed to return to Hungary earlier.

Conjecture tells me that it might have been the Russians who killed my brother. Servicemen captured by the Soviets were treated no better than regular Hungarian soldiers. Jewish prisoners who lived through the white death conditions of Soviet stalags were released only in 1947.

Chapter 18

Ferencz was apart from his wife, Rozsa, and young son, András, when they were deported to Auschwitz-Birkenau. I pray that, if he survived until that time, my brother never learned of this. It was left to the survivors to absorb the circumstances of their fate.

Ferencz Ingber

CHAPTER 19
Home: September 1941

History has no existence. All that exists are individuals, and of these, only individual moments as broken off from one another as shattered vertebrae.

—Joyce Carol Oates

I never should have mentioned to Tibor Lazarovics (I will refrain from giving the surname first, as is customary for Hungarians), my friend since he moved to Oroszvég as a kid, that I had received permission to visit my home. A furlough, even for one day, was now a luxury. My plan was to leave our camp early on a Sunday and stay with my parents that night, the start of Rosh Hashanah. Sundays were work days as well, but generally we performed lighter chores such as cleaning the grounds and the ditches that constituted latrines, peeling vegetables, scraping layers of dried dirt from our shovels and spades, and shaving and cutting each other's wild hair, like chimps grooming. Sunday also was a day for healing, when we would press the juice from wild onions to decontaminate wounds, and crush leaves

Chapter 19

and other plant parts to a mashed-potatoes-like consistency, heat them, and apply them to sores to increase circulation.

When I showed Tibi my pass, signed by Commander Dominik Nagy's adjunct, he pouted, cursed, and insisted on joining me. Mind you, not only was Tibi irreligious, but he avoided returning to his mother's home while she remained married to his stepfather, a *shochet* (ritual slaughterer) who viewed humans as marginally more worthy than chickens. Tibi had used up his quota of furloughs for visits to the *Kuplieri*, whose doors never closed, sampling the unspoken menu of delights. Its two-story building, where American ragtime music played in the lobby all night and his girlfriend, Gizi, occasionally worked, had a maze of individual rooms on the upper floor.

Before his last trip there, Tibi had urged me to join him.

"It won't take long. You'll still be able to see your family."

"But it will cut into my time with them."

He hushed his voice, to let me know that one of the great mysteries of life was about to be revealed. "Did you know that insects can have sex in a few seconds while flying around in the air?"

"That's why they don't need a brothel."

"Come on, Béla. Haven't you been deprived long enough?"

"True."

"Think of King David. Once he saw Bathsheba, he couldn't help but have her. Even though she was married to one of his warriors."

"There's someone as beautiful as Bathsheba in the *Kuplieri*?"

"Who cares?" He smirked. "Did you know that Bathsheba only took showers?"

"You're an idiot."

At the cusp of the following dawn, when the harshness of our lives was tempered by a drowsy calm, I arose to a fully clothed Tibi standing by my bunk.

"Why are you dressed already?"

"I'm going with you."

Tibi, without a pass but armed with the gift of gab, leisurely accompanied me out of the grounds for the hike down to the station in Ungvar. I had been to that modest city twice before, once for a bar mitzvah in the Central Synagogue, a garish, burnt-red temple built in the Moorish style, with three fluted arches for an entrance.

Years earlier, Ágnes and I had impulsively hopped on a train headed there for a walk along the snaking Ung River, within sight of the imposing castle overlooking the city. At one secluded spot, we stripped to our underwear and jumped in, dancing underneath the surface like wafts of smoke while the current caressed her body. So much of my life has been spent near a river, which continually flowed to the rhythm of replenishment.

I led as we pushed down the primitive trailhead, parts of which were thick with mud that sucked at our feet, clogged with fallen logs, or covered by dense brush strangling itself that masked the rustlings of animals. Maize yellow wagtails taunted us with high-pitched "jeets" as they darted by in pursuit of diving beetles and winking butterflies. Gray marmots warmed themselves on rocks and whistled to one another as we approached. Waking sunlight soaked through the leafy fingers of enmeshed birches and elms, sucked in by nature ravenous for life. Because of Tibi's sluggishness, which belied his hyperactive temperament, I paused repeatedly for him to catch up, until we arrived at a grassy plain waving in the wind, from which we could spot the railway station.

Soon we were in a cavernous building surrounded by lattice arcades, with a waiting room that could fit the entire town's population. In its center was a fountain on whose ledge sat a young couple, mischievously splashing each other. Single people and families sat on benches or on their luggage. A napping gendarme lay slouched on a bench near the ticket booth.

Chapter 19

As the crow flies, the distance to Munkács was not great, but the railroad took a meandering route through the mountains to get there. With little extra money after purchasing our tickets, we negotiated for black coffee and plum-filled cones from a vendor, a Great War veteran in a wheelchair who threw in gratis a couple of stale biscuits. The coffee, although watered down, was welcome, as a rumor had run rampant in the camp that our coffee was laced with potassium bromide to reduce sex drive. (The brown liquid that substituted for coffee only gave me diarrhea, which I suppose is a less direct way of achieving the same result.)

When our train was announced, we jumped up from our hard wooden bench at the back of the station. Tibi stumbled backward, as if he had been drinking already. We waited to board, examining the passengers ahead of us, searching for obscurity.

After ambling through several cars, we slumped down in the third-class compartment on buff yellow, straw cane seats next to a farmer smelling of compost and wearing a brightly colored peasant shirt over trousers tucked into boots. He had a gaggle of chalk white hairs protruding from the shadows of his nostrils and ears. His rumbling snores explained the empty seats around him. Tibi fell asleep to the clacking of the train's wheels, treating me to an unharmonious duet. He awakened when, with a series of unnerving jolts, we pulled into the next station at Csap, a sordid locale reputed to be filled with money changers and smugglers. Rising in his seat to check the location and let the farmer pass, Tibi passed gas and groaned.

"That coffee tasted like piss. Now it's eating a hole in me."

"What's the matter? You've been acting like an old man."

"I feel lousy all the time, Béla. I have indigestion constantly. My stomach feels weighted with an anchor, and I can hardly eat."

"You look like you've lost weight."

"All I want to do is sleep."

"Maybe your lovely girlfriend gave you some disease?"

He rubbed his stomach. "No, I may have an ulcer."

"You still intend to go to the *Kuplieri?*"

"Yep."

"I guess your dick still works."

"It's not for that reason. They have a doctor there. He's a friend. Hopefully he's got some medication."

I never doubted Tibi's honesty. One of his life philosophies was to bare himself to friends, on the theory that they eventually would come to find out who he was.

A middle-aged mother with her young daughter approached and hesitantly sat across from us. The woman was chesty, with snaking braids of almond-brown hair twisted around her head and fastened with bobby pins. Her daughter's plaited coils of hair, decorated with pink ribbons, glided down her shoulders. Upon taking her seat, the mother rummaged through her bag for a gold compact mirror; then she dabbed layers of powder on her face as the girl watched as if in the presence of magic.

In spite of a pug nose set in a bulbous face on top of a still-pudgy body, Tibi insisted that, at his whim, he could transform himself into a puppeteer of females. "They're not attracted to me at first, but give me an hour alone with any woman and she's mine." Ordinarily, Tibi would have struck up a conversation designed to constitute love-making with clothes on. Or at least offered a carnal wink or two. Instead, after staring at the woman while chewing on his lower lip, he resumed his nap for the remainder of the ride.

Tibi accepted my invitation to dinner and we parted, near a spot where as kids we would place coins on the tracks to have them flattened by oncoming trains. I trotted home from the station, where a lone taxi and several buggy drivers waited in a light drizzle. The horses, each with a jangling bell around its neck, stood idly flicking their tails and pawing the dirt as water teared down their sides.

Chapter 19

My mother was in the unlit kitchen, hunched over a copper pot of soup seasoned with herbs from our garden, stirring methodically.

"Mama, I'm home."

Without picking up her head, she answered, "Miki, you're back early."

I kissed her on an unexpectedly cold cheek. "No, it's Béla."

The woman whom I had once been one with had passed her fifty-seventh birthday. Atop a gaunt face, her coarse hair, woven into a sock bun that bulged like a jelly doughnut, seemed noticeably grayer than when I was last home. Her beauty, only leased, was trickling from her as sap from a maple tree. Did she even care? Had she ever been concerned?

Mama hugged me, her head at my shoulders, her palms digging into my back. "Béla, I'm so happy you're here. Why didn't you write?"

We had been reduced to a single postcard per week. "Would I miss your cooking?"

"You look skinny. Are they feeding you? Have you received the packages of food we sent?"

"It's muscle, Mama. Between what you send me and what they feed us, I need to work hard to keep from getting fat."

She nudged me toward a chair, her hand lingering on my forearm. "The vegetable soup is ready. *Ess* (Eat)." Mama would not have let me go unfed if she had only her own gnarled fingers to offer. By the time of the High Holidays, our backyard garden, subject to the ravages of raccoons and red deer, would produce a medley of radishes, scallions, tomatoes, cucumbers, carrots, string beans, peas, and cabbage (the last normally reserved for making into pickled sauerkraut), much of which was preserved for the winter in glass jars. She placed a bowl of her elixir in front of me.

"Where is everyone?"

"Papa is in temple with Miki and Libu."

I was relieved that the synagogue was still open. During the week before Judgment Day, it was Papa's custom to sit in *shul* for hours studying Torah, and he insisted that all the children living at home join him. The day before, he would journey to the city's fancy *mikveh* for a pre-holiday ritual immersion in its steam-heated indoor pools. (Munkács had first-class and second-class *mikvehs*, and a separate *mikveh* for women.) I sympathized with Miki, who also would be subjected to disrobing.

"Let's go meet Papa."

"You go, Béla. I still have much to do."

"I have something for you." I handed her a bag of loose chocolates and candies, along with a box of Darlings (Hungarian cigarettes) that still were plentiful in the camp. She pushed it away. "We don't need these. You keep them."

"I have plenty."

I dropped the bag on the kitchen table and pressed a chocolate into her hand. Mama's lone sin, so far as I could discern, was a sweet tooth, although even that vice did not rule her. She slid into a chair, studying the treat.

"What's wrong? You love chocolate."

"You're not telling me the truth, Béla. About your situation."

Had she and I as adults ever had a talk that stretched beyond elusive generalities? I grasped her hand. "We're both holding back, aren't we, Mama?"

She sunk her head lower. "I'm still your mother."

"But I'm not a child anymore."

Mama pretended not to hear. "Every holiday, there are fewer of us at home." Her hollow voice trailed off as she choked back tears. "Béla, what will be?" She stroked my cheek with the back of her hand. "I must believe that everything will turn out well."

"Of course, Mama. Papa is praying for us all, isn't he?"

Chapter 19

At last, a smile. "You are a good son."

I stood and kissed her brow. I was in my late twenties, and the central woman in my life remained my mother, who demanded nothing of me beyond staying alive. Imagining her pain would not allow me to give up. Nor to unburden myself as she suggested.

I pulled out a halfway finished cigarette pack and some matches. "Tonight is the birthday of the world, Mama," I said, parroting one of Papa's favorite sayings. "It's a time for celebration." Proud of elevating the mood, I proceeded incautiously.

"Mama, have you heard from Jenő?" Her eyes, now accentuated by crow's feet, narrowed, and the corners of her lips turned down.

"No, not for months now," she cried. "And Ferencz still is at the front. What will become of them, Béla?"

I rubbed the top of her back. What did we have left but the subtle torment of hope? "They're both smart and strong, Mama. They're probably running things by now."

"That's what Papa says." Mama dabbed the corners of her eyes with a handkerchief. "But I'm not sure anymore, Béla. I'm not so sure."

The intense, rapid refrain of dueling skylarks rushed in from the window. The kitchen had become stifling. I linked my arm through hers, our umbilical cord still intact. "Come for a walk with me, Mama. It's a beautiful day." She and I had taken hundreds of strolls over the years, back to the days when my shadow fit comfortably within hers and she could hear what I hadn't even said. We would shop. Visit friends. Meet Papa at the *shul*. Pick mushrooms, poppies, and herbs. Or walk with no destination in mind. She protested again, but I prevailed after devouring a bowl of soup infused with dill and parsley.

Along the Oroszvég side, the bronze terrain, pregnant with life, was familiar serenity. Holiday food scents floated about us. A sentry dog chained to a rusted fence post eyed us lazily. Portions of the path were lit by dense, violet mounds of bellflowers whose heads hung interspersed among spikes of white veronica, some of which I picked for Mama. They would adorn our table, and later she would dry them between the brittle sheets of Papa's five-hundred-page Responsa. We stopped to admire a slender sumac tree with graceful curving branches, cultivated by a neighbor, which Mama thought resembled a woman spreading her arms.

Crossing the bridge, we passed a gendarme inclined against a chest-high concrete balustrade. He glared at me as I groped for the pass in my pocket but, instead of asking for it, he leaned over the railing to gaze at the water.

Bells of clouds that had pin-holed the sun melted to wisps, leaving stark shadows and uncovering a bouquet of mountain peaks traced with frosting. Heaven opened for us. Mama removed her sweater and draped it over her shoulders. September was my favorite month. The summer's residue was fading, and the High Holidays would bring the family together.

During our walk, I described the places my unit had traveled to over the recent season and spun stories of winning money at cards and varied horseplay. Every tale was sanitized, revealing nothing of our normal state of hunger, sickness, and exhaustion. In the middle of a story about Tibi chasing after a farmer's piglet, Mama interrupted.

"Tibikam is a good friend, isn't he? You look after each other?"

"Yes, we do." In the camp, a world without women, one needed a close friend. To check your face in the winter for signs of frostbite. Apply a tourniquet to save a limb. Warn of an encroaching enemy. I had been drawn to Tibi during our teenage years, his anarchy an expression of impulses I dared not uncheck. But now, it was because he was someone who demanded nothing from me. Nor did he put on a pretense of caring more than he did.

"He was always a wild one. His mother couldn't control him, even before his father died."

"Mama, what do you know of Tibi's stepfather?"

Chapter 19

She stared ahead. "I've heard that he never learned how to be a father. I'm grateful that my own children have such a wonderful father. I wouldn't have married your Papa had I thought he would be otherwise."

"I am thankful, Mama. For both of you."

Arriving at the temple, we plopped down on a low stone wall near the entranceway, occupied by a lone garden snail whose extended tentacles had the good fortune of not being considered kosher food. Several men, without prayer shawls or books, studied us without interrupting their discussion. As I was completing the tall tale about the piglet, Libu, in navy blue wool dress with short sleeves and a white collar, emerged from the *shul* and passed us, along with several other young women. She rushed by as if anticipating that Papa would yank her back, although my father's expectations for religious observance by his daughters were not as strict. Mama yelled her name.

Libu squealed, racing to hug me, testing my reality. I lifted her off her feet as I kissed her. But now, this ritual was awkward. Last I was home, my sister was on the cusp of adulthood. Since then, she had crossed that threshold.

"I knew you would come home. I just knew it!"

"I heard you baked more of your sponge cakes. I couldn't miss that, could I?"

"How long can you stay?"

"I'm returning tomorrow."

I glanced at Mama, who was shooing us to go off together. Under a calm sky, our muted companion, Libu and I started down the brick path that circled the temple grounds.

"Béla, did you hear that the authorities have closed all the *mikvehs*?"

"No. Papa must be upset."

"Yes, although he won't admit it." She lowered her voice. "Nor will I admit being relieved."

In the camp, when water was scarce, we would take "air" baths when possible, stripping naked and lying in a sun penetrating us with its cleansing rays. "Why not use the Latorica anyway, primitive as it is?"

"Too cold, Béla. And one other reason. Which should be obvious."

"Not to a dumbbell like me."

"Lack of privacy, of course."

"Nonsense. Did you know that I once worked in the women's *mikveh*?"

"You did?"

"Yes, as a lifeguard."

As she chuckled, I perched my arm on her shoulder. "So enough of the *mikveh*. How are you doing, my baby sister?"

"How is anybody these days? We go about our business. In my case, school. And pretend that nothing has changed."

I was near bar mitzvah age when she was born. She had always been a child. "In your letters, you seem happy."

"Papa instructed us to write nothing alarming."

Our remaining refuge was lies—ones that we told ourselves and ones that we told to others. We reached the back of the building, discolored by egg stains. Shards of glass littered the ground, like sprinkled mirrors of ice atop barren soil. "I see that you're too old now for fairy tales. Which is too bad."

"I'm nervous, Béla. All the time."

I knew about permanent stomach knots. "Tell me about it."

"It's hard to describe." She lifted her shoulders slightly, as if to hide her neck. "Even in the happiest moments, there's a black cloud hovering. So real that I can reach out and grasp it. But no one will speak of it."

"There are cycles in life. We will get through this."

"I wish all my big brothers were with me."

"We'll be back once the war is over. Which may be soon."

Chapter 19

"What is the latest news about the war?"

Recent camp gossip held that the Germans were laying siege to Leningrad. "The Russians and British fight on."

"But they battle just to survive. They can't protect us from the Nazis."

I fought my instinct to shield her, wanting to maintain credibility. Hoping that growing up with six brothers had made her unbreakable. "I won't pretend that these aren't bad times. But we live in Hungary, which has not been taken over by Germany and won't be because we're an important ally of theirs. And we have each other, our friends, and our neighbors, and we all look out for each other."

Our loop near complete, Mama came into view, sitting with elbows on knees, fingertips rubbing the bridge of her nose.

"Béla, you haven't told me anything about you."

"Then we'll have to stay up all night to catch up. Or else we'll owe each other twenty-page letters."

Not long after the two women embarked for home, Papa and Miki, wearing their finest suits, came out of the building. Miki had turned eighteen and now was broader and taller than our father. "*L'shana tova tikatevu.*" We embraced and caught up on gossip.

"A few days ago," Miki said, "some people came back from the labor companies. One of them was your old boss."

"Ah, Pollack. Did you talk to him?"

"No. He's lost a lot of weight. He looked to me to be ill. And insane."

"Insane? Why?"

"He kept talking out loud, as if he were arguing with himself."

On the walk home, I fell back to reciting pointless camp tales. Papa listened while glancing around to spot gendarmes or troublemakers. But not so Miki, who was still too young to have built up the defenses and rationalizations necessary for us to accept reality. "Béla," he interrupted, "did you hear that the Nazis are about to take over

Kiev?" I asked for details, but he had none. He persisted. "I read that Moscow will fall by the beginning of winter."

"Don't believe everything you read," I cautioned. "I should know."

"And that the Russians will surrender by year-end," Miki shouted.

"Good," Papa said. "Then Ferencz will come back home."

Miki's face was bright red. "But it means that Germany will have won the war."

Papa raised his palms. "Let's not have war talk."

I had made a promise to Jenő. "Papa, if the British and Soviets are defeated and the war ends, the Nazis will rule us forever. We will have no hope of rescue."

"The Hungarians govern us, not the Germans."

"They are no better," Miki insisted. "I hate them as much."

Papa halted and grasped Miki's shoulder. "You mustn't worry so much. Remember your learnings."

"Learnings?" Waving outstretched arms, Miki added, "How do they help when the world is falling apart?"

"You learned of the coming of the Messiah. He will—"

Rabbi Gonzvi had told us that the Messiah would come if all Jews would strictly observe even one Sabbath. Miki and I made eye contact. "Papa," I interrupted. "you want us to wait? Wasn't it you who told me years ago that Judaism allows for choice, because that is the essence of what makes us human? And that often the worst choice is to do nothing. Papa, doing nothing now may get us killed."

Typically, my father, following the scholarly tradition, would attempt a reasoned response to any of our questions or statements, however blasphemous. Now he fell silent, his thoughts circling around a retort but unable to land. We resumed our trek, but Miki soon trailed behind us, his head down. My father slowed his pace. "Miki, I am not naïve. I'm well aware of what's going on in the world and the evil that approaches—"

Chapter 19

"Why is G-d letting it happen?" Miki said.

"G-d is not responsible for evil. People are. Do you remember the Bible's teaching about the Babylonian conquest of the kingdom of Judah?" After a pause, Papa answered his own question. "G-d allowed His people to be conquered, because of their sins. And now, look at what has happened in our community. Jews abandoning His laws and fighting and slandering one another. Violating the Sabbath. Visiting prostitutes. Gambling." Had Papa deliberately refrained from adding, "Children abandoning their parents?"

"G-d sees all this," Papa continued. "He is testing us, as he tested Abraham by ordering the sacrifice of his beloved son, Isaac."

If G-d is omniscient, why does He need to test us? "To what end?" I asked. "To be more observant?"

"Yes. But even more importantly, to recognize our sins and repent out of love. Especially on Rosh Hashanah. Now is our opportunity to reject past transgressions and transform and purify ourselves. Once we do that, we have the right to call out to Him to save us."

I had been taught in *cheder* that during these upcoming holy days, G-d determines the fate of all people. "Does this mean that it is G-d's wish that Hitler and the Nazis come to power?"

"I don't believe that, Béla. Hitler is evil, but he also is a human being. Every one of us is given the ability to make a choice—to love or to hate."

"But if G-d already knows what we are thinking and planning to do, doesn't this mean that He has predetermined our actions?"

"No, because for our decisions to be genuine, G-d allows for there to be consequences. If He forced everyone to be good, then goodness would be insignificant. Hitler has elected to hate. G-d waits for him to find his way back to true humanity."

Where does the test for us arise if Hitler continues down his chosen path? Miki and I glimpsed each other again. Miki's posture was rigid,

Béla's Letters

and we both frowned. Miki offered a final challenge. "Papa, remember the story of G-d agreeing to spare Sodom and Gomorrah if ten righteous people could be found? Once a person decides to hate, shouldn't G-d immediately prevent him from acting on it? Why should the good people suffer? Is that fair?"

"Life isn't fair, Miki. You're old enough to understand that. If the world were meant to be fair, then we would all be compelled to act in exactly the same manner. And we would lose our individuality."

"So G-d won't help us?"

"He's waiting. Waiting for each of us to develop a righteous character. And to make peace with Him and love Him, before we come to our final accounting." Papa hesitated, and then added, "Which will not happen without our suffering."

As I listened, my stomach turned rock hard. The future crystalized before me. And became the present.

Béla Ingber (under the X) in labor camp service in Kisbér, circa 1941

CHAPTER 20
The Hanging

Everything can be taken from a man but one thing: the last of the human freedoms—to choose one's attitude in any given set of circumstances, to choose one's own way.

—Viktor Frankl

Tibi joined us for the New Year's dinner, filling one of my siblings' empty chairs, allowing for more pretense. Mama set out plates on a corn silk, hand-crocheted tablecloth. We savored slices of bruised apples dipped in honey, as Papa wished for peace and health for us all, though in a hushed voice, as if the very request would prevent it. For the main meal, Mama served *tzimmes*, her sweet stew made of potatoes, carrots, and beef.

None of us can change the essence of who we are. Tibi's charm was that he never cared to try. That night, he was in rare form, chanting the *Kiddush* over the wine as would a cantor, praising food that he merely nibbled, and spreading gossip ridiculing our Hungarian leaders.

Tibi took a bath in a wooden trough and stayed the night, sleeping on a pile of blankets in the kitchen. Before the slate of dawn arrived, I woke Libu for a hug, one tight enough to bind the tears. As I released her, Mama appeared by my side. She was wearing a pearl white nightgown with faded yellow and red roses that lived in the fabric. Mama studied my face, as if she needed to memorize it.

"I will pray for us, Mama. Every day." She kissed the dome of my forehead. I kissed her back, my lips lingering on her cheek. They linger still, all these years later.

*

We caught a 7 a.m. train, the earliest one available, back to Ungvar. This time, Tibi stayed awake during the ride.

"What did the doctor say?" I said.

"Did you ever hear the expression, 'The cure is worse than the disease'?"

"What's the cure? No sex for a year?"

"That bastard told me to avoid coffee, tea, salt, chocolate, spices, and alcohol. And worst of all, no smoking."

"You're right. Better to have ulcers."

"At least Gizi was there."

"He didn't give you any medication?"

His face contorted as if his finger were stuck in an electrical outlet, Tibi pulled a bottle from his bag.

"Looks like piss, Tibi."

"Apple cider vinegar. I have to dilute it with water."

"It just keeps getting worse, eh?"

"I'll find some vodka to make it palatable."

We arrived at Ungvar before ten and trekked uphill to the camp, with Tibi periodically clutching his abdomen and grimacing. Racing through the creaking gatepost, we were yards from our quarters when there appeared in front of us, flanked by two

Chapter 20

guards, Sergeant Valler, who was in command of the camp in Nagy's absence.

Valler was an antediluvian creature, as broad as he was squat, with a thick neck, a wide shaved head, permanent black stubble, gaps in teeth set within shark-wide jaws, and acne that scarred one side of his face. He wore a tunic with asparagus-green collar patches and a gold braid marksman's lanyard with pompoms adorning his left shoulder. A butcher in his former life, his drooping mouth, which remained open as he chewed his food, maintained a permanent scowl. We servicemen referred to him as "The Beast." Tibi and I saluted overdramatically and stood at attention. His voice a sharp blade, he said, "Show me your passes!"

I handed him mine. Valler glared at Tibi. "Where's yours?"

Tibi gasped and stared back with a facial expression akin to one preserved by a taxidermist, his wide-open eyes gazing into an abyss of loathing.

I offered, "Mister Instructor Valler, that's his pass. I was holding it for him, sir."

"Why would you do that?" Valler challenged me.

"Because he loses everything, sir."

"And why are you out without a pass?"

"My mother was sick, sir. It was an emergency. I had to go home, sir."

The Beast puffed up his shoulders, like a blowfish in sudden danger, and then my head snapped back from the impact of his slap. The pain didn't register at first, only the coppery taste of warm blood on a swelling lip.

"You're a liar, and one of you scum left without permission. Go back to your quarters. The one without the pass, be at my barracks at noon."

With that, he left, his minions trailing behind him. Tibi and I trudged into our cabin and plopped on his bed, which was little more than a pile of straw with a rolled-up blanket for a headrest. My shirt was bloodied; the dull ache from my nose throbbed.

"He should die of leprosy," Tibi said.

"No, lepers don't feel pain. Better he should have cancer."

Tibi considered that as a shroud of panic encased his face. He whispered, "Nagy isn't here. Which means that The Beast will do what he pleases. Probably whip one of us. Or worse."

"You couldn't have realized this yesterday?"

"You know I'm a schmuck. Why did you cover for me?"

"Because I'm a schmuck also."

"Look, I'm ready to pay the piper. I'll go and get it over with."

I turned away from him. "No, you won't. I'm going."

He stood, waiting to meet my eyes. "I'm the one without the pass."

"Whatever punishment The Beast has in mind, you're sick and won't survive it."

"You might not, either. I'm not worth it."

"For sure. And the world could do with one less imbecile."

"I can't let you take such punishment for me," Tibi said.

"Don't flatter yourself. I'm not doing this for you."

"Then why?"

"Haven't you heard that the most wicked retribution G-d could devise is to make someone live forever?"

"C'mon, Béla, you're only twenty-eight."

I regretted not staying in Munkács, but reminded myself that it would have placed my family at risk. "Yesterday was a good day. Perhaps my last joyful memory." I stood, now understanding that every path I'd taken to avoid my fate led me back to it. "I don't want to be stuck in this everlasting hell. Where my only happiness comes from memories. So I don't give a shit anymore."

Tibi grabbed my arm and whispered, "I'm sorry, Béla."

Chapter 20

I shook him off. "If I survive and you do something stupid again, I'll kill you myself, Tibi."

I escaped to my pile of straw and let a couple of cigarettes burn my tongue, sucking the smoke deep into the branches of my lungs and holding it there. At twelve sharp, I was at The Beast's barracks. He was waiting. "I should have you shot. Next time, I will."

My insides quaked as the guards escorted me behind the building, where there stood a rusted flagpole with a pulley at the top. After I removed my boots, they bound my hands behind me with rope, and then my feet. (But I was lucky. Later in the war, they would add a rope linking the wrists and ankles, which caused intense pain and a dislocated shoulder.) I had seen others being hung by their feet. Depending on how long it took for them to let you down, and your general condition, you could asphyxiate.

I was yanked upward, until I could go no higher, a human bat in limbo. The Beast paced below, alternately smoking and yelling at the two guards over some matter I could not discern. I developed a pulsating headache. My heart pounded like a wrung bell, and I swallowed my breath before I could exhale. The attending guards studied me periodically as if they were scientists observing an insect under a microscope.

I shut my eyes to calm myself. The minutes dragged on, as if the hourglass had been laid on its side. I began to thrash about like a fish seeking submersion. Apparently waiting for this, they eased the tension on the rope, slamming me into the ground. The Beast stood over me, eclipsing the sun. He spat a wad of phlegm at my head. "Happy New Year, Jew boy."

Before I recovered, I was hoisted up again. This time, I began gasping for air before reaching the top. In the dizzying haze, with the moan of ghosts approaching to escort me to the other world, I sensed the image of Mama in her *Shabbos* dress. Drawing in the candlelight.

Capturing it for me. The light streaming through my body, dissolving the hardness. Illuminating a path to safety.

As I neared unconsciousness, Mama called to me, "Not now, my precious son. Now is not your time." Her voice was overtaken by the yell of a guard, "Nagy is coming back." Down hard I came again. The Beast, in a final ejaculation of his malevolence, leveled a kick at my chest. The guards untied me and dragged me back to my quarters.

I lay on the straw for the rest of the day immobile, the world gradually coming back into focus. Pain rippled through me with each breath, unfolding a hurt that I welcomed as a distraction. A weeping Tibi watched over me, chanting, "I'm sorry, Béla. I'm so sorry."

Béla Ingber and Tibor Lazarovics

CHAPTER 21

Miki Ingber: February 17, 1942
(Oroszvég)

My Dearest Béla,

We received your latest postcard and are very glad to hear that they are treating you well. Did you get the package? The mailman told me that he would arrange things.

I have found work in Ilosva as a dental technician, where I build bridges and crowns. I come out twice a week by bus, and for now have a fixed salary. I give most of the money to Mama and Papa. I can send you some as well. I know you always say you don't need money, but take some anyway, as I have enough.

I know that everyone is troubled that I did not finish my high school studies. I stayed longer than I wanted to, in order not to upset Mama and Papa. But when the math professor punished me for defending myself

151

in a fight and called me a name, I knew I could not stay anymore. It's better this way. I am learning and making money.

Write as soon as you can.

We all send you a million kisses,

CHAPTER 22
The Colonel: Spring 1942

Think you're escaping and run into yourself. Longest way round is the shortest way home.

—James Joyce

Throughout the winter of 1941-42, rumors proliferated of horrific slaughter and misery on the Eastern front. I was relieved to learn that the Nazis had not succeeded in capturing Moscow or Stalingrad. We celebrated the growing warmth and length of days until early May, when Commander Nagy was reassigned. For now, The Beast was in charge. Spending much of his time traveling to and from Budapest, he was distracted from using his unexpected omnipotence to indulge in creative forms of torment.

One morning mild enough to invite shirtlessness, with the air ripe with the odors of mud and manure, we lined up for roll call. The Beast soon appeared, interrupting the count. He had taken to wearing a cylindrical military shako hat, decorated with an ornamental metallic plate on the front and a peacock plume at the top. "Gentlemen, I have good news for you." The sound effects of a movie horror scene began playing in my head. "I've come from Army headquarters in 'Judapest.' And I am pleased to let all of you know that you will have the honor of serving your mother country where you are needed most." He thrust his finger into the distance. "On the Ostfront (Eastern front)!"

No doubt he had lobbied feverishly for permission to send us to our doom. "I can't tell you when this will happen. Hopefully, in just a few days. The transportation details are being worked out." Having bared his fangs, The Beast left, and roll call resumed.

We spent the morning in the sweet air of the forest, chopping down trees that scraped against the sky, each of which might weigh a ton or more, with handsaws and hatchets and removing their newly swollen branches. By now, hernias were common, and trusses precious. Spurred on by Valler, the guards scrutinized us, striking with their rifle butts at whoever worked too slowly or tried to catch a breather. A lunch of burnt soup and rancid meat was brought to us by horse-drawn cart.

Once a tree was ready, lying prostrate like a slain warrior, eight men were assigned to carry it. While struggling to balance the weight evenly, we were cursed at by the guards to speed up. We would lug the delimbed log to a wagon pulled by mules that were driven by whips to a boat at the river landing. However strenuous carrying the log was, we conversed through it, chattering about politics, books, movies, girlfriends, or that most taboo of subjects, food. This day, we speculated about what The Beast had told us.

That night, resting in our barracks, Tibi and I debated escaping to join up with the Czech resistance or a partisan group. But we had seen a number of captured resistance fighters strung up on tree limbs and had heard that many partisan units were anti-Semitic themselves. Nor were we even sure how to find them.

"Tibi, it makes sense to stay with our unit, but I am sure to freeze at the front next winter unless I get warmer clothing." One day a

Chapter 22

month earlier, when food was scarce and the weather warming, I had traded my overcoat, which was worn to the point that it had become an outer layer of my skin, for some rations. But nature's war on us was not over, and its onslaught again turned the trees and ground into stone. The gathering cold, too bitter for alcohol to overcome, was close to bearable while I worked, but not during the nights when the blessings of sleep were eroded by a piercing numbness that would gnaw on bones and claw away at one's reserves.

Most excruciating was when we were forced to spend the night outside in lean-tos made of branches or saplings. I would dig a hole and lie in it, on top of a rubberized sheet I had brought from home (my kingdom for a blanket!), with my hands under my armpits and my toes buried in the dirt. I slept so near the others that their exhalations mingled with mine, a bloodless bunch with our teeth chattering in unison.

The first night I was without a coat, we stayed in an enclosed wood paddock that stank of urine and droppings and had negligible insulation. Despite a pyramid fire that burned for hours, I shivered uncontrollably as winter reappeared to share my bed. The following morning, someone cautioned me that my lips had turned a bluish-white. Desperation emboldened me to risk punishment and undertake an unauthorized journey to a nearby town, although in the end I was able to obtain only a full fleece undergarment.

Not only was I without the semblance of a useful overcoat, but socks had been replaced with rags carefully wrapped around my feet to avoid blisters. I also needed winter boots and a thicker hat.

"Now I get to lecture you, Béla. You traded your coat for food and cigarettes? And I'm the fool?"

"You sure enjoyed those smokes, Tibi, didn't you?"

"I can lend you that sweater again."

"No, you'll need it."

No longer could one rely on help from the local Jewish community. Which led me, early the next Sunday, a day when roll call was not taken, to remove my yellow armband and crawl under the wires. But this time, I was headed home. Whether or not I was successful, I'd at least kiss my parents one last time before being shipped to the front.

I was again within walking distance of Ungvar. The Sunday trains stopped there every couple of hours. But if questioned, my military papers, with their distinctive "Jewish" stamp, would likely not prevent me from being jailed. Or worse. When a trio of Hungarian soldiers burst into my car, I feigned sleep. My luck persisted, aided by an elegantly dressed, flamboyant woman holding court in our compartment, who captured the soldiers' full attention. An actress in the State Theatre, she regaled them with tales of her performances and showed off her *Ahnenpass*, its gray cover embossed with an eagle bearing a swastika and its pages thick with genealogical information, to boast of racial pureness.

I slipped off the train during a rousing rendition of the national anthem and hurried through the city streets and over the bridge. On the Oroszvég side, the moaning wind picked up, pushing me along as if impatient with my progress. I passed near a juniper tree that was bent in the shape of a coat hook. A man was hunched behind it, his ebony fedora jammed down to the space between his hairline and eyebrows. With cupped hands, he strained to light a cigarette. Józsi. I was nearly past him when he spotted me.

"*Sholoim aleichem*," he said, and then repeated it in a shout to make sure the wind would not sweep his words away. "What a pleasant surprise. How long are you home for?"

I slapped on a plastic smile that didn't reach my eyes, and strolled toward him. With a joint effort, we emerged from behind the tree with two lit cigarettes. "Only a few hours. Józsi, are you on leave from the camp?"

Chapter 22

"I have a furlough granted by the highest authorities."

I had no idea what he was talking about, which was not unusual. I nodded. "How are Ilona and Feri?"

"Fine. And we have good news, Béla. Ilona is with child again."

Should I remind him that there was a war going on, that he had no steady employment, and that the prospects for a happy life for a Jewish youth in Axis Europe were dim? "Congratulations," I said, patting his back. "Józsi, I'm sorry but I'm on my way to my parents. I'm in a rush."

He studied me with eyes tearing from the gusts, as if he were peering down a deep well at my battered body, and said, "Are you in trouble?"

We all are, Józsi. I spilled out my story. Pulling at my arm, he urged, "Come with me."

My brothers had labeled Józsi the *Luftmensh* (dreamer), although good-naturedly, given his unquestioned love for our sister. To them, he lived in a world of artistic sensibilities, sheltered from the reality that lay beyond reach of his inspiration. I thought Józsi rather childlike, perceiving more but understanding less. Which made him a menace. I had no time to indulge in his self-absorbed madness. Holding up my hands, I pleaded, "I have to go home."

Józsi moved closer, crossing into my personal space. "No," he said, with evangelistic determination. "Trust me. Come to City Hall. I spent yesterday there with a very special patron. He is giving me more of his time today. You need to meet him."

"Who is he?"

"His name is Feder," Józsi stated. "Colonel Mihály Feder. He's in charge of the Hungarian Army regiment in Bereg County."

He had my attention, but for the wrong reason. Here was a likely path to summary execution. "And how do you know such a big shot?"

"A referral from a former client, whose portrait I also had painted. Come," he repeated.

Béla's Letters

On many a day, I was forced to make one or more decisions that might prove fatal. I relied on my instincts but, in this case, his insistence overrode them. I accompanied him to the Munkács City Hall, which sat across the street from the Csillag. The ornate multistory white structure was marked by a red and blue gable roof, a belfry, and distinctive spires. The lobby was jammed with Hungarian troops milling about and a roughly equal number of women engrossed in various administrative duties. Offsetting their urgency was a waltz melody incongruously spilling out from a hand-cranked Victrola near the staircase.

Nodding mechanically several times to familiar faces, Józsi led me up the stairs and into a conference room that had been converted into a studio. Paint cans, brushes, palette knives, and rags were piled in a toolbox in the corner of the room, which reeked of turpentine and was lit by a basket-shaped chandelier of cut glass. More than his talent, I admired Józsi's passion. There should be something uniquely precious in each person's life. A profession. A hobby. A body of work. Another person. A focus that one loses himself in and nurtures. When would I find mine?

One canvas, sitting on an easel, had taken life. The drawing, a head and upper torso, was of a handsome man in his fifties with an aristocratic bearing, a grandmaster of life. His eyes glistened with arrogance, observing a world meant to be centered on his pleasures. A man who would bet large without even glancing at his hole card. The representation would be in oil, which Józsi explained was the slowest and most costly medium.

"Is he paying you well?"

"Not nearly as much as I'd have charged before the war. But I'm in no position to negotiate." He launched into a lecture on the challenges of portraits, delivered in a tone normally reserved for prayer. The importance of preparing a proper foundation, and correctly sizing

Chapter 22

the person to the canvas and each feature in relation to the others. Avoiding a background that distracts from the subject. Capturing light and casting shadow. "And most important with this bunch, to downplay flaws, which I'm happy to do." Józsi's creativity, which was his health potion, did not to allow him to accept ugliness. He would gladly portray shit as fertilizer.

"Maybe you can build a business painting officers' portraits?"

"Not likely. They're mostly an uncultured bunch. I'm more liable to receive interest from their wives and girlfriends."

"Excellent. I can't wait to see your first nude."

"If they paid, I'd oblige. And your sister wouldn't care."

I was hungry, tired, and AWOL. Feeling trapped, like an insect in amber. Sensing the guillotine blade nearing the back of my neck. "Józsi, I can't linger here all afternoon."

Józsi pouted, his expression saying, "You hurry only to meet death earlier." As he opened his mouth to speak, into the room burst a man dressed in a mustard-brown jacket laden with gold buttons, medals, and insignias, with matching breeches, a silk tie secured by a pearl tiepin, and high, lacquered boots. He carried a riding crop under his arm, as did the Führer in his early days. His nose was chiseled like a Greek statue, and his oiled, thinning hair was slicked back. A demigod comporting a ramrod posture, he exuded military pedigree. Would it be so wrong for me to want to be him, just for today?

Equally impressive was the woman on his arm, who had stepped out of one of Tibi's wet dreams. Each one of which my friend insisted on describing to me in detail, asserting that orgasms, whether self-induced or not, were the greatest antidote for our misery, a reminder that all pleasure had not been lost.

Statuesque and half the man's age, with scalloped cheekbones and a freckled nose, she wore gold drop earrings and fire-truck-red lipstick. Her hair, peroxide-bleached filaments of light, flowed over a charcoal black lamé dress that stopped inches above her knees. I imagined that, at the slightest touch of its zipper, it would slide down her swaying hips and onto the floor like liquid, revealing an hourglass shape the proportions of which were marred by an over-ample tush.

Walking in strappy high heels with a carefree swing of her shoulders, a suitable lioness to her military lover, she headed straight to a chair by the window, lit a cigarette encased in a jade holder, and assumed a bored countenance. When I caught her eye, she stuck her chin out and stared through me.

Józsi introduced me. The colonel frowned, forming distinct vertical lines between his lowered eyebrows.

"Why is he here?"

"Béla is in town on furlough to visit his family. He will assist me in preparing the colors."

"That will be difficult after I have him shot for desertion."

I was in the antechamber of hell, subject to whims that could readily become law. The colonel had not brought any guards with him, unless his concubine kept a gun in her purse. If I flew down the stairs, I might have a chance.

Józsi ignored the comment. "Colonel, please sit and make yourself comfortable. As we discussed, this will be a lengthy sitting."

"Hopefully the last one." Before sitting with legs wide open and arms folded, the Colonel dissected me with a piercing, reptilian stare, allowing me to notice the dueling scar on his left cheek. Lavender-smelling cologne billowed about him. "Make yourself useful. Go downstairs and get some coffee for Szilvia and me. Tell them that it's for Colonel Feder."

Did the colonel ever entertain the thought that there were powers in the world greater than he? I raced out of the room, rejecting a thought to make a run for the train station. Wandering through the ground-floor labyrinth as if there were a spinning hoop around my

Chapter 22

hips that would fall if I stopped, the most generous response I received was one of puzzlement. A cleaning woman, whom I recognized as a former barmaid at the Csillag, pointed the way to the kitchen. The mention of the colonel's name earned me a tray with four demitasse cups of steaming Turkish coffee, a silver bowl of whipped cream, and a plate of pastries embellished with several chocolates. I stuffed a tart in my pocket and gulped down one of the coffees, wiping specks of foam from my mouth. Once out of the kitchen, I hid the empty cup behind a framed photo, perched on a nearby table, of Admiral Horthy, clad in full regalia.

When I returned, the blonde was cross-examining her fury-red fingernails while emitting a vortex of smoke rings, ones that shimmied through the air and kept their shape for several feet. As I glanced at her, she uncrossed her legs and slowly crossed them again. The colonel, perhaps pleased with the refreshments, motioned for me to take a seat on a side chair near his.

"Haupt informs me that you have a story to tell me. A sad tale, no doubt. Well, go ahead. It may relieve the tedium of sitting here and looking pretty."

What had Queen Esther said before approaching the king uninvited? "If I perish, I perish." So I again recounted my quest for a warm coat, hoping the colonel would not ask for my furlough pass. He gazed at a blank wall while I spoke. When I first mentioned The Beast, I came close to using that appellation, but caught myself. Upon hearing the reference to "Desző Valler," the colonel jerked his head up. His expression would have kept ice cubes frozen.

"Are you sure of that name?"

"Yes, Colonel."

"Continue."

When I finished, the colonel asked me to describe The Beast physically. "Tell me more about him. How is his treatment of the servicemen?"

Uncertain of whether to spin the story to guarantee that the colonel did not question my patriotism, or to ensure that word would not get back to The Beast that I had complained about him, I stated the facts, including highlights of The Beast's behavior. Enjoying the colonel's full attention, I threw in for good measure the tale of my hanging.

He stood, waiving to Józsi to stop painting. Glaring at me, he said, "Is everything you've told me the truth?"

"Yes, Colonel. On my honor."

The colonel said to the woman, "Szilvia, please go downstairs and find Sergeant Nosti. Tell him to locate a fur-lined leather coat. And a lined hat."

He glanced at my patched shoes. "What size are your feet?"

"Ten."

"Also ask him to bring up boots. Size ten or larger. Tell them to grease the boots first."

"Thank you, Colonel," I offered with a bowed head.

Szilvia sauntered away, the low-cut back of her dress revealing the outline of vertebra pushed against her skin like a pitchfork. He shouted after her, "And bring me a pen and paper. And an envelope."

During her absence, the colonel resumed the sitting, lost in pained thought as if his leather seat cushion were lined with barbed wire. Szilvia reentered, striding toward us with her curls bouncing off her shoulders. She was accompanied by a young, star-struck soldier laden with a coat and hat that appeared new, together with black boots glazed in greenish slime. The colonel again waved Józsi off. He scribbled out a note, sealed it in a tissue-thin envelope with a multicolored border, and thrust it at me. "Go back immediately and present this to Valler. To no one but him."

"Sir, I just need a brief time to visit my family."

The colonel gritted his teeth. "Are you deaf? I said to go back at once!"

In the Hungarian military, every order was urgent. I took my new clothes from the soldier, hastily thanked the colonel again and also Józsi,

Chapter 22

urging the latter not to tell my parents that I had been in town, and left. Halfway down the stairs, a shout froze me. Szilvia was standing at the top step holding the hat with a single finger. The hallway's grudging light threaded through enough to highlight the fringes of her hair.

"Forget something?"

I motioned for her to toss it, but she wagged a finger, summoning me. Her smell was of citrus, a subtle perfume to be worn during the day, Gizi had explained to Tibi and me. It numbed me, as though I had nibbled on the liver of a blowfish. The hook back in my mouth, I was reeled in.

As I approached, she leaned forward, revealing cleavage. I snatched the hat from an arm draped with loops of gold that shimmered against her ginger skin. Lowering her streaked eyelashes, she whispered, "You consider me a whore, don't you?"

"You and the colonel make a lovely pair."

"Bastard! You think I want this?"

"I make no judgments."

She gazed at me as would a blind man staring directly at the sun, knowing that no further damage was possible. How many men had she pulled into her web and then eviscerated? "Yes, you do. I can tell."

The colonel might open the door at any moment and spot me in conversation with his lover. "What do you want? My absolution?"

Her passionless voice answered, "Just know that I have a husband missing at the front and a young boy to feed."

Who was she trying to convince? I stepped backward down the stairs. "We all do what we must. I wish you and your family well."

*

Ignoring the exhausting heat, I wore the boots and coat, out of fear they would be appropriated if I carried them. During the train ride back, I savored the apple tart, nibbling at it, tasting the sliced almonds within, and licking the coating of powdered sugar. Hours later, during which time I contemplated tossing the letter out the window, I was back in camp. After leaving my new clothing with Tibi, I marched to The Beast's barracks. At the entrance, I was stopped by a sentry.

"I've been instructed to see Sergeant Valler."

"No serviceman can just come here demanding to see him."

"I have orders to give him a letter."

He chided. "Orders? From who?"

"From the highest authorities."

Out danced his right hand. He wiggled his sausage fingers, which had a patch of hair below the knuckles thick as pelt. "Give me the letter. I'll take it to the sergeant."

"My instructions are to hand it to him personally."

The guard advanced to within a couple of feet. "Give it to me!"

"My instructions come from…."

With a swift, practiced motion, he jabbed his rifle butt into my stomach, doubling me up. He again extended his hand.

I choked out, "From Colonel Mihály Feder."

The soldier froze. Would the invocation even of Horthy's name have an effect in The Beast's fiefdom? I braced for another blow, but instead he ordered, "Wait here!"

My assailant stepped inside, shutting the door behind him. When it opened, he motioned for me to enter. The Beast was sitting behind a wooden school desk with a slanted top and sheet-metal, foldable legs. With his feet sticking out in front, he looked like a truant who had been left back for decades. "You again! If this isn't genuine, I'll hang you in front of the entire camp. And you won't have Nagy to save you."

I placed the envelope in front of him. After opening it, The Beast called to Július, a soldier half his age who took care of The Beast's clothing and fetched him food and drink, to read it aloud. Tibi had nicknamed him "The Fegelah."

Chapter 22

As The Beast crossed his arms and locked his darkened eyes on me, Július read haltingly, "Sergeant Valler, it seems, once again, I must be disturbed by reports of your unsoldierly conduct. You are a disgrace to the...."

The Beast jumped up, revealing a mass of belly hairs under his shirt, and tore the letter from Július's hands. He approached and thrust his face inches from mine.

With a clenched jaw, and emphasizing every word, he said, "How do you know Feder?"

What to say? I couldn't reveal that I had left the camp without permission. Nor was it plausible that the letter arrived in the mail.

"HOW DO YOU KNOW FEDER?"

"Sir, he is a close family friend. He inquired of my health, sir."

The Beast would have me hung by the neck this time, I was sure of it. But he said nothing and motioned for his assistant to accompany him to a back room. I waited. The Beast returned alone.

"You Jews think you're so clever. You lie. Scheme. Manipulate. But your days of reckoning have come. Particularly for you, Ingber, who will soon run out of tricks," he snarled. "Then there will be no more fancy officers to protect you. Once that moment comes, I'll kill you with my bare hands. And shit on your corpse. Now get out."

Whether Feder himself canceled the order for my labor company to be sent to the battle lines or ordered The Beast to do it, I'll never know. Perhaps Feder had threatened to send The Beast along with us. No further mention of the Eastern front was made. I learned that Valler had labeled me "incorrigible" and worked to have me assigned to a company known to force servicemen to march shoulder-to-shoulder with spades and wire into mine fields to clear those areas, with the troops behind betting on how many would be killed. He was unsuccessful, and life's rushing tide continued to sweep me away from the waterfalls.

CHAPTER 23
Tetzi: October 17, 1942

Brother, come!
And let us go unto our God.
And when we stand before Him
I shall say—
"Lord, I do not hate,
I am hated.
I scourge no one,
I am scourged.
I covet no lands,
my lands are coveted.
I mock no peoples,
My people are mocked."
And, brother, what shall you say?

—Joseph Seamon Cotter

My favorite section of Hungary's capital is the steep hills of the old section of Buda. I first encountered them in the year of my bar mitzvah, when I accompanied my father to the "Pearl of the Danube" on one of his travels to sell range cattle. In my youth, I would lose

Chapter 23

myself in the cobblestone streets, each with its enigmatic pleasures, invariably ending my ramblings at the Elizabeth Lookout, to gaze at the lattice of mountains that guard the city before hiking down to the slate-gray river. However, it was across it, in Pest, where I made my greatest discovery.

Early on a Saturday afternoon, after a train ride from the labor camp passing columns of majestic bark lit aflame with fading life's palette, I arrived at the clothing shop on the Váci Utca, near elegant Vörösmarty Square. The storefront was surrounded by boarded-up establishments papered with scrawled notes offering services such as housekeeping and child care. Winter approached in fast-forward, stripping the woods bare, demanding its sacrifices. Again, I lacked a warm overcoat. Forced to use the coat that the colonel had given me as a blanket, it was now cracked and ripped, its holes stuffed with straw, one blizzard away from disintegration. By this time in the war, clothing was difficult to obtain. Even material was rationed. Not wanting to take from my family what they would need, and with meager means, I had written to Tetzi, who had moved to Budapest to work as a dressmaker.

I had passed several salons that were closed, with "Juden" painted across their doors in blood-red letters. In the window of Tetzi's shop, there was a large sign, next to a cream-colored, undressed female mannequin with a peaceful, welcoming demeanor, proclaiming the store to be "Christian owned." I was struck by the urge to remove the sign and tie it on the mannequin itself. Over the breasts would be the ideal spot. And perhaps bind her to her counterpart headless male, to whose groin I would attach a "Jewish owned" sign. Enthralled with my wit, I suppressed a chuckle as I entered.

Haphazardly taped to the interior walls were sketches of men's and women's clothing. A sewing machine sat on the counter, surrounded by a rainbow array of thread spools and stray pins and thimbles. Bolts of cotton and wool fabric in various bland patterns lay piled on top of each other on a nearby table, like corpses awaiting burial, along with pairs of shears and pages scribbled with customers' measurements. No one was in sight, the shop guarded by its innocence.

I waited, and then shouted, "Tetzi, Tetzi."

A voice of exaggerated sweetness emanated from a back room. "One minute."

As she entered, Tetzi offered a weary, "May I help…." Her glazed eyes focused on the tanned, muscular figure before her. "Béla!" She dashed around the counter, and we hugged. I did so self-consciously, as I was well past my last decent bath or shave. I was wearing my underwear inside out because I hadn't had the opportunity to wash them in a while. My fingernails were the dark-brown color of soil. Even my urine stank. "I didn't actually believe you would make it here."

Was she put off by my slovenly appearance? If only she would remember me as splendidly handsome. "So the little *pisher* from Munkács is now a city gal."

She laughed and pulled me to a swivel chair, perching herself on the edge of a nearby desk. An adventurous waif, Tetzi had long spoken of her desire to live in one of the great cities of Europe. "I am woven from strings of steel and silk," she explained, "too strong to be chained up in Munkács."

Six feet tall with Rapunzel-length chocolate-brown hair, Tetzi's rail thinness was highlighted by ample breasts. She was decorated with costume jewelry of base metals and synthetic stones that, on her, sparkled with joy.

"How are you? I want to hear everything."

"Well, I was going to wait until later to spring the great news. Horthy has appointed me as Kállay's successor. I've come to Budapest to assume my new office. Want to help me rule?"

She raised her arm, her sleeveless blouse revealing a thicket of armpit hair, and punched me. "Be serious."

Chapter 23

"What's there to say?" I fought a desire to describe daily life in the camp. No, best not to pierce her cocoon. "Like everyone else, I'm trying to survive until this stinking war ends."

She glanced downward. "I know. And your family?"

I shrugged. "Still no word from Jenő. And I just learned that Ferencz is missing at the Front…"

She laid a palm on my shoulder. "I will pray for them."

"Thank you. Tetzi, are you happy here?"

"Pretty much. I have an apartment nearby that I share with two other women. And I'm getting better at being a seamstress. Soon I'll have two years of apprenticeship…" She stopped in mid-sentence, leaving unsaid that Jews could no longer become licensed. "You'd be surprised at how many women still can afford to have us design and make blouses, skirts, dresses, and even gowns. Although, lately, mostly I do alterations."

"Your mom is well?" Tetzi's mother had followed her to Budapest.

"Yes. She lives with my Aunt Vera. Mama works with her in a manufacturing company as a bookkeeper."

"Please give her my regards. Tetzi, where is everybody?"

"In the summer and early fall, before the warm-clothing season begins, I'm the only one here on Saturdays. The woman I work for, Rózsi, is Jewish. She's the true owner of the place. She inherited it from her first husband. But we have a new legal owner, a Christian who gets a percentage of our revenue."

"In my next life, I will be a Gentile. So I can do nothing and get paid for it."

"Me, too. I would do whatever I wanted and then absolve myself through confession."

"That's the key. Absolve yourself through confession, but don't truly atone."

She grinned, "Although then you wouldn't be one of the chosen people."

"Apparently all people are chosen for something. The Nazis to kill. The Hungarians to torment. And we to be victimized. Speaking of which, do you think you can sew a coat for me?" *Don't just sew me a coat,* I thought to add. Look at me. Really look at me. Hear me. Save me, before I fall apart.

"Can it be made from cotton?" she said.

"No, it has to be wool. Cotton won't hold heat when it gets wet. And a hat and gloves would be helpful, too. I'm sorry to burden you with all this."

"Béla, stop. I would be happy to make these."

"So you can make men's clothing?"

"Sure. Although not a suit, which you will need as the new prime minister. One with deep pockets for the cigars you'll want, like Churchill."

I puffed out my chest, while she wiped imaginary dust balls off my shirt. "Tetzi, do you have material to spare?"

She waved her arm toward the fabrics spewed throughout the room. "At worst, we have some old blankets I can use. You may not be fashionable, but you will be warm. I also can make a pair of gloves from a worn sweater I have. It will take a little while. I can squeeze it in after my other work. Can you come back in a couple of weeks for a fitting?"

She knows I'm not a free man. Or does she choose to be blind? "I can probably manage to come back once, sometime next month. I won't be able to make frequent trips."

"I can finish it by then, but it might not fit."

"It will fit, because I need it to fit. Look, just use your judgment. I know you'll do a fine job."

Tetzi searched for a tape measure. I stood before a three-paneled mirror, catching sight of someone with a stubbled complexion who remotely resembled me, while she measured and recorded my

Chapter 23

dimensions on a flip pad. As her fingertips exerted pressure against my waist, I felt a gust stoke a fervor that had been in hibernation for so long. Gazing from the exposed downy flesh on the curve of her neck to the endless scythes that were her legs, I imagined Tetzi rendered bare for my pleasure. Was it intentional when her breasts brushed against my back? I faked a coughing fit to deflect my awkwardness. Tetzi appeared oblivious, as she impulsively bear-hugged me again when she finished. "It's so good to see a friend from home."

A woman wearing a tailored wool bolero jacket, matching skirt, and flowered nest hat entered the store, leading on a leash a frisky poodle with a curly beige coat of hair. She was tall, with a bouffant, lacquered hairdo, while the dog was a miniature. Tetzi presented her with a smile as real as the one on a mannequin, and then she handed her various sketches of dress patterns. The woman sat on a stool, flipping through them.

"Béla, what are you doing later?" she whispered. "I'm going to a reading with my boyfriend, Zoltán. Miklós Radnóti's poems. I believe that, like you, he is in a labor battalion."

"Miklós who?"

"Radnóti. Zoltán taught me one of his poems." She clutched her chest dramatically, fluttered her eyelashes, and assumed an affected, breathy voice. "You hold me in your arms when I'm afraid. I hold you in my arms. I'm not afraid. In your arms even the great silence of death can't scare me. In your arms I'll survive death. It's a dream."

No, my dear Tetzi, death isn't a dream. It's our master, allowing for innumerable sparks of existence for the pleasure of imposing its will on them at precisely the moment of its own choosing. I clapped. "Never heard of him. But then again, the only poet I know is Shakespeare."

"Radnóti is better than Shakespeare. English poets have a vast selection of words at their disposal, while Hungarian poets must work with a more limited vocabulary."

"Who knew? Poetry never appealed to me. I find it just a string of pretty verses that each person interprets differently."

"No, a good poet inhales life and then breathes it out in his eloquence."

"I think that each one of us is a poet, but some have more of a talent for hyperbole."

"Why not think of poems as you would music or paintings? As another way of expressing beauty. Of finding meaning in life. What could be more important these days?"

In the childhood that Tetzi and I had shared, problems were mild enough to be toyed with theoretically. Now I had neither the time nor the inclination. "A warm coat."

She reached for my arm. "You must think me a fool."

I took her hand and kissed it. "I wish that I could write a poem about you. About your kindness. And gentleness. And...."

Her face brightened. "Béla, you were skeptical of Jabotinsky also, as I recall. Come and give this poetry a chance. Listen closely to it. Try to feel it."

"I have to be back in camp tonight." A fib, but I had no money for lodging. And I had already imposed on Tetzi.

"At least have some tea. I close the shop at five and am meeting a friend. Join us."

"Three's a crowd, no?"

"Nonsense, Béla. Who wouldn't want to mingle with the new leader of our country?" Her smile was inviting, despite the protruding teeth. The customer, now holding a pattern, was about to interrupt us when her poodle began barking and pulling her toward the front, where a cat had parked itself. The dog was unable to discern that the stray would tear it apart in a fight, a metaphor for Hungary's relationship with Germany. Incapable of halting the yapping, the woman murmured an apology and left, promising to return. I followed her and shut the door.

Chapter 23

"Why don't you close now and spend the afternoon with me? We can reminisce about the good old days. When you skied to work and dated ill-tempered men."

Another cuff to my shoulder. "You are mean, Béla. And to think that I was so smitten with you."

"You were?"

"Of course. It should have been obvious. But you had eyes only for Ágnes."

I didn't love Tetzi, but now I wanted her love. For her to ache for me. "I'm sorry, Tetzi. I thought Adolph was the Ingber you cared for. Did I ruin that relationship?"

Tetzi emitted a laugh that ended with a snort, causing her to redden. "Of course not. Adolph was a true friend and, beneath all the anger, good-hearted. But I enjoyed being with him most when you were around."

We stood facing each other, near enough for me to kiss her without taking a further step. Please Tetzi, just one. It would change everything.

Did my breath smell? That morning, I had brushed my teeth with salt, using the tips of my fingers. I edged my upper body closer, my eyes locked onto hers. Imagining that, at least for a few moments, I would be at the molten center of her world. But my inflamed heart stumbled before finding its rhythm again, and in that instant she raised her palms, figuratively pushing me back. "Béla, meet us at the Café Gerbeaud. It's nearby, on the square. You can't miss it. A fancy red brick and marble building. They say their patisserie is as good as the best ones in Vienna."

Tetzi noticed my discomfort. "Don't worry," she added. "They will treat us well. I'm friendly with the manager's wife, whom I've made clothes for."

"That will be nice. I look forward to it."

I turned to leave, but she grabbed my arm. "Wait." She raced to the back of the store, bringing back a rumpled brown paper bag stained with food grease.

"Take this, Béla. It's a chicken sandwich and a pickle."

I possessed little that was uniquely my own, beyond my thoughts and emotions. And a few precious relationships. "I can't eat your lunch, Tetzi."

She pushed it into my hand. "It will go to waste. I'm full from a late breakfast." I gave her a slender kiss on the cheek. Before I closed the door behind me, she murmured into the thin air between us, "If only our timing were better, Béla."

Under a veil of cloud cover that heightened the fall chill, I wandered the local streets, weaving in and out of the path of aggressive beggars, many of whom were in wheelchairs and had planted themselves in front of open restaurants and bakeries. Turning onto Nádor Utca, my reverie was interrupted by the sight of a Wehrmacht officer in a coal-black leather trench coat and jackboots, a holster on his yellow leather belt. He was slapping a vagabond repeatedly.

I resolved to head to Margit Island, passing grand hotels with terrace cafés decorated with apricot mums and plate-glass windows offering views of Buda: dull, square limestone apartment buildings in hushed shades of gray, statues of war heroes coated in dung, and a park where, on a wrought-iron gated entrance on which climbing honeysuckle vines cascaded down, hung a sign, "No dogs or Jews." Few automobiles trundled along the streets, which instead were rife with motorcycles, mostly undersized French-made Matras, which were not subject to gas rationing.

The island was a lush, tranquil oasis offering pigment to a colorless city. I sauntered over the side bridge and along a cracked path that bordered the Danube on the right and lily ponds and stately sycamore trees on the left. The trail led to a waterless fountain cluttered with fallen leaves, with a statue of Neptune staring down from the top. Nearby were stone tables and seats where chess players pondered their moves.

Chapter 23

Next to a teenager selling flowers and roasted chestnuts from a broken horse cart stood a Gypsy violinist, deeply tanned, with muddy brown teeth and a mane of wavy hair damp with sweat. Wearing a red silk bandana and multicolored chemise shirt, he seemed a mirror image of the Roma accordionist who had played Yiddish tunes at Ilona's wedding. There is music in the genes of these people, who live spontaneously and primitively, as if they still were in the Middle Ages. But now they are outcasts, as am I. Why do we not bond in alliance against a common enemy?

The man was vigorously playing the Csárdás, gold loop earrings swaying against his cheekbones. He closed his eyes, engaged in dialogue with his instrument. Infused with the passion of the violinist's distinctive interpretation of the dance, I let myself believe that Tetzi was here with me. Imagining that I'm holding her by the waist as her hands cling to my shoulders. As our momentum builds with the rising tempo, we kiss each other gluttonously while twirling around the fountain to wild applause.

Tired by my fantasy, I plopped onto a park bench, shaded by a giant oak whose thick branches had grown horizontally to form a dense umbrella crown. Savoring Tetzi's sandwich, I regretted not having given her a proper kiss. The fiddler exhibited enormous range, seamlessly switching to a concerto at the request of a passerby, a dapper man as dissimilar from the Gypsy as if the two were from different planets, drawn together by the narcotic genius of Mozart. In appreciation, he dropped coins into a cap held by a scantily clad boy, with a straight-up cowlick, who was sitting in the dirt at the violinist's feet, his chin resting on knobby knees.

I sought refuge in the music, being played as if my heartaches had been woven into its creation. But competing for my ear was an ever-present inner voice, one that often lacked wisdom, forcing me to replay the events of the afternoon like a movie newsreel. We servicemen joked about our high standards for whom we would be willing to have sex with—the person would have to be "female and breathing." But Tetzi was special. Why hadn't I noticed that years ago? How serious was she with her latest boyfriend? What did she mean by, "If only our timing were better?" And why was I obsessing about her?

Perhaps I should head back to camp. Those few minutes with Tetzi were the sweetest ones I had enjoyed in months. If left untouched, they would sustain me until I next saw my family. But how could I pass up the opportunity to see her again? Or disappoint her, or go back on my word? I glanced at the coins in the boy's hat. I hadn't sufficient money to pay for myself, much less treat Tetzi and her friend.

The concerto was followed by a melodic Lehár waltz, then Pachelbel's Canon, surrounding the fountain in His divine spirit. Time slowed, for once not in response to pain or boredom. Simmering musical notes, drawn long and tender, made me safe.

I opened my eyes. The violinist and his son had vanished, their music replaced by the piping of birds. A man in a worn dark suit with a stiff collar sitting adjacent to me displayed a watch face indicating it was half past four. I jumped up and half-walked, half-ran to Café Gerbeaud, where several hackney carriages and hansom cabs stood in front.

Last night, I was served dinner with a long-handled ladle, and I ate the gruel from a tin bowl with a spoon crooked as a corkscrew. I had slept in a barn that we insulated with earth and straw embedded with lice and worms, which sucked away our strength. Now I was surrounded by silk-embroidered walls, Persian carpets, crystal chandeliers, artificial palms, and intricate wood paneling topped by scrolling crown molding. A trio—violist, bass fiddler, and piccolo player—was tucked in a corner, passionately playing melodies from operettas. I snaked my way across the polished parquet floors, banging into varnished, hardwood chairs with high, carved backs and cutting

Chapter 23

off waiters in crisp black uniforms with cream linen napkins stuck under their arms, until I spotted Tetzi. She was waving from a table set with damask, china, and silverware, located on the terrace facing the Square and its manicured, fenced park. Sitting next to her was a woman with the lithe slenderness of youth.

"Béla, this is Marika. My newest friend. Marika, please meet Béla, my oldest friend."

Marika greeted me with a weak handshake. Tetzi flagged down a waitress and ordered for us. Coffee was no longer available to the public. "Three teas. And we will share one of the cakes. Whichever you recommend." I fidgeted, fingering the meager coins in my pocket.

Tetzi orchestrated the small talk, whose triviality contrasted with a city burdened with rampant poverty, oppression, lists of the dead appearing daily in the papers, rumors of mass murder throughout the continent, and the approach of armed conflict. Marika listened quietly, as if her contentment lay in being in Tetzi's presence. When I spoke to Marika, I could hold her eyes only fleetingly. She was a timid bird, and I was careful not to become her scarecrow. I did learn that she was the stepdaughter of the woman whose deceased first husband had founded the dress shop. And that Marika helped out there.

The waitress brought a tea tray laden with a Victorian pot, floral cups, and three moist petits fours, each coated with dark chocolate, arranged precisely on Meissen china with an onion pattern. With food now rationed, and much of the Hungarian crop being confiscated by Germany, how were these delicacies possible? I inhaled mine and waited politely as the two women ate theirs with lady-like bites, leaving crumbs clustered on their lipstick. I was rewarded when, at the same time, each insisting she could eat no more, they nudged their plates toward me. This time, I let my tongue tease out the walnut and fruit jam resting between layers of sponge, while resisting the temptation to lick my fingers clean.

"So, Béla, tell us something amusing and wonderful."

More frivolity, sweet as the food. My hours on the park bench now would pay off. I lowered my voice. "How does a Hungarian firing squad stand?"

Tetzi squealed, "I give up."

"In a circle."

The thunderous laugh resonating from Tetzi was not unexpected. But I was pleased to have enticed a cautious smile and titter out of Marika, whom I had been stealing glimpses of. All day, I had fancied Tetzi a beauty, but Marika truly was one, with wavy hair, full lips, and high cheekbones with concave cheeks, an oval face whose perfection was blemished only by a slight but agreeable gap between her two front teeth. She had warm brown eyes and a curvy figure. I judged her to be about the same age as my little sister.

The cake now gone, Tetzi insisted on ordering more food. "We will eat in reverse order," she declared. Our server arrived with slices of black bread and cheese. She whispered to the waitress and pressed money into her hand. How was this possible? How much could Tetzi earn at the store?

The sky darkened, as if it had donned sunglasses. We were joined by Zoltán, who made his way across the room with a perceptible limp. He kissed Tetzi and then Marika's hand, nodding to me. Grabbing an empty chair from the next table without asking permission, he banged it into a silver-plated bucket holding a cobweb-covered wine bottle and disturbed a young couple's romantic toast. Sporting a checkered vest, unkempt goatee, and a mop of tousled, copper-red hair that covered his ears, he towered even above Tetzi.

Zoltán was on medical leave from a labor camp. He explained that, a month earlier, while working on laying "Drachenzähne," the "dragon's teeth" pyramids installed to stop tank movements, his foot had been crushed by a fallen slab of reinforced concrete. He acted out

Chapter 23

the first moments of this event, the hurt of recollection outweighed by the theatrical opportunity.

As we compared our camp experiences, Marika piped up to note that her father also had been in a labor camp, but had become ill with dysentery and was allowed to return home, given his age. Zoltán, after glancing around to assess those within earshot, proclaimed, "By next year, Hungary will be out of the war." Staring at Tetzi, he added, "And you and I will be the toasts of this town."

"How do you figure that?" I said, hoping for reassuring logic.

"Don't you listen to the BBC?" In camp, at night, when the guards had returned to their barracks, we sometimes were able to catch the BBC's Hungarian-language broadcasts over a hand-built shortwave. First the sonorous opening notes of Beethoven's *Fifth*. Then those alluring illicit words, "This is London calling…."

"We haven't been able to lately," I said. "The broadcasts have been jammed."

Zoltán was a man who might be wrong but was never in doubt. "The Axis is losing the war in Africa. Germany is being bombed by the British. The Russians are holding on to Stalingrad and killing lots of Germans. Hungarians are being used by Hitler as cannon fodder."

"We were told in camp that Hitler has assured the German people that Stalingrad soon would fall," I retorted.

Zoltán reached for the looped handle on Tetzi's mug, emptying it with a long gulp. "What I wouldn't give for a perch-trout a la Mornay with sautéed potatoes and a bottle of Riesling. Then coffee with globs of whipped cream and a snort of Bénédictine." He smacked his lips, savoring an imaginary aftertaste, before continuing. "Even if it does, the Nazis have bitten off more than they can chew. Germany is fighting on two fronts. Maybe three if the Americans and British ever launch an attack in the West. In any event, the fighting is far from here and not likely to touch us."

"There are rumors that the Nazis have miracle weapons...."

He waved his hand at me dismissively. "We know how the Nazis and Hungarians use false rumors to keep us in line."

"Zoltán, you trust Horthy to get us out of this?" Tetzi said.

"Isn't it perverse that we Hungarians, who live in a landlocked country, have been ruled for decades by an admiral?" Zoltán elevated his chin, as if performing a soliloquy. "Yes, Horthy is an egomaniacal, unprincipled tyrant, but he's not a fool." He licked his index finger and pointed to the sky. "Our beloved leader watches how the wind blows, and when it clearly rages in favor of the Allies, he'll negotiate an armistice."

His reasoning was a comfort, although only mildly so, like receiving condolences from an acquaintance for a lost relative. Tetzi muttered, "We should be careful what we wish for if the Russians get here first." Without waiting for a response, she glanced at her watch. "Zoltán, it's getting late."

He reached for her hand to caress and kiss it, the intimacy of this magnifying my solitude. Zoltán recited with exaggerated somberness,

Marika Leiner, circa 1945

"Somewhere within me, dear, you abide forever, still, motionless, mute, like an angel stunned to silence by death." The displeasure his presence was causing me had reached new heights, elevated by the gnawing thought that Tetzi had selected this man, above all others, to receive the key to her secret places.

Tetzi's eyes flickered. Then she stood. "Béla, you and Marika, please stay and enjoy each other's company. The manager's wife took care of us."

Zoltán bowed dramatically to Marika and me. I gave Tetzi a crushing

Chapter 23

hug, thanked her, and assured her that I would write soon about when I might return for the coat. She kissed me on each cheek, leaving incandescent lipstick fingerprints of our everlasting affection, and winked. The sweet joy on Tetzi's face, reflecting expectations for a life yet to be lived, is my lasting image of her.

CHAPTER 24
Marika

The room of love is always rearranged.

—Donald Hall

As I sat back down, my hands trembled until I grasped them together. Food, sophisticated atmosphere, seats under the stars, and alone with an attractive young woman. And I had wanted to head back to camp?

"What does your father do?" I said.

"He's a printer," she answered, speaking more to the table than to me. "He has a shop near where we live, on Joszef Korut Street."

"He prints books?"

"No, most of his business is advertisements, like the ones you see pasted to walls and lampposts. Also invitations and wedding announcements."

So people still planned their lives? The perversity of mailing out a party invitation while the world was in its fourth year of self-immolation

Chapter 24

made me laugh. Which caused Marika to startle, and me to refocus. I could not let this opportunity slip. "I see. And Rózsi, the dress shop owner, she is your stepmother?"

"Yes. I have a stepsister as well. Klari. She's older than me."

"Your mother and father are divorced?"

"No, my mother died when I was five years old. Leukemia."

"I'm sorry. May I ask how old you are?"

"Sixteen. Seventeen in December."

Younger than Libu. I racked my fermenting brain and threw out questions before scrutinizing them. "So what do you do in the dress shop, Marika?"

"Sew clothes. I just finished trade school. You're not allowed to graduate until you pass a final examination, which is mostly making a dress from scratch. It's harder than you might think. Especially the sleeves."

"I bet you're good at it. Me, I would bleed to death from poking holes in my fingers."

Marika rose shyly, tracing with her fingertips the bottom half of her plain beige dress with a high neckline outlined by a thin pink ribbon. It was form-fitting, accentuating her figure. "You can judge for yourself."

I clapped vigorously, and she took her seat again. "Thank you. Do you often come to Budapest, Béla?"

I explained why I had come, prompting Marika to offer to help Tetzi with my coat. The waitress interrupted apologetically. "We're closing. We're not allowed to keep lights on at night."

Marika stood first and reached for my hand. "It was very nice to meet you."

"Please let me escort you home, Marika."

"I don't want to inconvenience you."

"Nonsense. You said that you lived on Joszef Korut Street. I believe that's on the way to the Keleti railway station."

The corners of her mouth lifted in a suggestion of a smile, as I calculated how many hours of conversation I could fit into what would be a short walk. After we each stopped in a restroom, the men's decorated with floral flocked wallpaper and a wedding cake chandelier, we headed east, venturing cautiously in the dark streets. Marika kept a polite distance. My mouth kiln dry, I told her of my trip to Margit Island.

"It's so lovely there, particularly the gardens." I imagined a stroll with Marika to the island, followed by dinner al fresco by the water. Sweat beaded on my lip.

"My family often had lunch at the Palatinus," she continued. "There's a pool there that has waves, like you're at the beach. The men have to wear one-piece bathing suits with shoulder straps, which looks so funny. That's where Papa taught me to swim."

We crossed into the Jewish neighborhood of Pest, comprised mostly of early-nineteenth-century buildings with businesses on the ground floors and apartments above. Through an open window, music from *The Merry Widow* was being played.

"I love that operetta," Marika said.

I refrained from telling her that I thought it a vapid tale of the insoluble tension between money and romantic love. Or that Lehár was rumored to have pandered to Hitler, despite having a Jewish wife. "Yes, it's quite beautiful."

Downplaying my own experiences in the city, I encouraged from Marika stories of her life. Not paying attention to the route, I was disoriented as we became dwarfed by the enormous red and copper-brick Dohány Street Synagogue. We paused before its two soaring Gothic towers, crowned by onion-shaped domes with golden ornaments, which shone through electric beams that transected a sky shaded in despairing darkness. Wasn't there a general lighting ban?

Chapter 24

Papa had dismissed the synagogue as a theater for "fancy Jews to show off."

I pointed to the building. "Do you attend services there?"

"Sometimes on Friday nights with my father. Although he prefers a small *shul* that's closer to us."

"To me, it's odd. It looks like a mosque."

"Have you been inside? The interior is gorgeous. They say that it was modeled after Solomon's Temple."

"How do they know?"

I meant my question seriously, but Marika laughed. What was preferable—being earnest or providing entertainment? While in the camp, I had turned inward, focusing on an imaginary life. My conversational and wooing skills were rusty. I couldn't let this spark die out.

She pointed to a building next to the temple. "Did you know that Herzl was born there?"

The Betar maniacs in Munkács had worshipped Jabotinsky and spoke of Herzl as a lesser god. "I assumed Herzl was German, since that's the language he wrote in."

Marika told me that, weeks earlier, during the High Holidays, policemen with white gloves had directed traffic and maintained order around the synagogue, a scene tauntingly reminiscent of normal times. We strode past on the other side of the street.

As the temple's lights faded from view, Marika and I reached a square on a main thoroughfare, barren except for a flock of pigeons pecking at crusts of bread. She raised her nose toward an ornate, baroque structure. "That's the Hungarian National Theatre." The setting conjured images of gowned women and tuxedoed men gathering in a glass-enclosed foyer, being photographed for the next day's news. Marika pointed to her apartment building down the block. Hanging kerosene lamps, their orange-blue veins of flame surrounded by fluttering moths, illuminated the ground floor. They showcased an outdoor café with stacked tables and chairs enclosed within a gated iron terrace and flanked by thick-trunked, leafless chestnut trees. I made a mental note for the next time—and hopefully there would be one—that she and I would meet there.

Marika directed me to the street that led to the train station. "It's only about twenty minutes away."

My heart pounded, and my skin was electrified. I considered a peck on her cheek but, instead, I offered a cigarette, buying a few more minutes. I lit two in my mouth at the same time, with a lighter whose wheel I had to flick repeatedly before its tongue of fire took hold.

"It was a pleasure meeting you, Marika. I hope your father fully recovers his health." For the first time, she observed me without wavering. "And that we see each other again."

"I would like that." Marika clutched my hand with both of hers. "Please take care of yourself."

I ambled away, smiling during the entire walk to the train station. Awash in a sensation that, at last, the caprices of life, pure and unrestrained, had inured to my benefit.

*

I will forever be indebted to Tetzi. As she instructed, I picked up the coat at Marika's apartment. In an inner pocket, I found the following note:

Dearest Béla,

Sadly, it was not fated that the two of us should ever be together as a couple. I realized that by the end of our evening at the Café Gerbeaud.

Marika thinks you are a good and handsome man, but she is concerned about the thirteen-year age difference. But do not let that stop you. Our hearts do not count the years as our minds do. I believe that, over time, all that each of us needs does come to us. I am sure that your strength and confidence will win her.

Chapter 24

I look forward to our celebrating together, hopefully very soon, the end of this cruel war and the eternal friendship that we share.

I kiss you a thousand times,

From the left: Rózsi, Anton, Marika, and Klari Leiner, circa 1937

CHAPTER 25

Ferencz Ingber: October 26, 1942
(Southern Russia)

My Cherished Family,

If you receive this postcard, I pray that it has found each of you well. Do not worry for me. I have what I need. And I understand now how little we truly require. I desire only your health and happiness. My love for you all is my faith.
Your loving son and brother,

CHAPTER 26

Libu Ingber: May 20, 1943
(Oroszvég)

My Dearest Béla,

We received your latest postcard, and were very glad to hear that you are well. We sent you a package yesterday and hope you receive it.

I have taken the written part of the high school final examinations. They have been held since Monday, every day from 7 a.m. until 3 p.m. It has not been difficult, but now we have to write in Hungarian, which I am not as good at. We start each school day by standing and singing the Hungarian national anthem.

It is strange to go to an all-Jewish girls school. I miss some of my old friends, but I am not so sure that they miss me. The other day, I passed Diana Kling on the Korzo. You remember her? When we were young, she was my best friend for years. We used to walk home from school holding hands. Now when we pass, I smile at her but she looks away.

We are so glad that you will be home next month for Shavuot. Mama and Papa need to see you, and hear you, and touch you. As do Miki and I. You are so brave and so strong.

Jóska got a letter from the attorney saying that soon United States citizenships can be arranged for us.

I kiss you many times,

CHAPTER 27
Sister Zsuzsa: June 1943

Dumbly she clung and wept.
Her broken wing sheltered me:
scattered to the four winds of heaven;
they are gone, and I am alone.

—Hayim Bialek

Last November, with the onset of the cold, my nose leaked eels of green-yellow discharge as thick as pea soup. All winter long, I discolored my shirt sleeves. A permanent headache stormed in, and my nose swelled and stopped up. By the arrival of spring, my breathing was labored. I could no longer ignore it.

We had access to a camp doctor then, a dour fellow named Gabor Sas. Sas recently had graduated from medical school in Budapest, one of the last Jews permitted to do so. One evening, after the sharp whistle that signaled the end of the workday, I sat on a stool by his bunk holding a flashlight. He examined me with a cracked pocket mirror and a flexible tube inserted in my nostrils.

"Tilt your head back…take a long sniff in…let me see the color of your mucus."

Sas sneered, "What a stubborn idiot you are. This must have troubled you for months. Why didn't you come to me sooner?"

"I thought it would go away."

Sas threw up his hands. "Stop thinking! Just come see me. We might have prevented this. If you still have these symptoms in the warm weather, it's too late."

"Too late for what, Doctor?"

"Your sinuses are swollen, blocking the openings of your nose. The mucus can't drain out. You need an operation."

"Can't you give me some medication?"

"I have none to treat you with, Béla. Nor would it help."

I removed from my jacket pocket a cigarette pack. Sas tsked, but then reached for one. "And if I don't have the operation?"

"Soon you won't be able to work. Or breathe."

If I couldn't perform labor, they likely would shoot me. "So you'll operate on me?"

He shook his head. "I'm not a surgeon. You need to go to the military hospital in Budapest. I believe I can get the camp commander to grant permission and provide you with an escort."

We arrived at the same thought. He spoke it. "I don't know who will be assigned to you. It might be a Nazi."

I raised my palms in mock defeat. Every day, I awoke to a gnawing disquiet seeping through my life's canopy. Should I instead escape and travel home one last time? Return to my true self. But no, that would bring my troubles to their door. And if I made it to Budapest, I'd have the opportunity to sneak in a stopover with Marika.

After several fitful nights, I half-filled an olive rucksack with my few spare clothes, a pack of cigarettes, and several chocolate bars, leaving my prized mess kit in Tibi's care. Since last October, I had managed a couple of trips by train to Budapest to visit with Marika. The second time, when I arrived unannounced, her reaction was

Chapter 27

muted. But she dropped other plans to spend the day with me. By its end, we stopped to sit by the Mihály Vörösmarty statue near Café Gerbeaud. I blurted out that I could think of nothing else but being with her, and I leaned in to kiss her, on the cheek. Instead, she married her lips to mine, and they lingered.

This time, I was escorted by two soldiers who drove up to the doctor's cabin in a Volkswagen jeep on whose hood sat a treadless spare tire. I scrambled wordlessly onto the back bench, forced to sit directly over the axle.

We drove on a snaking dirt lane, the jeep kicking up dust clouds as it shuddered over ceaseless waves of ruts. Our path morphed into a single macadam-paved road, passing squalid cottages surrounded by haystacks and weeds, but also gated summer villas with gabled roofs, screened-in terraces leading to bay windows, and manicured lawns cut by scythe. Turning a bend sharply, the jeep came a few feet from barreling into families of Gypsies. The driver jammed on the brake, his bull neck reverberating like an accordion. The children approached, thrusting out their hands to us. Watching over them were teenage girls wearing loose, half-buttoned blouses, women festooned with colorful bracelets and rags, many carrying naked babies, and ancient men with gold teeth, rolled-up pants, and glossy black boots. Only after rifles were lifted was our path cleared.

Soon, Esztergom's grand basilica, where the King once lived, came into view, perched on a hilltop. My high school history teacher, who taught us the great influence of the Roman Empire and the Renaissance on Hungary, had admitted that when he first visited the basilica's marble chapel, built in the Middle Ages by Italian stone carvers and sculptors and transported to Hungary, he wept at its magnificence. "Once you have seen it," he said, "you have seen all the beauty there is in this world."

As the glittering dome cupola of the cathedral shrunk and disappeared behind us, I was overcome by two desires. First, if I survived the war's undertow, to immerse myself in such man-made splendor. And, second, for a well-placed Allied bomb to demolish it.

Competing with us for road access were bike riders, farm tractors, horse-drawn drays, and soft-eyed cows wearing large copper bells that clanged chaotically, all unimpressed by our military markings. The route roughly paralleled the right bank of the Danube, offering views of skipping whitecaps and the weeping birches of Szentendre Island. In the final stretch, after worming our way through Buda's Castle Hill District, we arrived at a massive art nouveau iron gate. As I climbed out of the jeep, the driver tossed my sack out, informed me that he was about to have an intimate interlude with my sister, and sped off.

The ground floor of the hospital, whose tentacles led to numerous corridors and anterooms, was filled with a confused mass of nurses, orderlies, and soldiers. Patients lay on the tiled floor waiting for attention, while others were lined up for dismissal papers.

After presenting a letter from Doctor Sas, I was registered and then required to wait on a weathered wood bench in an admitting room whose walls were coated with discolored white paint of varied sheens. Numerous posters had been taped to the walls. Most were advertisements for cars, liquor, or cigarettes. One portrayed a hook-nosed, bearded man with a Star of David on his shirt, leering lasciviously at a blond, blue-eyed teenage girl.

I sat invisibly until a diminutive young woman approached carrying a blood pressure meter. The pendant light at the center of the room highlighted her olive skin. A service patch on her left sleeve indicated she was a nurse's aide.

Underneath a periwinkle chambray cap that matched her pinafore and hid her hair was an unfading smile. As she placed the inflatable cuff around my arm, I said, "Why do you need to take my blood pressure?"

Chapter 27

"It's standard procedure, sir."

"What if I have high blood pressure? Does my operation get postponed?"

She fidgeted with the top of her blouse. "The doctor will determine that, sir."

"What if my pressure is so high that I faint? Will you slap me until I revive?"

Success. She giggled. "I'm not allowed to do that, sir."

"Call me Béla. What's your name?"

"Ozlem, sir...uh, Béla. It's pronounced 'Ahs-lehm.'"

"What kind of name is that?"

"Turkish." I must have shown surprise, for she made a clucking noise. "There are lots of Turks in Budapest. Didn't you know that?"

"I've never met a Turk before."

"Then you can't have spent much time in Budapest. Long ago, the Ottoman Turks defeated the Hungarian Army and ruled this city and much of Hungary."

"I learned that. You Turks brought us roses, didn't you?"

"And hot baths. We are a cultured people."

"Although I was also taught that, 'Where the Turk treads, no grass grows.'"

Or possibly the phrase was, Where the Turk treads, no birds sing? She glowered. I attempted to recover. "Someone once told me that the Hungarians have never won a war."

"Well, I don't know much about that, but I can tell you that Hungarians and Turks are intertwined racially. Although many of us Turks remain Muslim."

"You're Muslim? Never met one of you, either."

She shook her head, ending the conversation, and motioned for me to follow her up a flight of stairs.

The fourth, top floor was a vision from Dante's Inferno. The hospital entrance had been bathed in antiseptic, while this level reeked of rotting flesh, feces, urine, pus, and vomit. Countless rows of beds were occupied by wounded soldiers, many missing one or more limbs. Some had been blinded. We passed a patient with one heavily bandaged arm and an empty sleeve, about Miki's age, crying out for a nurse to scratch his back. Next to him lay a soldier with no evident injury, tied to his bed and screaming for someone to take him to the bathroom. As I turned away, Ozlem whispered to him, "I'll be back soon to change your bedpan."

I was back in one of my recurring dreams in which I'm half naked in the middle of a roomful of people, all of whom are about to notice me. One man, who had lost both legs, spat at me from his wheelchair and yelled, "It's you Jews who caused this." Another called out, "Take a pail and clean the floor, Jew!" A nearby doctor, who I later learned was Emil Szabó, the chief of the surgical department, yelled out, "Shut up and mind your own business."

Ozlem directed me to a cot with adjustable side rails, a paper-thin mattress, and sterile white, drum-tight sheets covered by a pale blue wool blanket. I had not enjoyed the comforts of a bed in months, yet I lay restless. An attendant approached and, without acknowledging me, taped across the headboard a sign that read "Zsidó," as if my yellow armband weren't sufficient notice. I was a lone strawberry on an ivory white plate, before a hungry crowd.

When Ozlem returned, she led me to an office shaped like an elbow, with a view of the Danube shrouded in heavy, clinging fog, discernible only by the horn of a distant barge likely carrying oil or bauxite upriver to Germany. There, a haggard middle-aged man, clad in a blood-smeared lab coat covering a shirt and tie, introduced himself as Doctor Jákob Tóth. An unlit cigarette lay glued to his lower lip, its ashes sprinkled on his jacket. He read

Chapter 27

Dr. Sas's note, although scant explanation was needed, as my nose was twice its normal size and I spoke as though my nostrils were cemented.

As Ozlem held a light, I recoiled from Tóth's probing fingers. He did not apologize. Shaking his head like a dog that's climbed out of a pool of water, Tóth advised, "Doctor Sas was correct. You need an operation, young man."

Everything can heal. I wanted to believe that. "How bad will it be, doctor?"

"We can only reach the sinuses through your cheek. We'll try to limit the scarring, but I can't guarantee anything."

I sighed in resignation. A scar on my rheumy face was the least of my worries. At least he was willing to perform the operation.

"There's one more matter, Béla."

I gripped the arm rests of my chair. "I'm not sure we will have enough anesthesia for you. We'll have to tie you to the operating table. I can't have you thrashing around." He patted my shoulder and strolled out of the room. Ozlem followed him, after whispering to me, "You are in good hands."

An orderly escorted me back to my cot. On it, next to my sack, had been placed chocolates, coins, and writing paper. Was this a test? If I kept anything, I could be accused of theft. I gathered the items and placed them on a semicircular table next to the bed, then jammed a pillow over my head to block out the moaning and wailing of death, and to absorb my tears.

*

The next morning, I was brought to a surgical room on the second floor and directed to a table, where Doctor Tóth was rummaging through an assortment of tempered steel lancets, amid a pile of tools that resembled saws. At his side, dressed in matching gown, rubber gloves, and cotton gauze mask, was Ozlem.

"Doctor, I don't want to be tied down. Whatever the pain, I can handle it."

"I doubt that, Béla," he mumbled. "However, you're in luck. We have some Pentothal to spare."

Why was I entitled to a sedative? "Then why all the screaming on the fourth floor, Doctor?"

"We have only a limited amount. It wears off quickly. The post-surgical discomfort for amputees is severe."

Ozlem taped a strip of cotton under my potato nose. "To monitor your breathing," the doctor explained. "Here's the situation. You'll be unconscious for a while but may awaken before I finish. As the drug wears off, you'll start to feel pain." He pointed his index finger at me. "Béla, you must stay still. Otherwise, I won't be able to continue. Understand?"

I nodded, not in confirmation but in submission. He took my arm and injected the anesthetic with a syringe whose length caused me to turn away. Ozlem pressed my free hand within both of hers. The next thing I recall were whirling movements around my face. I recognized pressure, but no pain. Seeing that I had awoken, the doctor stopped to give me an additional dose of Pentothal.

I dreamt of being chased by a wolf, which had clenched in its teeth a rose that dripped blood and stung me with its thorns. When I came to, I was back in my fourth-floor bed. My bandaged nose and cheeks ached, yet I was hungry. An elderly nun, not much taller than the bedpost and a hundred pounds at best, was at my side. Along with the traditional tunic and scapular, she wore an outsized rosary and a gold cross pendant on a chain around her neck. I sat up, banging my elbow against the railing. Hadn't she seen the sign proclaiming that I'm a Jew?

The nun appeared as puzzled as I was. "Why didn't you eat the chocolates?"

"They're not mine. Someone put them here by mistake."

She patted my arm. "There was no mistake. May I?"

Chapter 27

Without waiting for an answer, she pulled a chair to the edge of the bed and sat, making direct eye contact. "Does it hurt badly?"

"I can manage, thank you."

"I am Sister Zsuzsa. And your name?"

"Béla."

"Ah. A distinguished name. Many Hungarian kings were named Béla. And your last name?"

Why was she asking these questions? Why wasn't she caring for the seriously injured patients? I had never said more than two words to a nun. As a child, they had scared me. "Ingber is my last name."

She laughed. "Mr. Ginger. Wonderful! I drink ginger tea whenever I have a cold."

Ingber means "ginger" in Yiddish and German. Throughout my school years, teachers and classmates would exhibit their humor by calling me "Ginger" or some variant thereof. It had stopped being amusing long ago. I once broke the nose of an older boy who kept taunting me with the moniker "Ginger Rogers." Yet now I didn't mind.

"My father's family came from Poland, Sister."

"I would have guessed that!" I was startled by the sight of Doctor Tóth dashing by, but the sister remained unperturbed. "I see that you are still bleeding," she continued. "I'll get more pads for you."

"Thank you."

"I'm here to help you."

Your loving words can't mend an unkind world. "You know I'm Jewish?"

"Yes, I do. It says so quite clearly on your headboard."

"Yet you still want to help me?"

"We are all G-d's children. Some, like me, are also His servants. I would think no more of you if you were born Catholic. What matters is that you are alone and in need. I'll be right back."

Yes, I was lonely. But even more than that, I was frightened. Frightened that my last moments would be spent in this hellhole apart from everyone who would care. But I refused to cry, choking away my vulnerability in the back of my throat.

She returned with the pads, a topical ointment, and a new bandage. After replacing my original dressing, the sister peered up and down the floor before whispering, "Béla, come with me. Immediately."

"Where?"

"You cannot stay on this floor. Not tonight. Please trust me."

Her tone allowed for no argument. I grabbed my bag, into which she had placed the chocolates, coins, and paper, and slowly followed her down the hallway. With my head tilted back, my walk was staggered. Sister Zsuzsa led me toward a staircase. In front of it was a nurse with her hair floating in a net, kneeling to speak with a moaning amputee in a wheelchair. The nurse glimpsed my armband.

"Where are you going? Get back to your bed!"

"He's with me," countered Sister Zsuzsa.

The nurse straightened up, exhibiting the calves of a weightlifter, which were covered in nude-colored hose. "No one can leave the floor without permission from Doctor Szabó," she insisted.

"I'm responsible for him," Sister Zsuzsa responded.

The nurse shouted at me, "You do as you're told. You're lucky we even let you in here."

If we Jews were such abhorrent creatures, why did it take the yellow star to point that out? I was preparing to turn back when Sister Zsuzsa, her back erect, stepped up to the nurse, who was a good forty years younger and a half foot taller than herself. They stood inches apart, a grape bobbing in the air underneath a ripe watermelon. Jabbing sharply with her index finger, she instructed the nurse, "You tell Doctor Szabó that this patient is in Sister Zsuzsa's care."

Chapter 27

Her face frozen like a porcelain doll, the nurse slumped back down to a kneeling position.

Sister Zsuzsa reached to draw a cross with her thumb on the amputee's forehead. We hustled down the stairs. "Sister, I don't want to get you into trouble."

"The only ones in trouble are those who do not follow the teachings of the Son of G-d. They have forsaken him and dishonored his anguish."

"Still, you are brave."

"A true believer has no fear, Béla."

Back on the second floor, Sister Zsuzsa grasped the rusted key dangling from a hook on her woolen belt and opened the door to a corner workplace room. It was dominated by a worn wooden desk bolted to the floor and a folding bed that would accommodate me only if I lay in a fetal position. Above the bed, solemn eyes gazed down at me from a wooden cross.

"You sleep here, Sister?"

"Most nights. There are so many to comfort."

"To live among the dying must be difficult."

"Everyone perishes. What we must seek is resurrection in the spirit of G-d. Our death is only a sleep that His voice will awaken us from."

Papa once had tried to explain the difference between our religion and theirs. "With Christians," he said, "sin is unavoidable, and salvation is based on unquestioned acceptance of faith. But Judaism insists that sin is a matter of choice and requires each of us to mold our faith and actions based on a consciousness developed over a lifetime."

Sister Zsuzsa lowered her voice. "Béla, you will stay here tonight."

"Please, tell me what's going on. And where will you sleep?"

She tapped my arm. "Shhh...I will explain tomorrow."

"Doctor Tóth told me he would see me first thing in the morning."

"Yes, after breakfast. I will bring it to you." The sister addressed me as sternly as she had the buffalo who was two flights up. "Listen carefully. Do not step foot outside this office until I have brought you food." She pointed to a corner of her cave. "Use the urn for your bodily needs. Make no sounds. No one can know that you're here."

I reached for her arm. "Thank you for helping me."

She squeezed my hand and vanished, her space replaced by dim amniotic light trickling in from the corridor through the doorframe. With her faded presence tucking me in, and in spite of a rhythmic throbbing, I lay my head on a freshly laundered pillowcase and fell into a bottomless sleep that cloaked me from misery.

*

I awoke to lavish sunlight that brushed across my eyes and ripened the room. My shirt was streaked from blood. Sister Zsuzsa was at my side, with bandages in hand.

"Are you rested, Béla?"

"Yes. Thank you, Sister. But again, I must ask, aren't you taking a big risk by helping out an undesirable?"

She curled her lips together. "Why would I think you an undesirable? Jews and Christians share a common history, don't we? All Catholic liturgy and ritual is based on Jewish tradition. Your people were the first to acknowledge that there is one Almighty Creator."

The qualities of G-d are unknowable, I was taught, even though we cannot help but personalize Him. The Bible contains no command to believe in G-d, because His existence is not subject to debate. "The rabbis told us that G-d is all-seeing and all-knowing. But I don't see much evidence of Him. Has He abandoned us?"

"No, it is we who have abandoned Him. He remains everywhere."

So Catholics, too, believed in G-d's omnipresence. "Then He is…truly bad."

Leaning forward to place her hand on mine, she revealed a faint welling of tears. "You're mistaken. G-d's love is everywhere. But we must have an open heart to accept it."

Chapter 27

The sister ran her thumb methodically over my knuckles. Her radiant strength was soothing. "I see only death and misery, Sister. Is that what He wants for us?"

She tilted her chin to the side. "You, Béla, should comprehend better than most G-d's special relationship with His chosen people."

"Then why...why does He allow us Jews such pain? I understand that we were chosen to honor His commandments. But if we collectively are responsible for those who deserve punishment, though we ourselves are righteous, what is the point of it all? Why do we even pray to Him?"

She wavered, ever so slightly. "The question isn't why G-d allows unbearable hurt, because we cannot answer that. We pray to find the strength within ourselves to achieve a higher morality so that we can return to Him. So the proper question is—what will we do in reaction to such suffering?"

"My father believes that suffering is the path to purifying ourselves."

"Your father is wise. Suffering exists to show us that we have fallen."

Sister Zsuzsa appeared to experience this world more benignly than I did. Had she dulled her senses, or was her level of awareness far greater than mine? "Sister, sometimes I think that G-d allows misery as a way to make sure we beseech Him. To keep us in check."

"No! He loves you unconditionally. He wants His creations restored to their original state of perfection."

"Religious Jews believe that this will happen only when the Messiah returns."

"But the Messiah has come. In Jesus, who was an exact reproduction of G-d's essence."

"Then why are we so hated?"

"Because many do not appreciate the meaning of being a Christian. They believe in the son of G-d but fail to understand that faith isn't enough."

But faith, however blind, was the only hope left for most of us. "What do you mean?"

"One must be transformed. And live with the constant awareness that Jesus' lessons impose a common morality upon us. Which originate in your Torah. Do you know which ones I am referring to?"

In *cheder*, they taught us that the goal in life is the performance of good deeds. And that the study of Torah is necessary to understand the nature of those deeds. I chose the first commandment. "I am the Lord, your G-d, who brought you out of the land of Egypt, out of the house of bondage. You shall have no other gods before Me."

"Yes, Béla. That is the basis for Jesus' instruction to us to love G-d with all our heart, soul, and mind." Was she learned in the Old Testament, which taught that Yahweh was a jealous god and that's why only He was to be worshipped? "But what is Jesus' greatest teaching?"

I shrugged. Jesus was not sacred to me.

"Love your neighbor as yourself. From Leviticus. This is what the world has forgotten." She rose from her chair and brushed my cheek with the back of her hand, as Mama would do. "I must tend to others now." Before closing the door, she added, "I will pray for you, Béla." Then her fleeting light withdrew.

Next to my cot was a tray containing a decorative teapot with a hinged lid and matching cup and saucer. On a chipped plate lay two slices of white bread with marmalade. Tucked under the plate was a note in neat, penciled script that read, "Love your enemies, and pray for those who persecute you. Matthew 5:44."

*

After finishing the meal, I returned to the fourth floor. All the beds were empty. I stood, confused and unnoticed, as if the night's darkness had carried itself past the awakening dawn. One attendant passed with a bucket of rubbing alcohol, which he was wiping on

Chapter 27

mattresses to kill bedbugs. Nurses were scurrying about, laying out clean sheets and blankets, while orderlies were wiping bedposts and scrubbing the white tile floor with ammonia. The ubiquitous stench of death had been bleached away.

I located the bed I had occupied yesterday, which had a new sheet on it. The sign on the head board was gone. Spotting Doctor Tóth enter his office, I trudged after him, still holding on to my sack. When he noticed me, his jaw slackened.

"Béla, where did you stay last night?"

"On the second floor."

Tóth pondered that; then his medical instincts kicked in and he nodded toward a chair. The doctor removed my bandage and examined my nose. As he tilted my head back, I grimaced, but he persisted. He finished his examination and raised his thumb.

"I performed on you an operation as good as I would give my own son."

I clasped the doctor's forearm. "Thank you! I'm so grateful. What happened to all the injured men who were here yesterday?"

He pointed to the ceiling. "The Angel of Mercy came down and healed each of them." Searching my face, he added, "They are all home now, busy fucking their wives and girlfriends." Tóth reached into his jacket pocket for two clean handkerchiefs. "Tilt your head back whenever possible. And when you need to, keep one of these pressed against your nose to absorb any bleeding."

What kind of alternate world had I entered—in which life was so disposable? "Why did you even bother to operate on me?"

He shrugged. "I'm only a doctor. I don't play G-d."

"Please tell me then…how long do I have to stay here?"

"Ordinarily, I'd want to keep you for a couple of days. But it's safest for you to leave now. I'll ask Doctor Szabó to issue discharge papers and request an escort back to camp."

He began to scribble a note on his pad, then looked up. "Tell me, Béla, how did you end up sleeping on the second floor?"

"Sister Zsuzsa brought me there."

Tóth beamed. "So, you met Sister Zsuzsa." He enunciated her name reverentially. "You are indeed a fortunate man."

"Doctor, why did the sister choose me to save? Why not someone of her own faith?"

"I wouldn't know for sure. She did once tell me that we Jews must survive at all cost."

Perhaps Sister Zsuzsa felt I was in need of saving because of her belief that faithful Christians live forever? Tóth continued, "And... in order to bear witness."

I grabbed his hand and pumped it. "Thank you again. For saving my life."

"I only fixed your sinuses."

"Same thing."

The doctor lowered his voice. "*Ven me zol got danken far guts, volt zein kain tseit tsu baklogen zich oif shlechts*" (If we thanked G-d for all the good things, there wouldn't be time to weep over the bad). He winked, turned, and was gone.

*

During the early 1960s, Pope John XXIII summoned Roman Catholic bishops from across the globe to Vatican City to clarify Catholic doctrine and practice. Out of the Second Vatican Council came "Nostra Aetate," which reminded Catholics that Jesus was born a Jew and died a Jew. The pope, in a prayer for unity, condemned the belief that Jews killed Jesus:

Even though the greater part of the Jewish people has remained separated from Christ, it would be an injustice to call this people accursed, since they are greatly beloved for the sake of the Fathers

Chapter 27

and the promises made to them. The Church loves this people. From them sprang Christ the Lord.

Reading about the council, I was reminded of Sister Zsuzsa. She would have been pleased.

Despite the sister's urging, I have never forgiven the Germans or Hungarians. Nor will I. Anger paces inside me, which overwhelms at times, threatening to dissolve all the love that I've ever felt. Struggling to contain it, I concentrate on the blessings of my later life. And the angel sent to protect me in the midst of the horror.

CHAPTER 28

Eszter Mermelstein Ingber: August 22, 1943
(Oroszvég)

My Dear Child,

It has only been the day before yesterday that I wrote to you, but we got your package of clothing today. I am going to wash them and send them back to you right away.

Will you be able to join us for the holidays? If you would be home, everything would be easier and my heart lighter. The house will look a little different, because we took down the white fence.

If you cannot come home, I hope that you can be with a Jewish family during these holy days.

Today, some people serving in work labor companies arrived here. There is no news still about Jenő. We did receive a notification from the Red Cross, and that is why I am writing to you again so soon. It says only that Ferencz disappeared on January 14th on Russian soil. I pray for him every day.

Chapter 28

I am very glad that T.G. you are in a good place. If you need money, I will send you some. I would have sent you some before, but you wrote that you don't need it.

Ferike is so cute. Ilona is well, H.I.

I like to write everything to you. When I am writing to you, I feel as if I am talking with you.

There is nothing more. Write to us all about you. Believe me, my sweet son, you are not out of my mind for even one minute. I pray that the good G-d will watch over you.

I send you kisses in everybody's name and especially I, your loving mother, kiss you a million times.

Eszter and Kálmán Ingber

CHAPTER 29

Picnic in Buda: September 3, 1943

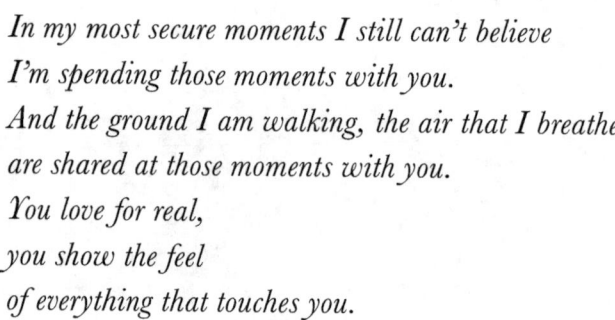

*In my most secure moments I still can't believe
I'm spending those moments with you.
And the ground I am walking, the air that I breathe
are shared at those moments with you.
You love for real,
you show the feel
of everything that touches you.*

—Terry Kirkman

    The rust-red trolley crept through meadows and valleys, piercing them delicately as a ladybug gnawing through clover. Marika and I were pressed together on a narrow bench, with our palms caressing, fingers laced, and wrists touching so that we could feel each other's heartbeat. A picnic basket sat on my knees. The streetcar was filled with families similarly escaping the city streets. New riders stood on the edges of steps, clinging to the brass handrails and waiting for others to gracefully jump off, often while the car still was moving.

    The trip began in Pest, at a station where on the wall next to the schedule was plastered a poster depicting a maliciously grinning black bear thrusting his enormous claws into a birdcage that enclosed a terrified girl. The streetcar trudged past desolate streets and dreary neo-Renaissance apartment buildings whose windows were covered by blackout paper. On several walls, the Arrow Cross had painted in large block letters, WE ARE COMING FOR YOU. (The symbol of the Hungarian Nazi party was, in imitation of the swastika, the sign of the crucifix with the head of an arrow at each of its four points.)

After a transfer, we were on to the Margit suspension bridge, tinted by the wine-red sun's reflection. Dr. Tóth had told me that many city residents arrived daily at the bridge to hurl themselves to their deaths. The bridge offered a view of the Danube forking around the island and enfolding it. I imagined Marika and me on a river boat, sailing down to the Black Sea and freedom. The foot of the bridge on the Buda side was flanked by a canopied beer hall and boarded-up café. As we rode on, the landscape changed to open markets, one-story shacks with fenced-in, leafy gardens and tree-lined drives leading to farms and manor houses with stables.

The trolley climbed to the Hűvösvölgy district, where the city dwindled and the "country" began. Bikers raced us, some performing wheelies, as we passed panting dogs and matrons wearing colored babushkas. When the burning brakes squeaked to a complete stop, we disembarked at the top of Hármashatárhegy Mountain, under a radio tower. Steps away stood a century-old Austrian wine tavern painted in Schönbrunn yellow, known as the Boar's Head, a popular winter refuge for skiers, enticing passersby with its scents of smoked bacon, soft cheese spiked with red pepper, and vinegar-marinated sausages. Marika pressed down the hem of her skirt as a fragrant wind, opposed by trembling trees, nudged us forward until we found a short trail that rolled downward. As the slope leveled off, the trail wound among several spacious wooden chalets with large, glassed-in verandas and then led to an open field.

Béla's Letters

We claimed a trestle table shaded by the branches of a willow tree bowed toward the earth of a slanting meadow. Below us lay an expanse of verdure broken by dotted white and red roofs. Later, when the haze lifted, we were treated to the dome and spires of the Gothic Parliament building and the dense forest of houses and buildings interspersed among the concentric half-circle boulevards of Pest, with the great flat plain of Hungary beyond them.

Brushing off black garden ants, Marika unzipped an insulated floral basket and removed forks, napkins, and a thermos full of iced tea. We sat nibbling on slices of dark rye bread slathered with *lekvár* (fruit jam) and bits of *nokedli* (dumplings) and chicken spiced with sweet paprika, which was still available from the farm wagons at the Custom House square market. Green-headed mallard drakes strolled up to us from a nearby pond, begging in raspy voices and leaving their waste.

As we ate, tree sparrows with chestnut crowns and a black patch on each white cheek called out from their nests. A father and son scurried past, the boy connected to the smoky blue sky by a kite with a vent between the upper and lower sails, painted in the colors of the Hungarian flag.

"Marika, your food is as delicious, as the camp food, to the extent they give us any, is odious." I pressed into her hand an oversized, frayed postcard that I kept close to me. The white space was covered with tiny, slanting letters narrowly spaced, written by the person who had taught me to write, whose words I traced ceaselessly with my fingertips.

Marika turned her body, reading as if the postcard had been written for her eyes only, her lips moving. "Your mother is sweet. She worries so for her family."

"I wish you had experienced a mother like her."

Marika became shrouded in a stillness like the deep silence after a lightning storm so violent as to fill every seam in the sky. Finally, she said, "I still think about my mother."

Chapter 29

She had been denied the singular love that childhood reminiscences are encased in. "Can you remember her?"

Marika knitted her brows. "Very little. Thankfully, I have a few pictures. I often imagine her hugging and kissing me. Listening to me, even when I am saying nothing. We would be the best of friends now."

Marika never had the opportunity to rebel against her mother. To recognize her as a flawed human being, freeing Marika to seek her own identity.

I hugged Marika and said, "You can talk to me," which provoked a shy smile. I pulled from the picnic basket two Szalon Sör pale ales, purchased at the station, and opened them.

"I wish we could spend every day like this," Marika said. She took a long swig. "What news is there of the war? Is it true that the Allies are bombing Rome and other parts of Italy?"

"Yes, but I have better news. Mussolini has been arrested. They say that Italy soon will surrender."

Four years of war had gone by. Though its flames had not charred this idyllic spot, we tasted the ashes.

"So maybe the war will end soon. When it does, where do you want to live, Béla?"

"Back in Munkács. What about you?"

"Budapest, I suppose. This is what I know. I've never been away from here."

I had not visited Marika for several months now. Nor did I tell her of my surgery, realizing that she had little capacity to absorb any negative news. But I had memorized her features. After we were last together, during the monotonous, oppressive ache of labor, I had changed. The heat, hunger, and weariness all bothered me less. I heard the voices of others more faintly, their wind chimes suddenly stilled, as I wallowed in daydreams of the future. Sitting here in the Buda hills, a speck in the world's vastness, I was at home. Tomorrow was now. If only time would take a vacation, at least for a day.

"But then we wouldn't be together," I said.

A smile opened, thin as a penciled line. "Is that what you want?"

"Yes."

She leaned back, to better assess my body language. "What are you saying?"

I took her hand and kissed the smooth skin. "Marika, before you met me, were you ever in love?"

"No. I did have a boyfriend. What about you?"

She was an empty page that I would write upon. "Me? No boyfriends."

She giggled. "You know what I mean. Any lovers?"

A thirty-year-old man should have had many loves. I had left few footprints. Now I was hungry for them. "Two. The first one was many years ago."

"Do you still know her?"

"No, she's in Palestine now. We've lost touch."

"Do I remind you of her?" she said.

"No, not in any way." I waited many years to shed the notion that my first love had been incomparable, and to admit to myself that my relationship with Ágnes had been a dress rehearsal at best. We had been oil and vinegar, unable to dissolve into each other. "Because I knew, deep down, that she wasn't right for me."

Marika hesitated. "Are you still in love with her?"

Many people had offered me their opinion about women and romantic love. Mama maintained that there was a single star in the vast galaxy meant for each one of us. Ilona whispered that love can sneak up on us from various openings, and that one's capacity to love is infinite. Ferencz described women as glowworms—"If their light burns, you don't necessarily know if they mean to mate with you or

Chapter 29

feed on you." Papa took me aside one day, winked, and said, "Women have their own seasons. Best to avoid them in their winter."

"If I did, I wouldn't be here."

She took a heavy breath. "And who was your second love?"

Nothing outside this moment existed. I leaned toward Marika, losing myself in her. I was a laborer, with no education or possessions. I had, at best, a 50-50 chance of surviving the war. But I would cast myself into love's deep, purifying waters, even if its currents might overpower me. "You, of course. I love you, Marika."

She was only on the cusp of adulthood. Without a mother or sister to interpret my intentions. "Is this a proposal?"

A handful of meetings with a woman would not ordinarily lead to an offer of marriage. But these were not normal times, and I no longer had the luxury of treating my remaining years as if they were unlimited. I finished the bottle, flung it into the woods, and gripped her elbows. "No. Not because I don't want to. But because we can't be together while the war is still on. But if it were a proposal, would you say yes?"

I braced myself, feeling as panicked as I did in my Army training days when you pulled the pin on a grenade but couldn't toss it until you counted off a few seconds. "I care for you deeply, Béla. I know that. But…there's such a large age difference between us."

"Do you love me? That's what matters."

She reached out and stroked my cheek. "Yes, I do…Béla, I would like you to meet my father."

"Of course. When the time is right. When I can answer all the questions he is bound to ask me. Like, 'Don't you think that you and my seventeen-year-old daughter should first spend some more time together?'"

She took me in at slow shutter speed. "I would tell my papa that a woman knows when to accept a marriage proposal." Marika removed her hand and slapped mine playfully. "Even a young one." With all

215

the other tables occupied, newly arriving families and couples spread an array of brocade tablecloths nearby on the worn grass, laughing and speaking noisily as if they were in their backyards. We packed up and strolled along a murmuring brook, crisscrossing it at narrow points, stopping under lush linden trees to embrace.

In the white noise of the forest, we lost track of time and our bearings. Heading back, the trail took us through bends and forks. We would begin down a path only to have it disappear a few yards later into a tangled thicket of shrubs that tore at our legs. The tree cover prevented our use of the setting sun as a guide. We resumed with more purpose. Night was approaching, and it was rumored that wild dogs and boars roamed the woods.

We were Hansel and Gretel, but without bread crumbs. With every sudden rustling, Marika's grip on my hand tightened. Then, the rhythmic clatter of a trolley and the trill sound of a band serenading tavern guests led us to a clearing within sight of the radio tower.

Back on the trolley, Marika leaned against my shoulder.

"When will I see you again?"

"I can't say. It's difficult to leave camp these days, but I will try."

"Write to me. Often."

"I don't think they even deliver mail anymore. But trust that I will write to you."

In the deepening dusk, the frozen lights of the city seeped through dense foliage. "What if I never see you again? What if I wait and wait, but you never come? What if I lose you, forever?"

"No, I will find my way to you." I thought to give her a time and place to meet me after the war ended. Something romantic, like the middle of the Chain Bridge at noon on the first Sunday after the end of the war. If I wasn't there, she would know. But no, better to rush to her as soon as possible.

Chapter 29

She clutched my hand. "Béla, you can't leave me. Find me. Promise!"

I would depart Budapest early the next morning, after a day of hallowed perfection, and not return until the war was near its end. Once again, I would not be there for a loved one's worst moments.

Antony Leiner and Malvina Simko, Marika's parents, on their wedding day, circa 1920

CHAPTER 30
Cluj, October 1944

As a boy I got the idea that death was an animal which lay curled inside waiting to swallow us.

—Jerzy Kosiński

In my youth, I held clear images of what my life's work might be. Gazing at magazine pictures of the Empire State Building and Golden Gate Bridge, I longed to become a civil engineer and design great structures that would outlast me. Papa wanted that for me also. He sold his gold watch and other possessions, but they could not cover the cost of tuition.

Over the years, my reveries of what I could have become grew more painful, only to be salved when my children, and theirs, all obtained a higher education. Although, if the purpose of knowledge is not to comprehend the world but rather to understand more about oneself, then I must thank the Hungarians for generously providing me with much learning.

Chapter 30

As part of our interminable, all-expenses-paid tour of the greater Hungarian Empire and environs, in early October 1944 our unit was stationed near Cluj. A Roman settlement that had succumbed to the barbarian hordes (the latest one being the Germans), Cluj was now the capital of Transylvania. During the day, shades of yellow and orange contrasted against the evergreen forest, providing the warm season's final act. But the nights, when the skies were filled with red arcs from anti-aircraft gunfire, again were biting.

Since the Nazi occupation, we had been prohibited from leaving camp, listening to the radio, or receiving mail, except that, for a time, we were allowed to send one "dumb" postcard per month—a printed card with choices such as "I am healthy," or "I am well treated," that could be checked off. I sent my last one to Marika, not expecting her to receive it.

Excluding rumors, like one that flashed through the camp proclaiming that Hitler had been killed by his own officers, we knew nothing of the war's progress beyond the great invasion by Allied forces in France. We were, however, cursed with intimate knowledge of weather patterns. Of the necessities for survival—food, water, shelter, and warmth—food was the most difficult to obtain, and we struggled daily to supplement the watery cabbage soup and transparent bread slices that constituted most of our meals.

We servicemen, clothed in disintegrating outerwear, slept in the lengthy trenches we were constructing for the remnants of the Hungarian Army straining to stave off the Soviets. Once the snow arrived, we melted it in water bags using our body heat. Layers of tree branches and vegetation formed our insulation. As the trench deepened, we cut holes in its sides to sleep in.

One morning, roughly sixty of us, accompanied by several Hungarian militia whose boredom had now been alleviated by the threat of flying shrapnel and Russian snipers, were laboring in the hills overlooking the ancient city. As a fog curled past, the clock of the gothic St. Michael's appeared, a reminder that, too often, our toils had been in sight of churches. Hadn't Christians been watching from their windows and bell towers?

The partially frozen ground, no longer answering to our shovels, yielded only to pickaxes, which were excruciating to wield. Although we were not building military ditches for long-term use (such as the fighting trenches lived in for months by soldiers during World War I), they required hollowing out, to a meter wide and two meters deep, in a zigzag pattern to lessen the impact of a bomb or shell. Had this been earlier in the war, we might also have constructed adjoining barbed-wire fences, lined the walls and floor with wood, covered the trench with a layer of wire netting upon which withered leaves and chopped grass would be heaped, and reinforced the sides of the channel with sandbags. But most of these materials were no longer available, nor were there dynamite sticks to blast away thick rock.

For days now, we had been continually tense from artillery fire and the high-pitched screech of Katyusha rocket launchers coming from the surrounding forests, ever increasing in volume and intensity. Silver flocks of Soviet fighter planes periodically flew overhead. Injured German and Hungarian troops, decorated in filthy, blood-crusted bandages, streamed by on foot, on stretchers, or in Red Cross vehicles to patchwork hospital facilities in Cluj itself. All the colors of autumn now were the red of human chum. Ah, such *Schadenfreude*. Tibi quipped, "Dracula would be proud."

Hearing of servicemen being shipped to Germany, we debated a night attack on our guards, who were much older than ordinary Hungarian soldiers. I fantasized about taking their weapons and provisions, mimicking their barking, and pounding them with the sticks they beat us with. We then would flee into the forest. A consensus, the building of which is not a strongpoint for Jews, had been growing to do so, with argument centering on whether or not to kill the guards as well.

Chapter 30

As the Russian bear laid siege, my ennui surrendered to a gnawing fatalism. Working in the open, we would be targets for the inevitable mortar barrage and enemy soldiers, crazed with blood lust, who likely would make no distinction between servicemen and armed troops. Nor did I relish trading my bondage to the Hungarians for slavery in a gulag.

Hollering from two nearby Hungarian officers broke the melody of swinging axes. I glanced up to spot The Beast, who recently had been promoted to a lieutenant through twisted logic that makes sense only in a dream. He was quarreling with a Hungarian captain clad in a peaked cap and service tunic laden with medals memorializing his days of glory. Captain Molnar was one of the few who remained wedded to protocol regarding the treatment of servicemen. Their open spat was surprising, as The Beast tended to be deferential, if not obsequious, to more senior officers. Pacing in his taupe leather overcoat, he screamed at the ground and air until spent.

An open Horch command car with room enough for six, with extra wheels above its running boards, sped into our midst, depositing a German official. He was dressed in a crisply cut gray-green uniform and black jodhpur boots. I could make out the SS eagle on his cap and the death-head insignia with skull and crossbones pinned to it and on his collar patches. The Beast marched up to the officer, shouting and pointing at both Molnar and us servicemen. Molnar joined to plead his case.

While we might occasionally straighten up to stretch or massage our backs, or to glance at the treetops for shifting winds that indicated the coming of unsettled weather, it was dangerous to be seen watching rather than working. So I had my head down when the first shot rang out. When I looked up, Molnar was on the ground, writhing. The German, not six feet from him, shouted "*Judenfreundlich*" (Jew-friendly person) and fired his revolver again, stilling the captain.

This unusual breach of military discipline was followed by The Beast's ordering us, as would an animal trainer in a lion's cage, "Lay down your axes!" As we complied, our guards raised their rifles.

The Beast approached, while the German officer remained in place, nonchalantly lighting a cigarette. Standing with splayed legs and speaking rat-a-tat, he ordered, "Line up by the edge of the trench."

Tibi and I exchanged wide-eyed stares. Eternity circled like a vulture.

"Hands behind your heads."

No sound could be heard above that of my heart, pounding as if my skin had been stripped bare. This could not be. I must know what the rest of my life will bring.

We stood motionless in the sights of our guards' raised guns while The Beast inexplicably charged back to the German for a further conversation. Seconds became minutes. We became trapped in a slow-motion replay. I slowed my breath. "Focus," I told myself.

I could step back and fall into the channel we had dug, but that would leave me an easy mark, particularly since it was not yet deep. The woods were at least a hundred feet away. Our best chance was to collectively rush the guards. Some would perish, but most should make it. Someone had to go first, bursting out of the fear.

An approaching plane emerged through a cloud, whirring as if struggling to stay in the air and interrupting our knell. Inured to the presence of reconnaissance planes with five-pointed red stars on their wings, I ignored the grinding sound until it overwhelmed all other senses. The aircraft veered toward us, its pilot visible through the glassed-in cockpit. (Later, I learned that this was the Russian "Ilyusha," also known as "the flying tank," one of the heroes of the war on the Eastern front.)

For an instant, the plane lay suspended above us. A cacophony of machine-gun fire erupted. I dove into the ditch, landing hard and

Chapter 30

biting the ground. Staying low, I crawled frantically toward the woods as dirt smacked my face from the impact of searing bullets striking the topsides of the trench. Screams mingled with the whine of the propellers. I peeked over my shoulder, confirming that several others had followed me, one clutching the side of his head. By the time we reached the end of the trench, the blare of the plane had receded, but the pop-pop of gunfire continued. I scrambled over the top, only to come face-to-face with an armed soldier wearing a uniform I didn't recognize.

"Halt," he yelled in Hungarian. "Hands up." Three other servicemen climbed out of the ditch and were similarly instructed. I considered rushing the soldier, but he raised the barrel of his gun, which had a round drum in the middle as if designed to carry a doughnut.

We were marched back to where we had been lined up, joining those who had fled in other directions. The salvos had died down. We passed the shattered bodies of several campmates, eyes hollow, lying in pools of blackening blood. Good men, whose body odors, rattling snores, and favorite curses were intimately familiar. Men who confided to me their dreams of freedom and family. Who late in the war had been teased with the prospect of survival. Safe passage, my friends.

Scarcely offsetting their fate was that of the SS officer, who lay prostrate, his mouth agape and run red. The heat of his being dissipated. But no sight of the corpse of The Beast.

Surrounding us were twenty or so soldiers, whom I guessed to be Russians. We were made to stand shoulder to shoulder, although not near the edge of the trench. Their guns were pointed downward. Tibi, his posture sagging, was three down from me. I shifted my weight methodically from one leg to the other to calm myself. My thoughts, bursting scattershot, no longer were of flight but of resignation.

An unhelmeted soldier stepped forward. "I am Lieutenant Andrei Grigore of the newly constituted Romanian Army. You are now our prisoners. But you have nothing to fear. We know that you are Jewish laborers."

As we servicemen together took a long exhalation of relief, he explained, nearly apologetically, that Romania had switched to the Allied side two months ago. "You men have a choice. One is to join us in fighting the fascist occupiers. You will not carry arms and will be expected to perform the same services for us as you did for the Hungarians." Grigore pointed to the woods. "If you refuse, we are obliged to hand you over to the Russians, who will treat you as enemy combatants."

And so, at the beginning of the sixth unyielding winter of war, in the inhospitably of a foreign land, I found myself in a third army—one that weeks earlier would have shot me for several reasons—among soldiers who for years had followed the emblem of the swastika. Now tainted with guilt, their collaboration exhumed, would they remove my label as an *Untermensch* (subhuman)?

CHAPTER 31
Horthy's Speech

*In rage's house nothing rules but rage, and the waters
cannot drown it nor the winds blow it away
nor the fires burn it down.*

—Donald Hall

We buried our comrades in the hard ground of the hill on which they perished, their graves marked by slats of wood bearing their names. Days later, on a crisp Sunday afternoon, with a careless breeze rustling our newly acquired tents (courtesy of the Romanians), many of us servicemen and our liberators gathered in Piata Unirii around a Telefunken radio adorned with miniature Nazi eagles, on whose glass dial was printed the names of cities in Germany and Austria. Horthy was speaking to the Hungarian nation. Although numbering in the dozens, we occupied a mere corner of the solemn square that lies at the heart of Cluj.

In a weary voice accentuated with a noticeable tremor, the Regent decried the pain that his nation had endured from the injustices of the Trianon peace treaty. Our leader proclaimed his disinterest in acquiring territories by force, and he complained of Hungary being pressured into war by Germany. We loudly mocked each of these fabrications. Horthy made mention that the Gestapo had tackled the Jewish question "in a manner incompatible with the demands of humanity" and further accused the Nazis of robbing Hungarians of their freedom and independence. "Today it is obvious to any sober-minded person that Germany has lost the war."

As Horthy spoke his final line, the square hushed. "I informed a local representative of the German Empire that we are signing a preliminary cease-fire with those who have been our enemies until now, and I am stopping all hostile action toward them." My fellow servicemen erupted, thanking a newly rediscovered G-d, pounding and climbing on each other's backs, and planting kisses on dismayed Romanians. Not sharing the general mood, I kept replaying Horthy's words as I hustled over to Tibi.

"What did Horthy mean?"

"What the hell are you talking about? Isn't it obvious?"

"Tibi, stop and think. What did he mean when he talked about the treatment of Jews?"

He shrugged. "The killings in Poland and Russia, no?" As the radio played funereal music, we rushed over to Grigore, who was smoking while slumped on a waist-high stone wall surrounding a crumbling, pock-marked statue of an ancient Hungarian king. He had exempted himself from the general frenzy.

"Lieutenant, a word, please?" I said.

Grigore motioned for us to sit by him. He curled his lips around his teeth and let out a circular smoke ring. A trick I could never master.

"Sir, did you listen to Horthy's speech?"

He ignored my question, instead responding, "Where are you fellows from?"

Chapter 31

"Munkács."

Grigore took a last drag and with his index finger and thumb flung a still-burning cigarette in an arc over his shoulder, sending sparks flying. He patted his pockets for a matchbook, then lit a wooden match on the sole of his shoe. "I grew up in Sighet. A beautiful place. At least it was. Right near the Czech border. Do you know it?"

"Yes," we both acknowledged.

"We would cross the bridge over the Tisza and go shopping in your country," he reminisced. "Mostly for fun, because our markets were better."

I knew of Sighet from Pollack, whose brother had taught the Talmud there. Grigore's cadence slowed, as he measured his words. "My birthplace was a town of thirty thousand people, a mix of Romanians and Hungarians, many of them Jews. Actually, it was a very Jewish place, filled with synagogues and yeshivas. The Chassids we had little to do with, but my best friend was one of the Zionists."

He let those words hang in the air. "What did you fellows think of Horthy's speech?"

"It's what we've been waiting to hear," Tibi said. "That Hungary will leave the war."

Grigore snorted. "I was in Cluj, back in 1940, when Horthy came riding into the city on a white horse ahead of his army, with the banner of the Virgin Mary waving above him." I pictured a scene similar to the one I had witnessed in Munkács, with the local ethnic Hungarians cheering madly. "That pompous old fool can say whatever he wants," Grigore continued, "but the Austrian paperhanger still calls the shots for Hungary."

"Don't you think this will at least speed up the end of the war?" I said. "Now that the Hungarian government won't actively support the war effort?"

"Which war are you referring to?" Grigore responded.

"What do you mean?" Tibi snapped.

Grigore stood and stretched while methodically grinding out a butt, one still substantial enough in size to have been fought over in the camp. He lit another and dropped down again. "You've been in this city for a few days now. Cluj once had a substantial Jewish population, as large as the one in Munkács. A centuries-old community."

He raised his right arm, sweeping it in a semicircle. "Have you met any Jews here?"

"No," I replied. "But we haven't looked, either."

"Don't bother. You won't find any. You know why? Because several months ago, they all were rounded up and deported. Sent to their deaths. The same for the Jews in Sighet, starting with the foreign ones." Grigore stared at us the way a dog would stare into a mirror. "What is it you fellows wanted to ask me?"

Tibi and I jumped up in tandem, as if handcuffed together, and shouted, "What about the Jews of Munkács?"

"I don't know anything for sure. But I would guess that, except for you servicemen, they're all dead."

A scream revealed itself as my own, but, in truth, more like a feral animal caught in a leg trap. Leaping at Grigore, I grabbed him by his shoulders. Grigore pushed me away. Gathering to rush back at him, I was tackled from behind by Tibi and thrown to the ground, pinned by his knees and arms.

A nearby Romanian soldier raced toward us, his rifle raised. Grigore held up his hand. He snarled at me, "Do you want to be shot?"

I shoved Tibi off me, and pleaded, "I need to go home, Lieutenant. To find my family."

He shook his head. "That's still German-occupied territory. You might as well commit suicide."

Chapter 31

"All I ask for is a rifle and ammunition. At the very least, I'll take out some Nazis first."

"I can't do that. Nor would I."

"Then let me at least go to Budapest. My fiancée is there. I have to protect her."

"No, Budapest is even more dangerous." Grigore softened his voice. "Béla, be smart. Stay here. Help us kill more Germans and Hungarians and finish the war." He smirked. "And if we take any prisoners, I'll let you interrogate them."

I glared at him. "If you were me, Lieutenant, would you take this advice?"

"I don't know," he whispered.

I spat out a curse and let Tibi lead me away.

*

The following evening, servicemen from various Hungarian cities and towns, summoned with unspoken words, conducted a service in the square. As we began, a raw wind stilled, and the shrill, tawny owls on the looming steeple fell mute, worshipping the night silently. Most of our lamps had gone dark and were replaced by a bonfire fueled by wooden pews, a sacrilege condoned by the church ordinaries in barter for food. We had refused an offer to worship in the chapel, although we gratefully accepted several boxes of self-standing white candles of varying lengths, now surrounding us in a ring of gentle light.

I recited the Mourner's *Kaddish*, for the first time not as a rote prayer but a true lamentation. An Aramaic poem dating back to the first century, which contains not a single mention of death, its essence is the glorification of G-d, as the mourner is to be comforted by the divine order of the world. Since that day, I have chanted no other prayer more fervently.

My personal translation of the *Kaddish* is the following. "My love could not protect you in life, let it keep you in peace now. The pain you suffered I carry in my heart. You are free of it. And I take comfort that your immortal and holy spirits, which illuminate my path, have now been returned intact to their rightful owner."

CHAPTER 32
The German Occupation

*I lived on this earth in an age when man fell so low
he killed willingly, for pleasure, without orders.
Vile obsession threaded his life, he believed in false gods.
Deluded, he foamed at the mouth.*

—Miklós Radnóti

By 1941, additional oppressive measures further restricted life for Hungarian Jews, including the Third Jewish Law, which introduced "race protective" orders and prohibited intermarriage. Jews now were defined, in the manner of Germany's Nuremberg Decrees, on racial extraction (those whose parents or two out of four grandparents were born Jewish). Over 100,000 persons were added to the roster of those considered Jewish.

Also, in the summer of that year, deportations and massacres of Jews living in Hungary who could not prove their citizenship began, including about 300 families of Polish origin in Munkács. Throughout Hungary, about 18,000 "aliens" were expelled to the Kamenetz-Podolsk district in Axis-held Ukraine, where they were led to a massive pit and machine-gunned by SS men assisted by Ukrainian militia.

231

Despite Hungary's alliance with Germany, the aristocratic Hungarian Prime Minister Miklós Kállay, who had assumed office in March 1942, and his superior, Miklós Horthy, were unsympathetic to Nazi fascism. Horthy was a Protestant landowner who had been a long-time aide to Habsburg Emperor Franz Joseph and the Austro-Hungarian Fleet's last commander. Despite his self-description as an anti-Semite, Horthy had quietly let the early anti-Jewish laws lapse, and he had maintained relations with prominent Hungarian Jews, having received substantial financing from them over the years. Three of his regular bridge partners were Jewish.

Throughout 1942, Germany had pushed Hungary to act more decisively against its Jewish population. Kállay's government procrastinated, and then they rejected most of the German demands, refusing to round up and deport Jews. Among the reasons cited was the indispensability of the Jews to the economy. However, to curry favor with the Nazis, various government ministries issued regulations and decrees increasingly restricting Jewish participation in everyday life, which were vigorously enforced by provincial, municipal, and village councils. Kállay pledged the resettlement of Hungary's 800,000 Jews as the "final solution of the Jewish question," but he determined to implement this only after the war's end.

By 1943, millions of European Jews had been murdered in concentration camps and ghettos or in mass shootings. Although native Hungarian Jews had suffered humiliations, beatings, and economic privations, no formal attacks against them by government troops had taken place. And the Allies had refrained from bombing a nation that they expected ultimately to join their side, as Italy would do days after my picnic with Marika.

At the battle at Voronezh in January 1943, the inadequately clothed, fed, trained, and equipped 200,000-man 2nd Hungarian Army

Chapter 32

Division (together with about 40,000 Jewish forced laborers), fighting in historically bitter cold, was annihilated in a Soviet offensive. Horthy and Kállay, recognizing that the Axis would lose the war, sought to negotiate a separate armistice for Hungary while avoiding provoking the Nazis. They conferred in secret with the Western Allies through neutral countries, making numerous peace overtures. To enhance Hungary's position with the Allies, Horthy ordered his troops to cease firing upon Allied planes and prevented the establishment of German airfields in the western part of the country. In the face of repeated requests from Hitler to relocate Jews to undisclosed sites in the east, Horthy complained, "I sent a Hungarian army to be destroyed on the Russian front, declared war on the Allies, and restricted the rights of Jews. What more can this madman want from me?"

Life in Hungary in the winter of 1943–44 appeared to be returning to a semblance of normality, despite the rationing in place, since much of the supply of food and goods was being shipped to Germany. Cultural activities blossomed, and the end of the war was in sight. I fantasized a postwar life with Marika at my side.

But in March 1944, infuriated by Horthy's formal request for immediate withdrawal of all remaining Hungarian troops from the Russian Front, and concerned about Hungary's intention to desert the Axis, Hitler "invited" Horthy to the Schloss Klessheim palace near Salzburg, Austria. Horthy arrived early on March 18 and engaged in heated conversations with Hitler throughout the day over allegations of Hungarian treachery and favorable treatment of Hungary's Jews. On the following morning, before Horthy could return to Budapest, Germany began "Operation Margarethe," a military takeover of Hungary, accomplished without opposition from Hungarian troops. Accompanying the regular German soldiers was a *Sondereinsatzkommando* (Special Section commandos) unit headed by the "Angel of Death," Adolf Eichmann, who had been ordered by

SS-head Heinrich Himmler to sweep out the Jews and deport them to Auschwitz as quickly as possible.

The occupation took most Hungarians by surprise. Horthy was permitted to remain Regent, after consenting to the delivery of a hundred thousand Jewish workers for employment in German industrial and agricultural enterprises. Kállay took refuge in the Turkish legation, where he remained until October, when he surrendered and was imprisoned in Dachau. (He survived the war and later wrote his memoirs.) Horthy installed the pro-Nazi General, Döme Sztójay, once the Hungarian ambassador to Germany, as Prime Minister. The Nazi high command told Sztójay of Hitler's expectation that he "solve the Jewish question."

On March 20, trucks carrying columns of German infantry and SS troops, supplemented by tanks and artillery, entered Munkács and occupied the public buildings. Soon Jews were beaten in the streets as a matter of policy, and the remaining Jewish-owned shops were smashed and looted. By month's end, Eichmann implemented his annihilation plan. Reminiscent of medieval times, Jews above the age of six were required to wear, on the top left side of their chest, a six-pointed canary-yellow Star of David ten centimeters in diameter, with a matching armband. Ghettoization followed, accomplished with a precision learned from experiences in many other European nations.

The Sztójay government promulgated more than one hundred decrees that further excluded Jews from society. Employees of businesses and government offices had to present birth certificates verifying an Aryan ancestry going back to their grandparents. Jews were forbidden to practice a profession, to leave their homes after nightfall, to ride cars or trains, to use public baths or restaurants, to listen to the radio, to speak on the telephone, or to receive mail. Their realty and movable properties were confiscated, bank accounts frozen, and food rations reduced. They could shop only during a limited number of hours each

Chapter 32

day. The Gymnasium was turned into a military hospital. Hundreds of prominent Jews were imprisoned, tortured, and held for ransom.

Because of the deteriorating military situation—the Red Army was approaching the Hungarian border on the east—the Nazis and their Hungarian accomplices moved swiftly. In April, Eichmann and senior Hungarian officials, including newly appointed Interior Minister Andor Jaross and Secretary of State László Endre, agreed to deport all Hungarian Jews to Auschwitz, beginning in the countryside. However, the Hungarian Ministry of Defense resisted German pressure to deport labor servicemen, which is why I survived to tell my story.

On April 15, a Sabbath and the last day of Passover, thousands of Jews in the villages and towns of Bereg County surrounding Munkács were rounded up by Hungarian gendarmes blowing whistles, with lists in hand. Jews were given a few minutes to collect a parcel of clothing and food for several days; then they were herded—the healthy on foot and the old, sick, or infants in oxen- or horse-drawn wagons—to two brick factory yards on the outskirts of Munkács. Their homes, with Passover foods still on tables or in stoves, were ransacked and stripped bare by locals.

At the brickyards, Jews were commanded to undress—adults in front of their children—so that they could be searched for money and valuables. Penned in by a wire fence near train tracks, they lived for weeks in the clothes they arrived in, lying on blankets under drying sheds with no walls or under tents in muddy fields strewn with broken clay, glass, and concrete. One day, in a driving rain, all, including the sick, were made to work for hours moving huge piles of bricks without purpose. Clean water was limited. Food was a thin soup brought daily by the local members of the Jewish Governing Council (*Judenrat*) in bathtubs. Ditches serving as latrines were positioned in full view of guards and passersby. Medical care was nonexistent. Typhus, which alone had killed millions earlier in the century, ran rampant.

Meanwhile, in Munkács itself, on April 18, posters and proclamations by drummers announced that all Jews must relocate to one of three areas designated as ghettos. More than 13,000 people were jammed into a few streets of the Jewish quarter around Latorica Street that were isolated from the rest of the city by high barbed-wire fencing that welcomed their blood. My parents, along with their Oroszvég neighbors, were ordered to lock their homes and place their keys in an envelope on which they were to write both their old address and their new one. They were allowed to take only a meager number of items.

As in the brickyards, the language of hunger and disease was spoken by all. Youths risked death daily to find food, even attempting to steal from nearby gardens. Non-Jews ventured near the ghetto fence to sell food at exorbitant prices or to trade for precious items such as wedding bands.

Seeking to remove what remaining identity the Jews clutched on to, police would cut off men's beards and side locks as they ridiculed them. Orthodox men, who every time they removed their *tallis* from its soft velvet bag would kiss its embroidered neckband, were forced to burn them. One Sabbath, later known as the "Black Saturday of Munkács," gendarmes burst into the ghetto, rounded up numerous Chassids, and ordered them to demolish the sanctuary within the Darkei Teshuva, Rabbi Shapira's renowned yeshiva. They were compelled to do so while singing. Afterward, their reward was to be beaten or shot.

One building was set aside as a "mint," where militia tortured victims into confessing where they had hid their valuables; then they hanged some hanged some publicly in the square. Husbands were abused in view of their wives and children. Males were beaten on the testicles, while females, including the young, were searched vaginally by volunteers with disregard for cleanliness, often with male interrogators watching.

On May 11, long trains pulling rust-covered freight cars, still smelling of cattle dung, arrived at the brickyards, initiating the

Chapter 32

deportations of the Bereg County Jews. Before being loaded, every person, including mothers carrying wailing children, was callously searched for remaining valuables. Each carriage was intended to carry forty-five persons, but eighty to one hundred or more were crammed in. After the thick sliding doors were slammed shut, those interred inside were shrouded in darkness except for a few slat openings covered with tangled barbed wire. Before the trains departed, the guards would randomly shoot into the carriages, leaving the corpses in place.

On May 15, the liquidation of the Munkács ghetto, including all those convalescing in the nearby hospital, commenced. Day by day, police and soldiers, with bayonets fixed, burst into buildings to roust the inhabitants. Shooting in the air and striking with rifle butts, they ordered the ghetto dwellers to be outside within fifteen minutes with only what they could carry. They were marched through the city streets to the brickyards while being beaten and whipped. Locals gathered along the sides of the street, clapping or spitting at those within reach while screaming "Christ killers." At the brick factory, they were made to fully undress, their clothes ripped in search of valuables sewn into hems and pockets.

The journey to Auschwitz-Birkenau lasted at least three days, during which men, women, and children were crowded together so tightly that one could not sit or lie down unless someone else stood. Each car was provided with two large metal buckets, one filled with water and the other for use as a toilet. When it overflowed, those caged inside were forced to stand or sit in each other's excrement, urine, and vomit. They were given no food or additional water. During the day, the sun bore down on the train's tin roof, baking them and magnifying the stench. Thousands, particularly the elderly and children, died in transit. Some committed suicide. Their bodies were stacked in a corner of the car to provide more room for the living. Others found refuge in madness. None knew their destination.

I imagine Mama, Papa, Ilona, Libu, Miki, Feri, Marcel, and András huddled together and whispering comforts to each other. They and any of my friends and classmates who survived the trip would have disembarked on a platform covered in white ash, only a few hundred yards from the gas chambers. Most of these arrivals, particularly the elderly and children, were gassed and cremated within the day. If the chambers could not accommodate the volume, Jews would be shot and burned in fire pits. Those who did not go quietly, such as sobbing children, were thrown alive into the hungry flames. The rest were enslaved.

On May 23, 1944, the final train left Munkács, carrying more than three thousand people. Thereafter, the city was pronounced "*Judenrein*."

This was the fate thrust upon my beloveds in the spring of 1944. I offer these facts antiseptically—who am I to provide commentary? When those I cherished were subjected to merciless blows, I was not there to shield them. When they wept, I was not there to kiss away the tears. When their hunger or thirst grew unbearable, I was not there to relieve it. When the children screamed, I was not there to comfort them and assure them that they were loved. And when those who had given me life were being led to their death, I was not there to walk with them. I did not help. I did not know. I was not there.

Ilona carrying Marcel (her second son), with her mother, Eszter, in the background, shortly before they were sent to Auschwitz

CHAPTER 33
The Destruction of Budapest Jewry

In the winter of 1944–45, I thought of death as I might have thought of, say, firewood: there was nothing unusual about it. It was outside my control, like drawing the wrong card.
—George Konrád

Within three months after the Nazis occupied Hungary, close to 450,000 of the country's Jews had been murdered or transported to Auschwitz. Only the Jewish community in Budapest remained, consisting of a quarter of a million Jews who were surrounded by territory and nations controlled by the Third Reich and submerged in horrific rumors that carried varied shades of truth.

In early April, Allied aerial bombing of Budapest began. The targets were industrial sites, with residential neighborhoods as collateral damage. By the end of that month, nearly all the German occupying troops were removed from Hungary. Yet the torrent of anti-Jewish decrees continued, one of which was the setting up of clearing stations where Jews were forced to stand for hours to surrender their valuables.

Daily deportations of Jews also began, with police routinely picking up men, women, and children from the streets, trolleys, and trams. Many left their homes to buy a newspaper or to make a phone call, never to return.

By June, the Budapest municipal authority had designated more than 2,500 buildings, each marked by a yellow star, into which all Jews were required to move. Also in that month, a comprehensive account of the Auschwitz concentration camp (the "Auschwitz Protocols"), written by Rudolf Vrba and Alfréd Wetzler, two Slovak Jews who had escaped from it, was widely circulated in the Western press. The Protocols described the geography of the camp system, its construction and organization, how the prisoners were numbered and categorized, the "selection" method, the sterilization experiments, and the various methods employed to torture and kill them, including the gas chambers.

A copy of the report was given to Horthy, and it was reported on by the BBC on June 15. Numerous articles appeared in the world press publicizing the recent mass murder of Hungarian Jews.

On June 25, Pope Pius XII, writing from a liberated Rome in an open letter that failed to mention Jews specifically, called on Admiral Horthy to "spare so many unfortunate people further sufferings." Several world leaders, including Franklin D. Roosevelt and King Gustaf V of Sweden, publicly appealed to Horthy to stop the deportations. (The king pleaded "in the name of humanity" that Horthy "interfere on behalf of those among these unfortunate people who can still be saved." In response, Horthy assured that he "will do all that is within my power in the present situation in order to secure that the fundamental principles of humanity and fairness be upheld.") On June 26, Richard Lichtheim, a senior representative of the Jewish Agency in Geneva, wired a telegram to England detailing the mass exterminations at Auschwitz and calling on the Allies to help stop the killings, suggesting that members of the Hungarian government would be held personally responsible. The unenciphered cable was read by the Hungarian Intelligence Service and shown to Prime Minister Döme Sztójay, who passed it to Horthy.

On July 7, following a heavy air raid on Budapest that destroyed government buildings (the American planes also dropped leaflets over Budapest stating that the United States government was closely following the persecution of the Jews "with extreme gravity" and warning that "all those responsible would be punished"), Horthy chose to act. Backed by loyal troops, he ordered the deportations ceased, fired the two Interior Ministers in charge of them, and demanded that the gendarmes who were carrying out the deportations leave the city immediately. He also offered to allow the immigration of a large number of Jews to any neutral states that were willing to take them. In response, certain consulates issued thousands of protective passes.

With Germany weakened following the Normandy invasion, neither the SS nor the Wehrmacht took action. Instead, Hitler sent an angry message to the admiral declaring "that the Hungarian Government will take measures against the Budapest Jewry without any further delay." Horthy agreed to recommence the deportations on August 25, but two days before, the pro-German government in Romania fell, and that country switched sides, as it had done in World War I. This hurt the Nazi war effort, as Romania had been a significant source of manpower and oil.

Emboldened, Horthy dismissed Sztójay, replacing him with General Géza Lakatos, who had served Horthy loyally since 1920. Horthy declared that Hungary's Jews were Hungary's concern, and he assured Samuel Stern, the president of the city's *Judenrat*, established in April at Eichmann's insistence, that there would be no further deportations. The Regent also resumed efforts to reach a formal truce with the Allies.

In stark contrast to their brethren elsewhere in Europe, the situation of the Budapest Jews eased. They were permitted to move about more freely. Many who had been imprisoned were freed. In September, the curfew was loosened for the High Holidays. The Soviet Army pushed closer but was slowed crossing the eastern Carpathian Mountains. Rushing rivers, steep valleys, plunging ravines, and limited natural passes made difficult the movement of troops and mechanized military equipment, while aiding the German and Hungarian Army's defensive position along the 220-mile fortified Árpád line. By October 6, though, the Soviet Army had reached the Hungarian border. Refugees from the countryside coursed into Budapest.

On October 11, Horthy's delegate in Moscow signed a preliminary armistice agreement with the Soviet Union, a development quickly revealed to Hitler through a network of spies. Four days later, in a prerecorded proclamation, Horthy announced on the radio that he was suing for peace with the Allies. Budapest Jews celebrated, and many discarded their yellow star.

But on that same day, Horthy was informed that his son, Miklós Jr., a leader in the preparations to leave the war, had been kidnapped by SS storm troopers. Realizing that he did not have sufficient military or political support for the proposed armistice, and to save his son, Horthy agreed to abdicate his position. Pro-German factions seized the radio stations and then broadcast that the alliance with Germany remained in full effect. Hungarian troops were ordered to remain in their fighting positions on the borders of the city.

Without resistance from the Hungarian Army or protest from the Hungarian Cabinet, the Germans installed a new puppet government under Ferenc Szálasi, the founder and long-time leader of the fascist Arrow Cross party, who had been imprisoned by Lakatos. Szálasi was a virulent anti-Semite who believed in a worldwide Jewish conspiracy. Horthy was placed under house arrest in Bavaria, while his son was sent to a concentration camp. (Both would survive the war, with the elder Horthy testifying at the Nuremberg trials but not charged with war crimes.)

Chapter 33

By October 1944, an exhausted, poorly equipped, and outnumbered Axis Army faced a superior Russian force bent on vengeance. Nonetheless, in spite of Budapest's desperate military needs, forces of terror raged on there. One was the unrestrained mob of Arrow Cross who had been armed by the Germans, recognizable in their green shirts, black ties, polished mountain boots, and armbands with the ancient symbol of the Magyar tribes. Carrying torches, they rounded up thousands of Jews from the yellow-star houses to dig anti-tank ditches around the city. In November, a squalid general ghetto was created, its streets enclosed by high timber walls. Within weeks, most of the city's Jews had been moved into it, where many either perished from starvation, cold, or disease, or committed suicide.

Meanwhile, tens of thousands of Jews under the protection of neutral states, such as Sweden, Switzerland, Spain, Portugal, and the Vatican, or the International Red Cross were sheltered in a section of Pest near the Danube that had been designated by the Hungarian government as the "International Ghetto." Raoul Wallenberg, who arrived in Budapest in July 1944 as Sweden's special envoy, alone rented or purchased more than thirty buildings from which he flew Swedish flags and offered letters of immunity and the protection of the Swedish government. In these protected houses, Wallenberg set up hospitals, schools, soup kitchens, and a special shelter for thousands of children now orphaned.

Wallenberg also designed a protective passport, known as the *Schutzpass*, emblazoned with the symbol of the triple crown of Sweden. Their distribution, organized by Carl Lutz, the Swiss counsel, saved the lives of numerous Jews as well as a great number of anti-Nazi partisans. Wallenberg himself demonstrated enormous courage in personally distributing *Schutzpasses*, at one point handing them out to Jews imprisoned on a train leaving for Auschwitz and then escorting them off the train.

Another Swede, Valdemar Langlet, an unpaid cultural attaché to the Royal Swedish Legation in Budapest, had arranged for a ring of apartments, houses, estates and convents to act as Red Cross sanctuaries. Langlet produced thousands of supposedly legal *Schutzbriefe* (letters of protection), an identity card imitating a passport, with a photograph, personal data, and Swedish Red Cross stamp. (Other neutral legations, including the Spanish, Portuguese, Swiss, Salvadorian, and Nicaraguan missions, followed suit.) The Swedish Legation issued international identity papers—forged and distributed by Zionist organizations—to an estimated 70,000 Jews.

For the sake of maintaining their few existing diplomatic relations, the Arrow Cross Foreign Ministry formally accepted these protective papers. But the effectiveness of the diplomatic shield was inconsistent. Until mid-January, Arrow Cross hoodlums routinely invaded ghetto houses and hospitals to beat and shoot Jews and forced thousands of them to the lower quays of the Danube, where they were murdered. They carried off Hungarian Jewish employees of the Swedish Legation, shot citizens with Vatican passes, and committed robbery and murder in houses "protected" by the Swiss. On Christmas Day of 1944, after the Arrow Cross senior leadership had fled the city, a gang of drunken militia broke into the Swedish children's shelter and machine-gunned seventy-eight children. On January 19, after the Pest side of the city had been liberated, Arrow Cross units attacked a nursing home in Buda, killing more than 300 patients and staff.

Adolf Eichmann returned to Budapest after the takeover by the Arrow Cross. In early November, when train transport to Auschwitz was no longer possible, he organized death walks to the west. Tens of thousands were marched for days, through muck, snow, and ice, more than a hundred and fifty kilometers to the Austrian border to build fortifications or to be deported to the camps. Women (many in high

Chapter 33

heels or slippers, and some heavily pregnant who later would go into labor by the roadside), children, and the elderly were forced to keep pace with the gendarmes. They ate worms and snails found along the roadway. Those too weak to continue, in a cold bitter enough to freeze their tears, were shot. More than ten thousand died on the way. Their bodies littered the route and were stripped of clothing by local farmers, picked at by crows and stray dogs, and feasted upon by maggots.

The marches lasted until early December, when the Allies and neutral states pressured Szálasi to halt them. Eichmann was ordered back to Berlin by Heinrich Himmler, who was planting peace feelers with the Allies. Himmler instructed Eichmann (without informing Hitler) to cease all liquidation efforts.

By early November, in the slipstream of autumn's fading decorations, the Soviet Army, bolstered by Romanian troops, reached the Budapest city line and gradually encircled the city. Acting as a modern-day Nero, Hitler forbade surrender and declared Budapest a *Feste Plätze* (fortress), in part to protect oilfields in nearby Lake Balaton. This decision removed from Nazi commanders the discretion to allow several German armored divisions to retreat to more vital defensive locations.

In the midst of Christmas preparations, barricades and tank traps were assembled throughout the city, and buildings were altered to accommodate firing positions. There followed, beginning in Pest, a block-by-block defense by German and Hungarian forces (although many of the Hungarian soldiers would defect). The Battle of Budapest was one of the war's longest and bloodiest conflicts, labeled in many German memoirs as the "second Stalingrad." More than 160,000 perished in the shelling and fighting that ensued. Many of these were civilians ensnared in the city's damp, unventilated, unheated cellars and shelters lit by tallow candles, emerging only to scavenge for sustenance. Some survived by carving up one of the thousands of horses that had been brought to the city by the Hungarian and Germany infantry and artillery units in the absence of sufficient mechanized vehicles or fuel for them.

Each day, mutilated bodies, wrecked vehicles, and overturned carts piled up around snow-covered mountains of sandbags, refuse, and excrement. Every bridge across the Danube was destroyed, but not before hundreds of civilians were killed by gun and mortar fire while trying to cross them.

On a frigid night in mid-January 1945, after hearing stories of widespread raping of women by Soviet troops, Tetzi and Zoltán attempted to leave the ghetto. They were spotted by a group of teenaged Arrow Cross carrying submachine guns, who surrounded the couple. Zoltán was forced to pull down his pants and underwear, revealing that he was circumcised. The two were beaten and marched to the bank of the turbulent gray Danube.

What were my dear friend's final thoughts, as she and Zoltán were taunted mercilessly while shivering from exposure? As they were made to face the river, a bombed-out Margit Island in front of them. Perhaps tied together, with only one shot in the back of the neck while the other died from exposure.

Their bruised, naked bodies would have lain on the jagged ice until the next morning, when an onlooker might have dignified them by breaking open a hole and allowing the corpses to sink out of sight. I imagine that I would have been that passerby. That I would have gently lifted Tetzi's lifeless face and kissed it. And that she would have felt it.

*

Only in mid-February, after a massacre of German and Hungarian troops attempting to flee the brick carcass of the massive Royal Castle in Buda, did the entire city fall under Soviet control. The living found themselves in a city of burned-out buildings, with live explosives

Chapter 33

abounding in the rubble. Streets, alleys, and backyards were littered with bodies buried in snow drifts. To avoid starvation, residents jammed the trains headed to the countryside. It was said that no dogs or cats remained alive in the entire city. Compounding it all was the pervasive criminality of roaming Russian soldiers.

Survivors emerged from the two Budapest ghettos. Another group of survivors were those who had assumed false identities and lived as Aryans, hiding in unmarked buildings, homes, convents, church basements, and other sanctuaries. The Arrow Cross, preferring murder to combat, had searched for them incessantly.

Marika, will I find you? Please, G-d, allow me this.

CHAPTER 34

Jóska Ingber: September 20, 1944 (Paris)

My Dearest Brother Béla,

I am posting this letter to the International Red Cross and pray that it will reach you.

The mind can be a terrible enemy. To write a letter to a brother who may no longer be alive is a cruel exercise, ripping open the scabs on my heart. I pray that I'm not speaking to a ghost who has taken the place of someone precious to me.

The truth is that I pen these words as much to myself as to you. I feel their certainty more when I put them in writing. And I now have a sign that life's tides do both ebb and flow. At the very moment the storm had finally pierced me, Providence reached out its hand with an offering, H.I.!

You must be thinking—what madness has overcome me? I will tell you. In May, while I was still in London, I went with some Army friends to a

Chapter 34

West End theatre one night to see an American war movie. Soon after we were seated, several British soldiers filled the row behind us.

You should know that, over the previous years, I had approached hundreds of Brits to ask about Adolph. Showing a picture of him, again and again. Spelling his name. Speculating as to where he might have fought or been stationed. Straining to bear the insensitive or unintelligible responses. Until I surrendered to the futility of finding a particular grain of sand on a swirling beach.

Then, just before the lights dimmed, I heard a voice. Even though disguised in English words, it was familiar. I felt it viscerally, as if it had body and temperature. I turned to look. Staring back at me was Adolph.

I leaped over my seat and we embraced. I will admit to you that I hugged and kissed him unabashedly, in front of my soldier friends. So much so that we disrupted the start of the movie for many, although I suspect they were as much amused as annoyed.

Adolph is presently again somewhere on the battlefront, I believe. It is now my most important task, and my solemn mission, to seek the whereabouts of all our family and to ensure that, after these terrible times, we are together again.

I am writing this letter from Paris, where I have been with my unit for several weeks now. Once we entered the city's suburbs, we could hardly advance past the Parisians flocking the streets in celebration. As we marched down the Champs-Élysées, the roar of the crowd even drowned out the bells of Notre Dame. Although we arrived days after De Gaulle and the Free French held their parade, I was told that a million Parisians came out to hail us. My face was covered with the lipstick and tears of grateful women.

Earlier this week, a friend and I attended Rosh Hashanah services at La Grande Synagogue. There were some two thousand people crowded into the main floor and balcony. Hundreds of women, dressed in black. A cantor chanted Kaddish for all the victims. There will not be enough days until the end of time for all of the individual Kaddishes needed. American, French, and British soldiers in battle uniforms stood in the aisles and wept. Outside, many men and women came up and hugged me and invited me to their homes.

My division has moved on to the front, while I have stayed here to conduct interrogations.

If you receive this letter, please respond immediately through the Red Cross. They have set up a service for American soldiers to get in touch with relatives.

I hope that hearing from you will be my next miracle. Your loving older brother,

Jóska and Adolph Ingber, London, 1944

CHAPTER 35

Adolph Ingber: September 30, 1944
(Caen)

My Dearest Béla,

I have finally the chance to post a letter with the Red Cross.
For years, I've been tormented for having abandoned my beloved family. Knowing that I left you all in the path of evil, while I fended for myself. And as the news of the unimaginable continued to be unveiled, a part of me came to believe that I was an orphan, not because of destiny but as punishment for my selfishness.
I tell you that the terrors of battle do not compare to the anguish I feel not knowing the fate of my loved ones. I have written separately to our dear parents and to each of our brothers and sisters. You all are what fills my lungs, and I wait, unable to breathe, until I hear of your safety.
If you receive this letter, please know that you have two brothers at least who have survived. I know this because, by marvelous coincidence, Jóska and I were seated in the same movie theatre in London just before

D-Day. We clung to each other, driven by fear that if our grasp was not strong enough, the other would evaporate. He is alive and well. And somehow I believe that he will endure to the end of the fighting.

I implore the Almighty every day for your survival.

Your loving brother,

CHAPTER 36

Marika Leiner: March 7, 1945
(Budapest)

My Darling Béla,

I have posted this letter with the Red Cross, in the hope that it will find its way to you.

I'm sorry to start this letter with terrible news. I cry as I write this. My Papa is gone! All I knew was that he had received papers from the Vatican and was living with Rózsi and Klari (who T.G. have survived) in the General Hospital building in the International Ghetto. When it finally was safe, I went looking for them. I ran from person to person, begging for information, until I found the superintendent of that building, who told me that Papa had been killed during an air raid. I don't even know where he was buried.

How frightening the past few months have been. My survival is due to the kindness of Kati Tibold, a friend of mine. In October, she offered me, without my even asking, her identity papers (fortunately, she and I look alike) and the keys to her apartment in a non-Jewish building.

She was going to live with her grandparents in the country, where food is easier to obtain.

I had to memorize all sorts of facts, like her date and place of birth and her parents' names. My story was that I was a non-Jewish refugee from the fighting in Yugoslavia. To earn money, I got a job in a factory that put fur lining around motorcycle glasses. I could not contact my family.

Every day, I lived as a shadow within a shadow, taking side streets to dodge the Arrow Cross and often staying hungry to avoid identity searches at ration halls. When the sirens went off, I remained in my apartment rather than leave for the shelter, for fear of being exposed. I knew some who carried cyanide, in case of deportation, but I was not brave enough to consider it.

One day in November, while the streetcars were operating, I headed to the market early so that I could barter jewelry for food [at regular prices instead of black market rates demanded of Jews after hours]. After I found a seat, I looked up to see opposite me a woman who had been a customer of our shop for many years. Her husband was a senior Hungarian Nazi Party member. She walked toward me, and I stopped breathing, sure that she would denounce me. But, instead, she asked how my family and I were faring. Then she laid her hand on my shoulder and whispered, "I'm so sorry for what is going on." I jumped out almost before the train stopped at the next station, and ran. My heart still is pounding.

Pest was liberated several weeks ago, and I have returned to live in my old apartment with Rózsi and Klari. The building is one of the few in the area that remains intact, although all the windows are shattered. The Russians finally restored the water supply, but there's no electricity or wood for the fireplace. We sit at night in an invisible dark under blankets, the only touch of warmth creeping in from the flames of burning buildings nearby.

Chapter 36

Russian soldiers and tanks are everywhere. They frighten me. If I need to go outside, I try to dress and act as a beggar. I know women who before they leave their apartments smear their faces using lumps of coal and put dust rags on their heads so that none of their hair shows. Rózsi told me that if the soldiers stop me, I'm to fake a coughing spasm and tell them that I have T.B.

The other day Rózsi was able to trade the watch I received for my 12th birthday and an old camera on the street near our building for a small bag of crumbly yellow corn flour, some bacon, and a piece of bread hard as a football. We gladly ate the bacon, white with greasy fat. We also made noodles with the flour and water. It was heavenly.

Béla, I think of you constantly. Of walks along Andrassy Ut, lost in our dreams. Our picnic. Our first kiss. I long for more of those moments. I long for you.

I pray that you receive this letter, that you are well, and that you come to me as soon as it is safe to do so.

I send you all my kisses,

CHAPTER 37
Return: March 1945

*Where you used to be, there is a hole in the world, which I find myself constantly walking around in the daytime, and falling in at night.*

—Edna St. Vincent Millay

In the sadness of a wind-swept rain that crystallized into miniature hail, punishing uncovered skin, Tibi and I disembarked at the Munkács station. Each feeding the other precious morsels of hope. Neither of us with a plan.

I could tell you that we had been absolved of labor camp obligations only days ago, but that is not the entire truth. No chains would have restrained us had we tested them. Tibi and I likely could have received permission from the Romanians weeks earlier to leave the camp. But with the advent of spring and its uncurling of nature's bounty, food was more plentiful. Vodka and cigarettes, too. The workload lightened. We became blanketed from much of the war's tentacles. Tibi and I now were pet birds whose cages had been flung open after many years. We were secure only in bondage.

Chapter 37

Stepping onto the saffron-brick Munkács train platform, our hibernation over, I could no longer lie to myself. Before this day, I had not ventured back to my native ground for one reason. Fear. Of shattering memories. And of opening for renewed inquiry the truths of my childhood beliefs.

The station building was unheated, and a large ice dam covered a portion of its roof. Muscular tapered icicles, symmetrically situated as if lovingly hung as Christmas ornaments, adorned the edges and dripped onto the platform in a rhythmic tap.

One station wall, which Tibi came to refer to as the "wailing wall," was covered with letters and signs, mostly in Yiddish, pleading for information about loved ones. A few had photos attached. We raced up to scour them, my gut churning as I moved from face to face. After walking the length of the wall several times, passing windows with rain running down them like rivulets of unacknowledged tears, we were comforted by the number of Munkács Jews who remained alive. But no one had been asking about either of us. Not one mention of Tibi or me. Why hadn't any of our family posted?

Before the war, Model T Fords would have been lined up outside the station, waiting to chauffeur townspeople to Oroszvég and nearby villages. Now there was only a flat-bed drawn by a near-starved nag. No matter. We had agreed beforehand that we would walk, each of us toting a tattered suitcase containing our worldly possessions. We were in no hurry.

Our progress down *Cukor Utca* (Sugar Street) was slow, warranted by glazed cobblestones that had positioned at least one embarrassed traveler, a woman rushing to meet her beau, on her rear end. The first destination was City Hall. A fellow we had been chatting with on the train urged us to begin there, to register. "Let the Russians know you're back. That will facilitate everything else."

Reaching the Korzo, the landscape of streets, shops, and houses remained familiar, although fake, like a movie lot. One might have thought that the war had passed Munkács by if not for the abundance of Soviet soldiers. At a checkpoint near a barren field with faded chalk lines—where in another time I had listened to my older brothers yell, "Béla, shoot the ball!"—a militia guard asked for identification. We displayed proper papers, but he rummaged through our suitcases nonetheless before letting us pass. I owned a single valuable—which was sewn into the lining of my coat—a handsome Auguste Reymond watch, with a black band and face containing a delicate circle on the left side timing the seconds. Found on a dead SS officer, the watch was awarded to me by Lieutenant Grigore. (Tibi already had traded away all items of worth he had laid his hands on.)

We passed pedestrians trudging through the ramshackle streets, workers brushing away the slush, and children staring from windows raked with condensation. All were mannequins. Munkács was sterile, transformed into mere shades of gray. Block after block, Tibi and I studied the faces, sounds, and smells, straining for a glimmer of home. Where were they—the Chassids, the orthodox, the Zionists, the *schnorers*, and the street urchins? Where were the time-honored cries of the pushcart peddlers and newspaper boys? The seductive melodies of barefoot Gypsy musicians? Sing-song chanting exuding from a *shtiebel*? Rebbes immersed in scholarly debate on a street corner? The harmony of children's voices softly echoing from *cheder*? Cartons stacked with Yiddish newspapers? The sweet, buttery fumes from the kosher bakeries? In their entirety was my heritage.

A man wheeling a grindstone for sharpening knives stopped us to reveal beneath his frockcoat several pocket watches for sale, similar to the one worn by Pollack. Further on, a soldier with a bottle clutched to his breast lay passed out under the tattered awning of a butcher shop, next to a sheep's carcass hanging upside down, its blood dripping into a pan.

Chapter 37

We found ourselves in front of the windows of Pollack's store, which were dusty enough that daylight was powerless against them. Even in the days when the shop owners were predominantly Jewish, Pollack had not bothered to advertise the store under his name. Only a "General Goods" sign had identified it, which remained. I tugged at Tibi's coat, pulling him inside. The place was desolate except for a haphazard assortment of sundry items on shelves directly behind the counter, including cartons of cigarettes and cans of meat and condensed milk. Hunched over the counter, staring at a newspaper, was a scrawny man with ash blond hair cut close in military style, one of the few middle-aged civilian men we had seen. His drooping eyelids and drained face, dimpled by acne, were familiar. We recognized each other at the same time. Tóni. The *Shabbos* Goy.

Tóni climbed over the counter and locked his arms around me. "Béla, you're back," he repeated, emphasizing a different word each time. While I patted his back, Tibi edged away to avoid a similar reception. Having worked for years with Tóni, I appreciated his untarnished soul. He was a man whom children and dogs gravitated toward. But Tibi remembered him as the local fool ("They must have really clamped down on those forceps when he was born.").

I wriggled out of his grasp. "So good to see you, Tóni. I'm glad you're all right. Are you in charge?"

"I run it." He swept his arm across the room. "What's left. The Russians come in every day and take what they want."

I exhaled deeply. "Has anyone returned? Anyone from Pollack's family…or Tibi's?" And after a pause that rendered my previous questions moot, "Or mine?"

He shook his head tearfully. I waved my hands as if I were a referee calling off a goal, then wrapped my arm around his shoulder. "I'm sorry, Tóni. Forget I asked. How are you and your family?"

The tears gushed into puddles. "We've run out of food, Béla. And money. Since they took the Jews away...." He stopped, as his eyes widened. I nodded for him to continue. "Since Mr. Pollack has been gone, I've been trying to keep the store open. But it's too hard!" He clenched his hands and gazed to the heavens. "I don't know how to find new goods. Or how to pay for them. How do we restock for the spring? Mr. Pollack and his partner handled all that."

Poor Tóni. He didn't realize that he was one of the lucky ones. Over his shoulder stood Tibi, wiping away mock tears and motioning with his thumb for us to leave. I mouthed a curse for his benefit.

"Tóni, listen. I'll try to help you. Maybe we can work together. Like the old days. But I need to take care of a few things first."

Toni brightened. "Thank you, Béla. Thank you."

Tibi pulled me aside and whispered, "If he were a radio, all we'd hear is static. Tell him to close the shop, before he's robbed completely. He can take his remaining inventory with him and sell it from his house. Meanwhile, you and I will negotiate a deal with the Russians and reopen the store."

"Okay. But we include Tóni."

Tibi rolled his eyes. "*Mentsch tracht, und Gott lacht* (Men plan, and G-d laughs). Sure. Let's just get out of here already."

I repeated Tibi's suggestion to Tóni, who implored us to approach the Soviet authorities immediately, a surprisingly rational request. We assured him we'd soon be back.

Resuming our trek, we approached the Grand Synagogue. Its roof, which had been adorned by a large *Magen David* (Jewish star), now was licked green with moss and partially caved in. Woven fingers of ivy clung to its outer walls, which were surrounded by unkempt undergrowth. I prodded open the decaying door, letting Tibi enter first. We were welcomed by the stink of rotted skin and blood, which drove us outside. Tibi had railed at G-d many times during the war

Chapter 37

years and sworn never again to venture into a *shul*. I expected him to drag me away, but instead he screamed an obscenity, inhaled deeply, pulled his shirt over his nose, and charged back in.

The Holy Ark and its contents, as well as all the furniture, were gone. Straw littered the ground and, amid the charred remnants of box stalls, flies feasted on animal droppings. The gaping hole in the roof had allowed in the elements, turning the interior into a putrid soup. A swastika, with Szálasi's name in its center, adorned one of the walls. Tibi ripped at the stalls, tearing skin off his fingers. I joined in, flailing away at the wood planks with my scuffed boots, some pine breaking cleanly while some splintered, until we were spent. I caught Tibi allowing himself the slightest smile.

Leaving the *shul*, we passed the post office, where dozens were queued up to send and receive telegrams. Soon, we reached City Hall, which was as I remembered it from the encounter with the colonel. But the ornate lobby had been stripped bare, replaced with a mess of folding chairs, olive-green sheet metal cabinets, incandescent lamps, many of which were without bulbs, and an outsized framed portrait of a self-important Stalin, his walrus-like mustache streaked with white. In place of the Hungarian soldiers and their secretaries were Russian equivalents. Nonmilitary local functionaries were absent.

Searching the white-tiled floor for someone other than an armed soldier, I spotted a young woman in uniform, her thick brown hair pulled back into a smooth twist at the nape of her neck, sitting on a chair sifting through a file cabinet. Motioning Tibi to follow me, I summoned the language of my early schooling and addressed the woman in Russian. "Excuse me—may I ask you a question?"

She turned toward me, revealing wide cheekbones and a heart-shaped face marred by a web of pimple scars, and scowled. "Visitors need to sign in on the second floor," she blurted out.

"Please, we're trying to find our family members."

The woman muttered, "As I said...," pointing in the air.

Her words did not sting so much as the sight of her turned back. I wanted to pull photos from her purse, then stick them in front of her and scream, "What if you were searching for them?"

As we headed to the staircase, Tibi whispered, "Have you noticed that all the Russian women wear thick padding on their bosoms? They look like cows."

"She's pretty anyway."

"Yes, the wrapping is nice. But inside it is junk. She needs to get laid."

"Tibi, she's probably the girlfriend of an officer who will stick a bayonet up your ass if you make a move on her."

"No, you've got it wrong. I don't want her. I don't want any woman right now." Tibi stopped walking and faced me. "I just want to remind myself that I once was a man."

I gripped his shoulder. "You're more of a man than anyone here."

On the second floor, there was a queue of a dozen or so men and women outside an office with a makeshift sign in Russian identifying it as an "Information Center." Tibi lifted himself up in his shoes and then pointed across the hall to an oversized poster depicting a marching soldier. It proclaimed in large red letters, "The Communist Party Defends the Property of the People."

"When they say, 'the People,' who do they mean?"

"We're about to find out. Behave, and don't run your mouth."

When our turn came, we were invited into a spartan room where a heavy-set uniformed officer with a square, rugged face that hovered over a thick neck reclined in a crimson, leather-upholstered armchair. In contrast, his felt boots rested on a frail metal card table that held a fountain pen, a spiral-bound notebook, and a silver-framed sepia photo of a woman holding a toddler, with the shutter having caught her in a moment of reflective calm. A light-green pilotka hat with

Chapter 37

the red five-pointed star hung on a nail on the wall behind him, and a dull brass spittoon sat on the floor nearby. He motioned for us to close the door and sit on a ledge before a gingham-curtained window, through which a solitary beam of sunlight illuminated dust particles, and opened his ink-stained palms.

"Gentlemen, I'm Major Valery Konstantinova," he said with a whistling breath. "What can I do for you?"

"Sir," I responded, "we are looking for information on our relatives."

"What are your family names?" He pointed at me. "Yours first."

"I-N-G-B-E-R."

He casually picked up the pen and opened the notebook. "Tell me all the given names of your immediate family members."

I began with my parents, then Jenő, Ferencz, Miki, Libu, and Ilona. Mama and Papa had lived in Munkács since the nineteenth century. They had raised eight children here, built a life, established a career and a home, and were deeply involved in the community. A year ago, the two could have readily been identified by hundreds of locals. Now, except for me, the evidence of their existence had been eradicated, like the surface of a river closing to absorb the impact of a rock thrown into it.

The major wrote down each name, asking for the precise spelling. He shook his head. "These names don't appear on my list. I'll have Anna check what other records we have."

I had given him all the Ingber names, including Ferencz's wife and son. How could it be that not one is listed? Or were they just reluctant to engage with the Russians?

"Wait, I forgot to mention that my eldest sister is married. Haupt is her married name."

"Haupt." The major gazed upward, and squinted. "Yes, I think I remember a Haupt. He had a wife and two sons?"

I corrected him. "Yes, he has a wife and two young sons."

"He's back in his house."

"You mean they are back in their house?" I pleaded.

The major shook his head. Tibi gripped my arm, as Konstantinova said, "Are you here to regain yours?"

"Yes," I choked out. I had never considered the house as mine.

Konstantinova leaned forward in his chair. "There is as yet no law requiring the return of property. What proof do you have of ownership?"

Proof? I had no documents. Only the testimony of other survivors. The major tapped his pen on the tabletop and answered his own question. "Never mind. There are few municipal records left. Don't bother filing a lawsuit—the judges are all corrupt. Just go back to your house. If there's someone living there and he won't leave, come back. I'll send one of my men to question him. With a rifle pointed at his head, or at his family, the truth will come out."

Konstantinova repeated the process with Tibi, garnering the same result. "Come back in a week or so," he offered us both. "I might have more information. People keep turning up."

Knowing we were being ushered out, Tibi drew a pack of cigarettes out of his coat pocket. He shook one loose and offered it to the major, who declined. "I've got a small cigarette-making machine and tins of tobacco in the back. What I really could use is a cigar." He sat back and placed his big-knuckled hands together behind his neck. "Anything else? There's a line outside."

"Major," Tibi said while signaling to me to let him do the talking. "One more question, if I may. What permission do we need to open a store?"

Konstantinova chewed on the barrel of his pen. "What kind of store?"

"A general goods store. The one on Bereksas Street."

"The one run by the idiot?"

This much remained of the old Munkács—there were no secrets. Only deceptions. Was the major one of the store's looters?

Chapter 37

"Yes."

"You need a license. From me," he emphasized.

We had less than twenty *pengős* between us, enough for a fine dinner and a bottle of slivovitz. But Tibi was in his element. "Major, I'm assuming that there's a cost for the license. Which we will gladly pay once we are able to reopen the store under our ownership and stock it appropriately." Tibi beamed as if his face were elastic, a jack-o-lantern smile usually reserved for a young woman. "And, of course, there will always be a substantial discount for any purchases made by the major."

The man stroked his chin and burst into a roar. "You Jews are the best salesmen." He opened a drawer and pulled out a half-filled bottle of Moskovskaya, its green label torn and faded. Raising it, he declared, "Let our tables break from abundance, and our beds break from love." Konstantinova shaped his mouth around the bottle and threw a hearty swig to the back of his bullfrog throat, then belched before passing it to Tibi.

Tibi took a long gulp. "Major, may you die in bed at the age of ninety-five, shot by a jealous spouse."

My turn. I had become reacquainted with vodka, courtesy of the Romanians. Their version tasted and stank like rubbing alcohol, while his was smooth. I offered to our newfound friend one of Papa's favorite sayings, "He who has not tasted the bitter does not understand the sweet." I fought the urge to drain the bottle.

CHAPTER 38
Ecclesiastes

Vanity, fear, desire, competition—all such distortions within our own egos—condition our vision of those in relation to us. Add to those distortions in our own egos the corresponding distortions in the egos of others and you see how cloudy the glass must become through which we look at each other.

—Tennessee Williams

After stopping at the "Emergency Bureau" office to fill out a crude form registering us as Munkács residents, Tibi and I headed for Oroszvég. The sun had surfaced, and chunks of snow and ice were escaping from buildings and wires. Home was close, but I feared I could never find it.

Again we passed the Grand Synagogue. "I attended a wedding there once," Tibi said. "My cousin's."

"The inside was magnificent. You remember those stained glass windows, one for each tribe?"

"No. Back then, I spent my time eyeing the women's gallery."

He pulled a flask of plum tuică from an inner coat pocket, so stiff that it could not be sipped slowly. Another present from Lieutenant

Chapter 38

Grigore. I declined. "Béla, in all the camp years, did you ever stop to think about why anyone should follow religion? Whether it makes any sense?"

"Are we about to have one of those 'meaning of life' conversations?"

"Why not? What else have we got to talk about?"

"Yes, I reflected on that every moment when I wasn't hungry, exhausted, sick, freezing, or worried for myself or my family."

Tibi was immune to sarcasm. Perhaps because he had no sense of humor unless the wit was initiated by him. "I don't think there's any purpose. Live as you want, because there are no consequences. The Nazi bastards did whatever they wanted, and G-d never bothered to stop them. Nothing matters."

"Love matters."

"No, love only brings pain. Unless it's self-love."

"And what makes you such an authority on the meaning of life and love?"

"Béla, do you remember the story of Ecclesiastes?"

I had a recollection of Rabbi Gonzvi describing Ecclesiastes as a man who had lost his way. "How about if you enlighten me."

Along our path, cup-shaped crocuses, each mauve or cream-yellow with a delicate white stripe painted down its middle, fought through the ice. Mama planted them in clay pots as centerpieces, announcing the arrival of warm days. "The book talks about how unjust the world is. How evil people flourish while the good suffer and perish."

Perhaps it is unwise to pin all of one's hopes and dreams on today's existence. There may be other worlds to come. "You need a wise man to tell you that? After all we've been through?"

He ignored me. "It also tells of the futility of seeking wisdom or doing good deeds. That everything we create will eventually be destroyed."

"I find it hard to believe that the Bible would leave us with that meaning."

"Well, this book does. It isn't about laws, history, or covenants. It isn't preachy. It's philosophical. It reminds us that we will be forgotten, so why not live for the moment."

"I get it. Death levels all."

"Exactly. And it's a great insight. G-d reigns because we're all subject to time, while He is eternal. But He can't be counted on to help us."

"So that's why you see no purpose in being religious?"

"I'm not sure. I still worry about an omnipotent G-d."

Consistency was not one of Tibi's strong points. He lived his life intuitively, with no talent or patience for deep thought, but with the capacity for sudden inspiration. "So tell me, what does the Book say is the meaning of life?"

He smiled. As if he'd suckered me to go all in and then drawn a straight flush. "It's what I've always believed. That there is none. So enjoy yourself."

I looked away from Tibi toward the mountain peaks that formed my first memories, ones never flattened by distance, and which only gained weight with the passage of time. "Being realistic about life isn't the same as accepting that it has no purpose. Maybe the Book simply advises us to stop searching for some mystical meaning."

"No, Béla, it tells us not to be afraid to eat, drink, and fuck to our heart's content."

"So by that stupid logic, the Nazis understood the true purpose of life better than the rest of us did."

"No, killing the innocent isn't part of the deal."

As if narcissism could be calibrated that precisely. "Why not? If there's no purpose to life other than self-pleasure, that leaves a lot of room for evil."

Tibi scrunched his nose. "You have a point. But I still think that living for the moment is what counts. And you and I have a lot of living to catch up on."

Chapter 38

"I don't believe any of this, Tibi. If I did, I wouldn't have returned here." I glared at him, adding, "Nor would you have. There's plenty of women and liquor elsewhere."

The Latorica came into view, calling me yet again to its path. Tibi froze and, with a shaking hand whose thick fingernails were nicotine stained, ignited a cigarette. "Whose house do we visit first, Béla?"

"Yours is closest," I offered.

He took a long drag and coughed out a ribbon of smoke. "Let's skip my place."

Tibi and I each had our hopes. But they were kept in different places. "Don't you want it back?"

"No. My stepfather's ghost haunts it. I may go there eventually to dig up the backyard for gold pieces and jewelry he might have buried. Then I'll burn the house down."

I kicked at the gravel path, flinging pebbles against the dark green leaves of a ragged lilac bush that would never again smile with flowers. "You're a *putz*. We survive the war, schlep all the way here, kiss the Russians' asses, and you won't reclaim what's rightfully yours."

He turned and spit on the lilac.

"Your mother also lived in that house, Tibi. She raised you with love."

Had we lived in a paradise lost, or was it paradise because we had lived in it? Tibi tensed back, as if preparing to strike me. The grief spread across his face was tearless, as Tibi allowed himself to cry only for mundane reasons. "Fuck you, Béla. I'm not a mama's boy like you. Anyway, it's none of your concern."

Tibi's home life had been a topic off limits, unguarded only during drunken rants. "Fine, as you like. You can live with me."

Reaching the gushing river, we were disoriented by the gap in the landscape that had been the bridge Ágnes and I owned. A passerby informed us that it had been dynamited by the retreating Germans.

In its place was a cobbled overpass, without handrails, composed of wooden boards laid hot-dog style over thick support beams, which were attached to posts driven into the riverbank. We flew across it.

    Nearing the only home I had ever known, I forced Tibi to slow our pace. What was I seeking? No happy ending was possible, even in the haze of self-deception.

CHAPTER 39
My House

The flowers anew, returning seasons bring;
but beauty faded has no second spring.
—Ambrose Phillips

The pungent smell of a wood-burning stove beckoned, one that had served as my incubator when I was born in the dead of winter. Walking on ground where my siblings and I had run, the youngest of us naked except for chains of dandelions around our heads, I was eager to discern the scent of *cholent, kneidlach,* and *pierogi.* Listening for the hissing of geese. Hoping for the absence of squeals. My polestar, the walnut tree, remained, with its myriad of grasping branches, disdaining weather's attempt to age it. Would I find where my name had been carved into its trunk long ago? Would anyone be sitting underneath?

I halted a stone's throw away from sanctified space, consumed with counting the years backwards. Up the road was a hill, less distant that I had remembered, where under the low sun of winter that had lighted my childhood, we boys would pile onto an old door and speed down, aiming for a tree at the bottom, challenging each other to be the last one to fall off. Tibi wrapped his arm around me and nudged me forward. The narrow front walkway had been shoveled clean. The white picket fence was gone. Near the front door were sets of muddy footprints crisscrossing a lawn upon which memories breathed. There was a darker shading on the doorpost where an intricately carved wooden *mezuzah* once had been.

Before my eyes, the house swelled into a tombstone. I took a step back, confounded at my yearning for ghosts who could neither be found nor lost. Taking a deep breath, I leaned my suitcase against the front wall and rapped on the door, the sound echoing in my ears. Muffled voices were followed by footsteps, and then the door was flung open. A stocky, balding, unshaven man in his thirties, wearing work clothes that smelled of raw chicken, stood in the arched doorway. His upper lip was raised in a grimace that forced the lower one to protrude outward. Studying us, he snarled in Czech, "How are you still alive?"

For the whole journey back, I had imagined killing whoever was enjoying life in my home. We would engage in cold conversation, which would escalate into a shouting match and then justifiable self-defense.

In reality, I expected to remain calm. But after years of living as a captured animal, his five words were an unlocking of the cage. In a swift, unconscious motion, I grabbed the man's shirt with my left hand and punched him flush in the face with the other. His eagle nose burst open, and he staggered back, as if standing on the deck of a ship in a storm.

Tibi and I stomped inside. Recovering his bearings, the Czech raised his hands and lunged toward me. This elicited a vicious blow to the side of his head from Tibi, who stood awning-like over our sprawled-out foe, mutely daring him to rise. I scanned the room. Filthy. Cluttered. Unfamiliar. Papa never sat on that chair. Mama

Chapter 39

didn't light candles at that table. The leather-framed needlework on the wall was of interlaced flowers, not Old Testament scenes. Their lives should have left traces, yet nothing of my family's furniture, wall coverings, rugs, lightings, photos, or paintings remained, as if decades had passed instead of a single year. An incompatible past had been picked clean.

Should I walk from room to room, opening doors, crawling through the attic, looking under beds, until I find them? A shuffling sound directed our gaze toward the kitchen. A woman, clad in a shapeless frock that billowed above gouty ankles to cover her late-stage pregnancy, stepped forward. Her hair was cut short and evidenced some thinning. One side of her face was discolored. With eyes opened wide, the woman raised her hands to apple cheeks and wailed, "Gyorgy."

Distracted, we didn't notice her husband kick at Tibi's legs, causing him to stumble backward and fall to his knees. As Gyorgy rose, I leaped at him, pressed my knee into the small of his back, and placed him in a headlock. He bucked furiously, and I squeezed tighter. Someone was screaming out curses, a shrill voice that I recognized as my own.

Tibi tugged at me. I raised my head. The woman had waddled closer. Her sobbing now was an openmouthed moan. Clutching her thigh was a crying, cloth-diapered toddler grasping a silver rattle. I let go of Gyorgy, now struggling for breath, and stood.

I shouted at the woman, "What are you doing in my house?"

She lifted the child, hugged him, and called to her husband, "Gyorgy, are you hurt? Talk to me!" Her husband rolled onto his back, rasping out, "We were given this house by the authorities."

"YOU'RE A THIEF!"

"I have papers...."

I had rehearsed with Tibi rejoinders to any arguments. Accusing the trespasser of anti-Semitic actions would maintain the farce. Instead, I said, "You were awarded this house by the occupiers of our homeland.

By the fascist enemies of the Soviet Union. Your claim is no longer valid. It's only proof that you're a traitor. If you have a problem with this, speak to Major Konstantinova."

The woman pleaded, "Please, we have no place to go."

Gyorgy glowered at her. "Don't beg them."

Addressing only her, I demanded to know how they had come to be awarded my house. They were from Kuchava, a nearby farming village, she told us. She, Gyorgy, and their son had been living with his parents, who wanted them out. Last May, the local gendarme had "invited" them to resettle in Oroszvég.

Gyorgy stood as if doped, leaning on his wife. "You heard Polina. We are here legally. Go and make yourselves rich by stealing someone else's property."

I pointed a finger at him. "Because of the child, I'll allow you to stay here a few more days while you make other arrangements. But be assured, I'll be back. With a Russian soldier. If you're not gone, I'll have you and all your possessions thrown out on the street." Without waiting for a response, Tibi and I stormed out. At the curb, the flares of two cigarette tips already protruded from Tibi's mouth.

"You threw a pretty good punch," he remarked, handing me one of them.

"Should I go back and apologize?"

Tibi chuckled. "Even with his face messed up, his wife is still uglier than he is." He parked his hand on my shoulder. "Are you okay?"

He and I had developed a pact over the years. When one of us cried, the other pretended not to notice. I threw my suitcase to the ground and sat on it. Tibi crouched next to me.

"They're all dead, aren't they, Tibi? Your family and mine."

"We can't be sure. Let's give it some time."

Chapter 39

I shook my head. "They're all gone. Maybe Marika, too. And I'm all alone." Tibi's expression turned pained. Slapping his knee, I added, "Except for some yokel who keeps following me around."

Tibi dropped his case also and plopped on top, indenting its middle and straining the zippers. "Béla, are you sure you want to reclaim your house?"

Did I want to live in a house whose beating heart I was no longer acquainted with? "Yes. If for no other reason than to kick those trespassers out of it."

"We could go to Budapest," said Tibi. I had been hearing stories of the widespread assault on Jews in Budapest during the past year. Marika, fragile and unsophisticated, was somewhere in that perdition. Could she possibly have survived?

"You know that I'm heading there as soon as I can. But not to stay."

"Why don't we both go? Start new lives there."

My remaining life already was too short for all of my dreams. "And live happily ever after?"

Tibi began massaging the bridge of his nose, as if a headache had developed. "Look, I'm just thinking that it's not good for either of us to be back here."

I pointed back to my house. "Tell me, Tibi, why does that bastard get to live? Much less to have a family?"

"Because he got lucky, and we didn't. I don't think it's any more complicated than that."

"My father told me that G-d is constantly testing us. Challenging us to recognize our sins and repent. But that little shit, who will never repent, is the one He grants His favors to?"

Tibi wagged his finger. "Béla, I know you loved your father. But maybe he was wrong."

"Maybe." I sprung up. "Let's find my brother-in-law."

"I'm going to the *Kuplieri*. Come with me."

"I'm not in the mood. And, I feel committed to Marika."

He considered this. "Suit yourself. Anyway, if it's still there, they'll be no better source of information. Plus they may have contacts for obtaining liquor for resale. That's the best way to keep our Russian masters happy."

"I can think of one better."

"I'm sure that's already been explored. Where do I meet you later?"

"At Ilona's place." Those words now referred to a cemetery. "Hopefully, we can stay there for a few days."

We headed in opposite directions. Ilona's modest home, surrounded by a jumble of trellises, vines, and shrubs, was blocks away. Knee-high weeds and crabgrass, decorated by a pile of trash, now constituted the lawn. The roof shingles were buckling, and several of the windows had been boarded up. The veranda, once laden with carefully tended potted plants, lay bare except for a stack of firewood.

I knocked with my knuckle on a front door guarded by a broken lock and the delicate strands of a spider's web. As footsteps inside grew louder, I attempted to gauge how heavy they were. Józsi answered, clad only in underwear and heel-less slippers, his skin as pale as alabaster. Dark stubble, feathered with battleship-gray, outlined his jaw. He reeked of brandy. Józsi moaned, then threw his arms open.

Our embrace was more of a mugging, as Józsi and I sought to feel our family through a common spring. As a violent wind whistled through the floorboards and attacked our flesh, he led me to a kitchen table on which dust pirouetted. With a shallow carved end for eating food, it was the only piece of furniture in the house other than a bed. On the table sat a bowl containing a solitary blue plum with purple accents, surrounded by several pits.

The ruins of life throbbed through Józsi's quivering eyelids that framed red-rimmed eyes. He pointed to the soft glow of a naked light bulb, under which lay a portrayal of Ilona smiling at a world that had

Chapter 39

not yet betrayed her. In all the time that I'd known him, Józsi had never been without a stick of charcoal in his pocket. I reached for the sketch, being careful to touch only its edges.

"You have captured her, Józsi. Her joy radiates from the page."

His love remained intimate, transcending time and separation. "Ilona on our wedding day. A lifetime ago."

I traced the paper's border with my fingers, allowing myself to reach the cusp of reminiscence before turning away from its brightness. How could it be that the soldier survived while the innocents perished?

He shuffled over to the cupboard and took out chicory and sugar, throwing handfuls into dirty cups before setting up water to boil. "I have nothing to remember her by," Józsi continued, waving aimlessly a hand that still bore his wedding ring. "No clothing. No jewelry. No pictures even."

"I have one picture." I hesitated. "Of Ilona holding...Ferike. Mama sent it to me. I'll look through my suitcase later for it. Józsi, have you contacted the Red Cross?"

"Yes, I checked their displaced persons lists after I returned from Pest last week. I went by car, as they're still repairing the destroyed railroad tracks. You can't get to Buda, except by rowboat, because the Germans blew up all the bridges."

"Did you find out anything?"

No response as he poured hot water into our cups. The only sound was of rain tapping on the eaves like faint drumbeats. What if Ilona came back? Would she be the same person we knew? As a mother with young children, upon arriving at Auschwitz she would have faced the choice, which had to be made within seconds, of whether to hand her sons over to Mama to possibly save herself. She would have seen close up those precious to her turn into corpses. Could we bear to see a loved one whose humanity had been shattered? Could she bear to be near us?

"What's the city like? Did many Jews survive?"

"Hard to tell. Budapest is a hell hole. They're still removing horse carcasses. Money is worthless, and there's nothing to buy, anyway. I spent hours in the Swedish and Swiss embassies. In the refugee center established by the Russians, I was surrounded by large crowds of survivors also searching. It took days to make my way around a few-kilometer area. You have to be very careful. Loose bricks still are falling from buildings. There are bands of Arrow Cross roaming the streets at night. And the Russians are picking up military-aged men and shipping them off to gulags in Siberia. They make no distinction between Jews and non-Jews, because they've been given quotas of 'captured soldiers' to fill."

"Did you ask about…?"

"Marika? Yes. No one has any useful information. And Prague remains in German hands."

I sighed. "Thank you for trying. Is there word about your parents?" He shook his head.

I recounted our conversation with the Russian major and the confrontation with Gyorgy. "Józsi, did you have trouble reclaiming your house?"

"No, it was abandoned. Apparently, the bastard who took it over had Nazi sympathies, and he fled before the Russians arrived. We're both lucky. Many Jewish homes were torn down for firewood."

I picked up a half-empty bottle of slivovitz, a few sips of which could tip a room sideways, and flavored our coffees with it, being generous with Józsi's cup.

"What are your plans?" I said.

"Plans? I have no plans. I have only shame. Which suffocates me."

I forced myself to peer into his face. To take him in. His pain was exposed, while mine was masked like a fencer's. Fidgeting uncontrollably, Józsi flipped over the drawing of Ilona and commenced

Chapter 39

another one. I ambled to a cracked window, where ice had formed on the inside of the sill, and rubbed my finger against it to clear the moisture. The bottom of the sky was bathed in pink and magenta.

József's sketch, the lines of which were frenzied, was of a small boy holding his mother's hand. The boy was pointing to a deer grazing at the edge of a stream. I grasped József's shoulders and kissed the top of his head. "Get dressed and walk with me to the train station."

At the station, József and I were drawn to a "martyrs list" that had been tacked to a door post of the high-ceilinged main room. I hesitantly scanned it, as József posted Ilona's picture on a second wall that was filling up. Underneath it, he carefully printed her name, his name, and their address. Then he pressed his face against it, his salty tears smearing her image with love.

*

The next day, after Tibi and I caught up on sleep on the floor of József's house, we met with Tóni to plan the reopening of Pollack's store. Tibi would be in charge of the relationship with the Russians. Tóni would maintain the store's inventory. I would pedal to nearby farms to negotiate the purchase of their upcoming produce on consignment. I also assigned myself the job of traveling to Budapest to search for suppliers. We persuaded József to help the three of us man the shop.

On the following Monday, before the store had officially reopened, Tóni and I were in the front cleaning up when Polina cautiously opened the door wider and stuck her head inside. I nodded for her to enter.

"Sir, I am here to let you know that we are leaving today. We are returning to Kuchava."

"Good!" As she pulled the door closed, I said, "Wait." I reached for two cans of condensed milk that had been left underneath the counter and motioned for her to come take them. As she did, Polina reached into a pocket of her dress and pulled out what appeared to be a postcard. She thrust it at me, grabbed the cans, and fled.

I stared at a gold-edged prayer card, dominated by a portrait of Jesus on the cross. Across the top, it read "Prayer Before a Crucifix." To the right of the picture were a few lines in Polish: "Look down upon me, good and gentle Jesus, while before Your face I humbly kneel and, with burning soul, pray and beseech You to fix deep in my heart lively sentiments of faith, hope, and charity and true contrition for my sins."

Struggling with a language I had heard only sporadically over recent years, I read and reread the words, then gripped the card with both hands, poised to tear it apart. "No!" Tóni lurched at me. I flung the card at his face and marched out. Wandering aimlessly, like a leaf on a windy day, I found myself at the train station. Facing the sketch of Ilona, I screamed silently.

CHAPTER 40
Marriage: 1945

*It is an absolute human certainty that no one can know his
own beauty or perceive a sense of his own worth until
it has been reflected back to him in the mirror of
another loving, caring human being.*

—John Joseph Powell

Munkács is 350 kilometers from Budapest. A drive of less than four hours these days. But measured by my heart, the distance was forever.

A month after I returned to Munkács, train service to Budapest was restored. But would I find Marika, or had she also disappeared like a modern-day Eurydice, imprisoned in the war's underworld? I kept her face before me. Imagined holding her. Wiping away tears from puffy eyelids. Saving her. We were only at the beginning of our novel. She could not yet live within me as Ilona does in Józsi.

During the trip, I scanned the car for the appearance of Russian soldiers, who were reputed to be robbing passengers. Outside the window, the great Hungarian plain was littered with the ruins of cottages and barns, the skeletal remains of livestock, abandoned fields, and bomb craters.

Arriving in Budapest, I ran toward Marika's building. Its structure remained intact, but the ground-floor restaurant was a burnt-out shell. Mounds of rubble, glass, and garbage lay in the courtyard and across the street, where another building hung limply. Bullet holes defaced the dignity of the brick facade. I climbed the steep, narrow staircase, where the stink of smoke and sulfur permeated the walls, with a Sabbath candle that valiantly fought the yawning darkness. Once again, I would approach a home with the fear of love lost.

Near her door was a stretch of cracked floor tile stained with blood turned hard. I shuddered. Knocking but getting no response, I yelled, "It's Béla!" I heard scampering. The door opened a chain's length. A face with shadowed hollows around the eyes peeked out. "Marika," I whispered. She flung open the door and pressed herself against me, her dress hanging loosely from a body wracked with sobs. "You came for me!"

I discarded my pretext of pursuing business opportunities. Marika suffered from dizziness and fatigue. Less so her stepmother and stepsister, the latter of whom took me aside to report that Marika had not menstruated in months. I roamed the neighborhood in a search for food, particularly meat and milk, finding success by trading with Russian soldiers the whiskey flasks I'd brought for that purpose.

Marika and I lounged for hours on the redbrick stoop at the building's entrance, touching as if each of us were blind. The first time Rózsi and Klari passed us on their way to find work, Marika gripped my arm until they were out of view.

"How do they treat you?" I said.

"Fine."

"That's not much of an answer."

"Stop it, Béla. They took me in again once the Germans left. We've shared the hardships together."

Chapter 40

"Took you in? Isn't this your father's apartment?"

"It was. Now it belongs to Rózsi."

"So now you're a guest in your own home?"

"They help me stay safe."

Marika ended that discussion with a kiss, itself a work of art. She listened as I described my new circumstances in Munkács, while watching for passing soldiers. When I asked that she accompany me to Munkács, to understand my roots, I had her full attention.

"Béla, I already know your background. From all the stories you've told me."

"Then let me say it another way. I won't risk losing you again, so I'm not leaving without you. And this apartment isn't large enough for four." She smiled and laid her head on my lap.

Each night, before I left to walk to a hostel in Pest operated by the American Jewish Joint Distribution Committee, Marika clung to me as I assured her that no earthly force could prevent me from returning. At the shelter, I swapped stories with some survivors. It was there that I learned of Tetzi's fate, which I cautiously conveyed to Marika the next day.

Between spasms of sobbing, Marika said, "How did you find this out?"

"From a friend of Zoltan's who had been hiding with them but decided to stay put in the ghetto."

"When did it happen?" Marika choked out.

"Only days before the Soviets overran the main ghetto. This fellow told me that they could already hear the 'Internationale' blaring over military speakers."

Marika covered her face with her palms. "Why couldn't they have just remained inside? And why couldn't my papa have stayed in the bunker?"

That evening, with Marika insisting that she was fit, we made our way to the Danube and lit memorial candles.

On our last day in Budapest, while Marika packed her possessions in a modest suitcase, Rózsi pulled me aside.

"Béla, what are your intentions regarding Marika?"

Swallowing my fury and ceding parental status to Rózsi, I said, "I will act honorably, and protect her. And when we are ready, we will marry."

After we exchanged saccharine farewells and left the building, Marika looked back and cried, "Goodbye, Papa."

We boarded one of the few trains that stopped in Munkács. Upon disembarking, I led Marika to the drawing of Ilona, now smudged and partially buried under photos of men, women, boys, and girls blessed with life.

She examined the face, remarking, "You have your sister's features." Turning to me, she added, "You must pray for miracles, Béla. We know they can happen."

Marika moved into a spare bedroom in my brother-in-law's house, which I managed to have furnished with a bed and dresser. One of our first trips was to a reopened beauty parlor on the Korzo, where Marika's hair was washed in turpentine to remove any remaining bugs. We avoided discussion of the war and our families, concentrating on healing. With mail and telegraph service returning to normal, I checked daily for a communication from Jóska or Adolph. "G-d, you wouldn't be so cruel as to deprive me of all my blood, would you?"

A hostage to her lost childhood, Marika basked in the serenity of the Carpathian setting as we hiked and biked over the paths and trails of my youth. Learning the nuances of each other's personalities, our life's goals melded. Enriched by Marika's beauty and gentleness, my spirit was replenished. On a walk during an early evening made for reflection, as the last gleam of perfumed sunshine faded behind the peaks and a breeze whistled softly through the leaves, I pledged

Chapter 40

to Marika that I would always take care of her. That I would never abandon her. That her pain would be mine.

She hesitated, as if her fear of losing me overwhelmed her trust that I was hers. "Béla, aren't you afraid of being alone?"

"Why do you ask that? Aren't we together?"

"But it's different with you. You had both of your parents while growing up, and so many siblings. A large, loving family that you identify with so strongly. Can I make up for that?"

"No, but that's not your place."

"Why?"

"They'll always be with me," I whispered, pulling Marika to me. "And if they lived, I still would want you."

I told Marika that I wanted each of my dawns to begin with gazing into her eyes. For our future stories to be written on the same page. When I asked her to remain at my side until my final hours, she smiled, took my hand, and offered her heart. (As I write this, I recollect that my proposal of marriage was romantically tendered, with a profession of the love that had overcome me, while Marika's remembrance is that I was so nervous that I spoke the magic words while pacing behind her.)

We would accept the darkest parts of each other and emerge from the abyss together. Our gifts to each other were ourselves, although I had the pleasure of giving Marika a ring, the winking diamond meager in size but well cut, that I obtained after a negotiation with Major Konstantinova, who coveted my wristwatch.

By then, a *shtiebel* had opened on Józsi's street. On the Saturday morning before our wedding, Józsi accompanied me to the house, the living room filled with chairs and two benches, the scarred remnants of those that had lined the Korzo until the occupation. On a table along one of the cracked walls was a Torah scroll, minus its lavish embroidery and ornaments, which had been hidden in a crawl space underneath the house. Without prayer books or shawls, we conducted the service in everyday clothes from memory. Tibi arrived unexpectedly and sat in the back.

In honor of my impending nuptials, I was called to the *bimah* (podium) to deliver a blessing over the Torah. Józsi, presiding at the stage, chanted in Hebrew, "Dov, son of Solomon," my father's name intertwined with mine. Using his shirtsleeve in place of the traditional ornate silver pointer, one end shaped like an index finger, Józsi indicated the words in the decaying parchment that I was to recite. He grasped my shoulder and whispered, "Béla, you can do this." Facing the congregation, I wiped my eyes before reciting the first benediction, praising the Lord for choosing us, from all peoples, to receive His laws.

That week's Old Testament portion spoke of the mutiny against Moses' leadership, to which Yahweh responded by opening the earth to swallow those who would betray and bringing fire to those falsely seeking the priesthood—a reminder of another time replete with violence. Józsi read next, while I gripped the handle of one of the wooden staves. When he finished, Józsi pointed to the last word he had chanted and I again gently pressed against the scroll, kissed my shirtsleeve, and recited the second blessing. As I headed to my seat, the modest congregation rose and chanted "Siman Tov u' Mazel Tov."

On the following Thursday, June 7, Marika and I were married in City Hall by a judge. There were no rabbis in Munkács. My bride did not circle around me seven times. We did not stand under a *chuppah* (canopy) or sign a *ketubah* (traditional marriage contract). At Ilona's wedding, Mama and Józsi's mother together had shattered a plate, signifying that the bride and groom could no longer remain at home. Now here I was, back in the place of my childhood, without a single blood relative to share my happiness.

Chapter 40

As Marika recited to me the biblical chant, "I am to my beloved and my beloved is to me," I glanced at Józsi, our witness. He was struggling to hold back tears, and in that short eternity I could not help but regret that I had reunited with him.

Józsi, Tibi, Marika, and I, together with Tóni, celebrated in the lone restaurant operating nearby. Marika and I poured our two glasses of sweet, topaz Tokaji wine into one. Tibi stood and recited the blessing over the wine. He continued, "As a great man said long ago, 'One word frees us of all the weight and pain of life.' My dear friends, let us please toast Béla's and Marika's love, and wish them happiness and many children in a peaceful world."

"*L'chaim!*" chanted the group. I stood and hugged Tibi. "You are my family."

He squeezed my cheek and kissed it.

"So, Tibi, let me guess. That saying was from Maimonides."

"No."

"Rabbi Akiba?"

"No."

"The Baal Shem Tov?"

"No."

Perhaps the wine would excuse my ignorance. "I give up."

"Sophocles." Tibi patted my shoulder. "You see, my illiterate friend, not all the wisdom in the world comes from us Jews."

Béla and Marika, July 1945

CHAPTER 41
Dachau

This sea of faces...every one of them, seemed to be dead, but they were still alive.

—Jimmy Gentry, a soldier with the
U.S. 42nd Rainbow Division

As the Russians advanced through Poland in the summer and fall of 1944, thousands of slave laborers from Auschwitz and other concentration camps were evacuated to camps in Germany. One such camp was at Dachau, a medieval Bavarian town on the outskirts of Munich, where the first of the major Nazi concentration camps and "scientific" centers had been established.

Transports arrived continuously at Dachau, the nucleus of a system of Bavarian camps. Overcrowding, poor sanitary conditions, insufficient provisions, and weakened immune systems promoted an epidemic of typhus, an ancient illness that seems to surface in every war. In late April of 1945, as soldiers from the U.S. Seventh Army neared the camp, they found dozens of roofless coal cars maggoty

Chapter 41

with decomposing bodies and scraps of clothing. Some of the skeletal corpses lay in convulsed positions on the car floors, while others were wedged in corners sitting upright.

Upon entering the camp, the Americans discovered crematoria, as well as large rooms of naked corpses stacked floor to ceiling, alternately head-to-toe to conserve space and assure stability. Thirty thousand prisoners, many perched on the border of death, were freed.

CHAPTER 42
The Red Triangle: Summer 1945

The skin covering the memory of Auschwitz is tough.
—Charlotte Delbo

In spite of rampant inflation, which emboldened peasants with food and tangible items to bargain with us without conscience, the store thrived, to the point where we hired Tóni's cousin, Lenka, to help attend to customers. Lenka, who had grown up in Poland and been imprisoned in Dachau for idle anti-Nazi comments, occupied the front post, where Ágnes once stood. Tibi grumbled, "Why spend money on a salary?" Until he met this timeworn young woman whose dark eyes were permanently widened with terror. Scrawny as a plucked chicken with elbows like knives, her unassuming nature cast little shadow in the world.

"She's an angel," he declared, his starved eyes salivating. "Listening to her voice is like hearing a nightingale's song. I want to have babies with her."

Chapter 42

"No doubt she's pining for you as well, Tibi."

Our commercial success was built on the rapport Tibi had cultivated with the Russians, who were essential to obtaining surplus Army supplies and goods not produced locally. We paid the major a monthly "license fee," and he and Tibi were regulars at the postwar version of the *Kuplieri*, located next to the town's slaughterhouse. Among the concessions to that relationship was our participation in a May Day parade down the Korzo, where we marched with the Soviet flag while wearing white sashes with hammer and sickle. To avoid being labeled as Nazis, the populace lined up along the parade route. A week later, the Russians marked the war's end in drunken celebration, highlighted by rifle fire aimed skyward.

One Sunday in early July, soon after the quiet night changed to a whispering dawn, Marika and I embarked hand in hand on our customary stroll to the train station to search for new postings. Blossoming rose bay rhododendron had turned the mountain slopes into a lavender blanket. The tapping of woodpeckers, on pine trees heavy with dewy leaves, mingled with our soft footsteps.

"Béla, will the Soviets return this area to Czechoslovakia?"

"No, by treaty, the Rus has been ceded by Czechoslovakia to the Soviet Union. It was Beneš's gift to Stalin for liberating our country. At least the border with Czechoslovakia is open."

"Why does that matter?"

"It's good for the store. We've found a surplus supply of potato schnapps and brandy there. Not great quality, but the Soviet soldiers will drink perfume bottles if they contain alcohol. Sales to them alone will make us a small fortune."

"What if the major wants to increase his fee?"

"Don't worry, Tibi will manage that. What counts is that I've got a steady-enough stream of income for us to enjoy a good living."

Marika's mouth twisted to the side. "What are you saying, Béla? That we should stay here? Not leave for Palestine? You trust the Russians?"

"Not really," I admitted. "But we need to be practical. Palestine would be a difficult trip, and we can't be sure that we'd make it there. And the British are interning immigrating Jews in detention camps on Cyprus. I couldn't bear to go through that."

"Nor I. Can't we go to America then? Isn't your brother there?"

"I still haven't heard from Jóska. You know that."

"Don't you also have an uncle there? Can't he sponsor us?"

"I don't know how to reach him." I knew nothing of my "Uncle Lou," except that he lived somewhere in the New York City area. Once he sent twenty dollars to my mother, which Papa used to buy a chestnut-colored horse. Maybe Lou is rich.

"Béla, I know this is your home and that you're working very hard to build a business. But I'm so afraid to stay here. The Russians are savages."

"Marika, all you have to do is mention the major's name and no one will bother you. Let's give it a little more time. We'll talk about this again."

We neared the bridge, which again touched both sides of town. Its rebuilding, sans the ornamental flourishes of the original, had been completed a couple of weeks earlier. The Latorica was flush with water from the spring thaw, connected to the grace of the fertile earth as it unlocked its frozen joints. Amid the currents pressing against the riverbank were several fishermen in high boots and rubber overalls, likely local farmers seeking to supplement their income. We had heard of Soviet soldiers coming to this spot, tossing hand grenades into the water, and scooping up the dead fish that surfaced.

"If they're still here on the way back, I'll go talk to them. We can sell their catch in the store."

Chapter 42

Stepping onto the bridge, Marika exhaled. "I am afraid of remembering too much, but this walk reminds me of the bridges across the Danube during the Russian siege. Though I don't know why, because they always were crowded then."

"I would have thought the opposite. That people would have been frightened to be outside at all, much less in an exposed area."

"The bridges were filled with people from Buda rushing over to Pest because they felt it would be safer there. And vice versa. Dashing here and there, like goldfish in a bowl. With no sane choices."

Halfway over, the sun's golden sheen broke through, tracing a halo above a silver sky. Stopping to pull out the cap jammed into my back pocket, I picked up a sound, so faint that I did not understand it as my name.

Had there been any competing noise—so much as a gust of wind—this call would have been undetectable. We turned around. Near the foot of the bridge was a man dressed in a mismatched jacket and pants, appearing as a child playing dress-up in his father's clothing. Wearing heavy hobnailed boots despite the warmth, he crept forward, one hand clutching the guardrail while the other kept his pants from falling. His head, which was shaven, was disproportionately large for his shrunken body.

"That man. He's calling you, Béla. Do you know him?"

Staring, I dismissed him for a *schnorer* who knew me from the store. But in that muted voice there was an echo of a past utterly familiar. I struggled to find it, and then it arose. Of our house. Mama's candles. The Seder table.

I dropped Marika's hand and dashed toward the scarecrow figure. Chasing a fantasy. Hoping to grab on before he faded away. Before the present overtook the past. As I reached to clutch him, he fell into my arms like a bird shot from the sky. I hugged him, too hard, before understanding his fragility. As I kissed his waxy, yellowed cheeks, he observed me through flat, lifeless eyes. Marika hurried to join us, frightened.

"It's Miki," I choked out. "My brother Miki. My baby brother!"

Miki was unable to speak. I reached under his legs to carry him, but he resisted. We hobbled back to the house, with him leaning against me and my arm around his waist. At the doorstep, Miki gave up, and I lifted him and brought him to our bed.

I sat nearby for several hours as he slumbered in front of an open window under a thin eiderdown cover. At times, he would moan, or call out to Mama and Papa. When Miki awoke, Marika heated up tea, to which I added honey and then fed him with a spoon. I helped him bathe, cleaning off the filth and sweat that caked a body whose sallow skin was like melting ice cream. I discovered white eggs behind his ears, as well as on his eyebrows and eyelashes. Without a lice comb, I used my fingers to ply them off and squash them, their blood painting my nails red. This was a nightly task we had become practiced at while in the camps.

Before discarding his clothes, we searched the pockets, linings, and hems. In one of the pockets, Marika found a ragged red cloth patch, shaped in the form of a triangle pointing down. In the middle of it was the letter "N." Not understanding its significance, I placed it in a drawer next to his bed, along with his camp release papers.

Suspecting that Miki was anemic, we held up his head and spooned a piece of meat and morsels of egg yolk into his mouth, which he promptly retched up. Marika had the idea to serve him warm farina, cooked with boiling water. This led to a calmer rest.

Each day for weeks, Miki slept more hours than he was awake. Whenever possible, Marika attempted to feed him. Often after calling him to the kitchen table, he would respond and then fall back to sleep, with his eyes flickering like a telegraph key. An advantage of the farina was that Marika was able to prepare it within minutes. To

Chapter 42

bolster its nutritional value, she added cream or mixed in grated apples or jam. Cause for celebration was when Miki graduated to chicken broth with vegetables, followed by scrambled eggs.

Miki had difficulty concentrating. He would ramble and then stop in midsentence without explanation. He angered quickly, his emotional pipe bursting at the most trivial of misunderstandings. Our gestures were met with a numbness more disconcerting than his physical state. As if a part of him needed to fully die before the rest could reappear.

We treated his constant diarrhea with blackberry tea, and Miki gained weight. His alertness improved and his parchment-like pallor diminished. One evening, Miki said to me, "Mama, Papa, Ilona and her boys, and Libu, we all were taken together. Couldn't at least one of them also have survived?"

"I search every day for news, Miki. Every day."

While I worked, Marika, sometimes joined by Tibi, who had taken a brotherly interest in Miki, accompanied him on daily walks, first around the house and then through the neighborhood. Tibi told me of he and Miki once coming upon grazing red deer.

"Your brother stopped and stared at them for quite a while. Until the distant howl of a wolf sent them running. It was strange."

"Why?"

"There was a haunted quality to his expression. As if he were jealous of those creatures."

"Jealous?"

"Yes. For never having to experience evil so pure as to take away their will to live."

Miki would not speak of the German occupation while in the house, but at times when I joined those Saturday strolls, Marika and I learned more of his story. Of the roundups to the ghetto and then to the brickyard. Of the transport to Auschwitz.

Memory was no refuge, nor would Miki risk branding a false past in his mind through attempts to forget it. My brother communicated in generalities, which left Marika and me to read between the lines, choosing between truth and comforting rationalizations. One day, as we rested on a bench at the train station, I pressed for more.

"Do you know anything about what happened to Libu?"

"No. The men and women were immediately separated."

"You didn't see where she went?"

Miki turned his head in the direction of the screaming whistle of a train creeping toward us in a moonwalk, its engine headlights winking. The blood from his face drained as he watched the train, as if it were another transport. "Béla, you have no idea of what it was like. Or else you wouldn't ask."

"I want to understand."

Miki waited for the locomotive to come to a stop, in a hiss of steam and breath of hot oil and sulphur. "We reached Auschwitz in the afternoon. We saw only the specks of light that filtered through the cracks in the car walls. Smoke leaked into the car. I thought we were being engulfed in a fire."

Disembarking passengers streamed past us into the station. Miki stared at them, perhaps searching for someone who could confirm the nightmare. "We stood waiting for hours until the doors were slid open. Although it had become night, the horizon was red, as if painted with blood. Many began saying the Mourner's *Kaddish*."

"Papa?"

He buried his face in his hands. "I don't know."

I gripped his forearm, as I needed to hear this. "As soon as the doors opened, inmates in striped prison uniforms with shaved heads climbed up and shoved and kicked us, screaming in Yiddish that we must get out of the boxcar at once. As I jumped down, I noticed high wire fences and the glow of watchtower lights. We weren't allowed

Chapter 42

to take any of our luggage. They said it would be brought to us later. Through the searchlights I could see piles of bedding, clothing, and food. What may have been hours I remember as seconds. It was drizzling, and I was licking the moisture from my face. Alsatians were barking, straining against their leashes. The guards were screaming, *'Schneller, Schneller, Schneller.'* The children were bawling. Mothers wailed. I became deaf. I was kicked or hit with a rifle butt repeatedly. I ran to where they told me to go. I stood, and then I ran again, swept up in a crowd of men. We were driven to a bathhouse where they stripped us naked and shaved all our body hair off...."

His body shook, and he cried, a weeping without answer. Marika and I joined his sobs.

"I've already forgotten so much. I only remember Mama's white shawl as she stood on the other line. Then she was lost in the distance. I was trying to understand it all. To know how to survive."

"I'm sorry, Miki. So sorry...."

*

As the first summer of our freedom faded, the New Year came upon us. We listened to the blowing of the *shofar* (ram's horn), calling to mind the creation of the world. When Miki began mimicking the sounds with his mouth, I was reassured that, finally, someone lost had returned.

Later at home, we dragged chairs into the garden and celebrated with a jug of white Moravian wine, which Miki consumed with gusto. The time had come. Marika retrieved the red triangle from the drawer.

"Miki, what is this?"

He crinkled his forehead between the brows. "Where did you get that?"

"It was in your pocket when you first came back."

Miki reached for the badge and examined it, his hand trembling. I pulled the cloth from him and replaced it with a lit cigarette. He drew on it hungrily.

"Sometime late last fall, they marched us out of Auschwitz. We walked for days, without shelter and barely any food. Luckily I had worn my boots when they took us the previous May, and managed to keep them, because your footwear was your life. Many got frostbite in their feet, collapsed, and were shot. When we arrived in Rybnik (in southern Poland, near the Czech border), we were crammed into roofless freight carriages. I think the cars came from France, because they read on the side 'Chevaux' (horses). We were on the train for two more days. I had some potato peels on me. Otherwise, I would have starved like so many of them did."

"How did you get them?" I said.

Only when the glowing embers began to burn his fingers did Miki grind his cigarette out on the floor. He nodded for another, which I lit for him. "I traded cigarettes for them. Cigarettes were the most valuable currency in the camp. Even ones made from bark. And yes, some would rather smoke than eat."

Reflecting on this last comment, Miki exhaled a flood of smoke that would float to the sky and tell it stories. "On the second day, a *Muselmann* next to me, he closed his eyes and died. Without saying a word."

"*Muselmann*? A Muslim?"

"I don't know why," Miki said, "but that was the name used for anyone who had given up."

Despite the misery of the labor camps, I had never considered giving up. But would I have had Miki's strength to survive a concentration camp? "On his shirt was a red triangle, which meant that he was a political prisoner. I changed shirts with him."

"What does the 'N' mean?" Marika said.

"That he was from the Netherlands. The Nazis were meticulous recordkeepers."

Miki grasped the triangle, rubbed it between his fingers, and thrust it to the ground as if it were contaminated. "When we arrived

Chapter 42

at Dachau, all of us near frozen, I was placed with the political prisoners. We worked fifteen hours a day in a windowless armaments factory. It was dangerous work. We would finish large shells, pour in molten explosives, cap them using a wheel to clear the screw threads, and add the detonator. Stuff like that. Someone told me I was lucky, that because the Allies were closing in, in order to make us more productive, the Nazis had stopped the daily roll calls." He covered the top of his nose with clasped hands, as if in prayer. "In Auschwitz, they counted. Always the counting. For hours, as we stood silently. Even in the bitter cold. Near naked, while the guards were warmly dressed. Waiting for the *Selektion*."

The ensuing silence was frostbite, painting our hearts white. "So why did it matter that you wore the red triangle?" I said.

"As bad as we had it, those who wore the yellow star had it worse. We would often see the bodies of Jews who had been shot in the courtyard. Every day there were new corpses, covered with flies. They also did medical experiments on them."

Marika sobbed. Miki continued, "I don't know for how long I was in Dachau. By the end, there was no food. The last thing I remember eating was part of a field mouse that we caught. I was too weak to work and lay in the triple-decker bunk that was hard as steel, covered in mud, shit, and lice, waiting gratefully to be shot."

Miki stopped speaking and stared ahead vacantly. I leaned over to kiss him, which rekindled his narrative. "The next I knew, I was in a hospital bed. A nurse who spoke some German told me that I had been thrown into a pile of the dead in one of the freight cars. An American soldier had spotted me moving and pulled me out before the bodies were buried in a mass grave…."

I hugged him fiercely. "I can't imagine…Miki, how did you get to Munkács?"

"After a couple of months, as soon as I could walk, I insisted on being taken to the train station. But I was weaker than I realized. I could barely manage to get off the train. What would I have done if I hadn't found you?"

As if this memory triggered a chemical reaction, Miki dozed. "Marika, let's get him to bed."

I reached to help him out of his seat, but he opened his eyes. "No, I'm fine."

Marika stood. "You've had a long night. We'll talk more tomorrow." Marika picked up the triangle and dangled it. "Miki, do you want to keep this?"

"It's *dreck* (crap). Burn it."

"But it probably saved your life," she offered.

He pulled Marika's free hand toward him and kissed it, letting his lips linger. "You saved my life, Marika. You and Béla did. I knew that I would live, that I wanted to live, when I saw you both on the bridge." And with that, we opened a Riesling and imbibed until our memories were clouded, our wounds salved, and our calloused hearts flush with the grateful joys of the resurrected.

CHAPTER 43
Bergen-Belsen

If you could lick my heart, it would poison you.
— Itzhak Zuckerman, a surviving leader
of the Warsaw Ghetto uprising

Bergen-Belsen was a concentration camp located in a forest compound in northern Germany. A prison whose treatment of its captives was so depraved that it would be compared unfavorably even to Auschwitz. Bergen-Belsen's most well-known inmate was Anne Frank. Starving, covered in lice, suffering from festering wounds and typhus, and drowning in her own waste, she died there in late March 1945.

On April 15, 1945, after days of negotiation with the Germans, British soldiers from the 11th Armoured Division entered the camp. They found mountains of shoes and thousands of unburied corpses in various stages of decomposition, with rats darting among them, splayed in heaps throughout the camp. All interspersed with the living. Many had died from being given bread laced with poison by the retreating guards the night before. A week earlier, the authorities had severed the water supply, forcing prisoners to drink from rain puddles contaminated with excrement inches deep. The camp's stench could be detected ten kilometers away.

The British soldiers pushed cigarettes and sweets through the wire fence to skeletal inmates, including children, who dove at them. Despite medical care provided by the Army and Red Cross, including 96 volunteers from London medical schools, an estimated 14,000 died shortly after liberation, many "killed with kindness," unable to digest the food they were given. They were buried in unmarked mass graves, with the British forcing the SS staff to use their bare hands to handle those who had died of contagious diseases. (Many of those guards soon died themselves.) Civilians living in nearby villages were ordered to the camp to witness the interment of the dead.

The survivors were deloused and moved into the barracks of the German Army Training Center next to the camp. In July, six thousand of them were taken by the Red Cross to sanitariums in Sweden to recover.

CHAPTER 44

Jóska Ingber: September 10, 1945
(New York)

TELEGRAM

DEAREST BÉLA

YOU ARE NOT ALONE I HAVE FOUND LIBU AND WILL BRING HER TO THE UNITED STATES ADOLPH IS SAFE IN LONDON CONTACT ME VIA UNCLE LOU IN TRENTON DO NOT GO TO PALESTINE LET US ALL BE TOGETHER AS A FAMILY YOUR LOVING OLDER BROTHER

CHAPTER 45

Libu Ingber: September 22, 1945
(Helsingborg, Sweden)

My Beloved Béla, Marika, and Mikike,

I cannot tell you how happy your letter made me, the one you sent as an answer to mine.

You are alive! All of you! And so am I! And slowly recovering T.G.

For the longest time, I was cold, even in the heat, and could do little but lie in bed. Now I am warmer, but I will never again be warm.

Before, even the smallest piece of food was too much. Now I have regained some weight and can think about enjoying things other than food. I try to walk for at least a half hour each day.

I feel like one of those flatworms that we read about in school, whose head is cut off, only to regrow it. My hair has grown back, and I look and feel more like a woman. You can't imagine the pleasure I get from washing. It makes me feel that I can start living in the real world, rather than hiding in the world within me.

Chapter 45

This past weekend, we celebrated Rosh Hashanah. A rabbi came to conduct services. I am not ashamed to say that when he blew the shofar, I wept. Tears that blurred my grateful vision. We were given apples and honey, which I tasted with my entire body, along with some challah. They did not let me fast on Yom Kippur.

You know that Jóska is getting married any day now. To a woman named Suzanne Miller. His Army friend introduced them. She and her family are in the diamond business and Jóska says they are wealthy.

There is a dark evergreen tree whose crown reaches the flower box outside my window. As I write this, I am gazing at its pattern of branches.

Marika, I can hardly wait to meet you. I heard that you are young and beautiful. Please send a photo. I hope that we will be together soon and then we will not only be sisters-in-law but sisters and good friends.

I hug and kiss you all a million times.

Your loving younger sister,

Libu Ingber, circa 1946

CHAPTER 46
The Rape: September 1945

He who rides on a tiger can never dismount.
—Marianne Moore

    In the faltering days of summer, months of discussion had turned into debates with Marika as I struggled with when to immigrate to the United States. Miki and I held the same view—that to remain would betray an unspoken covenant with family.

    But in the illusory harmony of our new life, wallowing in the extraordinariness of the commonplace, inertia had set in. I no longer felt like a stranger in my own home. I was a partner in a flourishing business. More survivors were returning, some of whom I knew, a few who had been neighbors. Now they were dear friends, bound to me through common sadness. A hint of the former city had peeked through. Plus, I feared the potential downsides. The flight out of Russian-occupied territory would be illegal, and I could again face captivity. Being in America would require adjusting to different customs

Chapter 46

and culture, learning yet another language, and starting again with nothing. How many new lives were in me?

And so I disguised my inaction as strategy and fantasized spitting on the smoldering fragments of the Third Reich by staying in Europe and raising a Jewish family here. Since I could not love Munkács for the old reasons, I would find new ones.

On the Monday after Rosh Hashanah, Lenka and Tóni were manning the store. I had pedaled to a nearby village to negotiate with a farmer to purchase his cauliflower crop. The trip lasted longer than expected, as the road to his farm was muddy. Not to mention the ever-present barking dogs, bony and filthy, that needed to be circumnavigated. And once we were done, it would have been impolite to refuse his toast to seal the deal. My new friend's black-currant wine was sweet and plentiful. We drank to our health and that of the chickens. To his son, lost in the war. And, to my surprise, to Pollack's memory.

I returned to the store in the late afternoon, riding through lengthening shadows. As I was chaining my bike to the side door, a piercing shriek came from inside. I dropped the chain and charged up the steps. Bursting in, I came face to face with a startled soldier, a hammer-and-sickle pin on his lapel, who reeked of alcohol.

The Russian soldiers in Munkács were from diverse races. Some had monolids for eyes and sepia skin, while others were Tatars with fierce mustaches. A few were women, each without a trace of femininity. This man was a stereotypical Slav, blond and broad-shouldered with corded arms. His face, with pewter gray eyes that were bloodshot and a wide nose that was a web of ruptured capillaries, was distinguished by a jagged scar that spilled down his left cheek. The soldier balled his hands into fists and twisted his mouth into a sneer, revealing a capped gold tooth. Toni was lying near him, groaning, sobbing, and clutching his midsection.

Lenka was bent across the top of the counter, with her blouse pushed up to her neck, her bra unfastened, skirt up, and panties pulled down to one of her ankles. Astride her was a second soldier, his pants at his feet. His left hand was pressed against the scruff of Lenka's neck, while the other pulled back a fistful of her hair. He glanced at me as if I were a stray hound that had wandered into the store and then resumed, pumping away at his conquest with a vengeance.

"Stop!" I said in Russian.

The closer soldier moved toward me, his face now beet-hued, and snarled some garbled words that I processed as either "Get out" or "Fuck off." He was unarmed, although two automatic rifles lay on a nearby table.

"We are under the protection of Major Konstantinova," I shouted. "Leave now, or I'll report you to him."

The rapist, a smaller version of his comrade, groaned dismissively, accentuating his volume to add his own displeasure to his comrade's. Lenka's cries now were whimpers. He relaxed his grip on her, smacked her rear end to signal he was finished, and yanked up his pants. Lenka, keeping her eyes closed, pushed herself upright, only to be forced back down by the soldier, who motioned for his comrade to replace him. "Alexi," the rapist called, "I've warmed her up for you."

"*Spaseeba*, Boris," snickered Alexi. He pointed at me and then at the door, as he strutted toward Lenka, ogling her. In a flash, Tóni arose, jumped on Alexi's back, and dragged him to the ground. They tangled until the solider flipped over on top of Tóni and pummeled him. Lenka recommenced shrieking.

I thought to grab one of the rifles, but feared escalating the situation beyond control. Instead, I rushed to the grappling pair and attempted to drag Alexi off Tóni. This directed his attention to me, and he stunned me with a punch to the side of my head. Boris grabbed me from behind and pinned my arms. Alexi measured me for a blow, winding up his beefy arm, but I lunged with my right leg and kicked

Chapter 46

him flush in his groin. As he sank to his knees, he let fly a stream of curses. I flung my body as though possessed, throwing off Boris.

Boris and I faced off, each watching for the other's tells. He also kept a wary eye on Tóni, who now was struggling with the mutually exclusive tasks of helping his sister to dress while avoiding observing her. With rifles within reach, our potentially deadly confrontation was interrupted by the entrance of two young children and their grandmother. The woman glimpsed Lenka and yelled, "Police, police," as she yanked the children to a halt.

Boris screamed at her to shut up and leave. Needing no further encouragement, the family bolted from the store. Alexi rose to his feet, and the two retrieved their weapons. The Russians slung the rifles over their shoulders and, glaring at me, headed to the front door. They each grabbed a red-cheeked apple from a nearby produce bin and wiped it on their sleeve before kicking the bin over, sending an avalanche cascading across the floor. Alexi faced me as he bit into the forbidden fruit and let it dangle from his mouth. He drew a horizontal line across his throat with a flattened hand. Then they departed.

I raced over to a trembling Lenka, whose head was hidden in Tóni's shoulder. "I'm so sorry, Lenka. Should I run for a doctor?"

She shook her head. "I want to go home."

Tóni said that he would escort her. I told him, "Stay with her."

Alone, I grabbed a cigarette pack from the counter, locked the front door, and hung a "Closed" sign; then I slumped into a rocker in the corner. After chain-smoking half the pack, my heart rate dropped to normal. A banging on the front door propelled me off the chair. It was Tibi, returning from an afternoon with Gizi, still with the musk of sex about him.

"Why the fuck is the store closed?"

I related the events, after which Tibi retrieved a bottle of apple Pálinka and two snifters from behind the counter and laid them down on the table. His pours met the brim.

"Poor kid. I was fond of Lenka. Now they've ruined her." My friend had the rare gift of exhibiting a consistent persona no matter how much he drank. Except for the self-pity.

"You're such a sympathetic soul."

"Did you tell the *mamzers* (bastards) that we know the major?"

"Yes. They weren't impressed. I don't think the guy on top of Lenka lost any of his hard-on hearing your buddy's name."

Tibi drained the snifter and then slammed it down. "For all the money we slip Konstantinova, and all the times I've paid for drinks and gotten him laid, he owes us protection."

"Agreed. But these guys were drunk. This may all blow over."

Tibi filled my glass. "Who knows what Lenka and her crazy brother will do? If they go to the police, we will have to confront the Russians. The hell with that. Konstantinova runs this town. We'll tell him what happened. Let it be his headache."

As we drank, the conversation turned to Gizi, with the intensity of Tibi's accounts of carnal delights, described spiritually, dwindling in inverse proportion to his complaints of her persistent demands that they marry.

"I tell you, Béla, sometimes I think that lust is best enjoyed in one's imagination."

"Can it really surprise you that she feels a relationship that exists outside of when the two of you are *schtupping*? Or do you just keep relying on the whore's covenant to not show emotion?"

Tibi's take on life was narrow, as if he could view the world only through a sniper's scope. "She gets as much pleasure out of that as I do. Calling what we do 'love' doesn't make it all dreamy."

"Wasn't it you," I said, "who told me there's no pleasure without pain? That the apex of life is when the two meet?"

"You mean like fantasizing about a beautiful, naked woman, but not—"

Chapter 46

"I was thinking more of getting into a hot bath."

Tibi leaned his chair back precariously far and chewed his lip. "I said that? I must have been drunk."

"And wasn't it you who said that it's better to be burned than not to feel the fire?"

"Sounds like me."

"And that there's no such thing as free sex."

"I'm always willing to pay."

"Not her price."

"I thought Gizi was different. Not afflicted with the mental illness of 'romance.'"

I had once believed that Tibi and Gizi were from the same species—hungry animals who spun deceit as readily as they breathed, effortlessly enticing their prey and then devouring it. But there was more to each of them, so much more, as is always the case. Gizi could not give herself to Tibi as she did without at least the illusion of love. "If that were true, she wouldn't be a woman. And you wouldn't have wanted her."

"I do love her. As much as I'm capable of that. Maybe I can only love in the abstract."

Could it be that my friend found home only in flesh? "Don't bullshit me, Tibi. You're as able as anyone to love. What you're apparently incapable of is admitting—to yourself or to her—that you don't want her as a wife. Why? Is the mystery gone?"

"I don't need suspense. Life gives me enough of that. And she's been good to me."

"Is it her, then? Or that she's not Jewish?"

Tibi raised the snifter to his mouth but missed, and brandy trickled down his chin. "It's that she's been with every other guy in town, Béla. I can't get that out my mind."

"Even she was a virgin once. Gizi did what she had to. Anyone who didn't is dead."

He wiped the dribble with his sleeve. "So we're all prostitutes?"

Yes, in time, life makes each one of us a whore. "End it now, Tibi. For both your sakes. You can't be faithful to someone you want to be rid of."

"She says she loves me. And that we are meant for each other. What do you think of that?"

I shrugged. "All I know for sure is that I'm quite grateful my days at the *Kuplieri* are over."

*

The next morning, I arrived shortly before nine to open the store, only to be welcomed by shattered front windowpanes. On the floor inside lay two bricks. Taped to one of them was a note scrawled in Russian to the effect of "We will finish what Hitler started." I hurriedly removed all remnants from the window panes and swept up the shards of glass, crawling on the floor to hunt for any noticeable slivers before the first customers arrived. To those who inquired, I implied that we were undergoing renovation.

Tibi and Józsi each arrived near noon. I drew Tibi aside to show him the note. He brusquely told Józsi that we had business with the major, and the two of us hustled to City Hall, where an oversized red star had been mounted above the front entrance.

The usual queue prevailed, which Tibi was not able to circumvent. When we finally were ushered into to the major's office, I closed the door and recounted the rape, my intervention, and the smashed windows and then showed him the note. The major asked for certain details about the two soldiers. Then he opened his arms.

"How can I help?"

Tibi reddened. "What do you mean? You run this city. Order those bastards to leave us alone. Lock 'em up!"

"It's not so easy," Konstantinova replied flatly. "Not every soldier reports to me. And these two bad eggs are decorated 'war heroes,' which gives them some immunity. You're not the only ones they've harassed."

Chapter 46

His wandering gaze was unsettling. "Major," I said, "we are grateful for all you've done for us. Could you please advise how best to handle this?"

Konstantinova chewed on a thumbnail. "I could find their commanding officer and request they be reprimanded. After all, anti-Semitism is illegal under Soviet law." He winked at us. *"Der tayvl iz nit azoy shvarts vi men molt I'm"* (the devil is not as black as we paint him).

I glanced at Tibi, who was shaking his head in admiration. "So the major is Jewish himself."

"Only a quarter so. My mother's mother taught me some Yiddish phrases."

Tibi blew out a breath that rattled his lips. "So you're telling us that anti-Semitism is illegal but rape isn't?"

The major's glare was a weapon. "Rape is more complicated. Witnesses' stories will differ. But the note clearly proves anti-Semitism. Although not by whom."

Where was the blustering, self-confident major we had grown accustomed to? The one who handled every problem with aplomb? "Will a reprimand resolve this?" I said.

"No, it will make the situation worse. They play by different rules and won't stop until they've shed blood in revenge."

"Okay, Valery," Tibi said, "how much money will it take to smooth this over?"

Konstantinova aimed his index finger at Tibi. "You're my friend, but I'm warning you: Don't insult me." Turning to me, he said, "I'll give you my best advice, but it stays in this room. Understood? If you betray my trust, I'll become your worst enemy."

"You have our word."

The major rose and ambled to the window. "Things are changing rapidly in our lovely city. Greater control is now being exercised directly by Moscow. A political officer who monitors me has arrived."

With the blindfold now removed, Tibi's expression changed. He'd been kissing the wrong ass. The major continued, "I'll probably be transferred out of here soon, and they'll bring in a new commissar."

"I'm sorry to hear that," I offered. A condolence I meant.

"Such is life. Anyway, this matter has several implications for you gentlemen, beyond having to suffer with ruffians. One of which is that you'll have to deal with a lesser level of tolerance for your business. You see, at first, the Soviets were pleased to have people like you restore businesses throughout Eastern European communities. But when you get too big, hire too many employees, make too much profit, they accuse you of exploiting workers, and they confiscate your store. Successful businessmen often end up being shipped off to Siberia for their efforts."

"What's too big?" Tibi said.

"When booze, whores, and bribes become routine, and your gift of gab is ineffective. Because there's more value in seizing your venture."

Again, after gaining a semblance of control of my life, I am being forced to let go. "Can't we wait this out?" I said. "One day you Russians will leave."

"Yes," retorted the major. "And the Hungarian Stalinist toadies who replace us will be even worse. No private property will be safe."

"What if we join the Communist Party?"

"That might help on the margins. But you'll still be considered bourgeois."

"So we're screwed no matter what we do," I grumbled.

"Basically. So here's my advice to you both." The major paused to ensure our attention. "Leave. Now."

Tibi and I stared at each other, mouths agape.

"We just give up and run?" Tibi muttered. His inflection rising, he continued, "Two assholes come into our store, and we have to abandon all that we've worked for the past few months?"

Tibi pointed at the major. "It hurts you as well."

Chapter 46

Konstantinova drew a stubby cigar from his desk drawer and bit the tip off as he reached for a match. "That's the least of my worries, after what I've been through. Did I ever tell you that, of all the men I trained and served with in the officer corps back in '38, I believe I'm the only one still alive."

We nodded in understanding. The major offered us draws. Once more I learned from experience what should have been obvious: The shorter a cigar is, the closer the heat is to your mouth. "The best ones were taken in the night by the NKVD before the Nazi invasion, made to confess to high treason, and shot. Then came the great battles—Stalingrad, Kursk, and Smolensk—not to mention the fighting it took to claim this stinking country. And when I say I was in battles, I mean that I was at the front line. Stalin's military strategy has remained quite simple. 'I have more men than the Germans have bullets.' And if you didn't keep charging ahead, the political officers would shoot you."

Gray ash fell to the floor. "As for you two, you're not giving up," Konstantinova lectured, "you're being smart Jews who've come to realize that you'll never be welcomed here. That you'll keep getting raped, in different ways. That this country is quicksand, and the longer you wait, the more difficult escape will become. Until one day they ship you out to a forced labor camp in the East."

He lifted his thick-soled boots onto the desk. "Anyway, why would you want to stay in the shithole where your families were murdered?"

Because there once was love. But how could I explain that?

"To give the finger to all the Nazi-lovers who remain," Tibi snarled.

Konstantinova snapped back, "You want to let your pride overcome common sense? Okay, then, don't leave here. What the fuck do I care?"

"Where would you go if you were us, Major?" I probed.

He motioned with his rank cigar, part of which had dissolved in his mouth, to the window looking out toward the green weight of the mountains.

"Italy. That's where most refugees are going now. Once you've made it there, they won't send you back or kick you out. And I've heard that the transportation prospects from Italy to Palestine are good."

"How do we get there?"

"Go to Vienna. Locate the Zionist organization. They'll help you arrange transport to the Austrian border, to a spot where there's a pass leading into Italy."

"And if we get caught?" Tibi interjected.

"Don't. But if you do, it will depend on the guards. On the Austrian side, they sometimes can be bribed, so bring vodka, jewelry, cigars, sardine tins, and money. The Italian side is easier. They're not natural anti-Semites. Did you know that one of Mussolini's mistresses was Jewish?"

"That's supposed to make us feel better?" I said.

Konstantinova shrugged. "All their border guards are corrupt, so there's no need to fear them." He sneered, "Just remember to take along a wine bottle."

"And what do we do when we reach Italy?" Tibi said.

The major threw up his hands. "I don't have all the answers. Stay away from the British military police. I assume that the Zionists there can help you as well. If not, head for one of the United Nations' refugee centers. Or get to one of the port cities where the refugee boats leave from."

I wasn't sure which one of us I was sorrier for. Although my course of action was now clarified, and Marika would get her wish.

I pumped Konstantinova's hand. "Thank you, Major. You're a *mensch*, and you've been quite decent to us." The major and Tibi faced off plaintively, and then embraced in a bear hug. Tibi said softly, "What will become of you, Valery?"

"I'll be okay, as long as I don't piss anyone off." He handed the note back to me. "That's why I don't prosecute fellow soldiers for crimes

Chapter 46

against civilians. Of course, one day that attitude will change, and the next soldier who rapes will be shot. As will any superiors deemed complicit." He stood in front of the portrait of Stalin and half-bowed. "The key to survival in our socialist paradise is ascertaining on which day such a shift in policy has occurred."

*

Tibi and I trudged back to the store. He could not find a voice, but I knew his thoughts. Our carefully crafted truths had been shattered. Reality remained on the other side of a window shade now open, taunting us to glimpse it.

After relaying our conversation to Józsi, he snickered. "We were fools to think all this would work. To hope for the hopeless. We will be respected as human beings only in a country of our own. In Palestine!"

Instead of reprimanding Józsi for his pessimism, Tibi whispered, "Maybe." I told Józsi that Marika and I would follow the major's advice, leaving unspoken our intention to immigrate to America, to avoid a lecture.

That afternoon, we shuttered the store, now the bastard child of our fantasies. With Józsi's help, we divided up the cash and valuables among the three of us and Tóni, who also received the entire remaining inventory for storage in his basement. (Tibi dropped off with the major's adjunct a box of Davidoff hand-rolled Cuban cigars, obtained on a recent trip to Geneva.)

"I can't manage the store on my own," Tóni said.

I repeated what the major said. "A successful store is in danger of being taken over. Sell the inventory on the black market." We hugged, for longer than I was comfortable with. "Take care of your sister. And yourself."

Lenka was, according to Tóni, threatening suicide. She had taken to lying in bed, unwilling to accept visitors. We left a cash gift for her with Tóni. I vowed to reunite with them someday, an assurance admittedly made without true commitment. I could not hold on to a place, and a people, who wanted me to go.

Persistent pleading over the next few days could not convince Józsi to depart with us. He was determined to wait in Munkács for a full year before accepting his family's fate. I was tempted to remind him that Jewish tradition does not approve of excessive mourning (which is why embalming is forbidden). We were taught that the highest principle of ethics in Judaism is not love, but justice, and to grieve too much is to question divine justice. But I did not believe this gratuitous logic any more than Józsi would have.

After obtaining a death certificate for Ilona, Józsi ended his vigil and immigrated to Palestine. Thereafter, my sporadic contact with him dwindled. One day a package arrived, the last communication that I would receive from Józsi. In it was a colored-pencil depiction of Ilona, her eyes dull and stare distant. And the following note:

My Dear Béla,

I cannot bear that every year, my recollections of our treasured Ilona fade. Not the love that she and I shared, which is fixed in my heart. But her voice, her laugh, her touch. Those details become harder to recall. Maybe for you also?

I still reach for Ilona through a veil of sleep that only exhausts me, and mistake other women for her, to my embarrassment and theirs. Her kindness and devotion should be enshrined in my sons, may they rest in peace.

My beloveds were too innocent to survive by themselves. And I was not who they needed. Because there wasn't enough strength in my love to protect them. Or perhaps it was that I did not show my love sufficiently to make Ilona fight harder to stay in this world.

I await the next life, where my loved ones and I have never parted.

I remain your devoted brother-in-law and friend,

CHAPTER 47
Escape: October 1945

What we call the beginning is often the end. And to make an end is to make a beginning. The end is where we start from.
—T. S. Eliot

In our last hours in the house, which I had left to a returning survivor, we packed. I bound together a pile of letters sent from loved ones whose fingers had caressed them and whose tongues had sealed the envelopes, together with photos. I also stuffed into the rucksack folders of stamps, many with a swastika watermark, hoping they would have some value one day. Miki made room in his bag for a variety of black-market items. Marika carried with her a silver hip flask that had been her father's. As I stood in front of my house for the last time, I blew a kiss, deep enough to free myself from it.

We left Munkács on a midnight train. Marika sat self-hugging between Miki and me, as we had heard stories of women flinging themselves off moving trains to escape the intentions of Russian soldiers. Tibi was not ready to leave Gizi, although he would soon trace our route out of Eastern Europe, following our dream if not his.

We stopped in Budapest to say goodbye to Rózsi and Klari. In spite of the vast improvement since April, much of the capital remained uninhabitable. Rózsi had reopened her store, and people now could commute to it by streetcar, although she complained of limited materials and too few paying customers. Their apartment building had been partially restored with a working lift, new windows, and reinstated water lines that operated sporadically.

We dined on potatoes, strands of chicken, and sugar cookies, with Klari apologizing for baking them with powdered eggs and margarine instead of butter. I contributed a bottle of white dessert wine that I had bartered for at the Budapest train station, prying out the cork with a knife. We ended the evening with soulless toasts to our health and the future. After Marika and I retired to a makeshift bed in the living room, Miki, who had never been in a major city, excused himself to discover the remnants of a past nightlife, drawn to it like a moth to light. In the morning, Marika hugged both women, Klari longer than Rózsi, and promised to write frequently.

Following the major's advice, we headed for Vienna. On the train, after Miki had left us for the bar car, I asked Marika why her stepmother and stepsister expressed no interest in joining us.

"Budapest is all they know. Their work is there. Their whole life."

"That's true of us as well if you include Munkács."

"They're afraid, Béla. I am, too. I wouldn't have the courage to do this without you."

"They wouldn't be alone. They'd be with us. I think they resent me for rescuing you from them."

"You didn't rescue me. I'm not Cinderella!"

"Well, you're as beautiful as she is."

Chapter 47

"Rózsi isn't wicked. She took care of me when I needed help. I think she was a good mother to me."

"You think?"

"I can hardly remember my own mother, so who do I compare Rózsi to?"

Marika was staring out the window, her face opaque as if wearing a closed motorcycle helmet. "Marika, I understand that Rózsi was only a stepmother to you and couldn't be expected to love you unconditionally like she did Klari. But if there was any love, it would hurt to leave her."

"Does unconditional love even exist?"

"Absolutely. And I'm sad that you never felt it."

Marika moved close to me again. "But I have you, Béla."

I kissed the top of her head. "And I cherish you, Marika."

When we arrived at the Austrian border, Russian soldiers climbed onto the train and forced all the passengers to line up outside for an inspection of their possessions and papers. The equivalent of ten Reichmarks was demanded of each person, although many paid with jewelry or watches. Or, in our case, with Miki's premium vodka.

Ferencz had taken me to Vienna a month after Hitler's ascension to Reich Chancellor, in celebration of my twentieth birthday. We spent our days traipsing to pastry shops and coffeehouses, where newspapers were displayed on custom-made stands, men played cards, and waiters wore tailcoats. At night we shifted to taverns, sampling local wines and waitresses. Now, amid the filling of bomb craters and clearing of rubble, the city teemed with displaced persons.

Through word of mouth, we located the Jewish DP camp in the aging Rothschild Hospital, which only months earlier had been a Nazi military infirmary. The massive building, structurally reminiscent of the Budapest hospital where I was operated on, now was supplied by the U.S. Army and the United Nations Relief and Rehabilitation

321

Administration (UNRRA) and was home to hundreds of refugee families. We were vaccinated for typhoid, fumigated for lice, and given pea soup, pastry with raisins, and milk.

In the hospital yard, we made contact with the Bricha ("flight" in Hebrew), an underground organization formed by Zionist partisan survivors from Eastern Europe, which had ties to the Haganah and the Jewish Brigade. (The Brigade was the only military unit to serve in World War II in the Allied forces as an independent, national Jewish military formation with their own emblem. These troops, comprised mainly of Jews from Palestine, participated in the final battles on the Italian front as an arm of the British Eighth Army and remained in northern Italy after the war to assist refugees.) Our plight was a familiar one, although the large majority of the Bricha's clients were Polish, German, or Austrian. With financial assistance from the Joint, we arranged to join one of the guided groups to Italy.

We waited ten days, each longer than the one before. Using money earned from the store, we bedded down in a hostel rather than the hospital, where multiple families shared a single room, toilets overflowed, and the daily ration now consisted primarily of canned meat, over salted as if cooked in seawater, reheated acorn coffee, and brick-hard black bread slices slathered with butter. Our journey could begin only when there was a full moon to lay a silver pathway and the expectation of a cloudless night.

As the days grew shorter, I checked in each morning, choosing to ignore the pitying assurances, until we received instructions to arrive at the hospital by lunchtime with our belongings. The three of us, together with twenty or so others, piled into an army truck for a bumpy, winding ride to Gschnitz, a village south of Innsbruck, surrounded by dairy farms and dung-scented cow pastures, only a stone's throw from the Brenner Pass. We were told that we had traveled into the French occupation zone and that England had been increasing pressure on the French to

Chapter 47

halt the exodus of refugees to Italy, concerned that they would continue on to Palestine. There would be no leniency from the border guards.

We met our guides in the late afternoon in the backroom of a stone tavern near a Baroque parish church, where they were engrossed in a game of dominoes. On a trip to the restroom, I spotted, up high in a corner alcove, the faint remains of a painted *sig rune* emblem, a testament to the Nazi Party's ubiquity.

After beef soup covered by a golden glaze served with stale coffee, we were introduced to our lead guide, a fiery, shaven-headed Italian in his thirties in a maroon leather jacket. Following the Munkács tradition of giving nicknames to anyone deemed odd, Miki labeled him "Mussolini," despite his bushy mustache. Skipping pleasantries, Mussolini commanded in quicksilver, mangled Yiddish, "No talking, no whispering, no smoking, no eating, no drinking, no coughing, no sneezing, no farting, no belching." I translated for Marika, taking the liberty to add, "No tact, no manners."

Our coxswain, who communicated through outbursts not requiring a megaphone, marched from person to person, slapping the back of his right hand rhythmically against the palm of his left and eliciting an affirmation to, "When I tell you to shut up, there will be no sounds whatsoever. Understood?"

Marika gripped my forearm, her breath caught in her throat. "Béla, I don't have a good feeling about this. Maybe we've made a mistake. How do we know if this crazy man can lead us through the mountains? Or that he won't turn us in for a reward?"

"I have no reason to trust him. But I trust the Bricha."

Miki chimed in, "Many have done this before us, Marika. And more will follow."

Beads of sweat gleamed from her forehead. I put my arm around her. "I won't let you down. However I need to, I'll make sure we're okay."

In the dusk's purple afterglow, as if the sky were on a dimmer switch, we lined up with our knapsacks behind Mussolini, now wearing a slate-gray balaclava. He admonished us to stay together at all times. A second guide brought up the rear. My contribution was to name him "The Goat," in honor of his peppery white goatee set against his tanned potato head. One couple brought their infant girl, who had been given sleeping pills. "If she wakes up," Mussolini instructed her parents, "Hold her mouth and nose shut until she turns red, and then let go for a few seconds so that she can take a breath."

At first, the pace was relaxed and the terrain flat. Then the path, which followed an old rail line, turned rocky and steep. We crept single file, holding onto a twisted rope anchored on either end by Mussolini and The Goat. I kept Marika positioned between Miki and me. Rounding a bend, Mussolini cupped his hand over the front of a tubular flashlight. "Complete silence now, not to be broken for any reason!"

Under the pitted moon, a night light tempering the curtain of darkness, we climbed among the overlapping gray-streaked shadows. I would reach out to caress Marika's shoulder, or she would grasp my hand, which I would rub, squeeze, or kiss, each gesture our private code. Weighed down by our bags and without sturdy boots or walking sticks, our steps were clumsy.

Marika wore a Loden wool coat, with leather buttons, that Miki had bartered for. As for me, the coat that Tetzi had made for me, which caressed me through the last brutal winter, had disintegrated. I wore only a thinly lined jacket over a cotton vest. So intense was my shivering that I imagined the sound of it alone could be detected.

At one point, the trail narrowed so that we were required to cross it sideways, our backs pressing against rock. The line moved in spurts. A pebble knocked around maddeningly in my shoe. Cued by nature's orchestrator, boreal owls hooted. Startled, I halted. As Marika tugged my hand, I cursed my weakness.

Chapter 47

Traversing a stony patch, someone up ahead sent a large rock over the edge of the black earth, and it rumbled down the belly of the mountain. The line froze, and we took a collective breath. The corset of silence was strangling. But soon after resuming, the quiet was replaced by noises from Austrian sentries below. Relieving themselves. Laughing. Bantering. I could eavesdrop on their staccato voices. Our footsteps seemed as loud as if we were walking on crepe paper. Was it possible that we would not be discovered?

We trudged ahead, and after several hours, interrupted by periodic rests, the path plummeted steeply and gradually widened. We reached a clearing, at which point Mussolini and The Goat each plopped down, turned on their flashlights, and tore cigarette packs from pants pockets. "We are outside Brennero, in Italy," Mussolini announced.

Marika, Miki, and I embraced, my wife shedding tears for the three of us. After the break, we walked a mile to a makeshift cabin, from which flew the tricolor Italian flag. There to greet us were men and women of the Jewish Brigade, wearing uniforms embellished with a gold Star of David on a blue and white insignia bearing the words "Jewish Fighting Force." We collapsed on mattresses for the remainder of the night, in a blackness pierced meekly by the embers of a crackling fireplace.

As the night departed, we ventured outside into an evanescing mist and the welcome of a lake that soon would mirror light like a shattered crystal plate, embraced in a chilly stillness. The senior member of the Brigade introduced himself as Lieutenant Hardy. He was a giant of a man who sported a white handlebar moustache with tusk-like ends framing cheeks pink from rosacea. Elsewhere, his mocha skin was wrinkled from overexposure. A Star of David tattoo adorned his densely veined forearm. He pumped our hands and, in Yiddish with a pronounced British accent that elevated his words, congratulated us on taking the first step toward making *aliyah* to Palestine. With forested peaks in the backdrop, we celebrated our escape with tins of scalding coffee that warmed our hands, and cold toast with marmalade spread thick enough to coat our mouths.

Under the amber glow of a sun that lovingly presented itself to us, the lieutenant began singing, in a deep baritone, "*Kol 'od balleivav penimah....*" And so, in choked voices plaited together, we chanted of our two-thousand-year-old hope to reach the land of Zion.

As I sang, I reflected on the last time I had intoned the "Hatikvah," at the Jabotinsky rally. On that night, my entire family was within my grasp. I then could dream of all of us reuniting in Palestine and singing this anthem together. Now, after years under the yoke of the Hungarians, Germans, Romanians, and Russians, all I knew for certain is that at thirty-two, sustained by precious ones at my side, I would start my life anew.

Marika in Italy on a Jewish Brigade motorbike, 1945

CHAPTER 48

Jóska Ingber: November 27, 1945 (New York)

My Dears,

I wrote to you only a few days ago and here I am writing again. I am going to receive your immigration papers in about a week and will send them to the American consulate in Rome. I hope that you all have already submitted your names for the quota. I will not rest for a minute until we can all be together.

I will try to send a package every week, and in my next one I will send the medicines you asked for and also vitamin C. Write to me about what else I should send, maybe things you could sell there for a good price. Also write Marika's sizes so we can send something to her. I know that a girl needs a lot of things. Always have a trustworthy address we can use.

My dears, please be patient. Remember that you are not alone. Adolph and I will help you with everything we have. Each of you should learn some kind of a profession and a little bit of English because this way it would be much easier for you here.

Béla, I beg you to watch yourself and keep your diet strictly. Only if we are healthy can we hope for a better future.

Here there is nothing new. Both of us are working, but so far only Suzy is making any money. It will take months before my new business will make a profit. Hopefully, Libuka will arrive here from Sweden next month, so now we are very busy looking for a new apartment, which is terribly hard to find. Currently, we are living in a small flat. When Libuka and you all will be here, then Adolph will also come. For now he can stay in London; he has a good life there. I wouldn't like him to go back to Palestine.

I am surprised that each of you writes so seldom to me. Did you run out of ink? I do not believe that you all are so busy.

That is enough for today, soon I will write again. I kiss you. Suzy sends kisses to you all too.

Your loving older brother,

Jóska Ingber and Suzanne Miller, 1945

CHAPTER 49

Libu Ingber: December 15, 1945
(Motor Ship Stig Gorthon)

My Dear Beloved Siblings,

I am writing this from the ship I boarded on Wednesday in Goteborg. Two of my girlfriends came to see me off, which felt nice because I had at least people it hurt to leave.

This is the ship's first voyage. It was finished only two weeks ago. I have a cabin which I share with a Swedish woman, and we also have our very own bathroom. There are only six passengers because this is a "freight ship." My fare was paid by the Mosaiske Union, so I spared Jóska $300. I still received $100 from Jóska to have some extra money.

This is my third day on the water. In the first two I was lying in my bed all the time like a corpse. The waves were fearsome. Everything was flying from one corner into the next and I had to hold myself to the bed to keep from falling out of it. I believed that I would never live to arrive. But I started to feel well yesterday. I suspect everybody has to go through this. The trip to New York is supposed to last for two weeks and a day, more or less, depending on the weather.

Can you imagine how happy I am that after such times, and such a long time, I soon will be able to see at least one of my siblings again. You are the ones who can understand best how I feel at this moment, what America means to me. At home, we were only able to dream about it, but now the reality seems like a dream.

Did I tell you that Jóska has arranged a job for me in America? His best friend, who he sailed to America with, has a sister named Georgette Klinger. She runs a famous salon in Manhattan. Lots of celebrities go there. I will be one of her students.

We are about to arrive at a Scottish harbor, where I will post this letter. I will not be very far from Adolph and still we won't see each other.

My dear Marika, why didn't you also write in Béla's letter? And from now on, you will send letters to me to America!

I hug and kiss you a million times.

Your loving sister,

CHAPTER 50
Italy: 1945-46

Return, O Zephyr, and with gentle motion
make pleasant the air and scatter the grasses in waves.
And murmuring among the green branches
make the flowers in the field dance to your sweet sound.
—Ottavio Rinuccini

After two days recovering in Brennero, surrounded by a natural splendor that nourished, our group was transported to Venice. The last leg of the trip was by boat. As we leaned over the bow railing, the stone buildings of the city of lagoons surged upward. A place of decaying grandeur relatively unaffected by the war, we stayed there while identity papers were secured.

The three of us were housed in a second-floor apartment located in a piazza accessible through a narrow alley. Our building, studded with black top-hat chimneys that slanted to one side, was bordered by canals on two sides. The air smelled of camphor, used by our neighbors to ward off mosquitoes. Below us, stagnant water reeking of algae and sewage hazily reflected the city, its picture broken repeatedly by the slash of oars.

We walked by men in uniform who were friendly. Watched rowdy neighbors sit in a semicircular balcony lit by candlelight, passing around bottles of red Cinzano and plates of sliced cheese. Listened to the gondoliers who stopped to serenade with mandolins while perched on the noses of their boats. Nothing threatening, yet we could find little comfort here.

Our days were spent meandering through the ensemble of bridges and canals, lost in the city's labyrinth, recognizing its miracle. In one piazza that we stumbled upon, a crowd had gathered around young male and female singers accompanied by string and woodwind musicians. Poetic madrigals flowed from the group, who swayed gracefully as they performed. During one rhapsodic ode, honoring the west wind that brings spring and the opportunity for romance, the music's fluid swings of emotion brought me back to the congregational songs of my youth. Frozen in place, I carried its melodies for days.

On the Calle delle Botteghe, we passed a storefront displaying a variety of masks. Several reminded Miki and me of the one that Ferencz had worn to frighten his sisters on our family's last Seder. We stood pressed against the window.

"They make me uncomfortable," Marika said. "Aren't they hideous?"

"No, they're works of art," Miki answered. "Look how they differ. Maybe they're from theater productions, each a different character."

"Sure," I countered. "And we know who the masks with long, pointy noses are supposed to be."

"Let's go inside," Miki said.

"No," insisted Marika, pulling us away. "The store owner will take one look at us and know that we don't have any money to buy anything. He'll ask us to leave."

Chapter 50

Days later, I asked one of the UNRRA staff about the masks. "The reason for their creation centuries ago," he said, "was so a state inquisitor could question anyone, even noble citizens, without either of their identities being discovered. Citizens could answer without fear of retribution. With no faces, everyone had a voice."

If we all wore masks, might anti-Semitism be impossible? With identity shielded, wouldn't all persons be equal? But, no, men return to their natural state, as an abandoned lawn turns wild. The red masks would conspire against the blue ones, the jolly masks battle against the frightening ones, and the full-face masks persecute the upper-face ones, and so on. One would remain unprotected from the compulsion to hate. And from the immutable law of physics that everything seeks to victimize everything else.

*

Leaving Venice after several days, Miki, Marika, and I were assigned to a group traveling south through idyllic towns and vineyards near the endless shores of the immense Lago di Garda. We stopped in the village of Sirmione, hopping off our truck near a pier filled with fishing craft surrounded by swans as white as angels' wings, moving with a skater's liquid grace.

Again, we played tourists. While Miki chatted with a local female artist who spoke broken German, Marika and I wandered to the tapered spit of beach, rocky and curving. Marika clung to me as if she would float away like a balloon if she lost her grip. Under a searing sun that burned through clouds riding high, we strolled barefoot with rolled-up trousers along the water's edge, overstepping seaweed and smashed seashells. In sight of a Roman castle with moats and a drawbridge, we lost ourselves in the rhythmic lapping of the tide as its curling waves nestled playfully around our feet and then rushed away leaving traces of foam.

"Breathe in, Marika. Aren't the smells so different here?"

"I love them."

Our final destination for the day was Cremona, a panoramic city thick with violin workshops and churches clustered around an ancient piazza. With time to spare before meeting **UNRRA** officials, Miki suggested we climb the hundreds of steps to the top of the nearby medieval cathedral's colossal bell tower.

"No, thanks. You go. I'll watch you exhaust yourself."

As Marika and I sat on chairs beside an alfresco café, she dozed against my shoulder. Lieutenant Hardy strolled over. Seeing that I was intrigued by the astronomical clock on the face of the tower, he launched into a whispered explanation of how this mechanism tracked the location of the sun in the sky and phases of the moon. Lost in his esoterica, I remembered only his boast that I was viewing the largest one in the world, reminiscent of the Old Town Hall Tower in Prague, where on the hour a trapdoor opened and Christ marched out triumphantly ahead of his apostles. According to legend, Prague's councilors had the clock master's eyes burnt out with a hot poker so that he could not repeat his work, a parable of hypocrisy and futility.

I turned my gaze to the Madonna sculpture on the facade of the cathedral, tenderness frozen in the gentle trace of fingers across her baby's back. We had scarcely been in this open-air museum of a nation and already the magnificence of its creations overwhelmed. Had we Jews been mistaken in not also depicting throughout our history the beauty and power of G-d? But beauty and power also have their demands.

"How could there be such splendor and the Nazis in the same world?"

My question was rhetorical, but the lieutenant answered it. "There's a difference between physically exquisite works and true representations of G-d's love. Have you read Freud?"

"His books were missing from the labor camp library."

Chapter 50

Hardy forced a smirk. "Culture is the result of our suppressed drives."

"How so?"

"Freud says that man is fundamentally evil. That he needs to be domesticated by society and to have his drives suppressed. Without that, we're not civilized. The more suppression, the more culture."

"So you're saying that a Nazi can't create great art?"

"Exactly."

"What about Richard Wagner? A world-class anti-Semite who they say was the first Nazi. He wrote great operas."

"Yes, because he wasn't able to act on his evil impulses." I thought of Józsi, who in one of his final letters to me had described the memory of Ilona, Feri, and Marcel as "all the beauty that remains in this world." He would have spit in the lieutenant's face.

I shrugged, sending Hardy ambling away. Marika awoke. Miki waved to us from the top of the tower, smiling broadly. Does his light-heartedness reflect what he feels, or is it now a learned reflex? Was it a betrayal to Mama, Papa, and our other siblings for us to enjoy life? Not that I was yet living, only moving through space.

After being dusted by a hand pump containing an insecticide, we were lodged in a schoolhouse that had been converted into a field intake and eligibility office for displaced persons. The following day, we were interviewed to prove our Jewishness to the satisfaction of UNRRA staff. Were we Nazi collaborators? Had Miki or I been active Hungarian soldiers? I schooled my interviewer on the forced labor camp system, and Miki educated him on the concentration camps, but he was assuaged only after we passed his infantile test of our knowledge of Jewish holidays and customs. We were accepted and would receive UNRRA's assistance. The next morning, our group was driven five hours to the Cinecittà camp directly south of the Eternal City.

Cinecittà had been a cinema complex, created before the war by Mussolini and his fawning admirers in the film industry. Initially intended to promote propaganda, by the start of the war Cinecittà had grown into one of Europe's largest movie studios. Employing more than a thousand, with sixteen soundstages and a network of streets and piazzas, gardens, and flowerbeds, it remained in business. Having produced as many as sixty films a year, it allowed for art and entertainment to coexist with mass murder. When the Allies liberated Rome in 1944, Cinecittà, although damaged by bombings, was chosen to serve as a holding station for thousands of the displaced.

Had we not gained perspective from our years of suffering, living in Cinecittà would have risked descent into madness. We were gathered within faux buildings and colossal sets with backdrops ranging from Roman temples to French boudoirs. Two thousand stateless souls, a hodgepodge of nationalities, were housed in improvised cubicles subdivided with pasteboard, wood planks, or sheets. Most of the *profughi* (refugees) were teenagers or younger, orphaned children with heavy-lidded eyes in mannequin faces. Before coming to Cinecittà, many had sold themselves or their siblings sexually in exchange for food. Their inerasable pain exposed our own, yet they cocooned themselves from it, and from our kind gestures.

Marika and I were assigned a "room," adjoining Miki's. Lying on beds of worn cotton mattresses and thin blankets, sans bedsheets, we enjoyed a view of the elaborate nervous system of the structure—a ceiling crisscrossed by bridges, ladders, and cables that seemingly shifted with every glance at it. Our possessions lay in cupboards built of vegetable boxes, our clothes hung from nails. The three of us could not leave together without also taking them with us.

Around us, within fluttering laundry drying on lines, were filth and disease, yet only the desperate ventured into the hospital, with

Chapter 50

its grave shortage of doctors, drugs, and equipment. The heat was as if the skin of the sun was bleeding into us. And our drinking water had to be obtained from collective containers.

"Béla, I can't drink this water anymore," Marika said at the end of our first week in Cinecittà. "It smells like rotten eggs."

"I know. But they say it won't make us sick."

"Easy for them to say. They can go home and drink real water."

"So do what I do. Drink the coffee instead."

"Then I won't sleep. And I'll be living in the bathroom, which also smells."

"The soup isn't bad."

"Yes, it is. It's watery, and it still smells. And the potatoes are over boiled and look like glue. And the bread is slathered with pork fat that makes me nauseous."

"Me too. And whenever we're served meat, it's charred black and tasteless and hardly worth the long line we have to stand in to get it. But let's just be thankful to have any food."

Given all we'd been through, boredom might be considered a gift, and yet it was our most pervasive antagonist. We faced hours of forced leisure, playing checkers or cards, reading weeks-old food-stained newspapers and magazines, or listening to humorless Yiddish programs on the Voice of America. Waiting, always waiting, for packages, news, paperwork, and information on when we would leave. Stuck at a broken red light, and powerless to change it.

But Miki would not be contained, seizing any morsel of control. He delved into the thriving black market of the DP camp.

"What kind of stuff are you selling, Miki?"

"All sorts. UNRRA supplies. Extra rations. Red Cross parcels. The best items are filtered cigarettes. That's why I asked Jóska to send me cartons of Chesterfields and Lucky Strikes."

"How do you know what to charge for them?"

"I learn from others. Everyone's doing it. I mostly swap for higher-end stuff, like stockings, meats, chocolates, and liquor. Those you can trade up for diamonds and hard currency."

"If everyone's doing it, how do you compete?"

"I'm better than most at faking empathy and exaggerating without outright lying. Plus I have one big advantage, which you have also."

"Charm and good looks?"

"The ability to converse in just about any language needed."

In early December, a letter from Herbert Lehman, a prominent American Jew and director-general of UNRRA, was distributed, wishing all those in the camp a happy holiday season. (Years later I would vote for Lehman to become U.S. Senator from New York. This conformed with my established method of voting, to first check for the most Jewish-sounding name and, absent any qualifiers, to vote Democratic.) Two weeks later, posted in the dining room was a directive issued by Harry Truman mandating preferential treatment under U.S. immigration laws for all displaced persons—a reminder of the fundamental idea of America. We cheered, hailing this as the president's Hanukkah present to us.

A feature of the American immigration program was the "assurance," a promise from an American sponsor that the displaced person would be provided employment and housing for his family. After receiving our housing and employment affidavits from Jóska in late 1945, we arranged to receive International Refugee I.D. cards and to be transported by the Jewish Agency to the American consulate on Via Veneto in Rome. But the first open date we could book was in late March.

Days before leaving for Rome, we celebrated Purim in the camp. That year's merriment was particularly raucous. The campgrounds were laden with handmade paper tombstones for Hitler, who was hung in effigy alongside Haman. We refugees flipped the Führer dummy upside down, mimicking Mussolini's fate, before beating it piñata-style.

Chapter 50

My exuberance was sobered. Equating the hanging of Haman with the demise of Hitler was a cruel, papier-mâché analogy, as Haman had been prevented from realizing his wicked goal.

The consulate was in the Palazzo Margherita, a Renaissance-style grand palace. Near the entrance was a centuries-old fountain with a richly detailed statue of the Greek god Triton effortlessly blowing on a conch shell to spout water. Through French windows lay an emerald lawn on which stood a sculpture garden studded with marble heroes.

Halfway up an oak spiral staircase that wound to the second floor, under a frescoed dome, we encountered a statue (whose plaque dated it as two thousand years old) of Venus emerging from her bath, her long dewy hair braided, attempting with both hands to preserve her modesty. I stopped to admire the serene, symmetrical exquisiteness of her face. Miki caught my eye. Smirking, he quipped, "I knew you were a breast man."

Buzzed into a room with ceiling-to-floor bookcases lining the walls, we were greeted by "Professor" Richard Fuchs, who rose from behind a drop-front desk. He pumped Miki's hand and mine and kissed Marika's. Middle-aged and bespectacled in half-glasses with fingerprint-smudged lenses thick as paperweights, he spoke in a Western Yiddish dialect, stressing vowels comically.

"Sir, my wife doesn't speak Yiddish. Would you please speak slowly, so that I can translate for her?"

He reviewed our papers and said, "You are brothers, born and raised in Czechoslovakia, correct?" We nodded, and I ignored the technicality that in the year of my birth Czechoslovakia did not yet exist. "And she was born and raised in Hungary?"

"Yes."

"This is somewhat unusual. Thankfully, you've each survived and made it here. But I must be frank. It may take time for all three of you to obtain United States entry visas."

While the professor stopped to allow me to translate to Marika, Miki ran his hands through his sweating hair and spit out, "What do you mean? Our papers are in order. How much longer will we have to wait?"

"I'm sorry. I'm not sure." He shrugged.

"How can this be?" I snapped. Marika, breathing faster and shallower, placed her hand on my arm. "What about President Truman's directive?"

"People misunderstand that decree," he cautioned. "The current U.S. immigration laws establish quotas for each country. But these limits are based on the nationalities resident in the U.S. decades ago, before the wave of immigrants arrived from Eastern and Southern Europe—"

I interrupted. "What does this mean for us?"

"It means that you'd be a lot better off if you were British. The entire yearly quota for all the Eastern European nations amounts to only 39,000, two-thirds of which are allotted to Germany. And under the law, in any single month the number of visas issued cannot exceed ten percent of the annual quota. A pittance given the million-plus refugees in Europe, most of them natives of Central and Eastern Europe and the Balkans."

I did not translate these last remarks to Marika, but Miki's savage kick to the leg of the desk was translation enough. I patted her fidgeting hand.

"So I'd be better off if I had been a German concentration camp guard than a Czech inmate," Miki snarled.

The professor removed his glasses and chewed abstractedly on one of the frame ends. In a tone softened and slowed, as if he were a plantation owner reading the Bible to his slaves, Fuchs said, "Listen, there's hope here. I have some flexibility for what we deem 'hardship' cases. Particularly with regard to you two fellows."

Chapter 50

I translated his first two sentences, weasel words and all, then said, "And my wife?"

"You brothers are from a country that was occupied by Nazi Germany and aligned with the Allies." He paused to push his clouded glasses back up his nose. "Your wife, on the other hand, is from a country that joined the Axis, so for her it's more difficult."

The incision cut even deeper. Did the professor not consider Marika sufficiently Jewish because she didn't speak Yiddish? "So let me get this straight," I bellowed. "My wife, who had to go into hiding for months, who was hunted constantly, in danger every moment of that time, is treated as if she had fought in the Hungarian Army alongside the Germans."

He bobbed his head sheepishly. "Yes, that's the rough illogic. But please, I want you to know that we have greater discretion for brothers of a U.S. citizen who fought in the war for the U.S. Army. That carries much weight."

He hesitated. "Béla, would you consider going to America first and having your wife follow later?"

His words decayed as he spoke them. "How can you ask me that? I'm not going anywhere without my wife!" I had stopped translating and avoided eye contact with Marika. "Just help my brother. I want him reunited with our siblings."

Miki opened his mouth to protest, but I motioned for him to stop. The professor touched his fingertips together, forming a steeple. "I'll need some time to work on your cases. My secretary will give you appointments to see me again in a month. I should have made some progress by then."

Every one of my chapters seemed to end with torn pages, while I waited to live the life meant for me. We shook hands and left. Once in the lobby, Marika pulled at my arm. "Béla, what did he say? Tell me the rest of it." I reviewed the untranslated parts of the conversation.

341

Her hands trembled. "Will you leave me?" Kissing and hugging her, I swore that she wouldn't be able to rid herself of me so easily.

Standing outside the building, waiting for our ride back, Miki stepped between Marika and me and grabbed our shoulders. "We've come this far together. Let's stay together."

"Miki," I answered, "if you can get out of here, you should. We'll be right behind you."

"I'll think about it." He pursed his lips, pulling his brows together. "But one thing is not negotiable. We don't live in that DP shithole anymore. I've made enough money for us to rent an apartment in the city."

We left Cinecittà within the week and moved to a one-bedroom apartment with a separate living room on the Via Carlo Alberto. Our building was within walking distance of Rome's imposing National Stadium. I still could hear Ferencz regaling me with stories of the 1934 World Cup final played in that arena, capped off by his bitter complaints of how the officials had stolen the match from Czechoslovakia in favor of the host country.

I encouraged Miki to rekindle his dental-technician studies.

"It's not for me," he insisted. "I like the sales business."

"Why? Just because you need to do it now to make some money doesn't mean it's right for you."

"No, I've known I wanted to do it for a long time. You remember the restaurant that Abrahámovics ran on the Korzo? The police kept coming in and ordering food and beverages and not paying for them. Then the gendarmes closed it down. I knew that he should have found a Christian partner. If he was too old to manage it anymore, I could have done so silently on the side. I kicked myself for not offering that to him."

"But why not develop a skill? Dentistry is a good profession."

"What do you know about it, Béla?"

Chapter 50

"Not much. I've never been to a dentist. I always used string and doorknobs to fix tooth problems." Actually, that was not the entire truth. Once, in the camp, I had a cavity filled with candle wax.

"So let me figure it out for myself."

Miki and I became regulars in the market on the nearby Piazza Vittorio, hawking goods such as nylon stockings that we had obtained from HIAS or received from Jóska or Adolph. (Adolph by now had changed his name to Oliver and asked that he be referred to as Oli. Why Oliver? Because his girlfriend's girlfriend had suggested to him that he resembled Lawrence Olivier.)

Like yarn on a loom, one month stretched into four. Our meetings with the professor were sporadic and his faux sincerity increasingly grating. When Miki and I received an invitation from a cousin, now living in Paris, to visit him, I insisted to Miki that he accept, hoping that, once there, Miki could more easily apply for a visitor's visa to the U.S. Jóska would send funds for the transatlantic passage.

On a day in July with the humidity spitting at us from buildings and pavement, Marika and I accompanied Miki on the metro to the Termini train station, which was in its final stages of construction. Marika insisted on joining us in spite of ongoing fatigue and nausea from a lingering virus.

We sat on backless chairs, below a vast, iron-laced vaulted ceiling, in the central room, where the air was trapped in our chests like wet cotton balls. Our sweat-soaked necks, which we fanned with train schedules, glistened as Miki chattered. "This past year has been quite something, no?"

Marika's eyes reddened. Miki grabbed her hand. "Marika, we'll all be together again soon enough."

"Right after my little brother has had time to explore Paris—and its pleasures," I said. Miki uncovered a broad smirk. I smacked his back, not out of shared passion but in gratitude for the return of his soul.

As we waited, Marika clenched and unclenched her fists. When the arrival time for his train was posted on the board in the center of the room, she leaned against me and wept. Again, Miki gripped her hand. "Marika, remember how far we've come. You and Béla are happily married, I'm back to health, we've heard from three of our siblings who are your family now, and we'll all be reunited in America."

Dabbing her eyes with a saturated handkerchief, Marika sobbed, "Everyone abandons me."

"What do you mean?" Miki and I shouted in harmony.

"My mother left me when I was five. I was shuttled from aunt to aunt for years until my father remarried. Even then, he was in no hurry to take me back, not coming to visit before he did. Then he was gone forever." She stared into a blank space between us. "I know from experience. When someone I love leaves, bad things happen."

"You have me now, Marika," I said. "I will never leave you."

Miki kissed the top of her head. "I'm not leaving. I'm just going on ahead. This time is different, Marika. My heart tells me so, with certainty. G-d could not demand any more from us."

Marika smiled weakly as Miki, his feet sliding in monk's sandals, bounded toward the gate. "There will be a happy ending this time," he called over his shoulder. And I thought to respond, "Haven't we learned that happiness only brings His ire?"

Marika and I remained on the platform, continuing to wave even after the train was out of sight, as if we were toddlers who had been dropped off in day care. Near the station exit, she bent over and raced to the restroom. Marika returned pale, her eyelids heavy. One hand clutched her abdomen while the other wiped her mouth.

The following day, at a clinic supported by the Joint, Marika was examined by a female physician who told her, "I can't yet be sure, but I suspect that you're pregnant." As she made this announcement to

Chapter 50

us, the doctor's voice was tinged with joy, appearing to reflect a view that all of life's purpose was procreation.

Her diagnosis soon was confirmed. On the following Sunday, Marika and I woke early, celebrating the news with coffee and halvah on the Via. We strolled to the walled Villa Ada Park, where we followed a shaded path bordered by white-streaked hosta, breathing in the scent of a carpet of pine needles. As if on the edge of falling into a dream, we came upon a lake reflecting weeping trees cast upside down. We rented a canoe. I was both the bow and stern paddler, my strokes cutting the murky water and splashing us. Marika gripped the sides of the canoe with every sudden rocking movement. Slender ospreys wheeled above us in search of prey, their wings flat as ironed collars and forming an M-shape. Passing the hollow stalks of a jumble of reeds, we glided to a secluded corner thick with algae. I kissed my bride's hand and praised her loveliness. "Thank you for your faith in me, Marika. For accompanying me on life's journey. And for blessing me with a child."

Miki, Marika, and Béla in Venice's Piazza San Marco, 1945

Here was yet another beginning. And a sign that we must, at all costs, carry on.

CHAPTER 51

Miki Ingber: October 12, 1946
(New York)

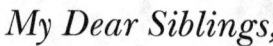

My Dear Siblings,

For sure you cannot have any complaints about me because I am writing to you frequently. When I arrived here from Paris I was sick, scared, and depressed, but I recovered soon.

We will be very sorry if you don't come out to America before the baby is born, but even in this case you shouldn't despair. We will support you as much as we can. We will send you a tenner every week. Sadly, we are too green here to be able to send more.

New York is as huge as a small country, with as many people, buildings, and cars. And so many are Jewish, including policemen. In the biggest restaurants, they serve you in Yiddish. There are programs on the radio in Hungarian, Yiddish, Czech, and any other language, all day long. So this is like the whole world in one city.

Jóska is so talented. He was born to work. Imagine that he started without a penny and today he has a successful office. And he is so good to

Chapter 51

us. It is as if he is our father. Did I tell you that he taught me to drive?

He and Suzy get along perfectly. Suzy has three older sisters. The oldest, Sterry, came to the United States before the war with a rich American who met her while he was on a tour of Europe and fell in love with her. Suzy and another sister, Regine, emigrated in April 1940. They had been booked to sail from Antwerp, where the family lived, in May of that year, on a ship that made a single voyage to New York each month. Then they decided to move up their departure by a month, to the day of Suzy's 21st birthday. Three weeks later, the Nazis occupied Belgium. Suzy's parents were taken to Auschwitz.

She and Jóska met because Jóska's Army buddy had a picture of her in a photo album. Jóska saw it and asked to be introduced. When he met Suzy, Jóska thought she was rich because she had a good-paying job in the Diamond District as a cutter, spoke French, and wore expensive-looking clothes.

Béla, Jóska will probably hire you to work for him. He plans to rent a storage facility and is counting on you to take charge of it. He also plans to hire me possibly. If I get married, I will have some money to add to his business capital. There is going to be an "Ingber" Co. in New York one day.

My Marika, it has been over a year since I was eating fried goose liver with onions and peppers in your kitchen. I went through a lot since then but still it seems as if it was only yesterday. The little remaining time that you have to spend in Italy will fly away just as fast.

I also am writing to you both discreetly about myself. I am looking for a wife. You know how I love girls. But the only way for me to stay here is to get married to an American citizen. I am now courting a pretty and intelligent social worker at Mount Sinai hospital. I met her when I went there for treatment for dysentery and bad stomach problems. Her father is the president of a big company and now she is working there. She is his only child. Her parents escaped Germany before the war, with only the shirts on their backs. They owned a hotel until the Nazis came and gave them five minutes to get out. Her parents are typical Germans—very selfish. They live only for themselves.

She and I have agreed that we will be each other's, but her parents know that I must get married, so they do not trust that I love her (which is actually true). So I don't know yet what will happen. But the girl said that she is not going to ask her parents' permission. I cannot say that her parents are against it, as they only asked me to wait awhile.

Jóska and Libuka met the girl, and we all have been together several times. They like her a lot. It is also true, though, that I brought several other girls to see them. After all, you know me. But with this girl, I believe there is money there, because if I would know that there isn't, I would move on.

My dear siblings, we would give up our chance of heaven just to see you here.

Now I think I wrote to you everything. You should also write.

I kiss you a million times. With much love,

CHAPTER 52
The Bells of St. Mary's: October 1946

There is no trap so deadly as the trap you set for yourself.
—Raymond Chandler

Our first year had passed in a country that was safe but not home, requiring constant adjustments to changed circumstances. Marika was approaching her third trimester, but Miki was no longer here to keep her company and make her laugh. Instead, each day, she waited in a sparse apartment while I mingled in local markets selling goods, typically purchased with rations or received on consignment, to buyers desperate for them. When I returned home, our conversation inevitably began the same way.

"Béla, you were gone for so long. I was worried."

"Sorry. How are you feeling?"

"Better, now that you're back."

Marika's pregnancy had been difficult, exacerbated by a lingering rash cured only by a prescription cream. Magali Devita, our kindly but meddlesome *vecchia signora* landlady, insisted that Marika take vitamins, but such a luxury we could not afford.

One Sunday morning, I was at the table, blowing on the surface of a scalding cup of coffee and reading Miki's latest letter. Hearing Marika's footsteps, I thrust the letter in between the pages of a local newspaper.

The paper's headline trumpeted the news of the Nuremberg trial verdicts. Twelve high-ranking Nazis had been sentenced to be executed, including Goering, who committed suicide the night before his execution, refusing to relinquish his position as master of death. But I was angered that many of the other defendants missed the noose, including seven sentenced to prison terms and three who were acquitted.

Marika was fully dressed. "Béla, I can't stand being stuck anymore in this room. Can we do something? Maybe go to a movie?"

"A movie? But whether it's in Italian, or dubbed in English, you won't understand it. We could just sit in the park."

"I don't care. As long as we get out of here."

Marika now became winded easily while walking. We strolled aimlessly until stumbling upon the Nuovo Cinema Palazzo, a palatial theater built during the war. Marika pointed at the poster near the ticket window, which depicted a nun and priest, each appearing saintly. "That's Ingrid Bergman, isn't it?" Marika said.

The marquee was framed by a ring of bald, yellow bulbs. "Yes, and Bing Crosby. So I guess there will be singing."

"I'll like watching her. Let's go in."

And so two European Jews, who spoke no English and knew nothing of Catholicism, sat through *The Bells of St. Mary's*. We arrived shortly after the opening credits, with the only available seating in the first two rows. Scanning the audience on our way to our seats, their expressions left scant doubt of their readiness to suspend reality in a manner I could not do.

Chapter 52

From what little I understood of the plot through body language and the action, it seemed childish. But I enjoyed the chemistry between the main characters. Bergman's real life, I later learned, had some similarities to Marika's, as both had mothers who died when they were young and had been raised by relatives.

Bergman was mesmerizing. In her Hollywood fabrication, I beheld Sister Zsuzsa. During a scene where she was singing in front of the other nuns, I glanced at Marika, who was humming along.

Afterward, we sat holding hands in a nearby park, piecing together the movie as best we could. I mentioned the person who Bergman's character reminded me of, telling Marika of my experiences with Sister Zsuzsa.

"You were so lucky," she said. "How frightening that must have been."

"Hollywood will make a great movie out of it," I teased, "once we get to the States and I tell everyone. Should I insist that Ingrid Bergman play Sister Zsuzsa?"

I had mistaken her calm sullenness for contentment. "Béla, stop with the joking and tell me—will we ever get to America?"

I recently had finished the arduous application process for immigration to the U.S., including having the two of us submit to background checks and health screenings. I kissed her forehead. "Of course, we will."

She shook her head. "Don't say that if it isn't true." She added, "I'm young, but I'm not a child."

Her words were a noxious ring of smoke. Didn't she understand? Some burdens must be carried in one's own heart, shielded even from a spouse. I smacked the wood slat furthest from me with my palm. "*Hock mir ein chinick* (constant prattle)! If you're not a child, then why do you keeping asking me that same question? You think I don't want to get out of here as much as you do?"

She looked down, swallowing a response. "Tell me about Miki's letter."

"He's doing well in New York. He says that it's as big as a country, and that everyone lives well there."

"Great," she responded sarcastically.

"And Jóska is very successful and about to make a lot of money."

She tried to hold back, but the dam burst. "I'm sorry I asked about the letter. Why do I want to hear this?" Marika let go of my hand. "They're all doing well, while we're stuck here for who knows how long. Me sitting alone in a stifling room all day. You running to the American consulate all the time, for nothing. Us dependent on your black-market trading to survive."

"Is our situation their fault?"

"No, but if your brothers and sister are so wonderful, as you're always telling me, then why aren't they helping us more?"

"They send money."

"I mean helping us to get to the United States."

"They're trying. I know they are." Was I seeking to convince her, or myself?

"How do you know? It sounds like they're busy making money and having fun. Even Miki, who knows our circumstances well."

Why is it such a struggle to celebrate each other, even those we're closest to? "They're living their lives. What else do you want them to do?"

"Help us! Use some of the money they're making to get us out of here. Béla, do you want our child to grow up among strangers?"

"No."

"Should we reconsider Palestine?"

"It's too difficult to get there."

"You just won't be apart from your family, at any cost. Maybe Miki would join us in Palestine?"

"No, Jóska is helping him make a life in America. And there's one more thing."

Chapter 52

"Suzy is pregnant?"

"No. Not yet anyway. Miki says that he's courting a rich American girl who he might marry."

"Soon they'll all be rich. And we'll be forgotten!"

Marika had penned my anger and frustration. Or was it shame at my powerlessness? One thing was clear. Nothing made sense anymore, except to rage against our unfulfilled desires. Through letters, my thorns reached out to draw blood from those I loved. Letters that I regret sending.

CHAPTER 53

*Libu Ingber: November 1, 1946
(New York)*

My Dear Beloved Siblings,

    We received your letter and really I don't know how to answer it. I know that we do not write frequently but Miki writes at least every second week and I also write into it a few lines.
    It was terribly hurtful that you wrote to us that all we think about here is having fun. I work from morning until evening and every Wednesday until 8 pm. Then I come home, cook, wash, and clean and I am so tired I can hardly stand on my feet and cannot wait for the moment when I can finally fall to bed. All I get from this is that I have enough to eat, but I must be careful even with that. If I want to buy something I have to save for it. I go to bed crying, thinking that it is not worth it and this is not how I imagined my life. I don't want to complain. After all, I can't blame anybody for my situation. But if I believed it would stay like this forever, I would despair at the unraveling of my dream.

Chapter 53

To make matters worse, I just came back from Trenton. I read there the letter which you wrote to Aunt and Uncle, and to be perfectly honest I got so mad. You were complaining to them about us! What they do for us you will see with your own eyes when you are here. They are good as long as it doesn't make them reach into their pocket. When we were talking about you I asked if they could pay for your boat ticket. Our aunt promptly declared that she won't pay for it, and that we should ask the other relatives. So I told them what I thought of them and I am not going back to them any time soon. On the other hand, Jóska would have paid for it even if he would have had to borrow the $600. He would do anything for us. There is no other sibling like him.

Yet you write to Uncle that you do not expect anything from your siblings. We are as mad as you are that we are unable to send you visas. Ask for your Czech quota number and write it to us and we will try to get information in Washington. Any one of us is willing to travel there if that would help your case.

But I want to write cheerful words as well, so thank you, thank you for the two photos that came with your latest letter. I love remembering my high school graduation. The one of our dear parents made me cry, but now I can talk to them every day.

As I told you, I work in a beauty shop. I receive $25.00 for a week. I'm not able to live on that, but am supported by Jóska. But... Dayenu, I must be satisfied if I think back to where I was last year. The miracles in my life make me trust that next year we will be reminiscing about this year's events together.

Béla, take good care of Marika and do not make her nervous also. We are all so glad because of the child to come, and you should be working on being happy about that, since we know what true unhappiness is. All the hardship now is like May snow, soon to be forgotten.

Promise me that you shan't write a thoughtless letter ever again, because if you would truly mean these things I would be very disappointed in you and it would upset me terribly. I know that one day you will be sorry that you wrote such words.

I kiss you both with love,

CHAPTER 54

Miki Ingber: November 4, 1946 (New York)

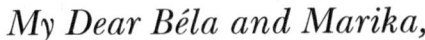

My Dear Béla and Marika,

We received the letter you wrote on the 24th of last month. I was very sorry to see that you paid our caring attention back with ungrateful words and assigned blame to us. How can I do anything from here about people stealing your mail over there? I will send this letter to HIAS, but now I am afraid they are going to steal it even from there.

I strongly ask you not to be angry with us. No one but your siblings truly cares about you. We do whatever is humanly possible to do and give everything we are able to afford for you. You write as if it would be our fault that they don't provide you with a visa. Remember, I wanted to stay with you and we would come over together but you insisted that I go ahead. Béla, I am sure that you wrote when you were in a bad mood.

Believe me when I say I wish I would have never come to America. You know that I came here illegally, and now they are harassing me for it. I never wrote to you that when I arrived here I was arrested for three days. I am telling you about this so you won't think we are constantly having fun. There are many other bad things, but I won't write to you of them because they are shallow puddles compared to the horrors I have known. And I know that you have enough troubles of your own.

We will send rubber stockings to Marika on Monday via airmail. Write to us what else to send. Perhaps it would be a good idea to send cigarettes?

My Marika, I would be sorry if you also believe that we are unfaithful siblings. Béla, promise me that you will make up with us.

You two take care of your health. My Marika, you have a duty to the child.

Write frequently, but write peaceful letters. I kiss you a million times,

CHAPTER 55

Jóska Ingber: December 7, 1946 (New York)

My Dear Siblings,

Finally I have some time to write to you. You cannot imagine how busy one can be here and especially after starting a new and difficult business. Know that you are always in my thoughts.

You think we don't do anything else but have fun, but you are wrong. In America only the very rich can have fun all the time. Lately, I have needed to put all my energy into my business. If I am doing well then you will also be doing well and all of our siblings too.

Béla, why do you ask me what to call the child? If he will be a boy naturally you should name him after our father. In English I think it would be Coleman. With Marika's father's name as his second name. If I remember it, Marika's father's name was Antal so you should call him Coleman Anthony. Here everybody has two names anyway. If she will be a girl then you should call her after our beloved mother, which is Esther in English and in Hebrew as well. This is a beautiful and well-known name here. And of course give her Marika's mother's name, Malvina, as her second name.

Are you are asking me this because you are considering a non-Jewish name? If this is so, aren't you ashamed of yourself for even thinking such a thing? We were born Jews and that is what we are going to remain and if you would remember our dear ones this wouldn't even occur to you. I ask you not to mention this anymore because Libuka is reading your letters and you would upset her.

Marika dear, now I would like to write to you a few lines. You are going to have your birthday on the 27th and you will be coming of age on that day. So I wish you many, many happy years to come, together with Béla, and may you have plenty of children. We hope that next year we will all be here together to celebrate your birthday. I am sending $20.00 in this letter. Out of this, $10.00 is for you, Marika, to buy a gift.

We are all T.G. well. Suzy is not working anymore and if we could find a suitable apartment we would like to have children. Libuka is well, only unfortunately she is always sad, even though I try to give her everything. Miki, I think, is disappointed in America because he thought that he would make at least $100 his first week here. He is young and too carefree. So far he hasn't got a job.

Have you learned some English? If you would know how important that is here then you would study English day and night. I could have had Libu working for me from the moment she arrived if she could have spoken some English.

We are going to send a package for the baby in a few weeks' time. I kiss you with lots of love. Your older brother,

CHAPTER 56

Miki Ingber: January 27, 1947 (New York)

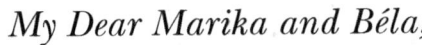

My Dear Marika and Béla,

You may congratulate me. I asked for Inge's hand in marriage this Saturday. We will celebrate the engagement next weekend among the closest family members. I can tell you that I am very happy.

We will be married on the 16th of next month. When I was in Inge's house the other day, I was telling them tales about you. I am sorry from the bottom of my heart that you can't be here for the wedding, but I know that you will be with us in spirit as you, Béla, have already written to us because you knew this might happen.

We are not going to have a big wedding. It will be held in a small family circle. Only her parents, Jóska and Suzy, and Libuka. Around noon with a rabbi we will have the usual ceremony, then lunch in a restaurant, then late in the afternoon we will leave for our honeymoon. We will go to the mountains for a week (the old folks are paying for it).

I want to ski all day and in the evening feast on the greasiest, tastiest meat.

So, my dears, you can understand how excited I am now. The whole family will be together on Saturday night and we are going to write to you together. I will also ask Inge to write to you a few English words, even though I know very well that all it will be for you is a riddle, but it will also be a good language practice.

Béla, you will have your birthday on the day before our wedding, and I wish you lots of happiness. Every day now we are waiting for the telegram from you saying that the baby has been born. Libuka told me that she dreamed that you had a baby boy. Well, we will see.

Miki Ingber and Inge Mitchell, 1947

We found an apartment last week, one bedroom, a kitchen, and a bathroom. As of yet, I do not know how much dowry they are going to give to me, at least a little one for sure.

By this time all my acquaintances have heard the news. Everybody is congratulating me. As a groom I feel fine, but I am nervous because I don't know how I will feel later. I think I am making an advantageous marriage, and the circumstances are such that I must do so. I know it will be hard for you to imagine me as a married man.

I am sending a few bad photos with this letter. Next time, I will send better ones.

I wish you good health and send millions of kisses,

P.S. I am going to write to you again later this week!

CHAPTER 57
Esther Malka

Woe to us that we have already come to remember, because memories are the hard shell over an empty heart.

—Yehuda Amichai

Upon arriving home from the Rome hospital with Esther Malka (Malka means "queen" in Hebrew) light in my arms, we were greeted by a sign on our door proclaiming, "*Congratulazioni per il vostro nuovo bambina!*" A basket, to which a pink balloon wafting above was tied, had been placed on our door mat by Mrs. Devita. Piled in it were stacks of freshly washed cloth diapers and hand-me-down knitted baby clothes.

From the start, as I entered our apartment, my first words to Marika often were, "She's crying. Why don't you pick her up?"

"I'm tired. I just changed her. And she's been fed."

Grabbing Esther up in my arms, I would say, "She needs comforting. Did you try rocking her?"

"Béla, you're home now. You try."

"It was a nice day today. Why didn't you take Esther out in the carriage that Mrs. Devita lent us? You could have met other women with babies."

"How am I going to meet anyone when I don't speak Italian?"

Jóska's latest letter sat on the kitchen table, awaiting response. Should I again tell him that I don't have time to wait for those visas? That Marika is not taking to motherhood as I had expected? She needs help with Esther. And I need help with her. Jóska, I'm not impatient. I'm scared. Should we have waited to become parents?

But no, I wanted—needed—to have children. To honor my lost ones. Although listening to my daughter's delicate cries, I could not help but reflect on the reality that all our baby would receive from her grandmothers were their names. She would never bathe in their attention, be soothed by their comforts, be nourished on their praises, or absorb their feminine insights. Nor would she experience our fathers' strength, confidence, and wisdom. None of our parents would be present in Esther's life to press her against them so tightly as to allow their hearts to meld. To multiply exponentially her own parents' love.

It would fall to Marika and me, while learning our new roles, to fulfill theirs as well. Only twenty-one-years old and still waiting for her own youth to begin, Marika had no memories of being mothered. But I carried with me Mama's embrace.

CHAPTER 58

Jóska Ingber: March 5, 1947 (New York)

My Dear Béla and Marika,

Yesterday we received your last two letters, and they made us exceptionally happy. We wish you much nachas with Eszterke. We all would love to see photos.

I am sending here a document that you should mail in right away (or take it in yourself) to the American consul. Hopefully, this will expedite the other visas. Since you have one already, Béla, they must give visas to Marika and the baby.

We are T.G. well health-wise and, as Miki and Libuka probably have written to you, we are expecting a child in early September. I cannot say much about Miki's wedding. It was a small one. Miki is a lucky boy that he found such a good girl like Inge, who we all love very much. Miki is not working but soon he will start.

Béla, when you arrive, I will help you get on your feet. Do not worry, as long as I have something to eat you will always have food on the table.

Write about everything and as often as you can. I kiss you many times.

With brotherly love,
P.S. I send extra kisses to Eszterke.

CHAPTER 59

Oli Ingber: March 25, 1947 (London)

Dear Béla and Marika,

I received your letter and am answering you right away.

You know, of course, about Miki's wedding. For sure he shouldn't have married. He could have waited 5-6 more years for it, and I believe this was Jóska's fault. When Jóska was here in London he was also saying to me all the time: "Get married, get married. What are you waiting for?" But I am not an idiot, and if you would know who he wanted me to marry you would laugh—it was an older Polish girl with a face like a gargoyle.

I could have married during my time in Palestine. I loved a Sabra, and she loved me. She was beautiful, a swan in a duck pond, although in an exotic way. Also artistic and intelligent. But it wasn't my time to marry. I wasn't ready.

Miki could have managed to stay in America in some other way. This was a wrong step, because first Libu should have gotten married and it would have been Miki's job as a bachelor to take her around, out to coffee houses, and everywhere else to meet eligible men, but now it is all over.

Libu wants to come here to London. She is impatient and hard-headed. No matter how much the others are talking to her she doesn't want to listen to anyone. Here they give you everything in exchange for stamps and points but you cannot buy anything with money, except on the black market. No, I do not think that Libu would like this situation at all and she will turn around and go back right away. In the meanwhile she would have lost her job and apartment over there.

The only reason for me to stay here is that I have been seeing a woman named Mary for several months now. She is a Gentile with some means and connections. She bought me an expensive silk scarf with patterns for my birthday and also a necktie and matching handkerchief. For Christmas she gave me a silver and gold cigarette case bearing both my name and hers.

Write soon.

I kiss you all, with many kisses just for the baby,

CHAPTER 60

Jóska Ingber: April 17, 1947 (New York)

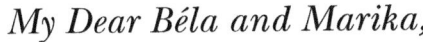

My Dear Béla and Marika,

Here we are impatient because Marika and the child still haven't got their visas. Béla, what are you going to do if they do not get their visas before yours expires? If they do not get them by the end of this month, then wouldn't it be a good idea for you to come over first and they will come after you? If you lose your visa at this point, you will have to start the whole process all over again. On the other hand if you are already here maybe it will go faster for them. What does the consul say and the HIAS?

Sadly, I have aggravation with Libu. She doesn't want to accept her situation. She is constantly in a bad mood and is writing to Oli that she is unhappy.

I do feel bad for her. If not for the war, we would have made sure that she spent her days going to teas and balls and flirting with young men and generally having fun. I have made sure that she is perfectly taken care of, but Béla you know what she is like, how she keeps everything to herself. This is rather painful for me because now that we are together we should be, must be, joyful. If she goes to London, it would cost a lot of money for Oli and there are a hundred other places that money would be more useful.

Write soon and as much as you can.
I kiss you many times,

CHAPTER 61
The Saturnia: May 1947

Girl, girl, I want to ask of you
What can grow, grow without rain?
What can burn and never end?
What can yearn, cry without tears?
— From "Tumbalalaika," a Russian Jewish folk song

Three months after Esther's birth, on the thousandth pull of the one-armed bandit, the cherries aligned. Under the weight of an uncovered peach sun offset by a Gulf breeze, Marika, Esther, and I set sail from Trieste, an unobtrusive location wedged between the mountains and Adriatic Sea where, only recently, Satan again had wiped his mouth with human lava.

We were third-class passengers, along with hundreds of other immigrants from an amalgam of Eastern European countries. The cost of our journey had been covered by the HIAS. Our ship was the *Saturnia*. Built twenty years earlier, it had been converted in 1935 for use in bringing transport troops to Italy's colony in Eritrea, from where Italy later that year attacked Ethiopia. By 1942, the tables had turned, and the ship was chartered by the International Red Cross for evacuation voyages from East Africa. After the war, the Italian government reestablished the Italia Societa di Navigazione, known as the "Italian Line." Steamships were refitted for service on a route from the Mediterranean to New York.

I won't complain about the conditions on the *Saturnia*. We hadn't expected better. Though I may have to correct my grandchildren's perception that we enjoyed the same atmosphere as that depicted in the *Titanic* movie that Marika dragged me to a half-century later. On the *Saturnia*, steerage travelers heard no musical instruments expertly played. No one offered beer and spirits to be generously imbibed. For entertainment, we lay in bunk beds with creaky springs in an airless cabin, sucking on lemons and speculating on which of us would vomit next.

Time on the ocean, as in Cinecittà, was plentiful, with languid moments among the harshest. At night, roused by the baby's cries, I would watch Marika breastfeed her. Other times, while the ship heaved and swayed, I studied the rise and fall of Esther's delicate chest as she sucked on a rubber nipple with her pink, detailed lips, taking in life like a dying plant absorbs water. What right had I to spawn? Would I be able to keep her safe? I had no assets, education, profession, or illusions. My comfort lay in the awaiting cocoon of my family. And a confidence that Mama and Papa remained close.

Esther was a chubby, alert baby. I diapered and washed her as I had watched Mama do with Miki and Libu, cleaning our few cloth diapers as best I could absent an ability to boil them. Esther would lie contentedly on my lap, turning at the sound of my voice and giggling at my whistles. The first time Esther returned my smile, I pressed her to me and cried, "My *Mamaleh*, I wasn't supposed to be here. And now you are here, too."

Between naps, with the baby now holding her head without wobbling, I showed Marika different ways to engage with her. Together,

Chapter 61

we sang "Tumbalalaika" to our newborn as I squeezed each of Esther's curled fingers.

"I know the words to the song, but what does it mean?" Marika said.

"It's just a silly love song, with a sweet melody."

Marika considered this. "What will be Esther's first language?"

"English, of course. We want her to be like the other children in America."

"It will take me a while to learn English?"

"You and Esther will learn together."

"But words in English won't sound right coming from me."

"Yes, they will. Because you're her mother."

Apart from meal times, during the first week, Marika and I kept to ourselves, either in our room or on the poop deck if the currents were calm and the wind and cold bearable. When Esther cried, I gathered her up, taking in her smells and softness, and paced the deck, letting sunrays glide toward her face. At times, Marika and I would lean over the side, the breath of the ocean slapping us with its briny odor, as we watched jellyfish propelling through whitecaps and the sudden splash of flying fish. There also were the occasional whales that the crew spotted, including humpbacks, which blew bubbles to trap schooling fish and then exploded out of the water in a feeding frenzy as playful as it was fearsome.

On our first day at sea, the captain had ordered a lifeboat drill. Each adult was required to don a carrot-orange, balloon-like life vest and traipse around to various parts of the ship. Esther's contribution to this effort was to wail when the emergency alarm was sounded. We repeated this drill with more urgency days later after being contacted by a sister ship heading the other way, advising us to "batten down the hatches." Within hours of the warning, our ship was immersed in a raging storm. Heavy ropes appeared in the passageways, and large objects that might shift were lashed down.

We huddled below deck on a floor tipping steeply, listening as the rabid ocean found its harshest voice. Hearing towering sheets of waves swallow rain and smash across the decks like steel barrel drums while a howling wind toyed with the ship as if it were paper. Clutching Esther, Marika hunched beside me with a wide-eyed stare. I slipped the baby into my arms, while Marika wrung her hands and rocked back and forth. "It's happening again. We're not safe!"

"Marika, we'll be fine," was my rote response.

When calm returned, Marika didn't reach for Esther, but accepted the saltine crackers handed out to quiet our stomachs. Once she regained her color, we circled the main deck, which had been wiped dry.

"I miss Klari," Marika said.

"What made you think of her?"

"When I was still living at home, she would hold my hand and talk to me during the air raids. And when I came back after the war ended, in the middle of the winter, we would sleep close together to keep warm."

"Well, now you have me. Don't I make you feel safe?"

"Yes, but in a different way. Klari was my sister."

"Your stepsister. Do you miss her, or just a female companion?"

"I miss her. We lived through a lot together."

"Marika, I can't make all your loneliness and fears go away, but I will protect you and Esther, and be here for you both."

By the second week of the voyage, if Esther cooperated, Marika and I would venture into the third-class common room to mingle. This was when I befriended Doctor Imre Sokolow, having heard him offering medical advice in Yiddish. A gentle soul from Budapest a decade my senior, he was traveling alone.

Survivors struggled to balance the remembrance of love against the hole that love's absence created. Sokolow appeared happiest when

Chapter 61

buried under his stethoscope, keeping several paces ahead of himself. I described my incessant stomach ills. "Doctor, do you have any advice?"

"Yes, but you won't like it. You've got to give up coffee for plain water, throw out the cigarettes, and eat more fruits and vegetables." Sokolow suggested that I could have an ulcer or simply be dehydrated. I followed his guidance, thinking, "Tibi, I'm sorry I belittled you about your ulcer. This is harder than I knew."

I looked for Sokolow when Marika and Esther napped. "I spent months in Auschwitz," he shared one afternoon as we stood on the deck.

"I was a laborer, Imre, but I know you had it worse."

"How I am here to speak of it I can't say," as he pointed his finger to the heavens.

"Do you want to talk about it?" I shut my eyes to perceive his story more intensely, as if sight might overpower his narrative. Sokolow continued, "I ended up at Mauthausen, having survived a death march to get there."

"Mauthausen?" I said. Until now, I had avoided probing questions. But I had recently learned through Jóska of Jenő's death in Mauthausen. "Please tell me about it."

Sokolow jerked his head back. "Such a terrible place, Mauthausen. That last winter, when even the sun was cold, we wore only lightweight sleeping attire. Our shoes were wafer thin. We were whipped up and down the hundreds of steps of a huge quarry as we carried heavier and heavier granite slabs, some weighing more than we did. No purpose in it other than to torment us. Every day, people around me dropped dead from disease or starvation, or they chose to hurl themselves from the top of the quarry to get it over with. The hunger was so bad that it drove some to eat the body parts of the dead."

"Imre, I'm so sorry you had to go through that."

"You couldn't live more than a couple of weeks there. I survived because I'm a doctor. They kept me alive so that I could treat the senior officials and their families. I was given a little more food than the rest. So I was lucky."

"Yes, and I was too," I whispered. In the labor camp, displaying any sign of vulnerability was dangerous. But now, listening yet again to a long-ago conversation under a walnut tree with a man who loved me, but whose devotion I had not properly acknowledged, I wept, etching scars of incomprehension. I leaned over the stern to gaze at the white froth topping. Letting the churning waves consume my tears. Taking in our growing distance from the place that once held all I had ever cared for. Finally, I was escaping its immense gravity.

How easy it would be for either of us to yield to the ocean's foaming embrace. To surrender now to the inevitable deep sleep. "Béla, I'm sorry I spoke of this."

"No, I pressed you to. I should have told you right away that my oldest brother had died in Mauthausen. He died in silence, but he continues to call out to me."

We stood together in a quiet that asked, "Why do you want to be near me when I am so distant?" Staring into myself, I said aloud, "What kind of loving G-d allows this?"

"I don't believe there's an all-knowing being in the heavens dispensing rewards and punishments, who loves His human subjects and who preserves the souls of the dead. If that's what you're asking."

I was reminded of my last conversation with Jenő. Had Sokolow also studied the philosophy of supposed heretics such as Spinoza? Or was it the war that had changed him? He continued, "I haven't believed in G-d in the traditional sense since I was a child."

"Because you're a man of science?"

"No. I follow Einstein's view that science and religion are not inconsistent. G-d is nature, and both science and religion are means to understanding it."

"Nature can be so cruel."

Chapter 61

"Nature simply is what it is. If a lion eats a zebra, it's not an evil act." He smirked, "Although maybe it is for the zebra. Only man kills out of ideology and hatred."

Sokolow patted my shoulder. "Come, let's play some cards." He took my arm, and we made our way back to the common room.

In the last days of our voyage, Sokolow joined us for meals in the third-class dining room, in an area where families with children would congregate. During our second Sabbath dinner, Marika recited the prayer after lighting candles provided by the crew. Though she lit three candles, I made out the glow of ten. The doctor chanted, through tearless sobs, "I love you, Yetti. I love you, Rebeka, my baby girl. Wherever you are."

I embraced Sokolow, understanding more. Watching Esther gurgling in Marika's arms, my words of comfort rang hollow. Would Imre ever risk reopening the roads to his bleeding heart? Józsi had. Through the refugee grapevine, I learned that after immigrating to Palestine, Józsi had remarried, discovering another whom he could hold close.

When we were seated together the next day for lunch, there was no mention of the previous evening. I pointed to an ice cream bowl filled with dark brown mounds of rubber cut in squares. "What is this?" I poked at it with my finger. "It's still alive!"

Sokolow let out a succession of laughs that sounded like dog barks. "It's called Jell-O. A chocolate gelatin. Not kosher, if you care about that, but you'll like it."

"They're trying to kill us."

"Don't be a baby, Béla," scolded Marika. She took a mouthful. "Taste it."

I placed a dab on my lips and said nothing more as I licked the bowl clean. The next meal was accompanied by a bound set of cylinders that were curves of sunlight. Not wanting to eat my words again, I waited until Marika and the doctor each selected one and peeled

377

it. Imre wolfed his down. Marika offered me half of hers, her fingers yellow with mush. And so I discovered bananas.

Each day, a member of the crew would announce our approximate location in the ocean, citing basins, ridges, and shelves as reference points. Our anticipation built as we passed milestone latitudes—the Azores, Greenland, and Newfoundland. At times during our walks, Marika's breathing turned rapid and shallow as she insisted that I repeat descriptions and stories of Jóska and Libu.

On Sunday, May 18, crew members passed out leaflets, in various languages, containing some facts about life in America. On the following morning, our fifteenth day at sea, as the dull-red haze hinted at the sun's appearance, ship stewards hurried through the halls knocking on doors and shouting that we would soon be sailing past the Statue of Liberty. Marika and I threw on clothes, wrapped Esther in a blanket, and joined the hordes pushing toward the upper decks. As we stood in a predawn that breathed frost, the man next to us pointed to the choppy waters and asked Marika if she had worn a bathing suit for the required swim to the Statue. Marika gasped. He laughed, raising the corners of his mouth to exaggerated height.

In the fading darkness, a kaleidoscope of iridescent lights illuminated the highways, bridges, and skyscrapers like necklaces on an enormous being. As my mother had done a half-century ago, we entered the harbor to the misty sight of the serene Pagan goddess. I held Esther high, letting her bathe in its glow. The ship crept past, moving as slowly as the sun, in a reverential silence broken by the accented voice of one of the passengers chanting, "God Bless America." Others joined in. I gripped Marika's arm. "Family waits."

We tied up at the Manhattan Cruise Terminal, a grimy, congested finger pier on the Hudson along the West Side. Our ship was dwarfed by an ocean liner one dock over named the *Normandie*, a floating city. We lined up on the main deck and waited for our names

Chapter 61

to be called. Marika said, "What will they ask us? What if we don't answer correctly?"

"Don't worry. I'll answer for us both."

Dr. Sokolow, who was traveling on to Boston, where he had been offered a teaching position in a hospital, hugged us as he recited the *Shehechiyanu* prayer, thanking G-d "who has kept us alive, and sustained us, and enabled us to reach this moment." I asked if he might one day find work in New York. Sokolow shrugged, suggesting that he would not seek anything or anyone he might come to love. We said that we would stay in touch, a promise as solid as air.

Once our names were called, with Marika and Esther in tow, I carried our luggage to the back of a queue in a spacious windowed customs section within the pier. Our interview was conducted by a young immigrations official with a flapper bob, wearing an "Anna" nametag on her uniform. After checking our passports and collecting the $6 entry fee for each of us, Anna fawned over Esther, allowing Marika to unclench her hands and breathe naturally. Conversational in Hungarian, Anna told us of her own family's emigration a generation earlier.

"Why have you made the journey to the United States?"

"To be with our relatives," I answered. "I have two brothers and a sister here."

"Where will you live?"

"My brother has found us an apartment in Manhattan."

"And how will you support yourself?"

"The same brother has a business. I'm going to work for him."

She smiled. "It must have been a difficult journey with the baby."

I kissed Esther's forehead. "We did this for her."

We were ushered to the medical examinations line. Nearby, there was a table manned by volunteers offering juice and donuts covered with powdered sugar. Rumors had abounded of immigrants deemed ill being detained indefinitely or sent back to Europe. After two weeks of seasickness, and years of deprivation, we were not models of health. The checkups were performed impersonally by an earnest nurse who spoke only English and communicated by gestures. She measured our blood pressure and heart rate, examined our throats with dry tongue depressors, and inspected our hair, eyes, ears, hands, and feet, including Esther's, frowning periodically. She handed me a card that listed, in Yiddish, "good health guidelines," including washing hands both before eating and after going to the bathroom. Another suggestion, that we take vitamin pills, had been underscored by her.

The final line led to disembarkation. Inching forward, we scanned the crowds. Would I be able to spot Jóska? Would he recognize me? Unexpectedly our names again were announced over a manual megaphone, and we were guided by an Italian Line official back to a corner of the boat's deck. Those nearby turned away from us. Marika whimpered. "Béla, did that nurse find something? Are they sending us back?"

I had to convince us both. "Everything's fine, Marika. If there's a problem, Jóska will help us take care of it."

In broken Italian, I said, "Why are we being taken off the line?"

The official waggled his hand. "Don't worry. Nothing is wrong."

We were introduced to a man wearing a suit, bow tie, and matching ironed handkerchief in the breast pocket, and a black, pinch-front fedora that had been popular among the Orthodox of Munkács. A Commando camera with a folding shutter hung from a strap around his neck. Shaking our hands, he said, "Hello, I'm Herbert Hecht." He switched to Yiddish. "Call me Herb." I exhaled fully.

"I'm a reporter for a New York newspaper. I'm writing stories about recent immigrants. I would like to tell your story."

Why couldn't I be seen as a person rather than a survivor? "Ours is like so many others."

Chapter 61

"Yes, and every one is worth telling."

Is this guy nuts? We've been on this damn boat for two weeks, we're cleared to leave, and we have to take time for this?

"My family is waiting."

"Please, just a few questions, and then I'll take you to the head of the line." Without waiting, he spewed out questions while scribbling on a spiral pad. "Where were you born and raised? How did you survive the war? What happened to your relatives? Why have you come here?" Our pain, one that constantly renews itself, would be traded for news.

Picturing Jóska and the others waiting on the pier and worried that we had missed the boat, I raced through our life stories, unconcerned about their coherency. I could not describe the indescribable, yet Hecht probed. The brief account that accompanied our photo on the front page of the following day's *Daily Mirror* was embarrassingly inaccurate.

As promised, Hecht brought us to the front of the line. "I'm terribly sorry for all you both have suffered. Thank you again, and *Zei Gezunt*." On the wharf, there was a confused crush of locals with welcome signs, passengers with carts and drays, porters piling up luggage, taxi drivers pushing their services, and vendors hawking beverages, pretzels, and other fare. "There's Miki," Marika shouted. Beaming, he was jumping up and down and thrashing his arm through the air. With a full, tanned face, he appeared healthier than I'd ever seen him. Aside Miki was a brunette with short, curly hair underneath a black cloche hat, sporting her own radiant smile. Inge, wearing an elegant, tailored, pleated red jacket with a matching skirt, could have been mistaken for one of the first-class passengers.

As we elbowed our way through the crowd, a clearer image emerged of the slim young woman next to them, dressed more modestly than Inge. Libu held her hands clasped in front of her, showing a grin tinged with persistent melancholy, as if sorrow was the inevitable cost for entertaining joy.

On her other side was the new head of the family—a dapper man in a charcoal-gray double-breasted jacket with wide-leg, creased trousers. Showing in Jóska were the changes that eight long years had engendered. He was heavier, balder, and now with a furrowed brow. Like Miki, he wore his hair with a "wet" look, which was all the rage. Puffing nonchalantly on a pipe with a self-confidence reminiscent of Jenő, his long-held assurances had been validated. Jóska's grin, knowing in a manner reserved for someone who had been with me since the first moments of my life, brought me home.

We traded hugs and kisses tasting of salt, switching partners until every combination had been paired. As I embraced my brothers and sister, we melted into each other. The solitude of our exodus dissipated with every touch. Esther was cuddled and kissed, her beauty proclaimed. Inge welcomed Marika into the family. When Jóska repeated Inge's greeting in Hungarian, my wife wept. Jóska explained that Suzy, still plagued with morning sickness, was sorry to have missed welcoming us.

Jóska grabbed Marika's hand, she took mine, and we continued until a chain was formed, so tight that the crowd could not break us apart. We

Béla, Marika, and Esther on the Saturnia

Chapter 61

crossed the street and headed to a parking lot several blocks away. Jóska would drive us to a hotel room in midtown that had been arranged for us by HIAS. We passed a deli crammed with dock workers and newly arrived passengers, with various unintelligible window signs. I focused on an electric one in blue and white that read "רשכ" (Kosher).

And so, we had arrived at the shores of our Zion, where G-d had reemerged to reclaim His glory. No more were Marika and I refugees, displaced persons, or undesirables running one step ahead of the dusk. My family would plant roots, never to be torn from the earth, in a place where true peace reigned, not the ugly form of it that settles after a great conflict. Now, time for Marika and me would finally travel straight.

Article from the front page of the Daily Mirror, *May 20, 1947*

CHAPTER 62
Assimilation

By conforming with the expectations of others, by not being different, these doubts about one's own identity are silenced and a certain security is gained. However, the price paid is high.

—Erich Fromm

"Marika, Jóska promised us. Don't worry. They need a larger apartment for themselves with their baby coming." And soon, we moved into Jóska and Suzy's furnished third-floor, one-bedroom apartment off Riverside Drive in Manhattan. Our building had no elevator or laundry room, and the only phone was in the dank lobby.

Although the *mamaloshen* (Yiddish) was commonly spoken in our neighborhood, adaptation to our new country was slow, frustrated by my being too ill to work. The nausea that plagued me on the ship remained, accompanied by frequent vomiting and weight loss. On top of that, I had periodontal disease and a mouthful of loose teeth requiring dentures. Fatigue was my constant companion, as I slept

Chapter 62

fitfully during the day and stayed awake much of the night. Life in America was normal, but I was not.

HIAS, which had been providing us with clothing and diapers, arranged for a medical consultation. Given the shortage of doctors and a surge in polio cases, it was weeks before I obtained an appointment. I waited in Dr. Stefan Wiener's crowded wood-paneled reception room, rife with his diplomas and Chagall prints. Flipping through photos in the *New York Daily News*, I came across one of the Hungarian Prime Minister, Ferenc Nagy, who had refused to be turned into a Soviet puppet. A patient seated nearby helped me understand that the article was about Nagy's ouster from office by the Hungarian Communists. Did Rózsi regret not emigrating with us?

Patients who had arrived after me shuttled in and out of the examination room. Only after I gently complained at the front desk to a receptionist hunched over her clacking Olivetti typewriter was I led into the inner sanctum, which was an office off a periscope-long corridor.

Wiener shook my hand rigidly, a king deigning to make physical contact with a pawn. His haggard face was blotched with a red rash that was blistered and swollen. Among the framed degrees hanging on a wall was one from CCNY, which Miki joked stood for the "College for Circumcised New Yorkers." Having learned that Wiener had been raised in Berlin and fled after Kristallnacht, we spoke in German.

After completing the examination, Wiener rolled his chair to an eggshell-white metal cabinet, opened a drawer, and took out a thick black canvas binder, which he flipped through hurriedly. With his mouth puckered like a giant anus, he ripped out a sheet and thrust it at me before snapping closed the rings.

I said, "Doctor, do you think I have an ulcer?"

"No, your condition is the result of poor eating habits." He spoke deliberately, as if every word he had chosen to enunciate was the perfect one to use. "Toxic substances that have built up."

"What does that mean?"

Wiener glared at me, as though I had failed a test that he had provided me the answers to in advance. "That your body is filled with *chazerie* (garbage), and we have to remove it."

"How?"

"I'm putting you on a lemon and maple syrup diet. Each day you'll drink six glasses of a mixture made of freshly squeezed lemon juice, maple syrup, cayenne pepper, and filtered water. This will gradually cleanse your body." He handed the paper to me and added, "Here are the exact amounts of each to be taken."

"How long before I feel better?"

"Everyone is different. In most cases, relief comes within a few weeks."

"I'll have to be on that diet for weeks? Only that? No food?"

Wiener stood. "Yes. You'll also have to do a saltwater flush each day to flush contaminated matter through your bowels."

"Can't you just give me drugs? My friend has similar symptoms, and that's what he takes for it."

Wiener strode to the door and grabbed the handle but didn't open it. "Is your friend a doctor?"

"No."

"Are you a doctor?" The arrogant SOB. I bet if he were lost in the woods, he wouldn't know how to light a fire. Build a shelter. Keep himself clean. Find drinkable water. Or, if he took a dump, all the different ways to wipe his ass. I shook my head.

"Well, I am. And one, I might add, who is taking your case pro bono. So stop listening to your greenhorn friends and heed my advice. Goodbye, Mr. Inger."

I gripped the edge of the examination table and glowered at Wiener. His eyes betrayed alarm as he silently exited. A nurse wearing heavy white orthopedic pumps came in to escort me out.

Chapter 62

Later that day, while Marika and I were walking through a grocery store in search of the syrup, which Wiener insisted must be of a certain grade, I doubled over with abdominal pain and was rushed by ambulance across town to Memorial Hospital. During an overnight stay, I was diagnosed with a peptic ulcer and prescribed antibiotics.

Weeks of bed rest followed. In spite of fans and open windows that welcomed the cacophony of street noise, I sweltered in a sun that had left its orbit and was hurtling directly toward our apartment. With each day of renewed idleness, murmuring waters rose further above my head, suffocating me into a death while still breathing.

And so, one morning, I determined to throw myself back into the world. I dressed, kissed Marika, marched out of the apartment, and hopped on a rusted southbound subway train, intending to ride to the garment district. Sitting on a woven wicker seat under a ceiling fan, I gazed at advertisements for soap and toothpaste. I exited at the last stop, where rats shuffled on the track. Drifting through a park, I was confused by the sight of the Statue of Liberty. Every person walking by appeared sure of where they were headed. Spotting a gray-haired man on a weathered bench reading *The Jewish Daily Forward*, I asked for directions.

He turned his shoulders sideways and pointed. "Walk up Broadway to Wall Street. Make a right onto William Street. Take that subway uptown to 42nd Street. The garment district is right around there."

"Thank you. May I ask where you are from?"

"Kielce."

"Kielce! That's where my father was from. My name is Béla Ingber. Did you know any Ingbers?"

The man laid down his paper and patted the empty space next to him. I sat as he pondered, his recognition of the past unfolding as does the dawn. "Maybe. My memory of the old days isn't so good anymore. Did they leave before the war?"

"No. At least not that I know."

He stuck his hand out. "I'm Zuchman. Morris Zuchman. Where are you from, Béla?"

"Munkács. I came here in May. When did you arrive?"

"We left Poland before the Nazis invaded, thank G-d. We fled east through Russia, taking the Trans-Siberian Railway all the way to Vladivostok. We were stuck there for a year. Got here in 1942. The stories I could tell. But we were lucky. Was your mother from Kielce also?"

"No, Kraków."

"Did your parents survive?"

My solemn look answered him. He plopped his arm on my shoulder. "Do you have family here? Are you alone?"

"Thank you, but I have lots of family here." Jóska was supportive in every way except that he was not able to hire me, for reasons that he never explained. "What I need is work."

Zuchman reached into his pants pocket and pressed two nickels into my hand. I pushed them back to him, but he persisted.

"We all need to practice *tikkun olam* (healing the world). Use these to go to midtown, where there are jobs, and then to go home."

I pumped his hand, thanked him for his kindness, and repeated, "Broadway to Wall Street. Then a right onto William Street." He nodded north, and I was off.

Leaving the "Tymes Kvare" station, I tightroped south along Seventh Avenue, where sunlight was an intruder, avoiding careening clothing, hissing manhole covers, and huddles of quarreling businessmen. People and structures and things everywhere—as if I had wandered into a hidden-objects puzzle. Coming from Munkács, I should have despised the madness of this metropolis, but instead I took comfort in its anonymity.

I knocked on doors until, on 37th Street, I spotted a second-floor window sign in Hebrew that contained my name. And that is how I

Chapter 62

came to apply for work at Bear & Sons Garments Company, a frenetic shop with fewer than twenty employees, mostly production workers. The manager sat in a space separated from the factory floor by a portable partition. "Can you start now?" he said in Yiddish.

"I can start yesterday."

I spent the afternoon packing coats, hats, and gloves on a non-air-conditioned, poorly ventilated, block-long floor lit dimly by widely spaced light bulbs, for the minimum wage of seventy-five cents an hour. Which was a lot of money compared to nothing.

And so the pattern began of short-term jobs.

"Béla, will you be home late today, too?"

"Sorry, Marika, yes. But they'll likely lay me off next week. Who knows what the next job will bring."

Not belonging to a worker's union, whose fees were unaffordable, I had no security. Every job I had required tedious hours over days on end. Marika, who had not picked up English, would wait until the weekend to go food shopping with me. I handed each paycheck to her, which I helped preserve by walking to work, weather permitting, for over an hour each way. (I admit that I'm a walker by nature, no companion or destination needed.) Marika made my lunch most of the time. Otherwise, I'd find an automat (invariably noisy and crowded, but which had the best coffee) or a cheap local deli. For months after we arrived, if there was no landsman around, I'd order "scrambled eggs and black coffee," words I could pronounce.

One evening burgeoning with the sounds of spring, Marika and I strolled with Esther to Riverside Park and found a narrow pathway that led to a sunset vista of the Hudson River painted with reflections of vivid cherry and auburn. In the distance, sailboats gently angled into the wind. We sat under a crabapple tree, its red-purple buds swelling like blood-engorged nipples, as a cool breeze blew. This grove had become my favorite spot, as the scent of any type of fruit tree was a caressing reminder of Munkács. In a nearby field separated by a chain-link fence, uniformed teenage boys were engrossed in a game, spurred on by goading buddies on the sidelines.

"Learn baseball," Jóska had advised. "Fit in." While Marika bottle-fed Esther, I studied the play, struggling to comprehend its rules and rhythms. I understood the essential goals: one team's players attempting to circle the bases to return to where they had batted, the other team trying to prevent this. Baseball appeared to be a democratic contest, one in which everyone in the field gets a turn at bat.

But the game's nuances escaped me, although I appreciated the displays of athleticism, such as a long-legged outfielder gathering cannonball speed, his muscles contracting in precise tandem with each other, to catch a ball on the edge of his glove an instant before banging into a tree trunk.

As the gloaming hour faded, we headed back, wheeling a sleeping baby.

"Béla, do you understand that sport?"

"Only that it's boring. I'd like to find a football match to watch. Maybe even join in."

Marika rubbed my hand. "They play football in Palestine."

"They play football everywhere but here. Why single out Palestine?"

Marika stopped pushing the stroller and faced me. "I think we made a mistake, Béla. Everything is different here. Life is strange. We don't fit in."

"We fit in fine. We don't have to be like the fancy Jews."

Her eyes were kindling. "We have no money. You don't have a steady job. We don't speak the language. I spend all day alone with Esther."

"That will change, Marika. And we have family to help us."

"*We* don't have family. *You* do. And Inge does—she has her parents and aunts and uncles and cousins. Suzy has her three sisters. Miklós has cousins here. But I have no one."

Chapter 62

Marika was stuck on the shores of America, caught in the Ingber family riptide. "My family is your family."

Was that true? Family is not, at heart, a social unit bound by defined relationships. Family is mutual experiences. Common struggles. Shared secrets. "Not really. We're the charity case. They look down on us. At least on me. I know they do."

"No, they love us. Both of us, Marika. So why would it be better in Palestine? We wouldn't have any family there."

"Because everyone's the same there. We would be valued as Jews and Zionists. Here, everyone just lusts for money and status. It doesn't feel like home."

How eerily familiar this conversation was with the one I had a decade earlier with Ágnes. My life was a circular trap. But Marika did not have a passion for Palestine. She only wanted to run from America. Or perhaps it all was my fault, for again choosing my blood over my lover?

"Marika, this country can be good for us, if we give it time."

"What choice do I have? My place is with you."

*

We spent most weekends with family. Jóska and Suzy had moved to Queens, a rural location that I had associated with my brother's descriptions of the World's Fair. On summer weekends, they drove us to Atlantic Beach, where our Esther and their son, Kenny, would frolic in air breathing of salt, and the two would team up with their fathers, competing for the most intricate sand castle, complete with moat, or the deepest dig to China. I had never been to a silken sandy beach before. Although the setting was dissimilar, lying on the caked grit before an infinite landscape aroused in me primitive sensations reminiscent of the forests of the Rus.

Jóska or Miki would drive us several hours to Trenton, New Jersey, to visit with Aunt Giza and Uncle Lou, after picking up strudels from

Lichtman's Bakery on Amsterdam Avenue. Aunt and Uncle's modest, well-kept box of a house in the North Ward was marked by a hand-painted birdhouse mailbox in front framed by dense evergreen shrubs. On their street, named after someone's sweetheart, braided welcome mats, emerald quilts of grass, swept sidewalks, and the mingling smells of bread baking and garlic sautéing greeted us. My aunt and uncle appeared so comfortable for Jews living in a Polish neighborhood near a large Roman Catholic Church. But this was America.

The first time we visited, Uncle Lou insisted on taking us to a nearby column of granite on top of a round pavilion that housed a statue of George Washington. "This is where the Americans defeated the British. They crossed the river in the middle of the night in the worst winter weather. It was an important battle, and it happened right here."

"You mean the Yiddish," Miki countered.

"The British," Uncle Lou repeated.

"No, I'm sure it was the Yiddish."

"Who told you that? There were no Yiddish. The Americans fought the British."

"How do you know?" Jóska said.

"How do I know! The same way I know that Columbus discovered America and that there was a Revolutionary War and that Lincoln freed the slaves. I read books."

Miki was unimpressed. "There must have been some Jews on the British side, or else they wouldn't have conquered half the world."

"You know the old saying," added Jóska. "Act British, think Yiddish."

"I never heard that."

"I read it in a book. I read books, too."

"What book was that?"

"A Yiddish book," Miki answered. Uncle Lou stormed away. We visited him less often after that.

CHAPTER 63

Oli Ingber: April 12, 1948 (London)

My Dear Béla, Marika, and Eszterke,

I have not written to you since Jóska and Libu arrived. Now they've returned to America, and I have a few moments to compose a letter.

Our younger sister has found a man she wants to marry. She professed to want to again live in Europe, and Mary and I tried our best to have her meet a suitable man in London. But Libu was sullen and disinterested. Then, Jóska accompanied her back to Czechoslovakia, and it was in Prague, through a mutual friend, that she met a fellow survivor, Miklós Hermel. I believe they are engaged now, and that he will soon join her in America. Jóska has promised to pay for their wedding.

These are good things done by Jóska. Otherwise, he is insane and, while I love him, I tell you that I'm glad that he's gone. He kept insisting that I must come to America, ignoring that I'm with Mary now and we have a daughter. 'You're not married,' he stupidly says. I finally told him to mind his own business, although I didn't say it as nicely as that.

I know he wants the best for me, but he says foolish things all the time, particularly that I will never be happy with a shiksa. This from a man already divorced once. What does he know of love? He is all about business.

I am planning to open a modest dental practice near where we live. The cost for all the required equipment is great, and I am in the process of obtaining the necessary loans. So my life is here now.

It's wonderful that your Eszterke and my Ilona honor our dear mother and sister. May they never know the suffering of their namesakes.

Jóska Ingber, Libu Ingber, and Miklós Hermel in Prague, 1948

I hope you are adjusting. Our distance will never diminish the love I have for you, my dears.

Write soon.

With kisses,

CHAPTER 64
Elmhurst

Where paths that have an affinity for each other intersect, the whole world looks like home, for a time.
—Hermann Hesse

In the spring of 1948, Marika and I again followed Jóska and Suzy, this time to Elmhurst, a "subway suburb" in central Queens that was largely Jewish, Italian, and Irish. A neighborhood known to Manhattanites for its two unsightly hundred-foot-tall natural gas storage tanks, which they passed on the way to their beach escapes.

There had been no new construction during the war, resulting in a crippled rental market. Jóska advised us to come to Elmhurst immediately to claim an apartment that had become available in their building. Marika worried whether we could afford not only the rent but also the required payoffs to the rental agent and superintendent. Jóska came to our rescue, and we moved into the elegant, newly built red-brick, six-story building at the intersection of Broadway and 81st

Street. Because it was rent controlled, we paid $60 a month in rent for years, which became cheap, even for us.

I was comfortable leaving the congestion of Manhattan, rife with urbanites whose idea of a day in the country was a walk in Central Park. After handing in our keys, we had no one to say goodbye to. Our neighbors had never become friends.

Elmhurst had a clean, naked face. I could find stillness there. Outside our building were parks and open spaces, albeit cemeteries everywhere as well. On the Broadway side was an evolving commercial strip that included a kosher butcher.

A block away, a traveling circus had pitched its tent on a field where the sprawling Elmhurst General Hospital would later be built. Its clowns and elephants reminded me of the *Cirque Medrano* that often traveled to Munkács. Marika and I would wander among the rows of booths offering stuffed animals and cigarette pack prizes. The nickel toss was my favorite game to watch, and I would chuckle at the frustrations of players trying to land a coin on a greased plate.

The Elmwood Theater, one of the largest in the city, was within walking distance. We enjoyed movie matinees, munching on snacks brought from home. On the opposite side of Queens Boulevard from the theater was the Fairyland amusement park, where Esther would ride the kiddie merry-go-round and water boat.

One late afternoon, walking into the apartment after work, Marika greeted me with a wide grin, an unusual occurrence. "Esther and I were coming back from the grocery store, and a nice woman with a daughter Esther's age invited us to come to her apartment so the girls could play. Her name is Lilly Panzer, and her daughter is Lenore. Her husband Jack works in Manhattan. They are Jewish." Marika never again brought up immigrating to Palestine.

Through Lilly and Jack, we met others in the building, many of whom became friends. We socialized, traveled, celebrated, and

Chapter 64

mourned together. Esther frolicked with their children on summer evenings as Marika and I sat with the other parents on folding chairs in front of our building. Marika joined a mahjong group that met Thursday evenings and rotated apartments each week.

Elmhurst was my new Munkács. Over the decades, the neighborhood grew into one of unparalleled diversity, with substantial Hispanic and Asian populations and a Chinatown of its own. The local Newtown High School benefited from often having the highest-rated soccer program in the country. Fairyland was replaced by the Queens Center Mall. Hundreds of modest one-family houses were torn down, supplanted by multistory buildings. Traffic increased exponentially, and the subway platforms during rush hours became impassable. Most of Elmhurst's kosher restaurants, butchers, bakeries, and delis relocated or closed down. The Young Israel of Jackson Heights *shul* that I prayed in for fifty years burgeoned with families until steadily leaking membership made it lock its doors.

But the neighborhood remained safe, middle-class, and welcoming. Marika and I would live in it for the rest of our lives.

Miki and Esther in Elmhurst, circa 1948

CHAPTER 65
Karpatalja Balls

*Words are easy, like the wind;
faithful friends are hard to find.*

—William Shakespeare

The Old Country remained close. Every year, Marika and I attended the Karpatalja Ball in the Grand Ballroom of the Manhattan Center on 34th Street. This gala event was hosted by a *landsmanshaft*, a hometown society of emigrants from Munkács and its environs that provided emergency loans, insurance, and burial plots. Among those who understood, we swapped boasts, advice, and gossip.

At each ball, Tibi held court at a long drop-leaf table. My life and Tibi's continued their parallel existence. After I left Munkács, he met and married Hannah, a Budapest native who had been sheltered in the Swedish consulate during the worst months, and they immigrated to the United States. Gizi now was a memory. She could not give up her life, nor could Tibi forgive her for it.

Chapter 65

Tibi and Hannah moved to Rego Park, a neighborhood within walking distance of Elmhurst. They lived in an aluminum-sided railroad home with a rectangular patch of front lawn too insignificant to warrant a mower and a narrow cement driveway in which children's names had been permanently etched. Often when I visited Tibi, we would walk to Ben's Best Deli on Queens Boulevard for corned beef sandwiches. Or, on Sunday mornings, we'd stop for coffee and buttered bialys at Murray's, where, no matter how many times I had been there, the proprietor greeted me with, "How do you keep someone from stealing your bagels?" (The answer, of course, is, "You put lox on them.")

During one Karpatalja Ball, after the apricot crepe dessert but before the brandy that would edge him into incoherence, Tibi rose unsteadily and clinked a fork against a water glass.

"Ladies and gentlemen, your attention please."

"Do we have a choice?" yelled Miki.

"No. So shut up." As he waited for side conversations to die down, Tibi reached for his wine glass and moistened his lips. "I'll be brief."

"You?" I offered loudly, which earned me a smack from Marika.

"I only want to say a few thanks," he continued. "First, I want to thank my lovely wife…for being stunning." He blew Hannah a kiss. "And for serving on the Karpatalja Ball Committee."

"You should thank her for staying with you all these years," shouted Jóska.

"You're right, Joe. Hannah complains about me almost as much as Suzy does about you. But let me carry on. I also want to thank all of you for generously contributing to this plaque that will be placed on the front wall of the Munkács City Hall." He held the bronze sign up. "Isn't it a beauty? It honors our lost Jewish community." Tibi paused for wild clapping.

"And finally…," he continued, finishing off his tumbler of Manischewitz Extra Heavy Malaga wine, "and finally, I want to thank G-d. Although I'm far from sure He exists. But in case He does, I thank Him for blessing me with the life that I have. A wonderful wife. A beautiful baby boy. A good job. A home near a liquor store. And—"

"Tibi, the trains stop running at midnight."

"Shut up, Miki. Just one more thing I want to give thanks for...." Tears dripped down his blotchy red cheeks like melted glass. Hannah reached to grip his hand. "I'm so grateful to live in this country. To be free to act like a complete asshole. And where no one gives a shit what I am." As Hannah reached to hand him a handkerchief, we all stood and applauded.

*Béla and Marika at a Karpatalja Ball,
early 1950s*

CHAPTER 66
The Butcher Shop: November 1953

A man that studieth revenge keeps his own wounds green.
—Francis Bacon

After moving to Elmhurst, I continued to hold a succession of random jobs, one of which was operating an oven in a local rubber-band factory. We lived a life built around the timing of my next payday. We bought on credit a Singer featherweight portable sewing machine, and Marika again was a seamstress, taking on odd jobs for neighbors. By 1953, the year we were granted citizenship (after passing an oral test in English), I had steady work as a welder in a unionized sheet-metal factory. It was in a desolate part of Long Island City where grime and smoke dense as steel wool smudged the landscape. We enrolled Esther in kindergarten in Public School 89, which was bursting with immigrants' children.

On the day before Thanksgiving, in the late afternoon, I stopped at the local kosher butcher shop, owned by a fellow Hungarian named Bernard Langerman, to pick up flanken (short ribs). The store, with a sawdust-covered floor surrounded by white-tiled walls, was crowded with pre-holiday shoppers. Back then, prepackaged meats and plastic-wrapped parts on foam trays were not available. If you didn't select from the various unnamed slabs displayed behind glass, Langerman expected you to have a precise order in mind. He would retrieve it from "the box," a refrigerated room in the back that held items such as chickens with the feet still attached or sides of fat-covered beef, which he would carve, trim, and weigh in front of you before wrapping.

I read *The Jewish Daily Forward* until I reached the front of the line, where Langerman stood in his blood-spattered apron. Behind him, various-sized saws and knives hung from hooks, above the iron meat grinder clamped to a table.

"How are you, Bernard?"

"Fine." Langerman engaged in small talk with the enthusiasm of a man confessing infidelity. "What can I get you?"

"Flanken. Four pounds."

He stepped toward the doorway of the refrigerated back room and bellowed, "Flanken!" Langerman normally manned his store alone but brought in temporary help before *Shabbos* and holidays.

A diminutive, stout man with dark-ringed and nervous eyes stepped forward, wearing a leather pouch holding his knives. Reflections from overhead lights snake-danced across his hairless dome. With a cleaver in one hand, he passed the meat to Langerman, to be wrapped in tan paper ripped from a large roll. The man was a stranger, and yet familiar. He now sported an angry gray moustache and had the jowls of a turkey. His teeth had been fixed, but the acne scars remained.

The man glanced at me and, in that flicker of a moment, he shed his skin. The Beast and I acknowledged each other, as gladiators before combat.

Chapter 66

"You!" I kicked the swinging waist-high barrier. He raised his hatchet while stepping backward. A woman behind me in line hustled out of the store, and others moved away, gasping. Langerman rushed toward me.

"Béla, are you mad? What the hell are you doing?"

"How could you hire this *fattyú* (bastard)?"

"You know him?"

"He was my commanding officer in the labor camp. A dog!"

Langerman turned to The Beast. "You told me you were Jewish."

The Beast stammered, "I...am Hungarian. I was victimized by the Nazis, just like you Jews. He's mistaken me for someone else."

His strength, derived from the vulnerability of others, was gone. I screamed into Langerman's raisin face. "I'm going to kill him." A man wearing a Pistol Pete black leather motorcycle jacket stepped forward. "A Nazi! I'll help you."

Langerman pushed his hands against my chest. "Béla, leave. I'll deal with him."

I might have shoved Langerman aside and rushed The Beast but for his grease-stained cleaver. I slammed my fist on the counter. Langerman quickly lobbed off a piece of the flanken and threw wrapping around it. As I stomped out, I was given a wide berth, except for the motorcycle man, who smacked my back.

Storming into our apartment, I shouted in Hungarian in Marika's direction, "The piece of shit lives."

Marika, holding a can of peach compote, jerked her head up. In the bedroom, *Howdy Doody* was playing on the veneer RCA television that Jóska had given us. "Béla, you'll scare Esther. What's the matter with you?"

I had told Marika that I would stop off at the butcher, since if I were home five minutes later than expected, she would assume I was lying dead in a gutter. "Here's the meat," I said, flinging it on the kitchen table. Marika placed the flanken in the refrigerator and then rushed over and grasped my elbow. "*Shhh.* Sit down." I plopped onto the forest-green sofa in the living room. Marika reached into a cabinet for a bottle of clear Hungarian slivovitz and a shot glass. In our home, temperance ruled, and bottles of booze survived for years.

I tossed down the first acrid shot and poured a second. Marika sat next to me. "So?"

"You know who cut that meat? The sergeant who ran my labor camp unit. The one we called 'The Beast.'" I raised my pant legs, exposing my ankles. "You remember I told you that these scars are from ropes. He did that! There were so many times when he would have gladly killed me if he could have gotten away with it."

"What can you do?" she said.

"If Langerman doesn't get rid of him, I will."

"And what good will that do? This man can't hurt you anymore. We'll find another butcher."

"Find another butcher? He needs to die!"

"Please, Béla, don't say such things. We have new lives now. Happy lives. Leave this in the past. The bad days are gone."

True, life is now, not a collection of past hurts. But some things you only pretend to bury, until they burst from the mound. I stood and paced. "Not for me." I pointed at Marika. "It was Hungarians like him who murdered Tetzi. She was a beautiful spirit, and they shot her as if she were a rabid animal."

The *Howdy Doody* closing song began. "It's time to go, till our next show. Goodbye from us to you…." Esther would be coming out of her room. Marika whispered, "I know. I'm sorry.

"Just report him to the police," she said.

As if our pasts were comparable, except that The Beast was wanted for a missed child-support payment. "They will do nothing."

Chapter 66

I finished the second glass. "Life will go on. It's a new decade, and nobody cares anymore."

"You'll get us in trouble. Leave his punishment to others."

My body shaking, I blew out a plume of breath through pursed lips. "That's the problem, Marika. Exactly that."

In the foyer, a few steps away, hung a glass-framed certificate in Hebrew honoring the memories of Jenő and Ferencz, whom I had been denied the chance of knowing as only the passage of time permits. Their black-and-white photos had been placed in the lower corners. I pointed toward it and covered my face with my hands. "They should be with us, not that bastard. And I can't even visit their gravesites."

"I know. Same with my father."

"No, it's different! My brothers were tortured to death."

Esther sprung into the room, racing toward me, arms raised. I mopped my eyes with the back of my hand and braced for her.

"Daddy!"

"*Mamaleh!*"

I raised her toward the ceiling and, with a practiced motion that we both anticipated, rubbed her belly across the top of my head, causing shrieks of laughter. After I returned her to the floor, Marika tugged at my arm. "Come help me prepare dinner."

*

The next morning, while Marika cleared away the breakfast dishes, I answered a knock on the door. Jóska, holding a black-and-white herringbone coat over his arm, nodded to Marika as he entered.

"I can't stay long, Béla."

"So who invited you?" Before he could reply, I added, "Sorry, you know you're always welcome. Come sit down. Have you had breakfast?"

Jóska waited as Marika scurried back into the kitchen. "Take a walk with me."

His tone allowed for no debate. We squeezed into the elevator along with a family of four from across the hall who were speed-babbling about heading to the Macy's parade. Under a penetrating drizzle spitting on every surface, Jóska and I turned right on Broadway, passing Langerman's butcher shop, now guarded by a folding lattice gate. Every few minutes, Jóska would duck into a doorway to relight his pipe in the face of a wind that scratched our faces.

"So tell me already. What's wrong?" I said. "You look like someone died. Are Suzy and Kenny okay?"

Jóska shook his head. "You want to go to jail? And leave your family without support? What were you thinking?"

Marika had called him. I hadn't expected that. In future years, she would refer to Jóska as "Uncle Tonoose," after the intrusive character on the *Make Room for Daddy* show. "I didn't commit a crime. I got angry. And you wouldn't? I thought the murdering lowlife was dead. Then he appears in front of me. Right where I live."

I relayed the story of my hanging as we crossed a playground, ringed with hunter-green wood benches. In the center were a seesaw with metal handles, several swings, and rusted monkey bars that Esther recently had mastered. An amalgam of fallen ocher leaves, each with an intricate grid of veins showing, swirled across the asphalt floor, forming ageless patterns.

Jóska listened, nodding from time to time as I recounted The Beast's intent to send us to the Russian Front and the tale of the firing squad at Cluj that was prevented by the Russian plane. "And if Langerman hadn't stopped you?"

"I'd have tried to choke him. Jóska, did you come here to recite the Ten Commandments to me? Don't bother. I already know them."

"I have a boatful of people I want to kill also. I'm here to talk sense into you."

Our path led us under the Long Island Railroad trestle and past the Dutch Reformed Church of Newtown, a stately snow-white

Chapter 66

building with Tuscan columns, so ancient that the inscriptions on the gravestones in its yard were eroded, like the impressions on an old penny. A place of worship had stood on that spot for more than two centuries, dating back to a time when much of the surrounding land was primeval forest.

"I know you suffered, too, Jóska." The ship on which Jóska crossed to Europe with the U.S. Army had been torpedoed. He clung to driftwood for hours in frigid water until he was rescued. And while fighting in the Battle of the Bulge, an exploding grenade sent shrapnel into Jóska's throat. Having refused surgery to remove the fragments, he was incessantly trying to clear it. I could not help comparing his misery against mine, a pastime we survivors were cursed with.

I continued. "It's easier for you to turn the other cheek. I was abused for years by anti-Semites like Valler, but not as a soldier. I couldn't fight back. You could. So don't preach to me."

We passed the tan-bricked Elmhurst library, half of whose space was devoted to children's books, a constant challenge to the quiet adult half. Why was I lecturing a man I respected above all? I couldn't read Jóska's expression. Reaching Queens Boulevard, by the Grand Avenue-Newtown IND subway station, we continued toward Rego Park.

"Béla, I never told you about my time at Buchenwald, did I?"

"I didn't know you were there." Jóska rarely spoke of his war experiences, while I could not stop. To bury the past would dishonor it. I was not ashamed to trumpet my survival.

"I was." Ahead, on the opposite side of the thoroughfare, twelve lanes wide, the Elmwood Theater was playing *High Noon*, with Gary Cooper. "In early April 1945, I was attached to Patton's Third Army. News filtered down that we had liberated a massive concentration camp. A gruesome one. I was ordered there the next day. I think it was around the time Roosevelt died."

Roosevelt's death occurred after I had returned to Munkács. I didn't shed a tear. The American president had not freed me, nor saved those I loved.

"Buchenwald was in an idyllic spot, surrounded by woods and pretty village houses. By the time I got there, thousands already had been buried. But there were thousands more in gray- and blue-striped rags with faded numbers on them, lying about or slouching blankly in the sun in a huge parade ground outside of rows of shabby, tarpaper-covered barracks."

Miki's image, as he appeared that day on the bridge in Munkács, flashed before me. Trapped in hell, all alone.

"The worst sight was the children. Even though their heads were shaved, they still had lice crawling over them. Their skin was yellow, barely covering bones." Jóska mumbled his last words, as would a shoemaker with several nails in his mouth. I patted his shoulder.

"We were taken on a tour. First, the crematorium, with its stacks of emaciated corpses. I remember taking a picture of a partially burned body on the grate and a mound of human ashes beside it. It's in a box somewhere along with other photos, which I plan to donate to the Holocaust memorial they're building in Israel." Jóska cleared his throat noisily. "For some reason, Buchenwald had no gas chambers, but there were execution rooms and a hospital used for medical experiments. We were shown a table lamp made from a skull, and wall hangings they claimed were made from the skin of tattooed prisoners. And a special vise designed to squeeze a man's head until his skull cracked." Again my brother halted his account, groping in his jacket pocket for Edgeworth Ready Rubbed pipe tobacco, which smelled like cocoa.

"As bad as all that was the stench. That first day, I couldn't stop vomiting. Before the SS left, they destroyed the pumps that provided the camp's water supply. The sewage system backed up, and it took

Chapter 66

a week for our engineers to restore it." Jóska chortled. "We made the Nazis haul excrement away until the sewer lines could flow."

"I can't imagine how it must have felt to be there."

"There's a famous quote about Buchenwald by an American radio broadcaster, Edward Murrow. When he got there, he said, 'I have no words.' I arrived there the day that Eisenhower and Patton got there, and before Ike summoned all the reporters and photographers to show the place to the world. Which was lucky for me."

"What do you mean?"

Jóska ignored my question. "The day after I arrived, I was assigned to screen one of the female guards for potential further interrogation. They had caught her hiding among the survivors. It was alleged that she stole Red Cross packages meant for them."

"You had been trained as an interrogator?"

"Yes, at a place in Maryland called Camp Ritchie." He stared ahead, his eyes fixed. "I remember that she was heavy-set, built like a teapot actually, with a lazy eye and a wart on her forehead. She had that typical short-bobbed Nazi blond hair. I forget her name. Or maybe I chose to...."

We neared Horace Harding Boulevard, which was rumored soon to become part of a major highway stretching from Manhattan to eastern Long Island. "They told me that this woman had reported to Ilse Koch, so she was fairly high ranking. Do you know who Ilse Koch is?"

The name sounded familiar. "No."

"She was the wife of the commandant. A complete sadist. They called her the Bitch of Buchenwald. For amusement, Koch would order a prisoner drenched in ice water in the winter so that she could watch him freeze to death. Or dangle food just out of reach of prisoners driven mad from starvation. She's in prison now. That they didn't hang her is a travesty."

Shuddering at the images, I said, "Did this guard know you're Jewish?"

"No. I claimed I was a German Catholic whose parents had immigrated to America when I was young. I didn't give her my real name."

"Did she believe you?"

"Yes. I took out a pack of Luckies and lit one for her. Then I went through her background. Like most of the other guards, she had come from a lower-class upbringing. She was a hairdresser who had volunteered for service after seeing an ad in a newspaper."

"What kind of information were you trying to get from her?"

"Any useful intelligence. Or something incriminating. But she gave just yes or no answers, until I asked about her own treatment. She relaxed a bit. Even had the gall to complain. How awful her training had been. How difficult the prisoners were. How if there were work slowdowns, she herself would be punished. She insisted that some of the male guards abused her."

"I hope so."

"I pretended to sympathize, although I believed nothing of what she said because she didn't confess to anything. She played the 'I was just following orders' game."

"Couldn't you have brought witnesses into the room?"

"Eventually. But it was chaotic then. And the focus of the first interrogations was on the male guards. My meeting with her was a preliminary fact-finding interview. I was alone with her."

I fantasized being there. Strangling her.

"We must have spoken for close to an hour," Jóska continued. "I encouraged her to talk. My questions were gentle, and my reactions muted. I wanted her to think I was seeking info about others, not her. And she did, in the very end, open up more."

"So what did she tell you?"

Chapter 66

He held up his hand, signaling that I shouldn't rush the punch line. "My final question to her was, 'Did you ever kill anyone?'"

"And?"

"She asked for another cigarette, took a long drag, and responded, 'Only some Yids.' Nonchalantly, as if she were telling me the weather."

"That bitch. But why was that your final question? Couldn't you have gotten more out of her?"

"Probably." Jóska inhaled, a violation of pipe-smoking etiquette according to Jenő. "It was the last question because I reached for my revolver and shot her. In the head."

I stopped and grabbed his arm. "Jóska! Why didn't you tell me this before?"

He shrugged me off. "The only one I told was Suzy. And until today that's how I wanted it to remain."

"I'm glad you finally told me. So what happened after you shot her?"

"The sentry outside—a friend of mine named Buckmaster—burst in. He examined the body, then said, 'Joe, just leave. I'll take care of it. We'll call it self-defense.' He didn't even ask me for an explanation."

We resumed walking. I whispered, "I'm proud of you, Jóska."

"Don't be stupid, Béla," he snapped. "I don't want you to admire me. I've told you this because, to this day, I can't get that moment out of my mind. I still can feel her brain tissue on my face." Jóska jabbed his temple with a finger. "As soon as I shot her, I became her. 'Murderer' is a label I'll take to my grave."

"Why, Jóska? The war was still on. And you had found out about Mama and Papa and our siblings. She deserved it. She might have been executed later for war crimes anyway."

"Because we're not them. We pay a steep price for our misdeeds. I spent a year in misery for what I did."

"I thought you said no one but the guard knew that you shot her."

"I'm talking about Rita."

"Rita? You're speaking in riddles."

"Looking back, I think that's why I married Rita. I loved her, but I knew that she was broken and that I would keep cutting myself on her shards. Yet I felt the need to help her stay in America. At any cost. To do some good to make up for my sin."

"Because you shot that bitch? That seems a stretch."

"Trust me, it isn't." He wagged his finger at me. "I tell you this. No matter what this guy did to you during the war, if you kill him, even if you get away with it, it will haunt you."

We arrived at the 67th Avenue subway entrance. Lying ahead was upscale Forest Hills, with its dull six-story apartment buildings offset by Tudor homes, cobblestone courtyards, and turrets that reminded me of Palanok Castle, which overlooked my hometown. Jóska's new apartment building was nearby. We hugged. I kissed his cheek and then headed down the steep station steps for the quick ride home, all the while considering the differing shadows my brother and I had stepped out from.

*

When I next picked up meat, Langerman maneuvered around the counter to greet me. "I fired the bastard." Slapping me on the back, he added, "But you still owe me for that flanken."

The Beast, who I prayed would spend the rest of his years looking over his shoulder, never again entered my life. I was not to be the instrument of His vengeance, or of man's justice.

CHAPTER 67
Fleischmanns: Summer 1954

*All journeys have secret destinations
of which the traveler is unaware.*

—Martin Buber

Our life was mundane. Predictable. Lived in black and white, just as we chose. Until, with another revolution around the sun, we were revitalized by the freedom of summer.

Starting in the early 1950s, Marika, Esther, and I spent several weeks a year in Fleischmanns, a sleepy Catskills community with fewer than 500 full-time residents. In the summers it shed its skin and swelled to 10,000 or so, mostly German, Austrian, and Hungarian Jews escaping the city. They would fill its Victorian-style hotels and inns, which welcomed Jews at a time when that was far from universal in America. During the summers in Fleischmanns, the locals (many of whom also were Jewish) became the outsiders.

Some of the more well-to-do visitors who ventured north of Route 17 to the central Catskills preferred imposing hotels such as the Breezy Hill, Takanasse, and Mathes, where they distracted themselves with *narishkeit* (foolishness). On weekends, husbands played tennis, followed by martinis and cigars, while their wives met for brunch, played cards, and drank tea on the veranda with their pinkies outstretched. For Saturday night dinner, the men sported tweed jackets, while the women wore dresses with lace at the throat, adorned with strands of pearls.

We stayed in the Palace Hotel, a "schlock house" to the moneyed folks. And we counted the days until summer arrived, when we could be among other families with an erased past. Who ate, dressed, played, prayed, joked, gossiped, and embraced the serenity and night chill as we did.

The hundred or so Palace Hotel guests, including some who stayed on the Mansard-roof level punctured by dormer windows, cooked and served their own food in an expansive kitchen area. Marika's stove was next to the one used by Eva Nowicki, who was also an annual Palace Hotel guest along with her husband and daughter. Even in the heat of summer, multiplied by a lack of air conditioning in the kitchen, Eva wore a long-sleeve shirt to hide the numbers tattooed on her left forearm. Marika told me of the following Friday afternoon exchange.

"Eva, Béla is coming tonight. I want to make chicken paprikash for him as good as you make. What do you use besides chicken breasts and paprika?"

"Ground black pepper."

"How much of it?"

"Depends."

"On what?"

"How spicy you want the chicken to be."

Chapter 67

"What else?"

"Garlic powder."

"How much? A pinch?"

"Depends."

"Mrs. Finel told me that she mixes the spices with some olive oil and then rubs that on the chicken."

"Does Mrs. Finel have a husband?"

"No, he died years ago."

"Do you know how he died?"

"How?"

"From her cooking."

Our assigned dining table was by a window with a view of a row of boxwood hedges, under which lost toys would accumulate. We wore shorts to dinner (except Fridays), and cleaned our plates with a piece of bread impaled on a fork. Often, while eating, we would be serenaded by children playing "Chopsticks" and other two-fingered exercises on a baby grand piano with yellowed keys that sat in the far corner.

One Saturday night during our first summer in Fleischmanns, Marika and I were persuaded by another couple (and the availability of their babysitter) to join them for dinner at the nearby St. Regis Hotel, overlooking Lake Switzerland. The entertainment began with a comedian firing out cheesy gags between warbling out classics such as "Bay Mir Bistu Sheyn," in the manner of a Jewish Crazy Guggenheim. After his last song, he announced, "And now, we have ten gorgeous women about to join me on stage. You will have the difficult task of deciding who is the most beautiful of them all."

With the audience judging via applause, the field was narrowed to two women. One was a stunning, buxom blonde in a light gray, dressy skirt and top, whom I clapped for vigorously—too much so for Marika's taste. However, in a close "vote," the brunette was deemed the winner. At a table next to us, someone grumbled, "Of course she won. She's the owner's niece."

I was to learn many years later that the blonde had been born in Vienna and, when she was seven, on the eve of Kristallnacht, had fled with her family to Switzerland, where they found sanctuary. Our spirits had been unalterably connected on that evening, and I would reencounter Inge a quarter of a century later, when her daughter became engaged to my son.

Like most of the husbands, I worked in the city during the week and commuted back and forth on Friday nights and Sunday afternoons. Only I didn't drive and relied on buses or hitched rides, helping to pay for gas and tolls and chipping in for the occasional speeding ticket.

On a Friday morning in late June of 1954, Miki drove Marika (beginning her third trimester), Esther (who had completed the second grade), and me (I had the day off, having worked the previous weekend) up to Fleischmanns, to begin another country vacation. We rode in his company-owned, tan Chevrolet Bel Air that still held its intoxicating new-car smell, with a grille featuring a row of "teeth" that delighted Esther.

After three hours of driving and two rest stops, we reached the final leg, Old Route 28, a two-lane twisting road that followed a rippling stream. The upcoming exit had a familiar look.

"Miki, get off here."

"Calm down. We only just passed Kingston."

"Well, it can't be far now."

"Béla, you talk like this is your first drive there. Reach for the map in the glove compartment. You'll see that we've got another hour to go."

When we reached Main Street in Fleischmanns, none of us could remember where the hotel was. Thus began a chorus of "Excuse me's" to passersby, which initially led to a medley of shrugs because we insisted on asking for the "Place Hotel."

Chapter 67

"That last half-hour is on you, Béla," Miki whispered to me when we finally arrived.

After hauling the luggage to our room and leaving Marika to unpack, Esther and I embarked on a tour with Miki, beginning with the inside of the hotel. Miki stopped by the front door to read a plaque.

"Béla, did you know that this hotel is more than forty years old?"

"Still looks pretty new."

"And that it was built by a guy who lived across the street."

"What's his name?"

"Harrison Mayes."

"Wasn't he president?"

"No. And he wasn't Jewish, either."

We were in no rush. Each day in Fleischmanns was deeply lived, offering boundless memories and the promise of perfection. And each was infinite, at first refusing to surrender to the dusk and then folding seamlessly into a hypnotic dawn.

On the wrap-around porch with its fluted balustrade, a cat lay languidly on the thick handrail of a bright red and yellow Adirondack chair, perilously close to a birdcage. Circling the hotel, we passed four women surrounding a metal folding table plumped on a gravel lawn amid a kaleidoscope of beach balls.

"Two bam."

"Three crack."

Esther took Miki's hand and led him to the back of the hotel, a grassy expanse where, after dinner, kids would gather to play "Red Light! Green Light! 1, 2, 3!" A gnarled oak tree with heavy fingers reaching in every direction sheltered a weathered ping pong table with wads of gum on its undersides and cracked edges like spider webs that you aimed for to make the ball spin wildly. Two worn paddles and a ball lay on top.

Miki unbuttoned his sleeves, rolled them up, and assumed a fighter's crouch. "You can't beat me!" But Esther did, in a rout, a highlight of which was Miki slamming a ball well over her head that smacked me flush on the nose.

Behind the ping pong table was Bushkill Creek, a narrow stream that snaked around jagged boulders in ever-changing patterns. With rolled-up pant legs, Miki joined Esther in dipping their toes into water as clear as glass—water in which the "city kids" would catch tadpoles in jars with holes punched in their lids. Esther again bested her uncle, this time in a game of whose flat rock could skip the most before being swallowed by the water. As I sat watching them, I wished the dance of my daughter's life would slow. She lived in a time and place where life was glad to exist.

Our next stop was a nearby public tennis court, notorious for its perpetually ripped net, which led to arguments over whether a shot had gone over the top or through the net.

"Uncle Miki, I can play tennis."

Summers in Fleischmanns were about living life large. "Can you teach me?"

Esther turned to me, jumping up and down. "Can we play, Daddy?"

"Maybe tomorrow, *Mamaleh*. Let's show Uncle Miki the town."

Esther borrowed from a shed in the hotel backyard a Schwinn—crimson with a banana seat matching in color and high, rusted handlebars to which a bell was attached. Bicycles, many with playing cards attached to their spokes, were ubiquitous. They lay unguarded on asphalt driveways and smooth lawns amid a flood of discarded jump ropes, naked dolls, and plastic bats and balls. Children as young as Feri was when they took him to Auschwitz rode tricycles through the streets of Fleischmanns, barefoot and unattended.

Esther rode as Miki and I ambled down Wagner Avenue, past the merry-go-round and grand ball field donated to the village by Julius

Chapter 67

Fleischmann. Above us were maple trees whose tops met in the middle of the street, forming a delicate green parasol. Esther was passed by several teenagers on their three-speeds, likely headed to Catskill Park, where they would find a secluded spot to smoke Camels and drink Canadian Club.

The rank perfume of the ball field's freshly mown grass enveloped us. Across the street, under an avocado-green canopy of the Belleayre Restaurant, a couple sat with cups of coffee in an outdoor seating section. After a few blocks, we came to a steep-roofed, ivory clapboard building. "That's Congregation B'nai Israel," I said to Miki while waving off a too-friendly yellow-black bumblebee. "Meyer, the local kosher butcher, is the rabbi. We'll go here tonight."

"Why don't you take a break from temple, Béla? This is your vacation."

"I enjoy going to service. It's only an hour on Friday nights. You'll survive."

"I'm past just surviving. Didn't you tell me there was a movie theater in town? Let's see what's playing."

"Why do you have to act like a goy, Miki?"

"I'm as Jewish as you are. But it doesn't mean that I have to spend every Friday night in temple. It's enough to go on the High Holidays."

The year before, I had attended Yom Kippur services with Miki at his Reform temple. As the entire congregation rose before the calfskin-covered Torah to chant the *Kol Nidre* prayer, he had wept, his tears dampening a canvas of lingering sorrow. "Why go at all then?"

"Twice a year, to pray and atone, maintains our covenant with G-d."

"Why do you even care about the covenant?"

"Because it defines us. It's why we're special. Chosen. But I don't… but I don't feel the need to follow other men's ideas about how I should be Jewish."

To me, the path had been set. "We have an obligation to pray with our brethren every Sabbath."

"If I pray out of obligation, it's worthless, isn't it? I'm not willing to achieve the level of spirituality that requires giving yourself up completely to religion."

"If we don't go to *shuls*, they won't exist."

"Béla, synagogues in America are businesses. Like everything else."

I had told Miki of my dislike of the temple practice of selling tickets to holiday services. And of the hefty membership fees that some congregations required. In Munkács, the well-to-do had paid for most of the cost of the temple. "But do you want to see our religion fade away? Too many of us have died to let that happen."

"Nonsense. We can still keep our culture and traditions. That's what counts."

My beliefs likely would be the most valuable possession I would bequeath my children. "If we don't go to temple with our kids, they'll become like all other Americans, chasing material goods."

"I hope they do. It's not a sin to live well." My brother, only a decade past his wrestle with death, had now fully embraced the American dream. In January of that year, he and Inge had their first child, Barbara, and Miki had become a salesman for the Independent Chemical Company in Brooklyn.

"So you know better how we should live our lives. My little brother is smarter than the collective wisdom of sages over the centuries. Even knows more than Papa."

Miki's face reddened. He turned so that Esther couldn't see it. "The real reason you go to temple is to pretend that you're back in Munkács. That Papa is *davening* (praying) next to you. Because you can't handle your remorse. Well, I have no remorse. It died in Auschwitz."

My brother had suffered, more than I could know. Wasn't he entitled to find his own meaning in it? Had I found mine? Was temple

Chapter 67

facile solace? "I need synagogue in my life, Miki. It comforts me. I don't know why. I only know that it does."

Miki grabbed my shoulder. "I know. Just don't assume that it's the same for me."

The tune of a Good Humor truck, parked by a playground where a gaggle of children were playing ring-a-levio, beckoned Esther. She pedaled ahead with churning legs, while Miki and I sprinted after her. By the time we caught up, she was pointing to a picture on the truck's side of an Eskimo Pie chocolate-coated vanilla ice cream bar wrapped in foil.

"Want a cone?" I said to Miki.

"No thanks, Béla. It might not be kosher."

I laughed. "I'd hate you if you weren't my brother."

We turned left onto Bridge Street, which climbed over harsh boulders hemming in the chattering creek, followed by a right onto Main, stopping at Schimmerling's Bakery for cinnamon buns for tomorrow's breakfast. Then it was on to Gale's sundries store to sit at the six-stool lunch counter, under the paddle blades of a creaking ceiling fan, and drink Cokes that had been floating in a metal box filled with ice water.

On the way back, at the Onteora movie theater, with its Art Deco facade, *Dial M for Murder* was playing. Miki checked the schedule. "A 7:30 showing. Maybe I'll enjoy Marika's cooking and then hustle over here. Just watching Grace Kelly is worth the admission price."

"I didn't know you liked blondes."

"I'm a Jewish male. I'm supposed to. Certainly her."

In the end, Miki skipped the movie and temple, and spent time building a popsicle-stick house with Esther and reading to her. After sleep washed over her, Miki and I brought beers down to the large TV room off the hotel's main entrance, now vacant and stifling. In a corner, on an overhanging ledge, sat a Nok Hockey board with several wood pucks and sticks. Next to it, a clock radio was broadcasting the Yankee game on WGY from Schenectady.

We took over a coffee table in the back, on which a checkerboard had been painted in red and black. A box of plastic chess pieces lay on a nearby window sill next to an empty Coke bottle and an assortment of dead insects. Through the double window, lightning bugs, which the kids would try to catch in glass jars, sparkled like rhinestones and flashdanced amid citronella candles. I shoved it open halfway.

"It'll be a hot weekend. Can you stay tomorrow and come with us to the lake?"

"I've got to get back. Inge's parents and aunt are coming over." In a scant few years, Miki had progressed from suspected gigolo to beloved son-in-law, as if he were a kidnapper who had resolved to marry and cherish his victim. "Did you watch any of the McCarthy hearings, Béla?"

"No. It's over my head."

"Mine, too. But I watched anyway."

"In case Grace Kelly was called to testify?"

His grin was still magical, as transparent as when he was a teenager considering whether to tie Rabbi Gonzvi's *tallis* to a chair. "To see if they turn anti-Semitic. Americans already think that all Jews are communists."

"I don't know about that. But the Rosenberg trial didn't help. All the defendants were Jewish. Although so was the judge."

Most New York Jews and Jewish organizations had dissociated themselves from the Rosenbergs and from communism in general. Already, Germany had become rehabilitated in America's eyes, while the Soviet Union, which had saved so many Jews from death, including Marika, was the pariah. Every day, millions of memories are wiped away, time's eraser working its pink nub down to the metal. "Think about it," Miki said. "A lot of those being investigated by McCarthy are Jewish. And most of their attorneys are, too."

Chapter 67

"You think McCarthy is an anti-Semite?"

"No. His two closest advisors—Cohn and Schine—also are Jewish. But the public may not care about that."

He had left me to burn in the fire of fears that would shadow me into eternity. "So what are you saying? That the Holocaust could happen again? In America?"

Miki had been staring out the flyspecked lower half of the window. He turned to face me. "Yes."

"No. This country is different. Special."

"It is. I love this country. It saved my life, and Inge's. But don't delude yourself. People are people. If they feel threatened, they'll do anything to protect themselves."

"The whites in America hate the blacks."

"They hate us, too. Anti-Semitism was rampant here before the war. The Holocaust made that unstylish. But only temporarily. We always end up being the scapegoats. We can't trust non-Jews. And we can't rely on G-d, either. Look how well that worked out for us."

A chill coursed through me, as if dark glasses had been removed, revealing Jenő, who again was begging me to face reality. Would I be able to hear him this time?

*Béla and Marika on the lawn of the Palace Hotel,
mid-1950s*

Inge Shumer (woman on the right) in a beauty contest at the St. Regis Hotel in Fleischmanns, early 1950s

CHAPTER 68
Bingo Night

G-d has many names, though He is only one Being.

—Aristotle

On the following Friday evening, I hitched a ride upstate with Jóska, Suzy, and Kenny, who were headed to Karasoffs, a Cape Cod–style bungalow colony off Old Route 17. The next afternoon, Jóska and Suzy left Kenny with a sitter and came back to the Palace Hotel. Before our babysitter arrived, they spent time with Esther, with Suzy playing "beauty parlor" and allowing Esther to restyle her hair.

The four of us drove to the Grand Hotel, which overlooked Fleischmanns and was said to have been fashioned after the Grand Hotel on Margit Island. A true palace, it had been built seventy years earlier to cater to the socially prominent. The "Grand" offered the most sophisticated services in the region, including a bowling alley, croquet grounds, and a nine-hole golf course.

"What's the big deal about all this?" I asked.

"Béla, you'll never be a true American."

That night, there was to be a fireworks show in front of the hotel. But we had come to play bingo. At seven o'clock, the ballroom doors opened, and the crowd swarmed in like an ant colony gorging on dropped crumbs. We raced to a table in the back, ordered Sea Breezes for the women and Schlitz beers for Jóska and me, and paid four dollars for eight playing cards, along with a stack of poker chips. The air was filled with the overlapping of various European tongues, as young waiters and waitresses in formal attire rushed about in a volcanic haze of cigarette smoke.

On the half-hour, a man with a coconut-shaped head and wearing a tailored plaid sport jacket with patches on the elbows strode onto the stage carrying a cage with numbered balls. He announced himself as "Landy of the Grandy." His limber glide and self-confidence reminded me of Fred Astaire. Landy was accompanied by a lanky, overeager woman whose shimmering silk scarf was corded around her throat. "My beautiful assistant is addicted to gambling at bingo," Landy announced. "That's why her name is…Betty!" When the expected, appreciative groan from the crowd died down, he continued, "But me, I'm not addicted to bingo. I only play on days that end in Y." After a slight hiatus, needed to mentally calculate the names of the days, Marika and Suzy laughed. Jóska and I flagged down a bow-tied waiter to order potato pierogi and pickled herring.

We were warmed up with three games of straight bingo, each for a $10 prize, during which Landy, while periodically swallowing a toothpick, unleashed a maddening supply of bingo one-liners. I did chuckle when a white-haired woman won a game and, as she hiked to the stage for her winnings, he announced, "How do you get a sweet grandmother to curse? Get another one to yell 'Bingo!'"

Chapter 68

The last game was in three parts, capped off by a full-card finale that Landy introduced by flashing a smile that spread across his face like taffy. "What's six inches long, two inches wide, and drives women wild?" he teased. Howls of laughter erupted, as much from the women as the men, when Landy answered, "A $100 bill! And I have two of them to give out."

As the game drew to a close, only the hum of the electric lights and the spinning of the ball cage could be heard. One of Suzy's cards was down to a single open space. The rest of us abandoned our cards and surrounded her chair. Marika and I strained our necks to determine from other nearby cards if the required "G52" already had been called, while also softly chanting that number to the bingo gods. The game ended when an obese woman near the front threw up her hands and screamed, "Oh my G-d."

Piling out of the ballroom, Marika protested, "With the money we're paying the babysitter, we would have been better off staying home and playing gin rummy." We grabbed an empty table on the deck for a view of Monka Hill, where the fireworks had been set up. Placed on the faded pads of each chair were a plastic case laden with sparklers, a coupon good for a free order of homemade ice cream with each paid order, and pencils with the name of the hotel printed on them, a miniature American flag attached to their erasers.

Jóska pulled out his pipe. A croaking welled from his throat. "Take a walk with me." Chatting aimlessly as we circled the hotel, we settled on chaise lounges around a desolate swimming pool illuminated by a solitary, outsized spotlight. Surrounding us were the mountains' fading silhouettes.

"Okay, Jóska, why are we getting our asses wet on these chairs when we could be sitting comfortably with our wives on the deck?"

His face congealed into an ominous hardness. "Béla, have you decided what you'll name the baby?"

"If it's a girl, we don't know yet. If it's a boy, we plan to name him Anthony, after Marika's father."

His tobacco smelled of vanilla and almonds. "You should name a boy after Jenő. We need to honor our brother's memory, like Kenny honors Papa."

"Marika's father doesn't deserve to be honored? Marika was his only child. She and I may not have another. How else will he be remembered?"

"Anthony is not a Jewish name."

"Why not? What about Tony Curtis? He's Jewish."

"And he's Hungarian. But that's a Hollywood name. I forget his real name, but it's not Anthony."

"So if Anthony isn't a Jewish name, we'll find another 'A' name." Jóska crossed his arms.

"Jóska, you want me to name my son Jenő?"

"No, that's not a name that Americans give their sons."

A slight wave of nausea washed through me, caused by the over-chlorinated pool. Or perhaps by the conversation. "Do you need to have an opinion about everything?"

"People should have opinions. Nothing wrong with that."

"How about this? We'll name him 'J. Walter Raleigh Ingber,' in honor of your tobacco. With a name like that, my son is sure to become president."

His response was the whoosh of the match, followed by a test draw. "I'm serious. You should be, too. Any name that begins with a 'J' will do. Except, of course, for Joseph."

"*Keinem seht sech* (no one sees himself)," Mama would say. "Libu's son is Jerry. Don't we have this covered?"

"No, Libu's boy is named for someone on Miklós's side of the family. His Hebrew name doesn't match Jenő's."

The din from the crowd in front of the hotel was growing louder. I was adrift from the shoreline, within sight yet unable to bridge the

Chapter 68

distance to rescue myself. "I've got it. We'll name our son Jesus." As he grimaced, I added, "I'll think about it, Jóska. That's all I can promise." I rose from my chair.

"Béla, what about the middle name?" His pipe began gurgling as he searched his pocket for a cleaner.

Across my tongue crept a curse, which I swallowed. "Can we at least use Anthony as a middle name? Or is even that not acceptable?"

Jóska displayed not the slightest hesitation. "We don't know if there will be any other boys in our family. We need to honor Ferencz as well. He saved my life."

"What? When?" I said.

"Ferencz could have gone to the World's Fair, but he offered the ticket to me instead. He did that deliberately. To send me out of harm's way."

A hood of darkness had covered us, erasing shadows. I grabbed the pole that served as an arm rest and flipped my chair over on its side, listening to it clang against the tile. "What difference does any of this make? Our brothers are dead."

"You know it matters. A bond forms between the soul of the baby and the relative he is named after."

"So let me get this straight. Because you believe that Ferencz saved you, I can't allow the mother of my son to honor her father?"

"It's the right thing to do. If Papa were here, he would tell you the same."

"Papa told me a lot of things. Including that the Messiah was coming to save us all."

"Some of us were saved," he mumbled.

I lashed out at the chair with my foot, sending it in flight, followed by a splash. "No! How can you say that!" I said, safe in the knowledge that no one else could hear. "The best of us weren't saved, Jóska. They choked to death in a gas chamber. And I was partly responsible."

"Béla, why are you talking this garbage?"

"Because it's true. I should have done more to get them out of Hungary, just like Jenő asked me to. Instead, I blathered to Ilona about how strong the Czech Army was. And about all the great allies that our country had."

"You were trying to comfort her."

"No," I shook my head with cold purpose. "I should never have said those words. G-d was angered by my presumptuousness." I glanced up to find a crowd of faint stars watching us. "If so, dear G-d, why did you choose to sacrifice my cherished sister and her precious child? You should have taken me instead."

I wiped tears on my sleeve, afraid they would signal surrender. My brother stood and set his arm around my trembling shoulders. I shrugged him off.

"What's this naming nonsense really about, Jóska? Your guilt for having left before the war started?"

Jóska knocked his pipe bowl against the chair leg, spraying ashes. "I have guilt," he muttered. "How could I not?"

"And I understand that. But it's no reason why my son can't be named after Marika's father." I spoke the last sentence in jackhammer style, sending spittle flying. "I'm going back up. You can stay here all night and think of 'J' names. Just stay out of my business!"

We returned to the swoosh of a skyrocket announcing the start of the display, an amateur production—mostly fireworks with a sphere of stars that burned without a tail effect. Some had no stabilizing stick and jetted around on the ground, whistling shrilly like a swarm of cicadas. There also were Roman candles arranged in a fan shape that fired at regular intervals, their sparks filling the sky. The finale was a wailing burst of shells, its center a cluster of red, white, and blue. Amid the bangs, crackles, and hums, I could make out the distant voice of rising trumpets, their timbre reaching to the heavens, proclaiming the impending arrival of my child.

*

Chapter 68

The next morning, warming our hands on oversized ceramic mugs of Maxwell House instant coffee, Marika and I sat on matching rocking chairs on the porch, gazing at a sky framed by spiny tree branches clapping in the wind. Marika huddled in a charcoal-gray pullover sweater, while I welcomed the chill, drawing it in before the sun took firm command.

I related my conversation with Jóska. Marika responded, "Did you tell him to mind his own business?"

"Yes. But he's my brother."

"So what? With him it's always about the Ingbers. No one else counts."

"Esther's middle name honors your mother."

"Yes, but he never would have agreed to have her first name be Malka, or some other 'M' name, for my mother. Parents come first. Everyone knows that except Jóska."

"Marika, what about the name Jeffrey?"

"Now you agree with him? Where did you get that name from?"

"The cowboy movie we watched last month. The star was Jeffrey Hunter. He's Jewish."

She tilted her head to the side. "You assume that each person you like is Jewish."

"He looks Jewish. Has a round Hungarian face." Ahead of us, on the concrete divider separating the two sides of the hotel lawn, Esther and two other girls were playing hopscotch. Touching Marika's hand, I said, "I'm not sure we should honor a man who abandoned his five-year-old daughter. He let you drift among relatives."

"Because he didn't know how to take care of me."

"Didn't you tell me that, while you were left with an aunt, he only came to your apartment building to wave to you as you watched him with your forehead pressed to the windowpane? He never went upstairs."

She pouted, fighting tears. "I don't remember many hugs or kisses from him. He didn't know how to do that, I guess."

"It's not brain surgery."

"My father didn't understand how lonely and guilty I felt."

"Guilty?"

Her eyes were downcast. "Yes. I never told you this before, but during the *shivah* for my mother, I overheard two lady friends of my mom talking. One of them told the other that my mother had never been sick a day until she gave birth to me. That giving birth to me and taking care of me made her sick."

"Two ignorant yentas babbling nonsense."

"Yes, I know that now. But then, I was only five years old. So on top of feeling that I wasn't good enough for my mother to have stayed with me, I also believed that I killed her."

"I still blame your father."

Marika's face tightened. With several residents within earshot, she kept her voice low, yet burning. "Did you ever consider, Béla, the pain my father felt? He had lost his wife, who he loved very much, when he was still a young man. Maybe he needed the same comfort that I did. And he did come back for me."

"Only after he remarried and stuck you with a wicked stepmother."

Marika's lips pressed together as she glowered at me. "He wasn't perfect, Béla. Certainly not as wonderful as every Ingber male is. But he was my father. And I keep telling you…Rózsi was a decent woman. She favored Klari, but she treated me well."

"And I keep telling you that Rózsi didn't show you love. That's what counts. And your father wasn't good to you. It was only guilt that drove him to come back for you."

Marika banged her mug on the rim of the chair, spilling coffee. "No, I loved my father. And I wouldn't have if he didn't love me first.

Chapter 68

And do you know why my father died? Because he grabbed a bucket and left the air raid shelter, before the safety sirens had gone off, to get an old woman some water. He gave his life trying to help someone else. So don't say such stupid things!"

Of the miseries I endured, none had involved being subjected to hours in an air raid shelter. Dozens or more crammed together in the darkness, breathing musty air, eyes raw from acrid smoke, plaster falling and dust floating from a fluid ceiling into sandpaper lungs, each shrill whistle a knife to your frozen heart, waiting for the reverberations to end and the siren to sound, fearing a final blast, knowing that a direct hit might bury you alive, praying for a miracle.

"You never met my father. How can you judge him?"

"From your dread of abandonment. That's more than enough evidence for me. Sometimes I feel that our marriage is your attempt to reconstruct your relationship with your father."

"I'm so glad I married Sigmund Freud. Why don't you psychoanalyze yourself and your insane brother?"

Was I fighting with Marika because I wasn't able to stand up to Jóska? Yes, and no. I was lost in the shadow of her childhood traumas. "Yes, Jóska and I both are crazy in our own ways. I admit that. But at least we know how to love. Because we were loved by our parents. Unquestioningly."

Tears welled. "What are you saying about me, Béla?"

I took back her hand and kissed it. "I love you, Marika. With all my heart. But I see every day the pain your father caused you. And it's what I have to live with, also." She looked away as I continued. "A baby's name is a reflection of his namesake's character. Do you want our son to have your father's traits?"

"If we're good parents, our children will have our values. And if we're bad parents, then their names won't matter. Where did you get this silliness about a name being a reflection of character, as if a person's entire story didn't count?"

"I was taught that a long time ago. And I still believe it."

"You and I were taught a lot of facts, Béla. Including that the good will be rewarded and the evil punished. Do you still believe that one?"

Her eyes were hot coals, searing both of us. "I loved my father. And be honest with yourself. You're looking for excuses because you're afraid of Jóska. You always give in to him."

"It is hard for me to say no to Jóska. And we owe him a great deal, don't we?"

Marika rose with her mug in hand, grabbing mine as well although I hadn't finished. "Fine, Béla, I won't argue anymore. Only because naming our child is more important to you than to me." She turned toward the kitchen. "And I see that your brother is more important to you than I am."

I resolved to name our next child after Marika's father, regardless of the gender. But we did not have another. Marika never brought up the matter again.

Death, a scent that had clung to me for decades, shrinks in fear before the power of love. Her father's soul does live on, incarnate in our son. Amen.

CHAPTER 69
A Son!

What cannot be repaired is not to be regretted.
—Samuel Johnson

Jeffrey Fred was born on September 26, two days before the Jewish New Year, at Physicians Hospital in Jackson Heights. After the delivery, I pumped the doctor's hand, babbling "Thank you! Thank you!" as if he not only had delivered our baby but also arranged his gender. Then I scooped up our blanketed boy, searching his face for Papa's features, or Jenő's, or Ferencz's.

Marika lay exhausted, but blissful. She would have to return the newborn-size pink sleeping sack that she had bought weeks ago, so sure this baby would wear it. We were soon brought several blue options by Libu, Suzy, and Inge.

Jóska and Suzy were among the first to arrive at our apartment a week later for the bris. Jóska and I embraced, and he smacked my back heartily.

A friend from temple, David Gintz, was the *mohel*. We gave Libu the honor of being the *kvatterin*, who brings the baby from the mother to the *sandek*, on whose lap the baby sits while he is circumcised. In America, the *sandek* often is referred to as the baby's "godfather," although it's not the same as the godfather relationship in Christianity. In Judaism, the parents remain responsible for the child's spiritual and religious development.

As Libu carried the baby to the circumcision table, Gintz explained the significance of the *sandek's* role. Jóska pushed his way toward us, readying himself. "I would like to ask," Gintz announced, "Doctor Kovesdi to come forward as the sandek." Kovesdi, our family doctor and friend, beamed and thanked me for this honor. Jóska froze and retreated toward the back of the room, pulling Suzy with him. Without being noticed, he departed the apartment, and my life. After our guests left, I told Marika, "I'll clean up. Go lie down." I let Esther hold the baby as they both sat in my arms with their faces touching, a pose I could have beheld forever. Then Esther left to play in Lenore's apartment.

As I studied my peacefully sleeping son, his face was replaced with the blurred image of Ilona. *One day you'll be here at Ferike's son's bris, assuring his wife there is nothing to fear.* "My dear sister," I whispered into the crib, "I am so sorry. What was I protecting you from? Please know that Jeffrey Fred honors Feri also."

Chapter 69

Béla and Jeffrey, 1956

Esther, Béla, Marika, and Jeffrey, at Atlantic Beach, July 4, 1957

CHAPTER 70
Klari Nosti: November 21, 1956
(Budapest)

Every generation needs a new revolution.

—Thomas Jefferson

In early November 1956, Soviet tanks and troops invaded Hungary and, over the next week, crushed the fledgling revolution, leaving a gushing wound. Thousands of refugees fled across the border to Austria, while thousands more were jailed or deported to the Soviet Union. Amid the death and destruction in central Budapest lived Marika's stepmother, Rózsi, her stepsister, Klari, and Klari's husband and son.

Every day, although she was not a regular newspaper reader, Marika devoured the front pages of the *Daily News*. We searched together the photos in *Life* and listened each night to Edward Morgan's foreign news report on ABC radio. Then Klari's letter arrived.

At a kitchen table smelling of cleanser, with eight-year-old Esther playing in the living room and her little brother napping, Marika

Chapter 70

reread it several times, hoping the words might change. She grabbed a pad and pencil to write a shopping list of food and household items to ship to them. "Béla, I can't believe this is happening again."

"It's not like before. The Jews are safe. It's the revolutionaries they're after."

"And when the Soviets leave, the Hungarians, who think all Jews are communists, will blame us for the destruction."

"Rózsi and Klari will survive this. And we will help them."

"You don't know whether the Russians will start killing again! And you don't know that a pogrom won't arise there, one way or another," she said. "Or even here." Was I once again giving a woman, a mother, empty reassurances?

I pulled my chair beside her and wrapped her in my arms. "We're safe, Marika. This is America."

She shook her head. "When I was growing up, I was constantly assured that I would be safe. Even through most of the war I was told that."

"The war's been over for many years now." Had time erased its own chalk marks?

"No, that war has just been replaced by other wars. Look at Israel, at what's going on there."

"There's always a crisis somewhere in the world, Marika. But we live in a different time now." I waved the paper at her. Its headline read, "U.N. Troops Arrive in Port Said."

A faint cry emanated from the bedroom. Marika slapped the paper away. "The United Nations did nothing to help the Hungarians."

"The Security Council condemned the Soviets."

"But only after they had taken over Hungary and done their slaughtering. What good is condemnation against tanks and bullets?" Marika rose, handed me the letter, written on onionskin paper, and walked toward Jeffrey's room. "As much as Klari wrote, it's also what she didn't write that worries me."

My Dear Marika and Béla,

The fighting finally is over. The despots have won. No more cries of "Russkik haza" (Russians go home). We Hungarians, who spit on the head of Stalin's giant bronze statue, have succumbed.

Abandoned by the West, Hungary still is paying the price for its wrong flip of the coin during the war. Our building remains with bullet holes from 1945, and now it's as if we were back in those days. There are bodies being cut down from trees. Rubble and corpses all over the streets. The tram cables are torn down. And the cobblestones have been ripped up to build barricades, a futile exercise, like trying to put fallen leaves back on a branch.

I'm afraid of being arrested by the military police if I go outside. The Soviets have built underground prisons, where it's rumored they starve prisoners to death and feed the bodies to a meat grinder. To buy food is risky, because we've heard stories of housewives being shot for hoarding. And if you get on line before the curfew lifts, you can be shot for that. We live on preserves, beans, and peas. Who knows when we'll be able to reopen our business.

I am sorry to upset you. We will all be fine. I just wanted you to know that you were wise to go to America. It's as if we were all riding on a carousel and then your horse broke free while mine had not enough courage. I pray that my son, Gyuri, will make it off the carousel one day.

We hug and kiss you all. Give extra kisses to Esther and Jeffrey,

CHAPTER 71
The Trial: July 1961

Forgiveness is the fragrance that the violet sheds on the heel that has crushed it.

—Mark Twain

After Jeffrey's bris, Jóska and I did not speak for more than six years, each one layered awkwardly upon the next. A silence heard loudly. We would nod at each other during family gatherings, like two prizefighters passing warily before a bout, or grunt out a smile-less hello too frigid to melt the awkwardness.

"He's your brother! Without him, where would you be, Béla?" Miki coaxed.

"Make up with Jóska. You are hurting all of us," Libu pleaded.

During the war, maintaining self-respect was a salve to the pain. But now I had allowed it to morph into self-importance. I carried the mark of Cain, cursed for my ingratitude.

A month before my nephew Kenny turned thirteen, the phone rang on a Sunday evening while Marika and I were watching a puppet act on *The Ed Sullivan Show*. Marika raced to the foyer to answer it, and I heard her say, "I'll get him." As I approached her, she was untwisting the cord to extend its reach, wearing a "brace yourself" expression.

"Hello?" I said, as I stretched the cord into the kitchen on the pretense of privacy.

"It's Jóska. It's time already. Let's end this. You are my brother, and I want you at Kenny's bar mitzvah." After the call ended, I stared at the speckled gray linoleum floor, shedding tears. Could reconciliation be this easy? Had we changed enough? Could we speak the truth to each other without fear of another rift?

The next weekend, he and I resumed our walks between Elmhurst and Forest Hills, where Jóska and Suzy had relocated to a three-bedroom apartment with Kenny and their baby daughter, Debbie. One evening, we picked up sandwiches at a corner deli and sat down in my living room to watch WABC's daily half-hour evening coverage of the Eichmann trial. Eichmann had been captured the previous May in Argentina by Israeli agents and flown clandestinely to Israel. The trial had commenced in April 1961, as Passover was ending. A fitting time—hadn't the Nazis often chosen Jewish holidays as dates to terrorize?

People everywhere were talking about the Holocaust, out in the open. But as the five-month trial droned on, interest faded. The public's attention was diverted after the Russians launched a man into space and the Bay of Pigs invasion occurred.

Our couch was flanked by metal folding tables from the John's Bargain Store in Middle Village. In front of us stood a black-and-white, 21-inch RCA television set that Miki had unexpectedly brought to us earlier in the year, insisting it was a present from a client. The news anchor, Jim Bishop, introduced the events that had taken place that morning, the start of Eichmann's cross-examination by Gideon Hausner, the chief prosecutor.

Chapter 71

A lean and partially bald Eichmann shuffled papers and adjusted his headphone, his dark suit set off by a white shirt and striped tie. I leaned forward to examine him. Confined in a glass booth as if he remained a lethal creature able to kill with only a touch, Eichmann habitually tightened his thin lips and swallowed while rubbing his right thumb against his left forefinger. He answered Hausner's questions mechanically.

"What a nebbish!" I said. "I bet either of our wives could kick his ass."

Jóska responded through a mouthful of a tuna salad on rye, a trace of mayo clinging to the corner of his lips like a stray snowflake. "You're missing the irony. He looks more Jewish than you or I do."

"So what would you like to see? A six-foot-five blond Hercules?"

Washing down his bite with Cel-Ray soda, Jóska continued, "Miki told me that Eichmann did have dirty blond hair when he saw him."

I raised my palm at him. "Miki saw him? Where? In Auschwitz?"

"No, in Munkács. Just before the trains took them. Eichmann came to inspect the ghetto. Miki said that the Jews were forced to stand for a long time waiting. Then Eichmann marched in, wearing jackboots, with a bunch of German and Hungarian officers trailing him."

"What happened?"

"Eichmann talked sweetly to the crowd. He assured them that they would be safe. And have wonderful lives. He actually said that."

I shook my head. Libu would have heard his words also, I thought, picturing her body quaking like a hovering hummingbird. "I bet he had the same nonchalant expression as you see now. As if he's being accused of a traffic violation."

A copy of the *New York Post* lay on the credenza, underneath a lamp whose dented onion-shaped base had been repaired with masking tape. "Jóska, did you read that the *Post* predicted this would be a 'show trial' and suggested that it should be held in Germany?"

"The *New York Times* is even worse. They called Israel's actions 'immoral' and 'illegal.' Where were all these righteous people twenty years ago?"

"They did nothing! Nothing that mattered, anyway. But now they ask all sorts of questions. Can he be fairly prosecuted in Israel? Is it appropriate to try him in a country that hadn't existed during the war? Is Israel entitled to speak for the victims?"

"Easy arguments to make from a comfortable desk in America."

"The only question they should ask is whether Israel will authorize the death penalty."

Meanwhile, Hausner continued to question Eichmann. "Do you in your own heart find yourself guilty as an accomplice in the murder of millions of Jews? Yes or no, yes or no!"

"Yes, from the human point of view, yes," Eichmann replied, denying legal guilt.

I smashed my fist on the tray table, tipping it over and sending soda spilling onto my lap and the carpet. The couch, with its upholstery sealed in a plastic hazmat casing, was immune. "What does it matter what Eichmann feels in his heart? What a stupid question! He has a heart?"

"They should simply present all the facts."

"And why is it that we survivors feel convicted, while the Nazis all believe in their innocence?"

"Jews are trained from birth to feel guilty," Jóska said. "Religious Jews go to sleep reciting a confession. And on Yom Kippur, we run to temple to pound our chests and tearfully admit to bad deeds we never committed or even contemplated."

"Morality is a curse."

"Did you know that at one point Eichmann had a Red Cross truck placed near where the trains let out the Jews?"

"I hope all the facts come out. There's plenty more time left in this trial."

Chapter 71

Jóska eyed the liquor cabinet, whose bottles were arranged by Marika in size order, with each label facing squarely front. I pulled out the Zwack plum brandy from the front row of bottles, filling two shot glasses. I tasted mine along the back of my tongue, as I was taught to do by my brothers.

"I read that the Hungarians wanted to begin the deportation of Hungarian Jews in Budapest," I said. "But Eichmann ordered it to start in the Rus?"

"Sure. The Russian Army was closest to the Rus. Also, it was easier in a place like Munkács, where Jews were less assimilated, to herd them into ghettos."

"Eichmann thought that if the deportations began in Budapest, they would attract more of the world's attention and provide a warning to all the other Jews."

Jóska chugged down the brandy and then picked up the bottle again. "It's worse than that. The Hungarians weren't thinking of killing their Jews, just relocating them. It was Eichmann who insisted on transports to Auschwitz."

Eichmann had lived two decades more than my parents and oldest siblings—years of enjoying life with his wife and children. "So if they started the deportations in Budapest, our family might have survived."

"How do you figure that?"

"Think about it. With a few months delay, who knows? Auschwitz would have been inaccessible by then. And the Nazis' growing need for slave labor might have prevented their immediate killing."

"Sounds like you believe in fairy tales, Béla. Besides, it cuts both ways. If the Nazis had begun in Budapest, Marika might not have survived."

Rabbi Gonzvi had taught that no mortal could stand before G-d if justice were the only standard, which is why we subsist on His mercy. "Will they put him to death, Jóska? That's what I care about."

"I think so." He downed his glass. "But so what? They can't kill him six million times."

*

That summer, Miki's family was spending a month in the Catskills at a camp for adults and kids disguised as a bungalow colony. One Friday night, Miki drove from his sales job in Glendale to Elmhurst to give me a lift to Fleischmanns. On my lap in the front seat of his car was a travel bag, in which I would later discover five $20 bills that Miki had slipped into it. Our drifting conversation wound its way to the Eichmann trial.

"A long time ago," I said, "someone—a good person—urged me to love my enemies. And to pray for them."

"Why? If you love your enemies, what meaning does love have? It's illogical. What idiot told you this?"

"A nun."

Miki raised the tips of his hands from the steering wheel. "A nun? Cheap advice coming from her, isn't it? What did she know of our suffering?"

"She was a witness to a lot of it."

His mouth was a thin convex line. "How do you forgive a man who murdered your parents? Your sister? Her boys? Our brother's wife and their little child?"

"She said to love your enemy, not to forgive him."

"What's the difference, Béla? How can you love someone who's hurt you terribly if you can't also forgive him?"

"I don't know. I can't do either."

"But this nun could?"

"So she claimed. But then again, she watched the brutality as an outsider."

I turned to face my brother. "I don't want to be a victim anymore."

"When he hangs from the gallows, you'll be free."

CHAPTER 72
Eugene Schachter

We pass through the present with our eyes blindfolded. We are permitted merely to sense and guess at what we are actually experiencing. Only later when the cloth is untied can we glance at the past and find out what we have experienced and what meaning it has.

—Milan Kundera

That Sunday evening, I rode back to Queens with Eugene Schachter, a friend from Elmhurst who had for many years operated a dry cleaning and laundry store on Broadway. Its blessings, along with the automatic washing machines in the basement of our building, were not lost on me. My mother devoted two days a week to laundry. We kids made repeated trips to the Latorica with buckets yoked across our shoulders, water sloshing over their sides. Mama would heat the water in the fireplace. Bed sheets were "cooked" in an iron pot, while clothes were scrubbed on a washboard using a bar of yellowish soap made from fat that she would cut into pieces and boil to make into a lather. They were put through a wringer composed of rollers attached to a hand crank, rinsed in fresh water, squeezed again, and hung out to dry on a long outdoor clothes line (or on hooks in the storage attic in the winter, where they froze). This ordeal culminated when the clothes were pressed with an iron on a waxed board laid across a couple of chairs.

Schachter, born at the end of the nineteenth century, drove as unhurriedly as he lived. Always in the far right lane. Never exceeding the speed limit. Which allowed for much chitchat.

"Eugene, what do you think of the Eichmann trial?" I said.

The grit of the highway warmed my elbow, which was stuck outside the lowered window. The radio began playing a song in which a woman repeatedly asks some guy if he will love her tomorrow. Schachter lowered the volume. "Don't watch the TV coverage. Don't read the newspaper articles."

"Why not?"

"It's just a big show. Let's get it over with."

"I like that it's taking months. Gives time to present all the evidence, which shows how fair Israel is being."

"No, it shows how weak Jews can be," Schachter snorted, raining spittle on the leather upholstery. "We're doing ourselves a disservice. Take the piece of vomit out of that stupid glass box and shoot him. In my day, people were shot for far more trivial things."

Schachter had fought in the Great War as an Austro-Hungarian soldier. After a stop for a restroom break, I mentioned to Schachter a scene from *Paths of Glory*, starring my favorite actor, Kirk Douglas, in which French soldiers are ordered on a suicide mission to recover a well-defended German position during World War I. "Eugene, was that true to life?"

"Absolutely real, Béla. The same thing happened to me at Isonzo. After days of heavy weapons barrage launched by our side, which some morons in the officer corps fantasized had destroyed the Italians' fighting ability, an attack was ordered. We huddled together at the

Chapter 72

base of a series of ladders, with gas masks on and bayonets fixed. Smelling each other's diarrhea. I was so certain of the outcome that I handed a nearby medic a final letter to my family."

His story transported me to the trench at Cluj, where we stood with arms in the air, before the plane and the Romanians arrived. I grew light-headed, though Schachter had no clue. Seated side by side, we remained in worlds that rarely overlapped. Lost in his own remembrance, he drove on autopilot as he continued.

"The whistles blew, and we charged over the top and across no-man's land. Most of us had loaded up on booze beforehand. If you refused to leave the trench, they'd shoot you."

At the end of the movie, three innocent men are executed. That was us Jews, wasn't it? Always balanced on the edge of a razor. Chosen to pay the cost of humanity's failures.

"Our side had thrown up a white smoke screen for cover, but it didn't help. We were so close to the Italian line that enemy fire began immediately. Even with all the artillery and machine guns, until a shrapnel shell burst above me and deafened me for a time, I could hear the drawn-out screams of the wounded. I hear them still. I found myself floundering in a crater half-filled with sludge thick as pudding. To keep from drowning, I had to let go of my equipment."

I pictured Mr. Slow frantically thrashing in the muck. "It took forever for me to climb out," he continued. "Which was fortunate. Everyone else had been mowed down. Those not killed instantly had their bodies riddled with bullets. None of them made it past the barbed-wire entanglements."

He paused, as if having completed a theatrical performance. "That's quite a story, Eugene," I said. "You know, I had my own dumb-luck survival experience. They say that your life flashes before you, but it wasn't the case for me. I had no epiphanies, no out-of-body revelation."

449

"What?" Schachter responded. His concentration had been interrupted by a billboard showing a tanned blonde girl in pigtails staring in surprise as a cocker spaniel sneaks up behind her and pulls down her swimsuit bottom, revealing her lighter-toned tush. "Did you know that Coppertone was invented during the war by a Jewish soldier?"

I pursed my lips and bobbed my head vigorously, to convey that I was duly impressed. The driver of a turquoise Ford Falcon in back of us leaned on his horn. Schachter remained oblivious. "I can tell you, Béla, that it was the first time in my life that I felt G-d's presence."

"Because you believe He saved you? I wrestle with that myself."

Schachter banged the steering wheel with the bottom of his hand. "No! Because I believed that He deliberately put me in that crater! That He was playing with me. Tormenting me. You know that my mother died while I was away fighting?"

"Both my parents were killed while I was away in the camps."

Schachter grew pensive. "I had to crawl for hours, covered in mud, to make it back to my line. With a bullet in my thigh. That's why I limp. All that time, I cursed Him."

In the rumble of a broken exhaust pipe, the Falcon passed us, its driver glaring at Schachter. This was the longest running drama in history. He would cut us off. Emerge from his car with gun in hand. Isn't that how it always ends for us? I rubbed my forehead with the butt of my hand. "I've never cursed G-d. But sometimes I wonder about His motives."

"I stopped caring about them when Lorraine was born. Holding her in my arms, I felt something new. Hope. Purpose. I didn't thank G-d for having given her to us, just as I realized He isn't responsible for the bullet in my thigh."

"Is that why you never go to temple? I'm the only one in my family who still regularly attends services. Funny how brothers can have the same religious upbringing, but such different attitudes toward it."

Chapter 72

"Your brothers are like me. I don't feel that I have to go to synagogue or follow His rules to be a good Jew. I'm a Jew my own way. And I tell you, it's quite liberating."

"Eichmann also had a set of rules that he lived by."

Schachter patted my shoulder before returning his hand to the steering wheel. "Forget him, Béla. You know that old proverb—it goes something like, 'If you hate someone, you might as well dig two graves.' Well, I'm not ready to dig mine yet."

I laughed to myself. From Rabbi Gonzvi to Schachter, I still underestimated old folk. In their certainty lay the seeds of wisdom.

"You're an interesting fellow, Eugene. And well-read, I see."

"Not at all. I learned that saying from a fortune cookie."

*

Once during the dozens of rides that I took with Schachter to and from Fleischmanns, I was a sympathetic listener as he railed against automatic washers and dryers and "wash and wear" clothes, analyzed the Mets' failures, *kvetched* about the bile that was rock and roll music, and told stories of Palace Hotel intrigue. We never spoke again of Eichmann, who was executed in 1962. Schachter's war tales dwindled. Steadily, I witnessed him let go of his past.

CHAPTER 73
Uncle Joe Visits: June 1963

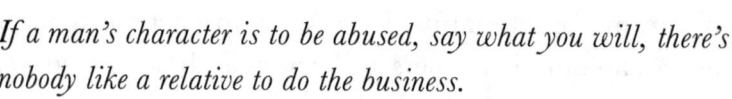

If a man's character is to be abused, say what you will, there's nobody like a relative to do the business.

—William Makepeace Thackeray

One Sunday morning, after breakfast, I reminded Esther and Jeffrey that their Uncle Joe was stopping by. "Put on nice clothes." My eight-year-old son, wearing a New York Titans tee shirt, P.S. 89 gym shorts, and a pair of dirty-white Keds Champion canvas sneakers, raced up to me. "But Dad, I want to go to the park. I'm meeting Simon to play basketball."

"You can play later."

"Nooooo! How many times do I have to sit and listen to him tell the same boring stories? It's not fair!"

As Jeffrey exited, Esther came out of her room, wearing a sleeveless dress of cornflower blue and white.

Chapter 73

"*Mamaleh*," I said, "You look beautiful." I turned to my wife. "Doesn't she?" Marika nodded without looking at her as she headed to the kitchen. I followed her and whispered, "You act like you're Esther's stepmother, not her mother!"

"I don't want her to get a swelled head."

An hour later, Jóska was holding court in our sunken living room, sitting with legs crossed in the middle of the couch, his leathery face a rich tint of cordovan. Acceding to the warmth, in lieu of his usual double-breasted plaid jacket, he wore a pale yellow knit cardigan over a sky-blue golf shirt. Completing the outfit were black pleated slacks that appeared custom-made, and tasseled loafers with whipstitch detailing.

"How was the cruise?" I said. "Did you get to walk on one of those pink beaches?"

Jóska gestured dismissively with the hand holding his pipe, as if swatting a fly. "I went a couple of times, but mostly I stayed on the ship. Bermuda is too hot this time of year. Anyway, it's the ship that makes the vacation. The 'Queen of Bermuda' they call it."

"Isn't that the ship you sailed on last year?" Esther said, reclining on a tan velour sofa-chair in the corner.

"Of course. It's the finest one in the Caribbean. And we had the best table on the ship. Next to the captain's."

I pictured a gray-bearded captain, in his phosphorescent white jacket with shoulder embellishments and gold buttons, jumping up and rushing over to where Jóska was seated, in the process knocking over a tuxedoed waiter holding up a tray of drinks and leaving his elegantly clad table guests to wonder. The captain would remove his gold-braid-accented hat, bow, and ask plaintively, "Joe, do you think that IBM is still a good buy?"

"Sitting across from us every night was a family from Scarsdale," Jóska continued. "The guy is a millionaire. You wouldn't recognize his name, but I did."

Rumpelstiltskin? I guessed silently. Perched on the living-room steps with his head in his palms, Jeffrey was alternating glances at the floor, where he imagined an escape hatch might be found, and his watch. Marika had fled to the kitchen.

"Did you have to wear fancy clothes?" Esther said.

"You should only know how many suitcases filled with dress clothing Suzy packed."

"That's why I don't go on cruises," I responded.

"Because you don't have a lot of dress clothes?" Jóska offered.

"No, because I don't have that many suitcases."

After giving me a what-the-hell-are-you-talking-about look, Jóska cleared his throat, momentarily silencing the drone of the window air conditioner. "At night, this guy at our table wore a suit that cost more than you would need for a down payment on a house." He waved his pipe distractedly, dispersing the aromatic blend that would degrade into a sour odor once Jóska left. "When we reached Hamilton, his daughter took a motorbike ride with Kenny. She was very interested in him!"

His monologue was shaping itself into a familiar pattern. No doubt, there would be an opportunity for a joint business venture with the millionaire. The guy's wife would likely invite Suzy to their country club for lunch. Jóska and his family would be pressured to move to Westchester, where Kenny would escort young ladies to debutante balls and Debbie would learn to curtsy, play golf, and sip tea through a lump of sugar. Nodding toward our new Silvertone TV, sitting on a cherry oak stand, I said, "I just heard on the news that Ben Gurion resigned."

Jóska leaned forward, releasing a slight whoosh from the cushion, and squinted at the set. "Where did you buy that?"

Maybe he hadn't heard me, for the resignation of the first prime minister of Israel had been shocking news. Perhaps I should have told him instead that Kennedy had resigned, to become Ben Gurion's

Chapter 73

replacement. After having himself circumcised. Or, better yet, of the announcement that all millionaires had been declared traitors by our government and were about to be deported. "Alexander's."

"Alexander's! You go to Alexander's to buy underwear, not TVs. Why didn't you ask me first? I could have gotten it for you wholesale."

Esther periodically shifted her bare legs to unglue them from the chair's plastic covering. I pointed to her dress, purchased at Fields Department Store in Jackson Heights, a neighborhood where, decades earlier, Jews—along with Catholics and dog owners—were overtly unwelcome. Fields was a store that hopefully my brother regarded as a step up from Alexander's. "Joe, do you recognize Esther's dress?"

Jóska glanced at it. "No. But she looks beautiful in it." He leaned toward Esther and winked. "A pretty girl like you should wait to marry a rich boy."

Yes, we all should be fabulously wealthy, blessed with every material treasure known to man. "It's what she wore at her Sweet Sixteen." Earlier that year, we held Esther's Sweet Sixteen party at Topsy's, a restaurant on Queens Boulevard known for its creamed chicken and corn fritters with gravy, served to patrons sitting in groups on wooden settle benches. In an attempted recreation of the Old South, all the staff were black, and the restaurant gave out baby-bottle nipples attached to a red and white mammy outfit as souvenirs.

At the party, Esther's friends had fawned over Miki. "Ouryay uncleway isway osay andsomehay!" While Miki bathed in female attention, Jóska sought out the owner of the restaurant, who shared with him the same passion for Merrill Lynch brokers.

Marika returned with a silver tray carrying a Lenox tea set, its pot and cups adorned with peach and blue butterflies. Then followed a plate filled with an assortment of Linzer torte and apple strudel that had been hurriedly purchased. Jeffrey glanced at the pastries and then at me. I signaled for him to take one.

While Marika poured a waterfall of steaming tea for Jóska, he reached into a colorful shopping bag between his feet, pulled out a white plastic wheel with BERMUDA *feel the love* stamped in bright red and yellow on it, and tossed it to an unprepared Jeffrey. "It's a Frisbee." My son stopped chewing on his pastry and examined the toy as if it were an ancient artifact. Again rummaging through the bag, building suspense in the manner of a magician about to pull out a rabbit, Jóska raised two small bottles of perfume and a red, buoy-shaped bottle of Old Spice.

"Chanel Number 5!" Esther exclaimed. "I always wanted that! Thank you so much, Uncle Joe."

"Aunt Suzy has a closet full of these bottles. Here, Marika. Here's one for you."

Once the food had vanished, Marika snuck back into the kitchen. Esther excused herself to meet friends at Jahn's Ice Cream Parlor, where they all would share a Kitchen Sink Sundae. Jóska's stories dwindled. We said our goodbyes.

Jeffrey sulked back to his room, banging his Frisbee repeatedly on his knee. "*Tataleh*," I yelled after him, "aren't you going to the park to meet Simon?"

"He's gone by now!" I took Jeffrey to the corner luncheonette for an egg cream and comic book.

CHAPTER 74
Flushing Meadow: August 26, 1965

This is a valley of ashes—a fantastic farm where ashes grow like wheat into ridges and hills and grotesque gardens; where ashes take the form of houses and chimneys and rising smoke and, finally, with a transcendent effort, of ash-grey men who move dimly and already crumbling through the powdery air.

— F. Scott Fitzgerald (describing Flushing Meadow in his 1925 novel *The Great Gatsby*)

Early in 1965, soon after turning eighteen, Esther became engaged to Jerry Rubin, whom she had met at a Queens College party. Jerry, two years older than Esther, came from a family with no European accents.

The wedding was set for the following year at the Fontainebleau in Westbury, Long Island. Jerry's father was friendly with the catering hall's owners and had struck up a deal for the Sunday of Labor Day weekend.

"Béla," Jóska said during one of our walks, "who is going to be Esther's maid of honor?"

Forgetting the audience, I answered, "Arlene, Jerry's sister."

"Not Libu? Shouldn't she have that honor?"

I wanted to shout, "Jóska, this is my daughter's wedding, not yours!" Instead, I mumbled, "I'll think about it."

That night, at the dinner table, I said to Esther, "*Mamaleh*, why don't you ask Aunt Libu to be your maid of honor?"

"Aunt Libu?" she responded. "Why?"

"It's the right thing to do."

"But I'm not close to her. And anyway, the maid of honor is always a sister, sister-in-law, or best friend."

"Béla!" Marika chimed in. "Libu is too old to be the maid of honor. You've been speaking to Uncle Tonoose, haven't you?"

"Yes. And I agree with him."

"So again he's going to run our life. Even this we can't decide?"

"This is different. It's the first wedding of the next generation. Shouldn't they honor their older relatives?"

Esther eyes reddened. "It's my wedding. That's not what I want!" She darted from the table. I searched Marika's face. "Okay, I'll tell him to mind his own business. (In the end, Esther asked one of her childhood friends to be maid of honor. Kenny was one of the groomsmen.)

*

"Béla," my wife instructed me, "I want a nice wedding for Esther. I want her to have the wedding I didn't have."

We needed money. Esther found a job at the Hollywood U.S.A. Pavilion at the World's Fair, behind the counter of its cafeteria-style restaurant. I applied for a second job to work nights and weekends as a short-order cook in the glass-enclosed restaurant at the Maryland Pavilion. That building, near the main entrance of the subway and close to the United States Pavilion, was built in the style of an Eastern Shore wharf. One of the more popular Fair destinations, visitors lined up at the pavilion entrance to watch a

Chapter 74

film that recreated the Battle of Fort McHenry and the birth of the national anthem.

"You got experience as a cook?" the line chef asked me.

"They taught us to cook in the Army."

He raised his pencil-thin eyebrows. "You were in the Army? Which unit?"

"You wouldn't know it."

"Why?"

"It was the Czech Army."

"The *what* Army?"

"In Europe. I also worked at the luncheonette at the corner of Broadway and Britton Avenue in Elmhurst."

"Don't know it. What did you cook?"

"Hamburgers. French fries. Omelets."

"Any fish dishes? Like crab cakes?"

"Yes…fish and chips."

He stared at me. "I think you're full of shit." But he was half-grinning as he said it.

"Mister, I need the job. I'm a hard worker. And a quick learner."

"Well, you're lucky, cause we need more staff. I expect you to pick up from the other cooks how to make our menu items. Can you begin tonight?"

I scrubbed grimy fryers and grills, washed dishes hardened with fat, and stocked supplies; then I graduated to preparing crab cakes, which I fried to a thin crisp. I never tried them myself but was told by a "true Marylander" that they were unpalatable and a disgrace to the state. At the height of my brief culinary career, I prepared blue-plate specials, Coney Islands (hot dogs), First Ladies (spare ribs), Jacks (grilled cheese sandwiches), and Noah's Boys (baked sliced hams).

I spent long hours on my feet inhaling a trembling heat that would set rocks afire, with my face bathed in steam. Always working on multiple orders and an ever-growing stack of order slips. Getting screamed at if it took too long to bring the food out of the grease-coated kitchen.

One humid Thursday, while on a week's vacation from the sheet metal factory, I worked a full day at the Maryland Pavilion. Marika brought Jeffrey there in the late afternoon. Before she left us, Marika whispered to me in Hungarian, "Remember that he is not yet twelve years old!" This was a reference to a Friday night in Fleischmanns a month earlier when, after arriving at the Palace Hotel, I slipped my son a brand new deck of cards with a different topless woman depicted on each of them.

"Jeffrey, don't let your mother or sister see this."

"Can I show my friends?"

"Only the boys. And only the older ones."

The gift made my son popular but it was soon uncovered, turning me temporarily into a pariah with Marika and the other mothers.

After Jeffrey and I shared a dinner of chicken and French fries, we headed north, walking past the monorail, futuristic street lights, and the General Foods information arches, finally reaching the elevated wooden track that crossed Roosevelt Avenue to Shea Stadium, where the Beatles had performed two weeks earlier.

I had bought tickets to the game weeks earlier, at the Mets ticket booth at Penn Station, for $2.50 each. Jeffrey was too young to reminisce about the Dodgers, but we had found out that the best pitcher in baseball, Sandy Koufax, would be starting tonight against the Mets.

Our seats were in left field, near the foul pole. At the bottom of the oversized electronic scoreboard past the outfield fence were various advertisements, including one with a picture of a smiling Yogi Berra holding a can of a chocolate soft drink called Yoo Hoo. Hanging from the railing at the front of our section was a bed sheet that read, "All the way with Sandy K."

Chapter 74

I bought Jeffrey a Coke from a barking vendor, the money and bottle passing each other with meticulous precision across rows of helpful hands. He drained it, his Adam's apple bobbing furiously. In front of us was a group of sailors in their service dress whites who kept up a steady stream of orders for watery beer.

Engrossed in trying to determine how the groundskeeper had created a perfectly mown checkerboard pattern, my education in baseball commenced, from a son who devoured the sports section of the local paper and the *World Almanac*. "Dad, do you know how many games Koufax has won already this year?"

"A hundred?"

"Twenty-one! It's amazing."

"I guess."

"Dad, did you know that Koufax has never lost to the Mets. He's thirteen and oh against them?"

"Thirteen and what?"

"Thirteen and zero. And once he no-hit them."

"No-what them?"

"No-hit. It means that he didn't give up a single hit. That doesn't happen much."

Jeffrey had mixed loyalties that night. Not me. I was rooting for the Super Jew.

Some kid named Tug McGraw was pitching for the Mets. He seemed to throw as fast as Koufax did. I couldn't conceive of how any hitter could make contact with a baseball. From my vantage point, there was an imperceptible interval of time between the pitcher releasing the ball and it disappearing into the catcher's mitt.

McGraw allowed a run right away, leading to a chant in our section of "Tuggie, you couldn't throw a party!" But in the bottom of the first inning, the Mets scored two runs to take the lead. Duly inspired, one of the sailors, while clutching his nth Rheingold of the young night with his left hand, used his right one to pull down the back of his shorts and underwear. Aiming a bared, hairy tush at the Dodger dugout, he roared, "Kiss my ass, you faggots!" He followed his chant with an extended fart. This demonstration led to a burst of giggles from my son and to Assman being escorted away by a bevy of security guards.

I tried to follow what the crowd did, to ensure that I reacted appropriately to different plays. Lucky for me, the man sitting next to me had the game's broadcast on a transistor radio. When the announcer became excited, I did also. Lulls in the action were livened by intermittent organ music and sing-alongs orchestrated by the scoreboard. After the banks of lights at the top of the stadium came on and darkness fully settled, we were treated to a view of the World's Fair fireworks.

Halfway through the seventh inning, while the organ blared out the "Mexican Hat Dance," I was admonished by my son to stand.

"Why?" I said, as the sailors, whose neckerchiefs now were unknotted, began arguing over whose turn it was to go for beer.

"It's the seventh inning stretch. Everybody stands."

We were in temple, but our roles were reversed. "But why do you need to?"

"I dunno. You just do."

The multitude was roused in the bottom of the seventh inning, when the Mets first baseman, a guy from the Bronx with the rather odd name of Kranepool, doubled off Koufax and scored on an error. Soon the Dodger manager came to the mound to take Koufax out of the game. After adjusting his cap for the hundredth time, Sandy ambled to the dugout, to concussive applause from a crowd standing as one. Before he left their sight, Koufax shrugged and threw his mitt into the dugout.

I was hoping to leave the game early, both to get Jeffrey away from the sailor in front of us—who had his head down, retching—and to

Chapter 74

beat the masses taking the subway. But the Dodgers came back with a run in the top of the eighth to make the score close. In the bottom of that inning, the energy in the stadium magnified as two Met players—one of whom, Ron Swoboda, sounded like he might be of Czech origin—each rotated their bats menacingly and then launched back-to-back homers.

"Jeffrey, the Mets are gonna win. Want to head home?"

"Noooooo. Maybe I can catch a home run!"

A Mets reliever named Jack Fisher, who I assumed must be Jewish, retired the Dodgers 1-2-3 in the ninth to nail down the Mets' win. Jeffrey raised his arms in triumph. "Dad, this is incredible. Nobody beats Koufax!"

*

In early October of that year, Koufax made history in a different way by refusing to pitch during the opening game of the Dodgers-Minnesota Twins World Series because it fell on Yom Kippur. This was the talk of the temple that day, as Koufax was known to be secular.

Walking home with Jeffrey in the late afternoon, he said to me, "I want to be like Sandy Koufax."

"You want to be a baseball player?"

"No. I'm not good enough."

"So what do you mean?"

"I want to be a Jewish hero."

CHAPTER 75
Oli Arrives: September 1, 1966

Man is not what he thinks, he is what he hides.
—André Malraux

On the Thursday morning before the wedding, Miki, Jóska, Jeffrey, and I (along with Suzy and her two children) stood at Pier 90, where Marika, Esther, and I had arrived a generation earlier, as the three funnels of the most heralded ship in the world, the *RMS Queen Mary*, appeared on the horizon—more than two hundred feet high and fivefold as long, a tipped-over skyscraper gliding toward us on the water's hem.

We adult men suffered through the ship's interminable disembarkation in ties and suit jackets that hid stained armpits. Spotting my brother was a challenge. The ship held two thousand or so passengers divided into three classes, each of which had its own gangplank. Adding to the confusion were the growing piles of luggage, which blocked lines of sight. Miki, Jóska, and I each picked a different walkway to monitor.

Chapter 75

"Is that Uncle Oli?" shouted Kenny. He pointed to a balding man dressed in a short-sleeved white shirt open at the neck and tan chinos who resembled his father. We all waved and shrieked, catching Oli's attention. He led his family and an overheated porter pulling a baggage cart over to us, weaving through breaks in the crowd like a fullback.

After tipping the porter, a man both unknown and familiar turned to face me. In his image was my youth. Oli opened his arms, and we bear-hugged; then kissed each other on moist cheeks, a reassurance that love had not been lost.

"You look good, Béla," he said in a Hungarian tainted with the slightest British accent. "Just as I remember you, except for this." He laughed as he pointed to my bald dome. I had not seen Oli since before the war (unlike Jóska and Miki, who had traveled to London on business), nor had I ever met his wife, Mary, or daughters, Ilona and Susan, eighteen and ten years old, respectively.

"Our curse." I nodded toward the ship. "Nice little boat you came over on. Not like the one that took you to Palestine, I imagine."

"For sure," he added, this time speaking in Yiddish, which made his face light up. "Plus this time I didn't have to jump overboard."

Jóska, carrying his daughter's jacket on one arm and a slender ebony pipe in his other hand, embraced Oli, as did Miki and Suzy. Oli introduced his family to Jeffrey and me, and Jóska and I presented our children. Mary was mild-mannered, her daughters shy.

"Everyone move together," I instructed. I took group pictures with an Instamatic camera. Then each man grabbed pieces of luggage. Bypassing a line of yellow cabs at the curb, we trekked to Miki's and Jóska's cars, walking double file, with Mary assuming the spot next to me. Unlike many of the other women who had traveled in cabin class (the equivalent of second class), she was modestly dressed in a plain white blouse and beige skirt, her only jewelry a wedding band and a slender gold chain.

The American brothers had speculated on the sustainability of Oli's marriage. Could he be happy with a non-Jewish wife? Could he trust her? Was she worth his betraying the memory of those lost?

"I'm so glad to finally meet you, Béla."

"The same, Mary. Oli has gushed about you in his letters over the years."

She blushed. "Oli says that you and he were close growing up and that you're the sweetest of the Ingber men."

"True, I'm the least likely of the brothers to cause his wife to throw a pan at his head. But that's only because Marika isn't violent."

She chortled. "So Joe and Miki are hotheaded also?"

"Stubborn, I would say."

"There is a wonderful bond between you brothers and Libu. I can tell from how Oli speaks of each of you. And how priceless your correspondence is to him."

Where was the evil *shiksa* we had imagined? "Esther apologizes for not being here to greet you."

"I suspect that she has quite a lot to do today. Ilona is thrilled to be a bridesmaid!" Ilona was directly ahead of us, walking next to Kenny, who towered over her. Sporting an Audrey Hepburn-like beehive hairdo that had been the rage early in the decade, she turned upon hearing her name. If, two decades earlier, Jóska had not been inhospitable to Oli moving to America with a non-Jewess, these two cousins, only a month apart in age, might have been close.

A block later, we reached the parking lot. Mary grabbed my arm. "We must find a way for our families to meet more often, Béla. My daughters have so few relations from my side. And Oli sorely misses you all, even though he'd never admit that."

"Yes. Hopefully we can return the favor when Ilona weds. If not sooner, Mary."

Chapter 75

"Wonderful, Béla. We'd love to show you around London. And you know, once you're in England, a trip to the Continent is a breeze. You and Marika could take the night ferry to Paris or Brussels. And from those cities there are plenty of trains to Budapest, where I understand Marika is from. Although you'd need a bit of time for that part of the trip."

Oli had written of Mary's life during the war. Her family had endured the Blitz. During that time, Mary was a volunteer firefighter, racing through the streets to join bucket brigades and search the rubble for survivors. But did she understand the war's lasting effects? "London would be nice to visit. I don't know about the rest."

"Does Marika still have relatives in Budapest?"

Rózsi was now dead. Klari and Marika maintained a sporadic correspondence.

"The years have taken their toll. I'm not even sure what family remains there."

"That's part of the adventure, isn't it?"

Pretending to react to a nearby car horn, I turned from her. "The Continent is one large cemetery to Marika and me."

"Sorry," she offered.

I shook my head, suggesting she needn't be. "No man ever steps in the same river twice. Isn't that the saying?"

*

Oli and his family stayed for a week in Libu and Miklós's split-level ranch house in Westbury, not far from the wedding site. In the early evening of that first day, the Hermels hosted a barbeque, laying out on several foldout tables grilled meats, salmon, and vegetables wrapped in foil. Miklós, chef and bartender, ladled fruit punch tanged with pineapples for the children, while the adults, including Kenny and Ilona, who were both over the legal drinking age in New York, helped themselves to a pitcher of Yago Sant' Gria. "The finest sangria available," Miklós declared.

Kibitzing in ever-changing clusters, the family traded stories, rushing to bridge a decades-long gap as if our shared DNA removed the stigma of being strangers. We spoke of the details that framed the edges of our lives. The bond between the two cultures was cemented when the next generation combined in off-key renditions of "Eleanor Rigby" and "Rainy Day Women" (with an alarming emphasis on the words "everybody must get stoned").

The wonders of the Queen Mary were recounted.

"I had my hair done in the ship's beauty parlor," Mary announced.

"We played shuffleboard on the deck and watched movies in the evening," Ilona said.

"I swam in an indoor swimming pool," yelled Susan.

"You couldn't have finer food in the best London restaurants," Oli said.

When Esther and Jerry arrived, we gathered in a circle and toasted our British cousins and the bride and groom to be. With Esther the focus of attention, Oli pulled me aside.

"What's Miklós like?"

"Why?"

"He seems nasty to Libu."

"Oli, you barely know your sister as an adult, and you just met Miklós, her husband of almost twenty years. And already you're making judgments? You see that he makes a good living." I pointed to Miklós, who, while talking to Jóska, was grasping Libu's arm as if it were made of delicate porcelain. "And can't you tell that he adores her?"

"I know what I see. An overbearing man bossing around his submissive wife."

You must have passed a mirror, I thought. "Oli, you remember Libu as an innocent, but that was taken from her long ago."

Chapter 75

"She's vulnerable. And we're her older brothers."

He could hear the scars in her voice and feel the ever-present tinge of remoteness. I had long ago acclimated to them. "So you want to save her? Is that right? Or is it that you only want to look like you're doing so?" Before he could object, I added, "Did it ever occur to you that she may be happy?"

Oli produced from his jacket pocket a box of Good & Plenty and popped some in his mouth. Ironically for a dentist, one of Oli's addictions, in addition to gambling and strip clubs, was candy. "Think about her situation, Béla. Libu grew into womanhood without a mother or older sister to teach her about men."

"That's not true. Libu had Mama and Ilona with her until she was eighteen."

"A girl needs the guidance of older females for longer than that. To help her choose a proper mate and start a home."

"I thought you were a dentist, not a shrink."

"When I was studying dentistry, I took psychology courses in a nearby medical school. I can recognize clinical depression."

"You know it all, don't you? Just like Jóska. Why don't you two share your guilt complexes?"

"I don't suffer from guilt. I fought. I risked my life."

Fighting with the British Army's Palestine Regiment, Oli had seen action against Rommel's Afrika Korps at Tobruk and El Alamein, before being sent to England for the Normandy invasion. Five years of active service in all. But the war had ended two decades ago. When would it stop consuming us? Had it no statute of limitations? "You did, Oli. And I'm proud of you for it. We all are. I'm asking that you not mess with Libu's life."

"I only want to protect her."

My dear brother, doesn't each of us want to go back to a time before it was too late? I pointed my finger at his head. "You Brits and the Americans should have moved up D-Day by a year. The time Libu needed protection was in May 1944. So that she wouldn't be wearing a long-sleeved blouse on a warm night."

Did I have the right to lecture him? Of the two of us, Oli had been the one courageous and wise enough to escape. Susan ran up to show her father a Beatles record that Miklós and Libu had given her. I whispered in Hungarian, "Just love her, Oli. Don't try to heal her."

*

The saffron sunlight faded into ribbons of peach orange and mustard yellow. Despite dangling flypaper strips and generous applications of insect repellent, mosquitoes illuminated by nightlights sawed the air around us in a frantic dance. The other celebrants fled into the house. As I moved to join them, Ilona grabbed my arm.

"Uncle Béla, can I ask you something?"

"Sure."

"The wedding, it will be a Jewish ceremony, right?"

"Of course."

"What I mean is...." Her eyes were moist. In spite of a rum-scented breath, my niece projected sobriety.

"Ilona, what's the matter?"

"What I mean is, there was never any question that Esther is Jewish, and that she would have a Jewish wedding?"

What nonsense had Oli filled her head with? "Did you think that Marika was Christian? She's Jewish." I stopped myself from adding, *So there's no conflict about religion in our household.*

Her mouth was slightly agape. "I didn't know, Uncle Béla."

"Didn't know what?"

The tears flowed, which she dabbed with a tissue. "That I'm half-Jewish. I always assumed both my parents were Catholic. That's what my Mum's family is."

Chapter 75

"How can that be!" I lowered my voice. "You've never celebrated Jewish holidays? Gone to temple? Heard about what the Nazis did to your father's family?"

"No. I only know that they died during the war."

"What did your father tell you about his religious background?"

"He never spoke of it. He and Mum are so mysterious."

Over time, all secrets are laid bare, including wounds lodged deep in the heart. We can only struggle to affect the timing. "When did you find out that your father is Jewish?"

"Last night. When he asked me to join him at one of the ship's bars. I was thrilled. We listened to a jazz band and drank sherry. And somewhere between glasses, my dad described his past to me."

Each one of us wears a disguise. But how could Oli have chosen to be clothed in this one? "I'm sorry that your father hid his upbringing. Sometimes, we do wrong things out of love."

"Perhaps." Ilona composed herself before adding, "But my father's never told me that he loves me."

I leaned over and kissed her forehead. "Of course, he does."

She considered this distractedly, as if a toothache suddenly had arisen. "I asked Mum this morning why they had denied me an understanding of who I am. She said that it was my father's place to tell me."

"Do you know that you are named after our sister?"

Ilona hesitated. "I thought…I was named after your mother."

"No, Esther is, since she was born before you."

"Well, I do know that your sister died during the war."

"Do you know how she died? And why?"

"No."

What was my proper role here? Shouldn't the details come from her father? But Ilona was an adult now. And my brother had opened the gates. "Your aunt wasn't merely a Jew who died in the war. She and her two little boys were murdered by the Nazis."

Wafting through the glass doors that led to the Hermels' family room were the faint lyrics of "Sounds of Silence."

"We learned about the Holocaust in school," Ilona said. "Not a lot, but enough. I just never thought it related to me directly."

How could I possibly translate her father's old life? "I'm sorry, Ilona. I'm not the one who should be explaining it all to you."

"I'm such a different person from who I was when we boarded in Southampton. Do you know that we aren't even going to live in our home anymore?"

"What?"

"My father told us on our first night out on the ship that he's sold our house. That we are moving in a month, and to start packing when we return. Just like that. Without asking us or even Mum." Her ivory cheeks blushed. "It's not so terrible for me—I'm out of school now. But Susan took it badly."

Hearing a buzz, I slapped the back of my neck, too late to avoid a bite. "We should go in, Ilona. I'm happy to speak more with you. But you should talk to your parents first."

From left: Oli, Kenny, Suzy, Susan, Mary, Debbie, Jeff, Miki (head partially hidden), Ilona, Béla (photo taken by Jóska) – September 1966

I moved to open the door, but Ilona reached for the handle, holding it in place. "Everything is changing for me. Soon I'll be in a new neighborhood and starting a new job. People who meet you for the first time often ask about your background. And I want you to know, Uncle Béla, that when they do, I'm going to tell them that I'm half-Jewish. I plan to tell everyone that from now on."

CHAPTER 76
Mamaleh

Men employ speech only to conceal their thoughts.

—Voltaire

On the evening before her wedding, Esther and I sat at the kitchen table, on dining chairs that scuffed the room's floral wallpaper, sipping hot tea fresh from a whistling kettle.

"*Mamaleh*, are you nervous?"

"Yes, but I know that tomorrow's going to be wonderful."

She stood and stretched to close the door. "Dad, can I ask you something? Yesterday, during our gown fittings, Ilona told me that she didn't know until a few days ago that she was half-Jewish. Why didn't Uncle Oli tell her before? Why did he keep it a secret?"

Is changing who you are the same as keeping a secret? "He was trying to shield her and Susan."

"From what?"

A voice lives in all Jews, even ones residing in paradise, which whispers that we will inevitably experience hell. "From suffering.

But you also have to understand that Europeans of our generation and earlier are different from you transparent Americans. Keeping secrets is our stock in trade."

"Why?"

"The pretentiousness of European society. Did I ever tell you about Mom's aunt?"

"The one who watched her after her mother died?"

"No, that was Mom's mother's sister. I'm talking about Mom's father's sister. She immigrated to New York before the war."

"I didn't know that Mom's dad had any siblings."

"Nor did Mom or I. Imagine our surprise when an old lady who somehow found us through the immigrant grapevine rang the bell at our apartment on Riverside Drive, telling us that she was Mom's aunt. We didn't believe her until she showed us photos of Mom's family. That's how we have some pictures of them."

"So, why didn't Mom's dad tell her about his New York sister?"

"Who knows? I remember that she told us she had a daughter. Maybe the daughter was born out of wedlock. Or maybe, like Oli, she married a non-Jew and was shunned by the rest of the family. I was so angry about it."

"You were angry with that woman?"

"No, I had no reason to be. In fact, she was very friendly. But I was mad that we hadn't known about her, because she might have been able to help us get to America earlier. And knowing that she had an aunt living in New York would have given Mom some comfort about coming here."

"So now you're telling me about a secret that you've kept from me," Esther teased.

"*Mamaleh*, I swear, it never occurred to me before now to tell you about this, because we didn't stay in touch. My point is that, for Europeans, lies and omissions are more acceptable."

"Does that mean you're not angry with Uncle Oli?"

Chapter 76

I sensed the tightness in my expression and tried to relax it. "No, I am." (In fact, after my conversation with Ilona, I had pulled Oli aside and heatedly whispered, "You name your daughter after our sister and you don't even tell her that!") "Because this is different," I continued. "He has an obligation to tell his children what was done to his family, and then they must tell their children."

"It will change her. On some level, I'm sure she's already been changed by living in a house of secrets, which all children of survivors do."

"I didn't think that you were affected that much by it."

Her eyebrows pulled up. "Of course I was, Dad. It's a big part of who I am."

My baby was grown. Leaving the house. Yet I still didn't know her. There had been too many silences. Was there any time left? "How so?"

"For one thing, I always believed that you and Mom must have been more courageous than others to have lived. And because I was your child, that I was somehow superior also. I definitely gained strength from it."

In my stories of the labor camp, I often made myself the hero. If only she knew. The truly brave ones—who spit in the Nazis' faces for the momentary satisfaction of it —were the first to be slaughtered.

"I also felt different from the other kids," she continued. "Not just because I didn't have grandparents or because you and Mom have accents. It's that I had to be more serious, and to grow up faster. To be prepared for life and what may come."

Were the happy moments in her teen years mere pretend? I rose and walked to the gas stove burners to boil more water. "Sounds to me like it kept you from being a child. I never wanted that."

She reached up to me and placed her hand on my forearm. "No, Dad, I think that knowing what you and Mom went through made me appreciate my childhood more."

The cold blueprint of my history had become my daughter's as well. She lived under the overhang of its shadows, which not even our love could erase. "I wanted to be the father to you that my papa was to me. To be a pillar of strength."

Esther eyes teared. "You are."

The Holocaust had rendered us far more than one generation apart. "Then why, ever since you became a teenager, did you stop telling Mom and me things? For years now, everything always is 'fine.'"

"Because I know that's what you both want to hear, especially Mom." I glanced toward the room where Marika and Jeffrey were watching TV. For how much of Esther's young life did she pine to be mothered, instead of having to mother her own?

"I'm sorry, *Mamaleh*. That's not the Holocaust's fault."

"No, but it didn't help. Dad, I'm proud of you, and I'm proud to be Jewish. I want my children and grandchildren to identify as Jews. I won't keep secrets from them."

Kissing Esther's forehead, I said, "I'm so happy to hear this. Now go to sleep, so that Mom and I can walk a rested young woman down the aisle."

*

Esther was resplendent in her wedding dress, her love and self-assuredness a confirmation of the choices that Marika and I had made. When Marika was nineteen, her world was a shroud. Esther, now nineteen herself, had never been forced to hide.

Over the ensuing months, I reflected on my wedding-eve conversation with Esther. Especially during Purim, which held magic in my house because its heroine was Queen Esther. During the Purim service, the rabbi spoke of her virtues. Queen Esther's father had passed away before she was born, and her mother had died during her birth. She was adopted by her cousin Mordechai, who instructed her from an early age to hide her Jewish identity.

Chapter 76

"The root of the Hebrew word 'ester' is 'saiter,'" the rabbi explained. "Which means 'concealment.' The lesson of the fable of Queen Esther is that we must discover G-d's purpose for us. In Esther's case, it was her ability to suppress her identity, revealing it at the precise time needed to save our people."

Could the Purim story hold a suitable explanation for Oli's behavior? But Queen Esther knew when to pierce her wall of disguise, while Oli would have maintained his deception forever if he could have.

I recited the rabbi's lecture to Schachter on my next visit to his store. We were in the back, and Schachter, shrinking from osteoporosis, was bent over a pressing machine. On the back wall, above a conveyor thick with laundered shirts sheathed in plastic, was a sign that declared, "We fight white grime!" I had not yet finished before he shrieked, "Béla, can't you see that so much of what rabbis do is simply mental masturbation? I tell you, if a baby were born with two penises, instead of worrying about his condition, the greatest Jewish scholars in the world would get in a room and spend eight days arguing over which penis to circumcise first."

I repeated Papa's words to Eugene. "There's a reason for scholars' interpretations. To get us thinking about what isn't obvious."

He waved his hand dismissively. "It's all a fraud. The rabbi decides on a theme he wants to preach about and then plays with words, intricately, as if he were splitting the atom, until he gets the desired result. They do this with letters and numbers, too."

"But isn't the purpose of spirituality to understand what's outside our perceptions?"

"Maybe there's some good in that. Lord knows—no one is better at theorizing than we Jews. But ignoring plain reality is dangerous. It clouds our reasoning, and leaves us without the answers we actually need."

"Reality is relative...."

Schachter observed me as if I had tracked dog poop into his shop. "Bullshit!" He jerked up the handle of the presser, releasing a hiss of steam and forcing Schachter to wipe vapor off his thick glasses.

"I'll give you an example. A fucking real-life one." He leaned closer, speaking in a reverent tone suggesting that the story to follow would be a valuable gift. "The Purim after Hitler came to power, my father rushed home from *shul* and told me that the rabbi had analyzed the Gematria (system of numerology) for the Purim characters and announced during his sermon that the numerical value of the letters in the name 'Queen Esther'—608—was identical to those in the name of the German national anthem. He was all excited."

"Why?"

"Because he insisted it was a sign that we were assured of there being a savior from the Nazis. My father believed that up until the day they took him to Auschwitz."

CHAPTER 77
The New York Public Library: May 19, 1969

Though a man conquer a thousand thousand men in battle,
a greater conqueror still is he who conquers himself.
—Udanavarga

The serene lions ignored me as I sped past them, turned left onto Sixth Avenue, and climbed the side-entrance steps of the New York Public Library. At the front door of the Jewish Division, a sign proclaimed a Holocaust Remembrance display, to be open for several more weeks.

In the Division's sparsely populated reading room, a clean-shaven man with cropped red-gray hair sat at the information desk, perusing the *New York Times.* In front of him was a plaque that read "Leonard Gold."

"Excuse me, Mr. Gold."

The man took the time to finish the sentence he was reading before looking up. "Sorry, Aryeh…I mean Mr. Gold, won't be in today. I'm Sam. How can I help you?"

Today was the twenty-fifth anniversary of my family's deportation to Auschwitz. Or close enough. "I'm trying to find books about the Jewish community in the town where I was born. Particularly what happened to it late in the war."

"And what town was that?"

"Munkács. It's now in the Ukraine."

"I know where Munkács is," he said, peering at me as if he were being set up for a swindle. His eyes, the color of a mountain lake in the midday sun, locked onto mine. And then I knew.

Mind you, over the years, I often had made a fool of myself by insisting that someone I noticed on the street, or in a store or restaurant, had been a friend, neighbor, or classmate from Munkács. After every "Don't I know you?" Marika would chide me to stop the make-believe. But this time, I was certain. My memory sprung to life, as it does when you're effortlessly able to sing along to the words of a song that you loved as a kid but hadn't heard in decades.

"Your last name is 'Gonzvi,' isn't it?" I said.

His stare turned inward, his mind a battlefield replaying flashes of a lost childhood. "How do you know me?" he said.

"I'm Béla. Béla Ingber. And you're the Shmuel I used to play with when we were kids. Whenever your father and mine would get together."

Sam's expression left me wondering whether he would embrace me or insist I leave immediately. Then, yielding to a connection as fragile as it was compelling, he rose and yelled to a co-worker in the back. "Hy, can you cover for me for a few minutes?"

Sam led me past a man asleep in the arms of a chair and into a back part of the Division, replete with carts laden with musty books to be wheeled into the massive stacks and refiled. We sat at a dusty desk on swivel chairs. He patted my hand. "So nice to see you again, Béla."

"Do you remember me?"

Chapter 77

"Yes, a bit. Your family lived in Oroszvég, didn't they?"

"Yes."

"How many of them survived?" he said, as if inquiring about the weather.

My answer was subdued as well. The passage of years had allowed for that. "Most were killed in '44. Or before then. Four of my siblings survived. What about your family?"

He chewed on the corner of his mouth. "Of nine, I'm the only survivor."

"I'm so sorry to hear that. Other than you, I only remember your papa. He was a fine and learned man. Like my papa. Older men like them had no chance."

Sam picked at crooked, saw-like teeth with his tongue, forcing his red-veined nose to widen. "That's not quite true. You know who survived? Of all the Munkáczer Chassids?" I shook my head as he pointed to the high, cracked ceiling as if it weren't there. As if heaven was merely ten feet above us. "Rabinovich survived. Our illustrious captain, who should have been the first one to go down with the ship."

"He survived Auschwitz?"

Sam dissolved frostily into himself and then resurfaced. "No!" His finger now was jabbing at his chest. "I survived Auschwitz. And Dachau. Where I said the *Shema* (a prayer to be recited before death) every day I was in that hell."

"Again, I'm so sorry. And Rabinovich?"

"He and his family got out of Munkács before the deportations. They escaped to Budapest and used their connections and money to obtain visas to Palestine."

"To Palestine? Wasn't he a fervent anti-Zionist?"

"No, that was his father-in-law. Rabinovich was more pragmatic," Sam said, while rubbing the back of his neck.

I changed the conversation. "Do you have a family?"

"Yes, my wife and I have four kids. They're all out of the house now."

"Grandkids?"

"A couple. They live not too far from us, in Bayside. And you, Béla?"

"Two kids. Our daughter is married. My son is finishing high school."

"I'm glad for you."

"And I for you, Sam. At least we and our families are proof that Hitler did not succeed."

"He didn't succeed? What the hell are you talking about?"

I raised my palm. "Sam, I'm sorry. I think you know what I meant. Only that our people have survived." I swept my hand across the room. "And I see that you've followed in the footsteps of your father and become a Jewish scholar."

Sam shrugged. "Scholar? Maybe. I'm a librarian who knows a lot about Judaism. But Jewish? Not like my father. I follow the teachings of Buddhism now. Though I still keep some of our traditions."

"Buddhism?"

"Yes. Don't look so puzzled. I don't sit silently with a shaven head wearing robes, or bow to anyone. But I've studied Buddhism for years. I've replaced prayer with meditation."

I pictured Papa in the *shtiebel*, a *tallis* draped over his head as if he were playing hide-and-seek with a child, absorbed in prayer. Wasn't that also meditation? "What's the difference between the two?"

"The difference is that I'm through with blind faith. Where does that leave us except always feeling like a failure because we can never meet G-d's expectations of us? Why pray to G-d to give us the strength to be who we aren't? Instead, I meditate to be who I am. To see myself and the world clearly. I still want to be the best person I'm capable of being, which is the goal of prayer, too. Not as one of many but as an individual."

Chapter 77

"I'm comforted by belonging to a Jewish community. And prayer helps as a collective yearning."

"Does it, Béla? Did it help your papa or mine? If *mitten drinen* (they suddenly) appeared now in front of us, how would they explain what happened to them, to all the six million?"

"They would say that we collectively had sinned."

"Okay, you can pray and wait for the Messiah. I'll meditate."

"So if your father were standing before you now, what would you tell him? That you're no longer a Jew? That you're a Buddhist?"

"They aren't mutually exclusive. Buddhism isn't a religion. It's a set of principles to live by without losing oneself. Without looking outward to a god. I am Jewish. It's in my blood, and in my children's, and so on. But would my father see it that way? No. Would he understand? No."

"I don't understand, either, Sam, honestly."

"I know. What's important is that we never stop talking about the Holocaust. That's what we owe our family."

"So on this we can agree. But I ask again. What would you say to your father?"

Sam glanced at his watch, and then stared hard at me. "I haven't seen my papa in twenty-five years. So you ask, what would I say to him? That's easy. I would hug him. I would kiss him. I would tell him over and over again that I love him." He rose from the seat, indicating that our conversation was over. "After all, Béla, what else matters more?"

CHAPTER 78
Yad Vashem: December 1977

*Courage is rightly esteemed as the first of human qualities...
because it is the quality which guarantees all others.*

—Winston Churchill

By 1977, Esther and Jerry were living in an idyllic neighborhood in Plainview on Long Island with two young daughters, and Jeffrey was studying at NYU Law School and engaged to Linda Shumer, whose mother had been the Fleischmanns beauty contestant. At the end of that year, in the fulfillment of a lifelong dream, Marika and I visited Israel. Forsaking the Holy Land in the spring of my life, I had reached it in the decay of autumn. I had come to my second home. A haven if the unimaginable happened. And the only possible explanation for G-d's permitting the Holocaust.

On December 11, we boarded an El Al flight from JFK airport. Over eleven hours later, nearing Ben Gurion airport, fellow passengers

Chapter 78

chanted the *Hallel* (prayer of thanksgiving) and broke into an impassioned "Jerusalem of Gold." We walked down the ramp into a chalky light made more illuminating by recent events. Only weeks earlier, Anwar Sadat had become the first Arab leader to officially visit Israel, meeting with Menachem Begin and speaking before the Knesset. Peace negotiations began in Cairo, inspiring hope for a permanent settlement with Egypt.

One morning in the middle of our ten-day guided tour, while in the City of David, we taxied to Yad Vashem, entering through heavy black doors on which welded iron bars formed broken shapes. We began at the Hall of Remembrance, built of large basalt rocks laid one on top of the other. The stone slab above them gave the appearance of an enlarged tombstone.

At the new Children's Memorial, the names of one and a half million murdered children were continuously recited in the dark eternity of an underground cavern. Soon Marika, with red the color of blood seeping from her sclera, tugged at my arm. "Béla, let's leave. I can't bear to hear this."

"Why don't you take a cab to the mall on Ben-Yehuda Street? I'll meet you in a few hours back at the hotel."

Searching for the caged spirits of my youth, I continued on to the Reading Room, where, with the help of Naomi, an enthusiastic librarian whose spectacles hung from a chain around her crinkled neck, I sifted through a catalogue of oral testimonies. On an impulse, I asked Naomi to assist me in locating old articles penned by Jenő Ingber. I held my breath. She emerged from a back room filled with microfiche files with a printed copy, of poor resolution but readable, of a March 1938 *Prager Tagblatt* editorial written in German. I guessed it to be the one he drafted the day of Feri's bris.

I read slowly, each word a rekindling of his flame. It was as if I had lived all these years in unbroken dialogue with my brother.

My Dear Fellow Citizens of Czechoslovakia,

As patriotic members of the only democratic nation remaining in Eastern Europe, one that continues to allow individual rights and to protect its minorities, we are all saddened by recent events in Austria. Our neighbor has suffered the influence of Nazism for years, from the assassination of Dollfuss to an ongoing campaign of terror. The latest outrage was the recent cancellation, under threat of invasion, of a plebiscite that would have asserted Austria's independence. Instead, the German Army was "invited" to march in.

To their eternal shame, thousands of Austrians have passionately welcomed the Nazis into their country. The photos from the Heldenplatz are compelling. What transpired in Germany over five years now has happened in Vienna in five days. Streets are covered with swastika banners. Leading politicians have been imprisoned, and anyone opposing Nazi rule is subject to arrest and torture. Jews are being attacked and humiliated in public, thrown out of universities, and their properties seized. Young hoodlums heave paving blocks into the windows of Jewish stores while crowds cheer. The cries of "death to the Jews" have reached another nation.

What are we to make of this? Some of my colleagues continue to maintain that Hitler sincerely wants peace. That he merely seeks to protect ethnic Germans. That he has no further plans for expansion. That we should welcome him as a bulwark against Stalin and the Bolsheviks.

When will our naïveté finally die? The Nazis' assurances of peaceful intentions are velvet ropes guarding a tiger. To trust them is to render oneself deliberately blind. To live in a fool's paradise.

As our nation's father once cautioned, "Dictators always look good until the last minutes." The Führer despises the Czech people. We are a barrier to his plan to gain "living space" in the east. He weakens us by aggravating tensions between German and non-German citizens. With his conquest of Austria, the underbelly of our nation is exposed. We cannot help but be the Nazis' next target.

Chapter 78

We Czechs now must prove worthy of the rights we have enjoyed for the past two decades. We must acknowledge the threat and prepare to fight it. And our Allies must understand that now is the time to join us.

I am a proud Czech and also a proud Jew from Munkács. And sadly, I have seen in my hometown a battlefield of a different kind. A spiritual one that corrodes and divides. Throwing stones at a mythical devil is sheer foolishness when Satan, hurled from heaven for seducing Eve, is back among us. He tempts us again, not with the sin of violence, but that of indifference.

There can be no further compromise. I urge you to believe in all possible evil. Its tide is ceaseless. Its waves wash over, pulling us under.

I kissed the page. "You are my hero, Jenő."

*

The practice of placing notes into the cracks and crevices of the Western Wall is ancient, founded in the belief that the Divine Presence remains there and that all prayers ascend to Heaven through the Temple Mount. I learned of the Wall in *cheder*, where I was instructed that a direct ancestor of the Munkáczer Rebbe had been the first, centuries ago, to inform the Jews of Europe of their obligation to come there to pray. Now, each year, hundreds of thousands of papers are collected from the Wall and buried on the Mount of Olives.

That day, after leaving Yad Vashem, I stood in a lengthy line of men, eyes closed and rocking back and forth in supplication. I pressed my forehead against the unyielding stones, and kissed them. In my pocket were two white, square-shaped papers. On the first, Marika asked for health for our children and grandchildren. I reached above my head and slipped it into a gap.

The second note had been prepared many years earlier. On it I had written, "When the time comes, reunite me with my loved ones."

CHAPTER 79
The Dream: May 20, 1979

*Time can do all sorts of things. It's almost like a magician.
It can turn autumn into spring and babies into children,
seeds into flowers and tadpoles into frogs, caterpillars
into cocoons, and cocoons into butterflies. And life
into death. There's nothing that time can't do.
Except run backwards. That's its trouble
really, it can only go one way.*

—Alex Shearer

Libu, Miki, and I stood in the tranquil orderliness of Mount Golda cemetery in Huntington Station, amid polished granite gravestones sprung up like the earth's teeth, the markers of time and memories. A series of sharp "seeps" from unseen warblers broke the calm. Nearby, an elderly woman wearing a pink button-down sweater despite the warmth was stroking the engraving on a tombstone, whispering final statements never made. Across the main road, workers were digging a perfectly rectangular hole, leaving soil sprinkled with worms chopped in half by shovels.

Chapter 79

Before us was a modest Holocaust memorial arch, erected by a Hungarian immigrant aid and benefit society. Drawing us, like paper clips to an immense magnet, to six million voices crying out.

"Jóska wanted us to wait until he got back from Europe," Miki said. "Too bad he didn't have a clear return date."

"Is this the thirty-fifth anniversary?" I said.

Miki had rolled up the sleeves of his white dress shirt and loosened his tie. "I'm not sure," Miki answered.

We covered our heads and recited the *Kaddish* to those who know the secrets of what follows this life. Afterward, Libu, in a black knee-length pleated skirt and beige silk blouse, picked up three loose rocks, each caked with an immovable coating of dirt as if fugitives from the deep earth. We placed these still witnesses on the arch's ledge and then tiptoed around grave sites to a nearby stone bench partially shaded by a red maple tree.

"If they had survived the war, Mama and Papa would be gone by now," I offered. "But Ilona would only be seventy-three."

"And her boys...," Libu whispered.

"Would be in the prime of life," Miki finished.

What is the prime time of one's life? Every day is precious, yet every moment fades. I tried to picture Feri as a man, but could only feel his tiny arms holding me tightly as he rode on my shoulders.

"Do either of you remember your last day in the Munkács brickyard?" I said.

"Too much so," Libu said. Sitting in the unshaded part of the bench, she pulled sunglasses from her handbag. "The night before we were taken away, Feri and Marcel sat between Mama and Ilona, who played button football with the boys, pushing buttons torn from Mama's coat. But the kids were scared and famished. They couldn't focus. So the women took turns reciting fairy tales until the boys gave way to sleep, curled up on Ilona's lap." I pictured my Jeffrey as a little boy, one for whom I would have gladly given up all my moments, past and future.

"The idle stretches were the worst," Miki said. "Who wanted time to think? We couldn't plan, only worry." A breeze blew Libu's spent Kleenex to his feet. He reached down, but it danced away. "Then the trains arrived. We were told that we were being resettled."

"Did you know to where?" I said.

Miki looked down, as if the answer were written on his shoe tops. "No, but we understood what 'resettlement' meant. All the rumors now made sense. But Papa and I never discussed it directly." He faced Libu. "And certainly not in front of the women."

Miki was only twenty years old then. How would I have coped at that age? "Papa and I sat together until late into the night, he doing most of the talking," he continued. "More rambling than purposeful. Like he was going through a box of old photos. Telling me of his childhood, of the first time he met Mama, of building our house."

Papa believed the Kabbalah's teachings on the immortality of the soul. Would he have taken comfort from them? Would his memories have consoled him or torn him apart?

A truck door slammed. The workers had piled their shovels and a wheelbarrow into the back of a pickup. The lady in the pink sweater had disappeared. We were alone.

In older days, I'm told, cemeteries were popular spots. Families would picnic in them. Now, they are places that you only whisper you've visited. Odd, because we live in a world filled with constant reminders of the dead, like old movies, history books, and family albums. We embrace death, so long as it's at a safe distance. Or sanitized.

Miki squinted as he followed the truck's taillights. "In the early morning, Papa told me of a dream he had. In it, he was walking. First in a flower garden, but soon he came upon rows of trees." Miki pushed his hands against his knees and stood, facing us with hands in

Chapter 79

his pockets. "More and more of them, until his path became a maze. He wandered this way and that, guessing at which direction would lead him out. Walking on and on. After quite a while, he came to a fork. This time, he chose with certainty. Then he woke up."

Even in sleep, the only time when the prospect of paradise was in reach, those in the brickyards couldn't escape. "What was his interpretation of the dream?" I said. Unlike me, who found dreams irrational, Papa was excited to hear about them. He believed that at night our souls ascend to heaven to replenish and to experience visions and encounters that are otherwise forbidden to us. Ferencz once commented that Papa could spend all day in a rug store, interpreting each of the patterns.

"Papa told me," Miki said, choking on the words, "that it meant G-d had accepted his bargain."

"His bargain?" I repeated.

A veil of purifying stillness fell upon us, which lasted long enough for Miki to find a lifeline. To reach back into time without being trapped in it. "His life...." Tears formed, each one a dagger. He took a deep breath. "His life, for mine."

Libu burst into sobs. We each rose and hugged Miki. Libu led him back to his seat, where we three sat fumbling with tissues. Studying the ground, with our hands creating space and distance.

We sat basking under a noon sky washed clear. Down the road, at the cemetery's entrance, a hearse with tinted windows was pulling into a parking spot next to the funeral director's house. "That last night," Libu said, picking up from where she left off, "Ilona slept a little, but I couldn't. Mama napped, too. When she awoke, she took my hand and kissed it."

"Did she say anything?" I asked.

"Only a few words." Libu removed her sunglasses and rubbed her eyes. "Mama said to me...'If you live, I live.'" Before burying her head on Miki's shoulder, Libu added, "That is my last clear image of her."

CHAPTER 80
Eulogy: May 1981

If I told my early history to a stranger, he might feel sorry for me. Robbed of a life as a carefree teenager, I lived for years in drenching fear and then endured two concentration camps. I watched as my parents, sister, sister-in-law, and three little nephews were led to the gas chambers.

So if I were to tell you that I have been blessed in this life, you might be puzzled. How is this possible?

My blessings are many. My husband and soul mate, Miklós. My beloved children, Evelyn and Jerry. My dearest brothers Joe, Béla, and Oli, and their families.

But I stand before you not to speak of them, but of Miki. Miki and I were only three years apart and a boundless presence in each other's lives. We played, studied, and explored the world together. He was the person who could best remember me as I was. Who from the earliest days knew my heart.

Miki was my constant teacher. I learned from his refusal to accept anything less than a full and rewarding life, which led him not only to survive but also to thrive and to find his own unique blessings.

I lived because the Angel of Death sent me to the right. And Miki as well, and I could bear what came after because my brother remained beside me even

Chapter 80

when he wasn't. All through the nightmare, and especially during the worst days in Bergen-Belsen, his distant music whispered in my ear. I imagined him as a candle approaching through a valley of darkness, somehow finding and rescuing me. I knew that my brother was capable of miracles. Miki saved me through my faith in him.

Miki was happiest when surrounded by his wife, children, siblings, nieces, and nephews. He kept us together, and played peacemaker when my other brothers—and you all know of the mishegas of the Ingbers—were warring.

Miki would do anything for his family, and he proved that time and time again. His greatest joy was being able to help us. If I mentioned in the slightest manner a problem that I had, he would try to fix it. If I was troubled, he suffered along with me. If I window-shopped with him and saw something I liked, I would not be surprised if he purchased it in spite of my protestations.

My brother came back from a world that most cannot fathom. He lived to comb gray hair and dance at his daughter's wedding. Yet, of course, he left us too soon. In the middle of his story. With so much still to give.

Am I being greedy in wishing he would return to us, as he did from the camps? I've learned to fill many holes in my heart, but this one is too deep.

Miki lives on within Inge, Barbara, and Ronnie. And, if memory is a form of love, we will all love him forever.

*

A younger brother is not supposed to die first. If anything, Miki was owed extra time for those years taken from him. But he had refused to go to the hospital. "I'm fine," he insisted, until he collapsed. Not accepting weakness had kept the Nazis from defeating him. But now, it prevented him from living.

We, his siblings, remained in shock. And during that time, the fabric of our extended family unraveled.

CHAPTER 81
Aviva's Letter: August 12, 1986

One lives in the hope of becoming a memory.
—Antonio Porchia

Esther's two children, Jessica and Dana, and Jeffrey's first, Arielle, all were daughters. In the summer of 1986, shortly before the birth of my only grandson, Craig, a letter arrived from Israel. Reading this fingerprint of a former life brought me back to that night with Ágnes, first at the Csillag and then on the Korzo, a night filled with longing.

After Ágnes returned home in March 1938, her father's declining health required that she and her mother stay in Prague for several weeks. Oskar Lőwie never left the hospital. After he passed, Ágnes and I met again, but now we held each other at arm's length, choosing our words carefully. The screen depicting our love had faded into darkness.

Chapter 81

Two months after the funeral, Ágnes immigrated to Palestine. She moved from kibbutz to kibbutz before joining the fledgling hotel business with her new husband and her mother, who escaped shortly before the war began.

Our correspondence was sporadic, each letter a fallen petal, and ended during the war. But Ágnes would reach out to me one more time.

Dear Mr. Ingber,

My name is Aviva Becker. I am the daughter of Ágnes Lőwie. I found your address with the help of HIAS.

My mother recounted many stories of her youth, which I still treasure. You were in many of them, so many that I feel I know you. She spoke of you fondly. I know that she and you once were lovers.

My mother and father had three children, of which I am the youngest. My oldest brother was killed in the 1967 War, a sorrow that none of us ever recovered from.

I am sorry to tell you that my mother recently passed away, from the same cancer that took her father. She felt fortunate to have lived long enough to enjoy grandchildren, and to see the blossoming of a primitive Palestine into the beautiful country we live in.

My mother and I spoke at length every day in her final months. I came to understand her more deeply than I could have expected. She had few regrets. One of them was not keeping in touch with you.

Mama asked me to write to you after she was gone. To say that she had always carried you in her heart. And to ask for forgiveness for calling you a coward. Through all the years of her life thereafter, her remorse for that accusation only grew.

Mama told me that you are a brave man. That it took more courage to stay than to leave. That she was blinded by her own desires.

I hope that you are no longer angry with her, if you ever were. Perhaps you don't even remember those words. But I wanted to honor my mother's wishes.

I wish you and your family much health and happiness.
Sincerely,

*

I handed the letter to Marika. She read it while I brewed a pot of Colombian roast.

"Ágnes was your first love, right?"

"Yes."

My love for Ágnes seemed long gone, taken by the same cresting wave that had carried away the yearnings of youth. But was it? At the least, I remained with nostalgia for the richness of days with a woman who knew me to the core and who gave of herself to her core. Days for which there was never proper closure.

"Do you remember the conversation with Ágnes that her daughter mentions?"

Maybe, with all your soldiering, deep down you're just a coward. Those hours with Ágnes were a memory that I tried to let go of, like releasing the string on a balloon, yet was burned indelibly. "Her words never bothered me. I didn't let them define me. And I knew she didn't mean them. That it was just her trying to be manipulative."

"I'm surprised that you loved someone like that."

Not expecting her jealousy of my affection for Ágnes, I shrugged. How could I explain?

"Will you write back to Aviva?"

"Yes, to thank her for her letter and send my condolences. And to assure her that I was never angry." As Marika reached for the coffee pot, I grasped her arm. "I was almost thirty when I met you. There were other women before you. But none after. You are the love of my life." She smiled, relaxing as if I had spoken those words to her for the first time.

Chapter 81

My response to Aviva would need to be carefully crafted. A tepid condolence from me might disavow her of the notion that I, too, carried her mother in my heart. I would tell Aviva that I still lament what I had left unsaid all those years ago. I should have praised Ágnes for the depth and beauty of her spirit. And for her courage.

Ágnes had followed her passions and enjoyed a fulfilling life. One might say that she had made her bed, as did I. But was this true?

For the longest time, I denied the conventional wisdom that we are the sum product of our decisions. That we have control of our fate. It appeared clear to me that the choices that outline our lives, ones as clear as white chalk on a tarred driveway, are made for us, not by us. Who we are born to and raised by. Our race and our heritage. How smart and attractive we are. The era and place that we live in. The economic, educational, and social opportunities allowed us. Who we stumble across in the marathon of our life. Who chooses to love us, in spite of ourselves. And who elects to hate us, however innocent we are. The war taught me that the impact we make on the established framework of our being is marginal.

Only with age did I unlearn that lesson. Our circumstances are not our destiny. It was true that in those last months together, Ágnes and I followed conflicting muses. But, over subsequent decades, we were fortunate enough to have been free to define ourselves.

I am proud of my choices.

CHAPTER 82
Clement Clarke Moore Homestead Park: June 1989

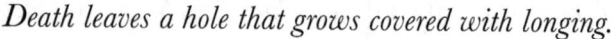

Death leaves a hole that grows covered with longing.
—Bernice Eisenstein

This was a day without distinction, its miracle drowned in the quicksand of routine. Marika and I shopped at the Key Food across the street, whose narrow aisles prohibited two people with carts from passing. I schlepped a full laundry basket to the clanking washing machines in the basement. Marika slipped into a discount store around the corner for a bargain on a new blouse and matching summer handbag (my wife had the rare ability to go into a store with a particular item in mind and not come out with any other). I read the *Daily News* and the *Jewish Press*. Marika prepared chicken soup and chopped liver with generous amounts of egg.

It was a Friday whose harbinger of freedom was misplaced on us retired folk. Esther telephoned to confirm plans to pick us up in

Chapter 82

the morning for a weekend visit. I called Jeffrey to remind him and Linda to light candles tonight.

The sun's web had burst its gold upon us. But this was overshadowed by a pervasive mindfulness that, less than two weeks earlier, Jóska had passed away at a hospital in Glen Cove. After weeks of lingering in a coma, trapped at the border between life and death. Last night was the first time I didn't think about Jóska before falling asleep. Had I already stopped mourning?

With the Sabbath arriving late and chores accomplished, Marika and I had time to spend in the blacktop park on Broadway. As we entered, I pointed to a plaque on the park wall. "Marika, did you ever notice that? All these years of coming here, and I never had read it until a few days ago."

"What does it say?"

"Who the park is named after. Some famous poet named Moore. I forget his first name."

She teased, "He must have been Jewish, right?"

"No, can't be, because he wrote a well-known Christmas poem."

"So what? Didn't Irving Berlin write 'White Christmas'?"

Why were we talking about poems and Christmas? "I keep expecting Jóska to come for a quick visit. Then I remember."

Marika took my hand. "I know. I'm sorry."

We arrived at our usual bench and positioned ourselves between hardened pigeon droppings painted on the wooden slats of the seats. Nearby, children dashed through spray showers, teenagers boiled about the basketball and stickball courts, and older men hunched over games of Chinese checkers. I tilted my face toward the pulsing sun, its rays pressing against my closed eyelids, soothing me. "He was always in my life."

"Was he always so difficult?"

"It became worse with age."

"When it should have gotten better. When he could have started letting go."

"He wanted to take care of all of us." As long as I could remember, Jóska had been shrewd and self-confident, someone who shaped his world. "All those years, even when I wasn't sure he was alive, just the idea of him was comforting."

I unveiled my eyes to peer at a Spaldeen rolling up to my feet, its pinkness marred by jagged cracks, and its new-tire scent long gone. I flipped it underhanded back toward the stickball players.

"Jóska was good to us. So generous," Marika said. "I don't know why I let myself get so aggravated by him."

Hurriedly pacing by were two orthodox Jewish women, each with their cut hair covered by a wig and wide hairband and wearing closed-toe shoes, long-sleeved shirts, and skirts cascading below the knees. After forty years in America, it still reassured me to see Judaism so publicly advertised. "Remember how Debbie began her eulogy?" I said. Jóska's daughter had told the audience, "I know that many didn't like my father."

"Yes. He was so complicated."

I watched as a boy standing in front of a chalked batter's box leaned into a pitch and fluidly swatted the ball, its trajectory launching it over the basketball court and park fence and onto the top of the bowling alley across the street. Park ritual maintained that, once players ran out of balls, one of them would climb onto the ironed-flat alley roof through a set of stairs in the back and toss all the wayward rubber and tennis balls back across the street. "Marika, did I tell you about Jóska's bad experience in France during the war?"

"When he shot the Nazi guard?"

"No, that was in Germany at the end of the war. I mean when Jóska was in Paris in 1944, after the liberation."

"No, I don't think you did."

Chapter 82

"He was walking by himself down a side street and encountered a crowd that had circled around a woman, half-naked with her head shaven. They were shouting, cursing, and throwing rocks at her."

"Was she a collaborator?"

"The mob believed that. Jóska thought she was just a prostitute trying to survive." A jet flew low overhead, preparing for a landing at Kennedy. I raised my volume. "He said that when she spotted him in his American Army uniform, she raised her arms, shrieking for him to help her."

"Did he?"

"No."

"Because he was afraid to?"

"Jóska insisted that wasn't the reason. He knew that if he had raised his pistol, the crowd would have backed away. And that they wouldn't have harmed an American."

"So why didn't he help her?"

"He admitted that he found satisfaction in letting the crowd act out his rage. Even though he didn't blame the woman for her actions."

"He was always angry," Marika said.

"What I don't understand is why Jóska was angry with those closest to him."

"Like Henry." Marika said. Henry Windish was the husband of Fellah, one of Suzy's sisters. He and Fellah had remained in Belgium during the war, surviving by hiding in various houses, enduring one miraculous escape after another. They now lived in our building. Jóska had developed a pathological hatred for Henry, claiming that he had cheated Miklós in some business deal. Jóska wouldn't allow his family to get together with Henry's, forcing Suzy to visit Fellah in secret.

"Even Suzy."

"You weren't spared, either."

Time had reversed itself. I was reliving those years of not speaking. "I shouldn't have let that go on."

"Like it was your fault?"

"No. But he was my brother. Who loved me, and cared about me. And knew me."

Marika frowned. "But I know you, Béla."

"I mean...he knew me before." An incubating sun retreated behind the windowless telephone company tower across the street, sending us into delicious shadow. "Before I changed." Marika studied me, as if ground fog were dispersing, revealing my true identity. "Before a part of me died."

CHAPTER 83

Oli Ingber: April 30, 1990 (London)

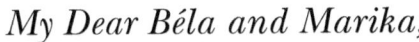

My Dear Béla and Marika,

It has been six months since Mary died and everything became so faded. There is not a day gone by that I haven't wept like a deserted bride. We were together ever since '44, and brought up Ilona and Susan. Here we lived a very good life. We never talked about the fact that one day we are going to die. This is why it was such a great shock when we buried her, like a sudden low thunderclap on a clear day. I cannot accept this emptiness. I know now that I've lived as if in a dream, because reality remained too painful.

Every day when I come home, when I go to bed, or when I get up, I am alone. I have never cooked or cleaned. I have never been domesticated. Yesterday they came and took all her things, even items that were nearly new but I didn't want them in the house. Every day I buy flowers and go to the boneyard for an hour.

> *Other than this I am bitter like I have never been. Mary started to love the Jews because of me and if somebody said something against the Jews, she would defend us. I was her everything.*
>
> *I am sorry to write this kind of letter. I hope you understand. Otherwise, there is some happy news which you may know already. Susan had a boy last September. I have sold my practice. I try to stay healthy. It has been ten years now that I am taking insulin once a day and it does me a lot of good.*
>
> *P.S. I wish I would have gone before her, like Miki and Jóska did.*

*

"I don't know if Oli is simply depressed or if he's lost his mind," I said to Marika.

"He's so alone without Mary. Can't he get close with his daughters?"

"He never had that kind of relationship with them."

"Too much craziness?"

"Or too many deceptions. And there's more." I retrieved a recent correspondence from Ilona and pointed to the penultimate paragraph:

> *I found out on the night my mother died that my parents weren't married to each other when I was born. My father said to me out of the blue, 'You know your mother was married before.' At first I thought he had gone mentally unbalanced. But it was true. During the war, she had gotten married to a Canadian pilot. After the war ended, the pilot returned to Canada and she was supposed to follow him, but Mum was too frightened to get on a plane. That man wouldn't divorce her for the longest time. So you see, I was a bastard until I was nine years old.*

"All these secrets," Marika said. "What did they accomplish?"

CHAPTER 84
The Bar Mitzvah: October 4, 1997

*No one saves us but ourselves. No one can and no one may.
We ourselves must walk the path.*
— Gautama Buddha

Tibi and Hannah raised three sons, the eldest of whom was Brad, named after Tibi's mother, Basha. The last time I saw Tibi happy, we were having dinner at Lou Siegel's on 38th Street in midtown, near Tibi's Garment District job. We sat at a table with a linen cover and cloth napkins, under a wrought-iron chandelier whose lights were translucent petals. On the wall behind us was an oil painting of a rabbi, his smoke-white beard gleaming, leading services.

"Tibi, how was your weekend in Atlantic City?"

"Terrific. We saw Ray Charles. Bally's comped our room. And I won big."

"You always win big. How can that be?"

"Luck. G-d is making up for my early years. Didn't you and Marika go there in the summer?"

"Yep. We took the bus. When we got to the casino, they gave each of us a roll of quarters. I lost mine in the slots in ten minutes."

"And Marika?"

"She kept her quarters for the washing machines in our building."

Tibi's voice was watery, as if he were perpetually gargling. "Did I tell you," he said, waving a pickle in his hand, "that my Brad is a *macher* (big shot). He works for the best law firm, *kayn aynhoreh*."

"Only a dozen times." My counter to the pickle was a *challah* roll. If Marika were here, she would have grabbed the roll from me, wrapped it in a napkin, and stuck it in her purse. "My Jeffrey is a lawyer, too."

"Brad's firm is four or five names together. Each name sounds like the guy was once a president of the United States."

"I'm sure each of them was," I mumbled through a mouthful of *challah*. At the next table, two grandmas were scrutinizing a group of young men in gilded yarmulkes (likely headed for Madison Square Garden to watch the Knicks game), assessing their potential as sons-in-law.

When the inevitable surly waiter approached, we ordered matzoh ball soups, gefilte fish prepared with black pepper, and stuffed derma rich in beef fat. Tibi glanced around the room, focusing his attention on a couple of bachelorettes at a corner table. In older times, he might have invented a need to go to the bathroom and then tried to schmooze with them on the way back. Now there was no need for invention, and his life was no longer veiled by alcohol.

"Look at us, Béla," Tibi said, as he shoveled some coleslaw onto his bread plate. Neither of us would allow for any leftovers. "Two Schleppermans from Munkács sitting in a fancy-schmancy restaurant like this. Being served the best food on the planet."

"Marika's food is the best."

"Did you ever think we'd end up with such great lives? If The Beast is dead, it should only happen, he must be turning over in his

Chapter 84

grave. I tell you, Béla," he said, with twin strands of coleslaw delicately protruding from the corner of his mouth, "it feels good. Good to have finally succeeded."

"I don't know that I'm a success. But my kids are."

"Same thing."

*

After Tibi died in the 1980s from a combination of cirrhosis and throat cancer, I lost touch with his family for over a decade. Then an invitation arrived from Brad and his wife to attend their son Jeremy's bar mitzvah in New Jersey. I RSVP'd our apologies and sent a gift. Hannah called.

"Béla, it would mean a lot to us to have you there."

"How will we get there? We don't have a car."

"We'll arrange to have you and Marika picked up and dropped off."

"That's too much trouble. And too expensive."

She honked out a laugh. "Trust me, Brad can afford it."

Her agreeable persistence illuminated my insensitivity. "Hannah, we would be honored to witness your grandson become a bar mitzvah."

"I am so pleased, Béla. And I expect at least one dance with you. I've insisted that they play some slow songs."

Early on a fall Saturday morning wedged between the High Holidays, during the days of repentance and judgment, a gleaming black limo arrived at the entrance to our building. I was dressed in a light-wool blue suit that had been Miki's. An hour later, after racing past an infinite number of shopping malls, fast food restaurants, and condominium complexes, we arrived at a spacious brick-and-glass Reform temple in a rustic setting adjoining a country club. The parking lot was laden with Beemers and Sadies.

Entering the *shul*, I snatched from a bin a carnation-pink linen skullcap. An usher approached. "Which family are you here for?"

"Lazarovics. Why?"

"Then you should take a yarmulke from the other bin."

And so I plopped on my head a shrunken black velvet *kippah* (skullcap) that requires a hairpin, a dilemma for a man with only a trace of hair.

Strands of a solemn organ announced the entrance of the rabbi, cantor, and a choir of two men and two women. The traditional psalms and hymns began, ones mostly meant to be sung to us, not by us. The sounds of music and prayer melded in a noise that scratched my eardrums.

"Marika, what's with this organ music and singing group? And all the English praying? Are we in a church?"

"I like the English readings. I can finally understand what's being said."

"Ach!"

My pulse quickened as a succession of elegantly dressed men and women were called up to the *bimah* for the honor of reciting a blessing, and most had no clue of what to do or say. Then there was Samantha, close to a foot taller than Jeremy, who was becoming a bat mitzvah. This made for duplication of readings, benedictions, and honors.

Samantha herself spent much time expounding in a monotonic, grating voice, while stealing glances at her adoring parents. The highlight of her discourse came when she explained that the color of the skullcaps, pink markers over a sea of black suits, was chosen in honor of National Breast Cancer Awareness Month. She proceeded, through tortured logic, to relate her Torah portion to that cause.

Often, the rabbi's speech is the finest portion of a bar mitzvah ceremony. In the best of their lectures, I would hear Papa. This rabbi, who appeared to be straight out of rabbinical school, explained with profound consideration every aspect of the service. He sought to exude Judaism, but I suspect that he understood less about our religion—its inherent humility, humor, and wisdom—than anyone you might have randomly bumped into on Latorica Street.

Chapter 84

A lifetime ago, after my own bar mitzvah ceremony, the family gathered back in our living room with select friends to celebrate over tumblers of slivovitz and home-baked pound cakes. The years had gone by as if I had deliberately skipped the beginning and middle of my life.

We were herded into a room with four bars, one of which offered multi-neon-hued martinis. Hard liquor was poured in copious amounts, confirming that, in America, even Jews drink to get drunk. Guests crowded around tables so thickly that even the air searched for space. On them lay a variety of ethnic foods that would have fed my labor battalion for a week. Marika and I guessed that this spread alone represented an expense greater than the entire cost of Jeffrey's bar mitzvah three decades earlier.

I consoled myself with a plate of herring, while enduring a volley of chatter from several men in their thirties who were boasting, in a language largely unintelligible to me (sprinkled with mysterious phrases such as "EBIT" and "arbitraging the yield curve"), of their financial prowess. Hannah came over to thank us for attending and to catch up, implanting splashes of lipstick on our cheeks, in stark contrast to the general air-kissing environment. We congratulated her, after which I let Marika duel with Hannah as to who has more wonderful grandchildren.

Chimes announced the end of the cocktail hour. Walking past booths where teenage boys were shooting hoops and dunking on a six-foot-high rim, we found ourselves at a table of *alta cockers* (old people) in a room filled with more than three hundred guests. Although we were seated in the back, pulsating music, played as if it could only be enjoyed if deafening, made speech impossible. The twelve-piece band was led by a male vocalist reminiscent of a young Louis Armstrong. Accompanying the musicians were several virile female dancers in bare feet, modern-day Gypsies gyrating like furiously played accordions in front of middle-aged men who discoed as if they were fighting not to drown.

There had been dancing at my bar mitzvah—Papa and my brothers and I, skipping feverishly in circles to a wordless melody hummed and clapped to by the congregation. We moved through and around each other seamlessly, like the twirling blades of an eggbeater.

Now, above the din, young Louis announced, "Let's get the rest of you folks onto the dance floor. Here's some Sinatra." Marika, color-coordinated in a powder-blue dress with perfectly matched shoes, earrings, and necklace, each purchased separately, pulled me to the middle of the room.

"Yes, you're lovely, with your smile so warm, and your cheeks so soft, there is nothing for me but to love you…." I wrapped my arms around her slim waist, as she reached for my shoulders, floating against me, her beauty evident to the entire room. We rotated, perhaps less than graceful, yet free, like butterflies pirouetting through a field of wildflowers. The floor filled.

"Lovely, never ever change, keep that breathless charm, won't you please arrange it…."

The song soon melded into "Strangers in the Night." Marika's eyes, dark full moons, took me in, caressing me. Her face curved in a smile at a memory, as if she had known from the first time we met that we would end up together in this time and place. She lowered her head against my chest as we lost ourselves in the music, swaying to it, absorbing it. "Dooby-doooby-doo…." Marika and I were one. Completing each other, however imperfectly. I had fulfilled my promises.

When the song ended, Marika and I curtsied and bowed to each other as we were encouraged by Louis to rush to our tables but remain standing. We clapped for the grand entrance of the bar mitzvah boy and his family. It occurred to me why Hannah had been so insistent. No doubt I had been tapped to say the blessing over the *challah*. Okay, I could handle that, and then I would call for the car service.

Chapter 84

The band launched into "Hava Nagila." All attention was on Jeremy and his parents and younger sister, each of whom had been hoisted precariously in the air on chairs. Hora dancers in ever-expanding circles of men and women enclosed them until, with the participants near collapse, the untamable music stopped as if the power cord had been pulled on a jukebox. Everyone was asked to return to their seats but again remain standing.

A towering layered cake, in the shape and colors of Yankee Stadium, was wheeled to the front of the room. Jeremy, wearing a black tuxedo with a white boutonnière pinned on the lapel, was waiting there with his parents, who, like all the others of this generation, had surrendered their lives to their children. I was familiar with the drill. A lengthy parade of family and friends would be called up to light a candle. Any flaws in the relationship with each honoree would be photoshopped into perfection.

I sat back down. Why watch when I hardly knew anyone? Time to take a nap with my eyes open, as I had done so often in the camps. Marika pursed her lips. "Stand up, Béla. You're being rude."

"Ach, leave me alone. I'm tired. When is the *challah* cutting?"

"The *challah* cutting? Why does that matter?"

Brad, while still catching his breath, accepted the microphone from the vocalist. "Dear friends and family, I'm so glad that you've joined us to help celebrate Jeremy's coming of age. Dori and I feel so fortunate to have here today everyone who is meaningful to us. We love you all." Did Brad really love each guest? Even the kid with spiked hair and a nose ring who was smoking in the men's room and, with a pronounced overbite, mouthing the words to "Da Ya Think I'm Sexy?" "We're about to begin the candle-lighting ceremony, during which Jeremy will honor some very special individuals, including his three living grandparents. I've requested the privilege of announcing the first honoree, in tribute to Jeremy's Grandpa Tibi."

"Marika," I whispered, "this is going to take forever."

"Shush!"

"As many of you know," Brad continued, "my father spent the war years in the Hungarian forced labor system. He suffered greatly and came close to death several times. One of those times, he was saved by a remarkable man, who was his best friend and who risked his own life to protect my father's."

Only half-listening, I wasn't sure I had heard correctly the reference to me. Maybe someone else had also rescued Tibi during the war? He was always finding trouble. I glanced up at Marika. Her smack on my arm confirmed my understanding and compelled me to stand.

"The Talmud tells us, 'Whoever saves a single soul, it is as if he saved the whole world.' There's a man in this room without whom neither I nor Jeremy would be here. I now call upon this saver of souls, who we are so fortunate to have with us. Someone who represents the finest qualities of Judaism. Béla Ingber, please come up and light the first candle."

Applause rang out. The band began to play "Tradition." One of the young dancers, clad in black spandex and sneakers, pranced over, hooked her arm under mine, and escorted me the length of the room to where the bar mitzvah family stood. Jeremy, straining to recall who I was, handed me a lighted candle and pointed to a shorter one that I lit.

I congratulated Jeremy, shook his hand, and kissed Dori. Then I turned to Brad.

"Thank you for your kind words." I stuck out my hand to meet his. Brad grabbed my arm, pulled me to him, and hugged me, leaning down to bury his head in my chest. Then he drew back. "My father always talked about you, Béla. He…he loved you." As the room quietly watched, Brad let tears fall. And so did I.

CHAPTER 85
A Passionate Life: January 1998

The more you struggle to live, the less you live. Give up the notion that you must be sure of what you are doing. Instead, surrender to what is real within you, for that alone is sure.
—Baruch Spinoza

I was about to chant the *Modeh Ani*, giving thanks for the restoration of my soul for yet another day, when the telephone's brittle ring startled me. Had I begun the prayer, I would have ignored its demand for attention.

"Hello."

"Dad, Esther just left me a message about Uncle Oli. I'm so sorry."

So much heartache enters our lives from a telephone ringing. "Thank you, *Tataleh*. I was going to call you later."

"When did you find out?"

"This morning. Ilona called and talked to Mom. I was out walking."

"What happened?"

"All Ilona said was that it was a heart attack."

"When did you last speak with him?"

"Not for a long time. We wrote to each other, mostly about the family." Jeffrey paused. "I can't say that I feel much. I didn't know Uncle Oli."

"I didn't, either. I knew who he was but not who he became."

"Still...it must be hard for you."

How can I explain to my son that getting old means losing so much of what is precious to you? "Yes, I feel sad, and guilty that I didn't make more of an effort."

"Dad, have you spoken with Aunt Libu lately?"

My sister and her husband had moved to Dallas, to be near their daughter and her family. "No. We don't speak much anymore. I should call her."

"Linda and I will come over tonight. Maybe play some rummy with you and Mom."

"Good."

"I love you, Dad."

"I love you, too."

*

On the top shelf of a closet, in a Tupperware container that smooched when you opened it, were the letters. Dozens of them. I searched for a recent one from Oli and reread the ending:

Ever since leaving home, I've felt as if each year was a gift. If Beneš had more of a backbone, we Czechs would have fought the Germans instead of capitulating. And you and I most likely would have been killed, either in combat or as prisoners.

But this gift has become a curse. To start life with such happiness, only to have it turn into an acid bath of pain. And now I suspect that even that happiness was a mirage.

Remember the night when we listened to Jabotinsky? Jenő congratulated me for scuffling with the Chassid. Our brother, the smartest and most logical person I've ever known, quoted Spinoza to me: "Reason is no match for passion."

Chapter 85

My dear brother, I wish that we had spent more time together. Revealed our secrets to each other. Suffered this world together.

I hope that you have lived a passionate life.

CHAPTER 86

Final Letter: December 2002

Dear Dad,

I'm sorry to see you in poor health. I know that walking and being active are so important to you. To me, you are still the strongest of Dads.
I want to share some recollections of you that make me smile.
One of my earliest memories is of you wrapping me up in the bedspread at night, so tight that I couldn't move my arms and legs. And then we would talk and laugh. Do you know that I still wrap myself in a blanket at night?
Over the years, many people have told me that they admire my self-confidence. Well, that's because you always made me feel that I could do anything. When you were teaching me how to ride a bike with two wheels, and I had such a hard time of it, you didn't let me quit trying. You kept running alongside of me until, all of a sudden, I looked back to see you had stopped and I realized that I could do it on my own.

Chapter 86

Friends tell me that I have a good sense of humor. That also comes from you, starting with those Yiddish finger games you would play with me. At the end of them, you would tickle me with your hands and face. When I was in kindergarten, my teacher's name was Mrs. Ehrlich. So every night, while putting me to bed, you would ask me what her name was and, right after I told you, you would ask, "Does she lick your ears?" And every night, the joke made me giggle.

You gave me my lifelong love of long walks. We would wander around the neighborhood on Sunday mornings. One day, we rang the bell of a friend from the "Old Country." He and his wife were hardly dressed, and I thought that was funny. They let us in and served me Thin Mints.

I knew that nothing could keep you from being there for me. I was sitting in Hebrew school when a citywide blackout occurred. The rabbi called all the parents to ask them to come pick up their kids. Even though you had just come back from work and we lived over a mile away from the temple, you were one of the first parents to arrive. We walked a few other kids home first.

One evening, when I had a lot of homework to do and it was late, I accidentally turned over the three-ringed binder, spilling all my work onto the floor. I was upset because I didn't know how I would put all the loose-leaf papers back in order. You said that you would stay up all night helping me if you had to. I calmed down and we gathered them up together.

I watched so many examples of your kindness and decency, like giving money that you didn't have much of to the needy. I remember once when you took us all to a large restaurant where there was entertainment. Toward the end of the evening, the lights went out suddenly. There was pandemonium. Some people walked out without paying, but you insisted on waiting until order was restored so we could pay the bill.

Now that I understand the depth of the suffering that you, Mom, and your families experienced, I am so amazed and appreciative that you didn't let it change you. When you had every reason to become bitter and selfish, and to perpetually lash out at the world, you remained the person that your parents raised you to be all those years ago. Those are the qualities that make you a survivor.

Do you know what I see when I look at old photos of you? Your pride. Well, I am proud of you. And proud to be your son.

Your love and support for me have made me the person I am.

I love you lots,

Jeff

CHAPTER 87
Bookend

Be near me when I fade away
To point the term of human strife,
And on the low dark verge of life
The twilight of eternal day.

—Alfred, Lord Tennyson

"Hi, Grandpa. Can I join you?" Craig said. Behind him, plastic drug containers are lined up on a wall unit behind clear baggies, each labeled by the time of day I am to take the various sized, shaped, and colored pills they contain. What should I tell him? That I miss his grandma, whom I can't visit because I'm not strong enough to take the ride to the hospital? He is sixteen years old. Full of anticipation. Unable to be checkmated.

On a rainy Wednesday weeks ago, Marika was helping me go to and from a medical appointment at Elmhurst General Hospital. Upon reentering our building, I slipped on the wet steps and an umbrella spoke punctured the skin under my eye. Blood gushed, requiring a return trip to the doctor.

Marika insisted that she caused the accident. What's the difference? Accidents and mistakes rule each of our lives. But Marika couldn't handle that it happened in the first place. Realizing we couldn't take care of each other, we relocated to Jeffrey's house to rest. But it didn't pull Marika out of her funk, and her doctor suggested that a more meaningful rest was required. So I am here, and Marika is in a Manhattan hospital.

I sit, with wooden eyelids, on the sofa in their downstairs den, now my sanctuary. The harsh splendor of winter is evident behind the chilled glass sliding door. The backyard is a snow globe, painted by silvered leaves that squirrels dance upon, with the occasional black one presenting a stark contrast.

On occasion, I am tempted to proposition G-d for more time. But often, I am overwhelmed with the sense that man was not meant to endure old age. That life was destined to be fleeting, a mere scamper across a field of flowers while jauntily taking in the sights.

Craig plops onto the sofa. "How are you, Grandpa?"

"Happy to see you, that's how I am."

For days now, he and Linda have listened to tales of my youth and the war. The chronology is muddled, vital details forgotten, trivia stressed, and names confused. Past facts have fused with modern perspectives, as if the story were unfolding backward. No matter, they are attentive. I am trapped in these stories, which flow feverishly. They are my wisdom. My identity. I want them to survive, as if they were my children's and grandchildren's own memories.

*

Earlier that day, with Craig in school, Arielle away at college, and Jeffrey at work, Linda brought me a bowl of fresh vegetable soup, sprinkled with dill. She sat facing me.

"Barry, can I get you something else?"

"No, thanks."

Chapter 87

"How are you feeling?"

"Useless. Burdensome. I can't stand myself like this."

"I know you don't like depending on your family. But try to look at it as a way for them to show you their love."

But am I lovable like this? The taste and scent of her soup send me back, across a boundless distance, into a kitchen where shards of sunlight spilled in through a window covered with diaphanous lace curtains. Into a room where a gentle woman, the first person to love me, spent hours each day hovering over a wood-burning iron stove. "I'm worried about Marika."

"She's getting the best care."

"I don't mean now…."

"You mean…when she'll be alone?"

"Yes. I promised her that she'd never be abandoned."

"You know that we all will look after her."

I looked away, hiding a tear, evidence that my body had not yet run dry.

"Would you like her to be in a place like Vera is in now?" Linda said. Vera Bornstein was our friend from the Old Country, widowed for many years, who had lived for decades in our building and had been a steady Rummy-Q partner. Her daughter had recently moved her to an assisted living facility, and our time with her ended.

"Yes. So she won't be by herself."

Perhaps I soon would have a dream about the next life. But Papa is no longer here to interpret. The room turns silent, except for my labored breathing.

"I understand, Barry."

*

"Dad, do you want to watch family videos? I transferred them onto this CD."

"That would be nice."

On a movie-theater-wide television, I watched Arielle and Craig grow up through celebrations of Shabbat, Chanukah, Rosh Hashanah, and Passover, complete with ritual, prayer, and songs. Jeffrey wandered in and out of the den, catching glimpses of his babies maturing into adolescence. I saw our traditions lovingly preserved for the future. How many times over the years did I call Jeffrey to ask, "Did you go to *shul*?" Or, "Did you put on the candles?" His monotonic response, "Yes, Dad," never felt reassuring. "Jeffrey, you made me very happy."

One day, Jeffrey came home from work and announced, "Dad, I've got good news. Mom will be released from the hospital in two days. I'll pick her up, and Linda will bring you home."

*

The end is not orchestrated. You can't rehearse the interminable game of medical Whac-A-Mole. I was rushed to the emergency room several times that year, despite my protestations, until my last hospital stay led to a transfer to a rehabilitation center in Queens. I am ninety years old. Are they planning on rehabilitating me?

One day blended into another. After meals, they wheeled me to where I could watch TV and socialize with men and women for whom, when death came, it would not be a noteworthy change. I did neither.

The facility was nondenominational. A staff member said to me, "Why is there a slipper on your head?" Not waiting for a response, she grabbed it, tossed it on the table next to me, and marched away. I returned the slipper to where I had placed it. Apparently Jeffrey was called and asked the same question. The next day, he brought me a baseball cap. It didn't need to be a yarmulke.

"No more medication," I told the staff. And no pity. I've defied the odds. Survived to play with my grandchildren. Assured that Marika will be cared for, I am ready.

*

Chapter 87

One evening in early November, Jeffrey and Linda enter my room. Dressed in a medium-sized sweatshirt and matching pants now large enough for two of me, I lay with closed eyes, arms and legs flailing reflexively. "I know you are here. I hear you. I feel you." My words did not reach them.

Jeffrey sits on a chair to my right. *I want to kiss you, Jeffrey. Don't be sad. I'm a lucky man.*

Linda stands next to me on the other side of the bed. "Barry, do you see your mother's face? Can you find her? Go to her."

My body stills as I search. *Mama, I've been away for so long.* Two days later, I am at her side, reclaiming my place as the fourth son, as she lights the candles of Heaven.

Cousins at Ron Ingber's wedding in September 2012. From the left: Esther Rubin, Ken Ingber, Ron Ingber, Jeff Ingber, Barbara Cooper, Debbie Deutsch

ACKNOWLEDGEMENTS

This book is a work of historical fiction. Many descriptions of events are based on stories told to me by my father. There were innumerable gaps in the known facts that I was compelled to fill in using imagination, deduction, and research. Nearly all the conversations are made-up. For the sake of continuity and ease of reading, I altered certain dates and timelines. Most of the letters are condensed and edited; some are fictional. Certain characters are composites of actual persons or entirely fictional.

Nonetheless, I strived to have the major facts presented in this book be grounded, to close extent, on historical reality. Each of the depicted members of the Ingber, Leiner, and Haupt families was an actual person. Tibor Lazarovics and Eugene Schachter are based on real persons. There was a woman named Ágnes who was a girlfriend of my Dad's. And there was a woman named Tetzi who was a friend of my Mom's and responsible for introducing her to my Dad.

The historical chapters are constructed on extensive research, and any errors are unintentional. Ze'ev Jabotinsky did visit Munkács in the summer of 1934, and all the statements that I attribute to him in the book are ones that he did make at differing times in his life.

Yaakov Pollack is loosely based on the person of the same name who was the chief rabbi of the Young Israel of Jackson Heights that I attended. I remember Rabbi Pollack as a moving orator, whose Saturday morning speeches often were the highlight of the Sabbath ceremony. Among my teachers in Hebrew school was a Mordechai Gonzvi, who I remember for his innumerable stories of the great Jewish scholars of history.

I am indebted to the new age of self-publishing, which has allowed so many priceless memoirs to come out that describe life in the labor camps and in both Munkács and Budapest before, during, and after the war. Many of them are listed in the bibliography.

Many friends were kind enough to read portions or all of one or more drafts and provide feedback. They include Dave Buckmaster, Mary Craig, Marta Fuchs, Aviva Grunwald, Dori Kam, Phyllis Kam, Brad Mirkin, Marlene Sokolow, Andrew Weg, and Leona Wish.

Others helped enormously with critical research. With regard to Fleischmanns, I received invaluable assistance from Marilyn Kaltenborn, the author of a memoir on growing up in Fleischmanns, who actively provided me with additional information and commented extensively on a draft of the book. In June 2015, Linda and I had the pleasure of spending several hours in Fleischmanns with Marilyn and her brothers Brian and Dean Mayes and friend Linda Armour. We walked down Main Street and Wagner Avenue, passing the Palace Hotel (which was up for sale) and the nearby house where Marilyn, Brian, and Dean grew up. In the decades since the early 1970s, tourism dwindled, and Fleischmanns became a depressed area. Many of the hotels, such as the Grand, burned down (although the St. Regis remains), stores closed, and the dam that formed Lake Switzerland was taken down. Fortunately, Fleischmanns is now in a period of renewal, helped in part by an influx of Chassidic Jews.

Acknowledgements

Thanks to William Laufer, who provided me with information on the Mount Golda Cemetery; Amanda Seigel of the Dorot Jewish Division of the New York Public Library; and Blanche Wesalo (the mother of my longtime friend July Wesalo Temel), who sadly has passed away. Mrs. Wesalo generously shared her recollections of life in Elmhurst immediately after the war. And many thanks to my Newtown High School classmates Dave Gintz and Ray Hoffer for their recollections of Elmhurst.

There have been many invaluable works of scholarship regarding Munkács published in recent years, including those of Anna Berger, Levi Cooper, and Raz Segal. And there is the renowned work of Randolph Braham on the Hungarian Holocaust, which is where I started my research (Professor Braham was kind enough to meet with me and encourage me to write the memoir).

I am thankful to help in some small way to preserve the memory of those who acted with great courage, compassion, and humanity during the darkness of the war years. One such person was Kati Tibold, a young woman who offered her identity papers to my mother without being asked, which saved my mother's life. Another was the nun who befriended my father in the Budapest hospital, a saint whose name is lost to history.

In 2012, Linda and I spent a wonderful weekend in Cleveland with Zsuzsa Racz, translator extraordinaire, whose talents brought the letters to life and whose insights formed the basis for the first chapter of the book.

I am grateful for the wonderful editing and strong support provided me by Jane Cavolina, whose love of her craft is evident, and whose enthusiasm for the book is much appreciated. And many thanks to Julie Salamon, a distant relative and NYU Law School classmate (not to mention a well-known and talented author in her own right), for introducing me to Jane, and for her consistent encouragement and support. Further thanks go to Pat Egner for her terrific, meticulous proofreading of the final draft of the book.

Much appreciation to my cousins Barbara Cooper, Debbie Deutsch, Ilona Ingber, Ken Ingber, and Ron Ingber, each of whom I have an ineradicable bond with, for their remembrances and encouragement. And to extended family members such as Steve Holt, Lilly Salcman (Julie's mom and herself an Auschwitz survivor), and Jackie Windish-Shager for providing their recollections. And thanks to Joe Minnelli for his memories of Uncle Miki.

To my sister, Esther Rubin, I am grateful for all of her recollections, engagement in, and enthusiasm for the book.

To my talented daughter, Arielle Morris, my deep appreciation for her crafting of the family tree and the book's cover (with additional thanks to Alexandra Hervish Jabs for fashioning the cover lettering). And much gratitude to my mother-in-law, Inge Shumer (the Fleischmanns beauty contestant—a true story), and my son-in-law, Adam Morris, for their multiple readings of and comments on drafts of the book.

It is impossible to overstate how much of a debt I owe to Linda for her support, wisdom, thoughtfulness, active suggestions, and careful editing of various drafts over a period of years. She and I spent many hundreds of invaluable hours passionately considering and debating innumerable aspects of the book. It would be a mere shell of itself without her.

I am so grateful for growing up in the comfort not only of my immediate family but, also, of my extended family. I will always remember my Uncles Joe, Miki, Miklós, and Oli, and my Aunts Inge, Libu, Mary and Suzy, with fondness and love, and great respect for those who endured the unimaginable. For my grandparents and other family members who perished in the Holocaust, writing this book helped me to better appreciate how wonderful it would have been to have known you.

Acknowledgements

I am so fortunate to have my Mom still with me. She continues to have great clarity of recollection and was able to provide countless helpful details in addition to loving support and encouragement.

Finally, thank you, Dad. For surviving, for giving me life, and for loving me so much. And for everything else.

—January 5, 2016

SELECTIVE TIMELINE

October 14, 1918: The WW I Allies grant recognition to a provisional Czechoslovak government headed by Tomáš Masaryk.

November 11, 1918: An armistice between the Allies and Germany goes into effect, ending the fighting in The Great War and marking victory for the Allies. By then, the Austro-Hungarian Monarchy, the largest state in Europe, had dissolved.

November 13, 1918: The Austro-Hungarian Emperor and King of Hungary, Charles IV, abdicates.

November 14, 1918: The union of the Czech lands and Slovakia is officially proclaimed in Prague, and the Czech and Slovak Constituent National Assembly unanimously designates Masaryk as President of the new Czechoslovak republic.

November 16, 1918: A People's Republic of Hungary is formed, the first Western-style liberal regime in Hungarian history, led by Count Mihály Károlyi.

March 23, 1919: Béla Kun, head of the newly organized Hungarian Communist party, and his fellow Communists, many who had returned from Russian POW camps, seize power and proclaim a

Hungarian Soviet Republic, the second Communist government in Europe after Russia itself. Hungarians became subject to repression by armed gangs that intimidate, rob, and murder enemies of the regime – particularly, the upper classes, landowners, Catholic Church leaders and intelligentsia – in a period of violence known as the "Red Terror."

<u>April 10, 1919:</u> The Romanian army launches an invasion of Hungary to forestall a Hungarian offensive against Transylvania.

<u>May 30, 1919:</u> Anti-Communist politicians form a counter-revolutionary government in the southern Hungarian city of Szeged, occupied by French forces. Miklós Horthy de Nagybánya, the Austro-Hungarian Fleet's last commander and a war hero, is asked to be Minister of War in the new government.

<u>August 4, 1919:</u> French-supported Romanian forces enter Budapest. The Communist government collapses, and its leaders flee. A two-year campaign of murder, torture, and humiliations against suspected Communists follows, known as the "White Terror." Those deemed enemies of the state often included Jews, because much of the Communist leadership had been Jewish. In one noted incident, in the forest near the southern Hungarian village of Orgovany, 300 Jews were hanged in a single night.

<u>September 10, 1919:</u> The Treaty of Saint-Germain-en-Laye is signed by the victorious Allies and the new Republic of Austria. It formally dissolves the Austro-Hungarian Empire and recognizes the independence of Hungary, Czechoslovakia, Poland, and the State of Slovenes, Croats and Serbs. Subcarpathian Ruthenia (including Munkács) becomes part of Czechoslovakia, along with the traditional Czech provinces (Bohemia, Moravia and Silesia) and Slovakia.

Czechoslovakia signs the Minorities Protection Treaty, placing its ethnic minorities under the protection of the League of Nations. In the treaty, Czechoslovakia commits itself to granting autonomy to the Rus. This pledge is reiterated in the new Czech constitution adopted on February 29, 1920, but never acted upon.

<u>November 16, 1919:</u> A day after the Romanian Army leaves Budapest after committing a final looting spree, Miklós Horthy rides into the city on a white horse at the head of a right-wing, counterrevolutionary army.

<u>March 1, 1920:</u> Horthy is unanimously elected by the National Assembly as Regent (a position expected to be temporary until a monarch was appointed—but Horthy later prevents the former Hapsburg Prince, Charles IV, who had changed his mind about abdicating, from regaining the throne) of the newly reconstituted Kingdom of Hungary with a new national government. Horthy is given the power to convene and dissolve Parliament, appoint and dismiss Prime Ministers, and command the armed forces.

<u>June 4, 1920:</u> The Hungarian delegation signs, under protest, the Treaty of Trianon (referring to the Trianon Palace at Versailles), which greatly redefines and reduces Hungary's borders. Hungary loses two-thirds of its territory, three-fifths of its total population, and five of its ten most populous cities to Romania (which is awarded Transylvania), Austria (awarded Burgenland), and the newly created Czechoslovakia (awarded Slovakia and Ruthenia) and Yugoslavia (awarded various areas, including Croatia). It renounces its rights to its only seaport (Fiume, on the Adriatic) and is deprived of some of its most valuable natural resources. The Royal Hungarian Army is reduced to 35,000 volunteers, with no heavy artillery, tanks, or aircraft permitted. In addition, Hungary is required to pay war reparations to its neighbors.

<u>September 24, 1920:</u> A report of the Joint Distribution Committee on the Jews of Carpatho-Russia (the Rus) states:

> [They] have suffered intensely as a result of the war...
> The people are impoverished, there is a great shortage of food, and epidemic diseases are raging. Because of the

lack of transportation facilities, it is difficult for the people to secure food and other necessities; thousands of refugees are living in hiding under most terrible conditions, because, officially, refugees are not permitted to remain in the country. Up to recently little relief activity was carried on among the Jews of the area, who, because of Orthodoxy, would not patronize the kitchens which the American Relief Administration conducted, and who were helpless in the face of the appalling want.

The Joint Distribution Committee decides to establish its Rus headquarters in Munkács instead of the county capital, Uzhorod, "since it is better situated for the distribution of food and is the central headquarters for the Czecho-Slovokian Red Cross and the American Relief Administration in Czecho-Slovakia."

September 26, 1920: After a wave of anti-Semitism and widespread demands that the civil rights of Jews be limited, the "Numerus Clausus" (closed number) law is promulgated in Hungary, the first anti-Semitic law to be enacted in twentieth-century Europe. It provides for admission to universities and colleges for only those "who are trustworthy from the point of view of morals and loyalty to the country, and even those only in limited numbers, so that the thorough education of each student could be ensured." As a result, although the word "Jew" is not mentioned in the law, the number of Jewish students in Hungarian institutions of advanced education plunges. (Hungarian Bishop Ottokar Prohaszka stated, in support of the law, that "I would feel scorn for Hungarian culture were it to ignore the fact that while the Jews trample it underfoot and turn its blood into water, it does not have the strength to raise its voice and to voice its protest...") These quotas were largely repealed by 1928.

November 6, 1921: The Hungarian parliament officially dethrones the House of Hapsburg.

January 31, 1923: Hungary is admitted into the League of Nations.

May 26, 1924: The Immigration Act of 1924 (known as "The Johnson–Reed Act") is enacted by the U.S. Congress, limiting the annual number of immigrants who could be admitted from any country to two percent of the number of people from that country who were already living in the United States in 1890, down from the three percent cap set by the Immigration Restriction Act of 1921. The law is aimed at further restricting immigration of Southern and Eastern Europeans, including Jews from Poland and Russia.

October 16, 1925: The Franco-Czechoslovak Treaty of Mutual Assistance is signed in Locarno providing that each country will offer military assistance to the other if either is a victim of unprovoked German aggression.

April 5, 1927: The Hungarian-Italian Treaty on Friendship, Mediation, and Arbitration is signed, providing for the delivery of Italian weapons to Hungary and for mutual support for the aggressive plans of the two states.

1930: Rebbe Hayim Elazar Shapira travels to Palestine to visit with elderly Kaballist and sage Rabbi Shlomo Eliezer Elfandri as well as his followers in Palestine. Shapira discusses with Elfandri ways to hasten the Redemption through the coming of the Messiah.

January 30, 1933: Adolf Hitler is appointed Reich Chancellor of Germany.

March 15, 1933: Rebbe Shapira's only daughter, Frima, is wed to Baruch Rabinovich. Over 20,000 guests attended the wedding, coming from all over Europe and even from the U.S. Special triumph arches are erected throughout the city in celebration. International filming companies document the event.

March 20, 1933: A concentration camp for political prisoners opens on the site of a World War I munitions factory in the town of Dachau, near Munich.

Selective Timeline

June 21, 1934: Shortly before a visit to Munkács by Ze'ev Jabotinsky, Rabbi Hayim Elazar Shapira, the Munkáczer Rebbe, proclaims in a sermon that, "Whoever sends his children to the accursed [Hebrew Reform Real Gymnasium] shall be wiped out and shall not be permitted to live to raise his children…A Zionist must not be called to the holy ark, and no one may partake of his wine. For the past ten years, I have spat whenever I passed the godless Hebrew high school."

July 25, 1934: Engelbert Dollfuss, the Chancellor of Austria, who had banned the Austrian Nazi party, is assassinated as part of a failed coup attempt by Nazi agents.

May 16, 1935: The Czechoslovak-Soviet Treaty of Alliance is signed. At the insistence of the Czech government, the treaty stipulates that it would go into effect only if France gives assistance to the victim of aggression.

December 18, 1935: Edvard Beneš assumes the presidency of Czechoslovakia after the resignation of Tomáš Masaryk.

1936-1939: The period of the Arab Revolt in Palestine, a sustained period of violence across the country, leading to the death of thousands of Arabs, Jews, and British soldiers. The Zionist movement builds 54 "stockade and watchtower" settlements to circumvent British regulations and brings tens of thousands of illegal immigrants into Palestine.

March 7, 1936: German troops occupy the Rhineland, a demilitarized zone created after World War I that had formerly been within Germany's borders. Hitler later admitted, "When we marched into the Rhineland with a handful of battalions—at that moment I risked a great deal. If France had marched then we should have been forced to withdraw."

August 1-16, 1936: The Summer Olympics are held in Berlin.

October 15, 1936: Germany and Italy sign a friendship treaty and form the Rome-German Axis.

April 28, 1937: Nine kilometers south of the Eternal City, a state-owned "cinema city," called "Cinecittà," is inaugurated by Benito Mussolini.

May 1937: Rebbe Shapira dies and is succeeded by his son-in-law, Baruch Rabinovich. After the outbreak of war, Rebbe Rabinovich and his wife and five children escape to Palestine. After his wife's death in April 1945, Rabinovich remarries and eventually becomes the chief rabbi of Holon.

September 14, 1937: Masaryk dies at the age of 87. His coffin is shouldered by six soldiers, one for each of the Czech "nationalities": a Czech, a German, a Slovak, a Hungarian, a Ruthenian and a Pole.

February 20, 1938: In a speech to the Reichstag, Hitler proclaims the duty of Germany to protect the more than ten million Germans living in Austria and Czechoslovakia.

March 9, 1938: Austrian Chancellor Kurt Schuschnigg calls for a plebiscite, to be held on March 13, to decide whether Austria should remain independent or opt for absorption into Germany.

March 11, 1938: After British Foreign Secretary Lord Halifax refuses Schuschnigg's plea for assistance, Schuschnigg steps down from office (and later is sent to a concentration camp).

March 12, 1938: Nazi troops enter Austria, with Hitler arriving in the afternoon and being greeted by huge, cheering crowds. Germany announces *Anschluss* (union) with Austria. Later that month, Himmler establishes the Mauthausen concentration camp near Linz.

May 20, 1938: In response to reports of German military concentrations along the Czech border, the Czech government instructs the Minister of National Defense to call up reservists and military specialists.

May 28, 1938: Having been convinced that neither France nor Britain would fight for Czechoslovakia, and concerned about the close association of Russia and Czechoslovakia (and between Stalin and Beneš), Hitler calls a meeting of his principal advisors and gives instructions to prepare for an attack on Czechoslovakia.

May 29, 1938: The "First Jewish Law" (formally known as "Act XV of 1938 on Securing Social Balance in a More Efficient Way") is promulgated in Hungary, stating that "for the sake of social and economic balance" certain white-collar professions could be practiced only by those who are members of the professional chamber." The number of Jews (defined as members of the "Israelite denomination" and, if they had converted, had not done so before July 1919) in each profession is limited to 20 percent. (Kálmán Darányi, the Prime Minister, stated in support of the law that, "There is a Jewish question in Hungary…A solution should be found whereby Jewish influence in cultural and other domains of national life will be reduced. Such a solution will grant the Christian section of the community a just share in the industry, commerce and finance of the country.") Over the next six years, up to the time of the German occupation, the Hungarian government would enact 21 more anti-Semitic statutes and 267 anti-Jewish ministerial and governmental decrees.

June 12, 1938: Édouard Daladier, the Prime Minister of France, declares that France's engagement to Czechoslovakia is "sacred, and cannot be evaded."

September 12, 1938: In a speech at Nuremberg, Hitler demands that the Czechoslovak government accord Sudeten Germans the right of self-determination. These demands result in widespread political disorder in Czechoslovakia and, on the following day, Prime Minister Milan Hodža declares martial law in an attempt to restore order.

Great Britain's Cabinet, in response to a query from the French Foreign Minister whether, if Germany attacks Czechoslovakia and France mobilizes in support of Czechoslovakia, Great Britain will do so as well, states that, "while His Majesty's Government would never allow the security of France to be threatened, they are unable to make precise statements of the character of their future action…"

September 14, 1938: The date on which "Operation Green," the invasion of Czechoslovakia, is to be announced. This announcement is postponed because of the news that Neville Chamberlain, the British Prime Minister, will fly to Berchtesgaden to meet with Hitler to discuss a solution to the Czechoslovakia situation. Some historians believe that this action by Chamberlain prevented the implementation of a plan by Hitler's generals to arrest Hitler and stage a coup.

September 23, 1938: The Czech government orders a general mobilization of a million and a quarter men. A blackout is ordered in Prague and other large Czech cities.

September 29, 1938: Germany, Italy, Great Britain, and France sign the Munich Agreement, avoiding a German invasion of Czechoslovakia. Under pressure, the Czech government agrees to abide by the Agreement, which forces the Czechoslovak Republic to cede to Germany its western and northern regions (known as the "Sudetenland"), which are mainly inhabited by ethnic Germans, including vital Czechoslovak military defense positions. Hitler announces that Germany has "no more territorial demands to make in Europe." Poland takes the opportunity to annex the Teschen region in the north, which has a Polish minority.

Chamberlain, upon returning to 10 Downing Street the following day, declares, "My good friends, for the second time in our history, a British Prime Minister has returned from Germany bringing peace with honour. I believe it is peace for our time. We thank you from the bottom of our hearts. Go home and get a nice quiet sleep." Winston Churchill, in a speech to the House of Commons, replies, "This is only the beginning of the reckoning. This is only the first sip, the first foretaste of a bitter cup…"

In the days that follow, the Gestapo arrest more than 10,000 Czechs suspected of being anti-Nazi and send them to concentration camps.

At the Nuremberg trials, Field Marshall Wilhelm Keitel, who had been Supreme Commander of the German Armed Forces, stated, in response to the question whether Germany would have attacked Czechoslovakia in 1938 if the Western Powers had stood by it, "Certainly not. We were not strong enough militarily."

October 5, 1938: Beneš is forced to resign, and Emil Hácha is chosen as President. Later in the month, Beneš would leave for London where, during the war, he would form and head the Czechoslovak government-in-exile. At the end of the war, he would return to Czechoslovakia in triumph.

October 10, 1938: Nazi troops complete their occupation of the Sudetenland.

October 11, 1938: The Subcarpathian Rus declares itself a Ukrainian autonomous region. On January 1, 1939, it is renamed the Republic of Carpatho-Ukraine.

November 2, 1938: By the "First Vienna Award," negotiated at the Belvedere Palace by German and Italian diplomats, the largely Magyar-populated territories in southern Slovakia and the southern Subcarpathian Rus, including Munkács, are separated from Czechoslovakia and awarded back to Hungary.

November 9, 1938: Following the murder of a German diplomat in Paris by a Jew avenging his parents' deportation, the Nazis orchestrate a widespread wave of violence against German and Austrian Jews, known as "Kristallnacht" (Night of Broken Glass), resulting in numerous murders, the imprisonment of thousands of Jews, and massive property destruction and murder.

November 10, 1938: the Hungarian Army enters Munkács.

January 6, 1939: Troops of the new Republic of Carpatho-Ukraine, angered by the Vienna Award, clash with Hungarian troops in Munkács.

<u>March 11, 1939:</u> An act is passed by the Hungarian Parliament requiring every man between ages 14 and 70 to perform national defense service.

<u>March 14, 1939:</u> Under German pressure, the Slovaks declare their independence and form the Slovak Republic, a puppet fascist state.

<u>March 15, 1939:</u> The German Army occupies Bohemia and Moravia-Silesia, which constitute the remainder of Czechoslovakia, including Prague, and declares the establishment of a German protectorate under the control of Reinhard Heydrich.

<u>March 16, 1939:</u> The Hungarian Army occupies the remainder of the Subcarpathian Rus, ending the Republic's brief independence.

<u>April 14, 1939:</u> Hungary withdraws from the League of Nations.

<u>April 30, 1939:</u> A World's Fair opens in Flushing Meadow in New York. It would close on October 31 of the following year.

<u>May 5, 1939:</u> The "Second Jewish Law" is passed in order to "prevent the expansion of Jews in public life and in the economy." It excludes Jews from Parliament, prohibits them from working for corporations, and further reduces their numbers in most white-collar professions (to six percent). The law also limits the right of Jews to purchase or hold property. (Béla Imrédy, the Prime Minister, stated in support of the law that, "Our country has an extremely delicate problem which we have to meet, just as we meet all our problems. I am speaking of the Jewish problem...")

<u>May 17, 1939:</u> British White Paper limits Jewish immigration to Palestine to 75,000 in total and restricts Jewish land purchases.

<u>May 22, 1939:</u> Germany and Italy sign the "Pact of Steel."

<u>May 28-29, 1939:</u> In the Hungarian Parliamentary elections, the new Arrow Cross party receives the third highest number of votes (14.4%).

<u>July 1, 1939:</u> The first unarmed labor battalions of "unreliables" (those deemed unsuitable for military service) are formed, led by Army officers and NCOs.

Selective Timeline

August 23, 1939: Germany and the Soviet Union sign a non-aggression pact under which each pledges to remain neutral if the other is attacked by a third party.

September 1, 1939: Germany invades Poland, initiating World War II. Hungary refuses Hitler's request to join in the invasion and over the next few weeks allows tens of thousands of Polish soldiers and refugees to flee into Hungary.

September 3, 1939: Honoring their guarantee of Poland's borders, Great Britain and France declare war on Germany. In Palestine, soldiers are recruited for the British Army. About 26,000 Jews and 6,000 Arabs join to fight with the Allies.

September 17, 1939: The Soviet Union invades Poland from the east.

September 27, 1939: Poland surrenders, and the Polish government flees into exile in London. Germany and the Soviet Union divide Poland between them.

November 30, 1939: The Soviet Union invades Finland, initiating the "Winter War." Volunteer Hungarian troops join the Finns, and Hungary sends war materials to the Finnish Army. By the following March, the Finns sue for an armistice and cede the northern shores of Lake Lagoda and the Finnish coastline on the Arctic Sea to the Soviet Union.

April 9, 1940: Germany invades Denmark and Norway. Denmark surrenders on the day of the attack; Norway holds out until June 9.

May 10, 1940: Germany attacks France and the neutral Low Countries. Luxembourg is occupied that day; the Netherlands surrenders on May 14; and Belgium surrenders on May 28. On June 22, France signs an armistice agreement by which the Germans occupy the northern half of the country and the entire Atlantic coastline. In southern France, a collaborationist regime with its capital in Vichy is established.

June 10, 1940: Italy joins the war on the German side.

June 14, 1940: The Soviet Union begins its occupation of the Baltic States.

June 28, 1940: The Soviet Union forces Romania to cede the eastern province of Bessarabia and the northern half of Bukovina.

July 26, 1940: The mayor of Munkács publishes a list of Jewish and Zionist organizations whose activities are banned.

August 3, 1940: Ze'ev Jabotinsky dies of a heart attack while visiting a Betar self-defense camp in upstate New York.

August 30, 1940: Under the "Second Vienna Award," Germany and Italy arbitrate a decision on the division of the disputed province of Transylvania between Romania and Hungary, awarding 16,790 square kilometers of northern Transylvania to Hungary.

September 6, 1940: Blamed for the land loss caused by the Second Vienna Award, Romanian King Carol's government collapses, and he abdicates in favor of his son, Michael. General Ion Antonescu, appointed President of the Council of Ministers, assumes dictatorial powers and establishes close relations with Germany.

September 27, 1940: The Tripartite Pact is signed in Berlin by representatives of Germany, Italy, and Japan, formally establishing the Axis Powers.

November 1940: Hungary (November 20), Romania (November 22), and Slovakia (November 23) join the Axis Powers.

December 2, 1940: A decree is passed in Hungary ordering Jewish draftees to be enrolled in special Jewish labor battalions. Jews already serving in the Army are expelled from their units.

December 12, 1940: Hungary and neutral Yugoslavia sign an "eternal friendship" pact.

March 27, 1941: In Belgrade, a coup is conducted by a group of pro-Western Serb-nationalist Royal Yugoslav Air Force officers, overthrowing the government of Prime Minister Dragiša Cvetković.

(Two days before the coup, the Cvetković government had signed the Vienna Protocol on the Accession of Yugoslavia to the Tripartite Pact). It brings to power the 17-year-old King Peter II Karadorđević, and a new government is formed, sympathetic to the Allies.

April 6, 1941: Germany, Italy, and Bulgaria declare war on Yugoslavia and invade, leading to its annexation and occupation and the creation of the Independent State of Croatia. (Pal Teleki, Hungary's Prime Minister, committed suicide three days earlier in protest of his country's breaking of the pact with Yugoslavia and its active support of the invasion. In his suicide note to Horthy, Teleki wrote, "We have placed ourselves at the side of scoundrels...") Greece falls to the Axis later in the month.

April 11, 1941: Hungarian troops invade the Yugoslav area formerly within Hungary. Horthy states that Hungary must protect the Hungarian population broken off from the country in 1918.

June 22, 1941: Nazi Germany and its Axis allies invade the Soviet Union.

June 27, 1941: Hungary formally declares war on the Soviet Union, based on an alleged Soviet attack by airplanes on the city of Kassa.

July 12, 1941: The Hungarian National Central Authority for Controlling Foreigners initiates the deportation of people with "unspecified nationality" (the "stateless" Jews, such as Polish refugees).

August 8, 1941: The "Third Jewish Law," formally known as the "Race Protection Law," is enacted in Hungary, intended to "defend the race." It prohibits marriage and sexual relations between Jews and non-Jews. Jews are defined in racial terms. (László Bárdossy, the Prime Minister, stated in support of the law that, "We must try as hard as we can to enable our fellow Hungarians by race to live their lives in racial purity...)

August 27-29, 1941: Approximately 18,000 Jews from Hungary are machine-gunned into mass graves by SS units in the outskirts of Kamenetz-Podolsk.

September 8, 1941: The German siege of Leningrad begins.

September 19, 1941: Kiev falls to the German armies.

November 27, 1941: The Battle of Moscow begins.

December 5, 1941: The United Kingdom declares war on Hungary, Finland, and Romania.

December 7, 1941: Japan attacks the United States at Pearl Harbor. On the following day, the United States declares war on Japan, entering World War II.

December 11, 1941: Germany and Italy declare war on the United States and United Kingdom (and vice versa).

December 13, 1941: Under pressure from Germany, Hungary (along with Bulgaria, Romania and Slovakia) declares war on the United States and the other Allies.

January 4-24, 1942: Hungarian soldiers kill close to 4,000 Yugoslav civilians, mostly Serbs and Jews, during an anti-Chetnik operation in what comes to be known as the "Újvidék Massacre." The responsible officers are prosecuted but escape to Germany.

January 20, 1942: At the Wannsee Conference in Berlin, the Nazi leadership decides that the "final solution to the Jewish problem" is relocation and, later, extermination.

March 9, 1942: Miklós Kállay, a moderate, is appointed Prime Minister, succeeding the more pro-Nazi László Bárdossy.

April 21, 1942: In a speech before the National Council, Kállay states, "I know there is no final solution to this problem other than the removal of the Jews...In the meantime, the Jews must be removed from each and every socially and nationally important position..."

June 5, 1942: After secret talks to set up a Hungarian government-in-exile fail, the United States declares war on Hungary.

June 15, 1942: The "Jewish Estates Expropriation Act" is adopted by the Hungarian Parliament. (Count Gyorgy Apponyi states, in support of the law, "According to the outlook of Christian morality, the right of the individual to property ends where it comes into conflict with the public interest.")

July 29, 1942: The "Jewish Religion Status-Lowering Act" is adopted by the Hungarian Parliament, revoking an 1895 law that had made the Jewish religion equal with others. This law also ruled out any government support for Jewish educational institutions.

July 31, 1942: The Hungarian Parliament passes a law providing formal authority for the existence of the forced labor camps and codifying the already-existing practice that Jews fulfill their military obligation exclusively through the unarmed auxiliary service. (The Minister of Justice, László Radocsay, stated, in support of the law, that "It will be catastrophic if within the army framework there will be those who do their destructive mischief…")

September 4, 1942: Budapest is bombed for the first time, by Russian planes. But the bombings do not continue.

September 6, 1942: The "Fourth Jewish Law" bans Jews from owning or purchasing agricultural property, estates, or tenures of land.

September 21, 1942: Horthy appoints General Vilmos Nagy de Nagybaczon as Minister of Defense. Nagybaczon immediately begins to issue numerous orders for the improvement of conditions for forced laborers.

October 22, 1942: The "Captured Personnel and Material Branch of the U.S. Military Intelligence Service" is established.

December 17, 1942: A joint declaration is issued by the American and British governments on behalf of the Allies, describing the ongoing events of the Holocaust in Nazi-occupied Europe and condemning "in the strongest possible terms this bestial policy of cold-blooded extermination…such events can only strengthen the resolve of all freedom-loving peoples to overthrow the barbarous Hitlerite tyranny. [We] reaffirm [our] solemn resolution to insure that those responsible for these crimes shall not escape retribution and to press on with the necessary practical measures to this end."

January 12, 1943: In weather that fell to as low as -45 degrees Fahrenheit, the Soviet Army attacks the Hungarian 2nd Army at Voronezh. Within week, the 2nd Hungarian Army is annihilated. About 50,000 Hungarian soldiers are killed or freeze to death. 70,000 are taken prisoner or disappear. Of the approximate 50,000 accompanying unarmed labor company members, only a small number return home.

February 2, 1943: The German Sixth Army surrenders to Russian troops at Stalingrad, in the first major defeat of Hitler's armies.

May 10, 1943: The establishment of the Bergen-Belsen civilian internment camp is officially declared.

May 13, 1943: Axis forces in Tunisia surrender to the Allies, ending the North African campaign.

June 8, 1943: Under constant attack by the extreme right, Nagybaczon resigns.

July 10, 1943: U.S. and British troops land on Sicily. By mid-August, the Allies control the island.

July 25, 1943: Italian King Victor Emmanuel III replaces Mussolini with Marshal Pietro Badoglio and has Mussolini arrested.

September 8, 1943: The Italian government surrenders unconditionally to the Allies. But the Germans seize control of Rome and northern Italy, establishing a puppet Fascist regime under Mussolini, who is freed from imprisonment by German commandos on September 12.

September 9, 1943: Allied troops land on the beaches of Salerno near Naples.

October 30, 1943: The Moscow Declaration is issued. In its final section, entitled "Statement on Atrocities," which is signed by Franklin D. Roosevelt, Winston Churchill, and Joseph Stalin, the Declaration points to "evidence of atrocities, massacres and cold-blooded mass executions which are being perpetrated by Hitlerite forces in many of the countries they have overrun and from which they are now being steadily expelled." It went on to state that Germans would be sent back to the countries where they had committed their crimes and "judged on the spot by the peoples whom they have outraged… as for those Germans whose criminal offenses had no particular geographical localization, they would be punished by joint decision of the governments of the Allies."

November 6, 1943: Soviet troops liberate Kiev.

November 9, 1943: The United Nations Relief and Rehabilitation Administration (UNRRA) is created at a 44-nation conference at the White House, with a mission of providing economic assistance to European nations after World War II and to repatriate and assist those refugees who would come under Allied control. The organization is subject to the authority of the Supreme Headquarters of the Allied Expeditionary Forces in Europe. Its first director-general is Herbert Lehman, former governor of New York. He was succeeded in March 1946 by Fiorello La Guardia, former mayor of New York City, who was in turn followed by Major General Lowell Ward in early 1947. It largely shut down operations in 1947.

January 22, 1944: Allied troops land successfully near Anzio, south of Rome.

January 27, 1944: The Siege of Leningrad is lifted, 872 days after it began.

March 19, 1944: Fearing Hungary's intention to desert the Axis partnership, the Germans occupy Hungary without a shot being fired and compel the Regent, Horthy, to appoint pro-German General Döme Sztójay as Prime Minister. This places the instruments of state power—the gendarmerie, police, and civil service—at the disposal of the Nazis. One of Sztójay's first acts is to approve the immediate deportation to Auschwitz of all Jews in the forced labor camp system, a move later stopped by Horthy.

March 20, 1944: German troops arrive in Munkács.

March 24, 1944: President Franklin Roosevelt broadcasts a message to the people of Hungary and Horthy warning them against participating in Nazi crimes. Six days later, British Foreign Minister Anthony Eden makes a similar public statement.

March 27, 1944: German troops enter Cluj.

March 31, 1944: By order of the Prime Minster, Hungarian Jews are required to wear a 4-by-4 inch canary-yellow six-pointed star on the upper left side of their outer garments.

April 2, 1944: The Allies begin bombing Hungarian military targets such as railway staging areas and oil refineries, although many houses and apartments also are destroyed.

April 7, 1944: The Hungarian Ministry of the Interior issues a decree, addressed to the representatives of the local organs of state power, stating that "the Royal Government of Hungary will within a short period of time cleanse the country of the Jews...by regions." The decree stipulates that Jews "would be concentrated in empty warehouses, factories, brickyards, and the Jewish community establishments, schools, offices, and synagogues. These Ghettos are to be near adequate rail facilities to make possible swift entrainment and deportation." Based on this decree, the Hungarian authorities begin rounding up Jews.

Rudolph Vrba and Alfred Wetzler miraculously escape from Auschwitz to Bratislava and subsequently document exhaustively the workings of Auschwitz. Their report, known as the "Auschwitz Protocols," is sent by Slovak Jewish leaders to the Jewish Council in Hungary and other prominent Hungarian figures, including politicians and church leaders. It is soon widely distributed in the Allied countries.

April 28, 1944: By the Prime Minister's decree, the April 7 Interior Ministry confidential decree is formalized, and "yellow-star" houses begin to be established in Budapest.

Selective Timeline

May 11, 1944: The deportation by cattle cars of the Bereg County Jews to Auschwitz commences.

May 19, 1944: The deportation of the Jews in the Munkács ghetto to Auschwitz commences.

May 25, 1944: Munkács and its surroundings are declared totally cleansed of Jews. By the beginning of July, more than half of the Jews in Hungary—approximately 437,000 persons—arrive at Auschwitz, with most being immediately killed.

June 4, 1944: The Allies liberate Rome.

June 6, 1944: Allied troops land on the Normandy beaches of France, opening another front against the Germans.

June 15, 1944: The Hungarian Ministry of the Interior orders the concentration of the Budapest Jews in 2,600 houses marked with a yellow star.

The BBC broadcasts details on Auschwitz from the Vrba-Wetzler Report.

June 24, 1944: The deadline for Budapest Jews to move to designated buildings. On the next day, a strict curfew is imposed for them.

June 25-30, 1944: Pope Pius XII, Franklin Roosevelt, and King Gustav V of Sweden publicly ask Horthy to stop the deportations.

June 26, 1944: Richard Lichtheim, senior representative of the Jewish Agency in Geneva, sends a telegram to the British Foreign Office giving full details of the mass extermination of the Hungarian Jews at Auschwitz. The Hungarian Intelligence Service reads the telegram and shows it to Sztójay, who passes it on to Horthy.

July 7, 1944: Horthy, responding to international pressure, orders an end to the deportations. "I shall not permit the deportations to bring further shame on Hungarians."

July 9, 1944: Swedish diplomat Raoul Wallenberg arrives in Budapest and proceeds to save tens of thousands of Jews by issuing diplomatic papers and establishing "safe houses."

July 20, 1944: An attempt by German military officials to assassinate Hitler fails.

August 23, 1944: King Michael of Romania dismisses the Fascist Prime Minister Ion Antonescu, and Romania leaves the Axis alliance and joins the Allies.

August 25, 1944: German General Dietrich von Choltitz surrenders Paris, ignoring Hitler's order to raze the city to the ground. Charles De Gaulle leads a victory procession down the Champs Elysées. Four days later, the U.S. 28th Infantry Division, on its way to the front, marches down the Champs Elysées as well.

August 29, 1944: Horthy dismisses Sztójay, replacing him with General Géza Lakatos, who holds a moderate view toward Jews. Horthy asks Lakatos to make preparations for Hungary's exit from the war, and assures Samuel Stern, the President of the Budapest Jewish Council, that there will be no more deportations.

September 5, 1944: The Soviet Union declares war on Bulgaria and invades it. Three days later, Bulgaria switches sides and declares war on Germany.

September 7, 1944: Horthy tells his council of the planned peace discussions with the Allies. But the council balks and advises that Hungary continue to rely on Germany as a protective ally and ask it to send troops to protect against the oncoming Russian invasion.

September 20, 1944: In a BBC broadcast, Churchill announces that "His Majesty's government have decided that a Jewish Brigade should be formed to take part in active operations. The Infantry Brigade will be based on the Jewish battalions of the Palestine Regiment..."

September 23, 1944: The Russian Army crosses the Hungarian border.

October 11, 1944: Soviet and Romanian troops liberate Cluj.

Horthy accepts the terms of a preliminary armistice agreement with the Soviet Union.

Selective Timeline

October 15, 1944: After a radio broadcast by Horthy announcing that he is about to conclude a military armistice with the Allies and to cease all hostilities against them (leading Budapest Jews to tear off their yellow stars and emerge from yellow-star buildings), Waffen SS storm troopers kidnap Miklós Horthy Jr. and force Regent Horthy to abdicate. The Hungarian Fascist Arrow Cross movement, with German support, assumes control of the Hungarian government.

October 17, 1944: Adolf Eichmann, head of the Reich Main Security Office for Jewish Affairs, returns to Budapest in order to complete the "Final Solution." By the beginning of November, death marches begin.

October 26, 1944: Soviet troops occupy Munkács.

October 31, 1944: Jewish Brigade troops arrive in Taranto in southern Italy.

November 3, 1944: Soviet troops and tanks reach Budapest's eastern suburbs after breaking through a semi-circular ring of German defenses.

Ferenc Szálasi is sworn in as Prime Minister and head of state of Hungary.

November 4, 1944: The eastern span of the Margit Bridge is accidentally blown up by German engineers fusing demolition charges, killing more than 600 civilians.

November 7, 1944: The German high command announces the successful launch of V-2 rockets against Britain, reviving hope among the Budapest defenders for an Axis victory.

November 8, 1944: 25,000 Jews begin a forced march over 150 kilometers in rain and snow from Budapest to the Austrian border, followed by a second march of 50,000 persons that ends at Mauthausen.

November 13, 1944: The Arrow Cross orders the creation of a general ghetto in Budapest.

December 6, 1944: Hitler designates Budapest as a *Feste Plätze* (fortress), requiring defense to the last man. Stalin, in turn, intent on capturing as much land as possible before the Yalta conference scheduled for early February, orders Marshall Malinovsky, the head of the Soviet forces attacking Budapest, to seize the city as soon as possible.

December 9, 1944: Szálasi flees Budapest.

December 21, 1944: A pro-Communist Hungarian Provisional National Assembly is formed in Debrecen, Hungary. Nine days later, the Assembly declares war on Germany.

December 26, 1944: The Soviet Army completes its encirclement of Budapest, trapping nine German and Hungarian Divisions within the city, together with 800,000 civilians.

January 13, 1945: Soviet soldiers reach the Central Jewish Ghetto, where they find hundreds of bodies in the interior courtyard of the Dohány Synagogue.

January 18, 1945: The Chain Bridge, the first permanent stone-bridge connecting Pest and Buda, is blown up, with only its pillars remaining intact, during the day at a time of peak traffic over it. As German troops evacuate Pest and cross the remaining bridges to Buda, they are raked by Soviet fire. Early the next morning, all those bridges are destroyed by the Germans by explosives, trapping 300,000 Buda residents.

January 27, 1945: Soviet troops liberate Auschwitz-Birkenau (although most of the complex had been evacuated earlier in the month). In spite of Nazi attempts to destroy the evidence of gas chambers and crematoria, the Red Army finds mounds of toothbrushes, eyeglasses, and shoes and mass graves. This date later becomes the United Nations' International Day of Commemoration in Memory of the Victims of the Holocaust.

February 1, 1945: The free Czech provisional government cedes the Subcarpathian Rus to the Soviet Union. In exchange, Stalin guarantees

Selective Timeline

the renewed Czechoslovakia a German-free Sudetenland. After the end of the war, millions of ethnic Germans are forcibly deported across the border into Germany, with thousands dying in the process.

February 13, 1945: Almost all the German and Hungarian defenders of the Royal Castle in Buda, who are out of ammunition and rations, are killed while attempting to break out and flee to the west. The battle for Budapest ends. During the siege, an estimated 160,000 soldiers and civilians died. Soviet troops are granted three days of free looting and rape.

April 4, 1945: The remainder of Hungary is liberated (a date celebrated for years after as Liberation Day).

A new Czechoslovak government is installed in Košice, Slovakia (recently liberated by the Red Army), consisting of parties united in the National Front and strongly influenced by the Communist Party of Czechoslovakia.

The American 4th Armoured Division of the Third Army overruns a concentration camp at Ohrdruf, the first one the American Army would liberate. The soldiers are unprepared to care for the hundreds of skeletal inmates living among thousands of unburied corpses.

April 11, 1945: Forward elements of the U.S. 6th Armored Division, along with the inmates' underground organization, liberate the Buchenwald concentration camp. (The Buchenwald clock tower's hands are permanently set at 3:15 pm, when the American soldiers entered the camp.) Twenty-one thousand prisoners were freed, one of them being a teen-aged Elie Wiesel. Many die in the following days.

April 12, 1945: Franklin D. Roosevelt dies in Warm Springs, Georgia. He is succeeded by Vice President Harry Truman.

April 13, 1945: Vienna is liberated by Soviet troops.

April 15, 1945: After negotiations with the Germany Army, the 11th British Armoured Division liberates the Bergen-Belsen concentration camp without a fight.

April 28, 1945: Mussolini and his mistress, Clara Petacci, are shot to death by Communist partisans. On the following day, a mob hangs their bodies upside down on meat hooks at a gas station in the Piazzale Loreto, south of Milan, where fifteen hostages had been shot by Fascists the previous August.

April 29, 1945: The 45th Division of the U.S. 7th Army liberates the Dachau concentration camp.

April 30, 1945: Hitler and Eva Braun, his wife of two days, commit suicide in his underground bunker under the Chancellery in Berlin. In accordance with Hitler's last will and testament, Admiral Karl Dönitz is named Head of State.

May 6, 1945: Mauthausen, the last concentration camp to be liberated, is taken without a fight by the U.S. 3rd Army.

May 7, 1945: Dönitz orders Germany's surrender, effective at midnight on the next day.

May 9, 1945: The Soviet Army enters Prague soon after a failed uprising.

June 29, 1945: By treaty, the Subcarpathian Rus is formally ceded by Czechoslovakia to the Soviet Union.

August 3, 1945: Earl G. Harrison, Dean of the University of Pennsylvania Law School, issues in preliminary form a report, which had been commissioned by President Truman, sharply criticizing the Army for its lack of proper treatment of Jewish survivors.

September 17, 1945: The war crimes trial of Josef Kramer, the commandant of Bergen-Belsen (and before that of Auschwitz), and 44 other former SS men and women, and capos, begins in a gymnasium in Lüneburg, Germany, before a British military tribunal.

September 30, 1945: The borders of the Rus are closed by the Soviet authorities.

November 20, 1945: The trials of 21 senior Nazi officials begin in The Palace of Justice in Nuremberg, where the Nazis had held their annual rallies.

<u>December 13, 1945:</u> Eleven of the Lüneburg defendants, including Kramer, are hanged.

<u>December 22, 1945:</u> President Truman issues a directive instructing various government departments to facilitate the immigration from Europe of displaced persons under existing quotas. ("I consider that common decency and the fundamental comradeship of all human beings require us to do what lies within our power to see that our established immigration quotas are used in order to reduce human suffering.")

<u>February 1, 1946:</u> The Kingdom of Hungary is dissolved, and the Second Hungarian Republic is established.

<u>March 12, 1946:</u> Ferenc Szálasi is hanged in Budapest.

<u>October 1, 1946:</u> The final verdicts at the Nuremberg Trials are delivered. Those who received the death sentence are hanged on October 16, 1946, except for Hermann Göring, who commits suicide the night before by taking cyanide.

<u>February 10, 1947:</u> The Paris Peace Treaties are signed by the Allies, restoring Hungary to its prewar borders.

<u>February 18, 1948:</u> Hungary and the Soviet Union sign a Treaty of Friendship and Mutual Aid.

<u>February 21-25, 1948:</u> The Communist Party of Czechoslovakia, with Soviet backing, assumes undisputed control over the government of Czechoslovakia.

<u>May 14, 1948:</u> The Israeli Declaration of Independence is proclaimed by David Ben-Gurion.

<u>August 20, 1949:</u> The Socialist People's Republic of Hungary is established, governed by the Socialist Workers' Party and subservient to the Soviet Union.

<u>June 19, 1953:</u> Julius and Ethel Rosenberg are executed in the electric chair, after being convicted of passing information about the atomic bomb to the Soviet Union.

April-June 1954: The Army-McCarthy hearings are held and dominate national television. A subcommittee of the Senate Committee on Government Operations seeks to learn whether Senator Joseph R. McCarthy used improper influence to win preferential treatment for Pvt. G. David Schine, a former member of the senator's staff who had been drafted. McCarthy countercharged that the army was trying to derail his embarrassing investigations of army security practices through blackmail and intimidation.

May 14, 1955: The USSR, Hungary, and six other European countries establish the Warsaw Pact in response to the integration of the Federal Republic of Germany into NATO.

July 26, 1956: Gamal Abdel Nasser, the President of Egypt, orders the nationalization of the Suez Canal Company.

October 23, 1956: The beginning of the Hungarian Revolution, with mass protests in Budapest, which are met with violence by the Hungarian Communist authorities. Over the next few days, battles break out in Budapest and spread throughout the country. Soviet tanks fire upon demonstrators. Imre Nagy, a reformer, returns as Prime Minister.

October 29, 1956: Israeli forces cross the Egyptian frontier and drive toward the Suez Canal.

October 31, 1956: Anglo-French forces attack Egypt in the Canal Zone. Israeli troops begin to occupy the Gaza Strip and key points in the Sinai Peninsula.

November 4, 1956: Soviet tanks and troops invade Hungary and, over the next week, crush the revolution. Many buildings in central Budapest are damaged or destroyed. Thousands of refugees flee across the border to Austria. Tens of thousands are jailed or deported to the Soviet Union.

November 6, 1956: A Middle East cease fire commences.

November 8, 1956: The Middle East hostilities end.

Selective Timeline

February 9, 1957: Horthy dies at age 88 in Estoril, Portugal, having never been punished for his activities during the war.

May 11, 1960: Adolf Eichmann is captured by Israeli operatives in Argentina.

May 23, 1960: Israeli Prime Minister David Ben-Gurion announces that Eichmann is in Israel and will be tried there.

April 11, 1961: The Eichmann trial opens in Jerusalem.

December 11, 1961: Eichmann found guilty.

May 31, 1962: Eichmann executed at midnight in Ramle Prison.

May 18, 1963: In a personal letter to David Ben-Gurion, Prime Minister of Israel, President Kennedy warns that unless American inspectors are allowed into Dimona to search for evidence of nuclear weapons, Israel would find itself totally isolated. Rather than answering, Ben-Gurion abruptly resigns less than a month later.

April 22, 1964: A World's Fair opens in Flushing Meadow in New York for the second time. It would close on October 17 of the following year.

October 31, 1967: The *RMS Queen Mary*, which for decades after the war had ruled the North Atlantic passage along with her sister ship, the *RMS Queen* Elizabeth, leaves Southampton for the last time and sails to the port of Long Beach, California, where she remains permanently moored.

November 19, 1977: Egyptian president Anwar Sadat makes an historic visit to Israel, where he addresses the Israeli Parliament.

December 27, 1977: Israeli Prime Minister Menachem Begin visits Cairo, laying the groundwork for a peace treaty between Egypt and Israel.

June 16, 1990: The last Soviet occupation troops leave Hungary.

August 24, 1991: After the collapse of the Soviet Union, the Ukraine is formally declared an independent democratic state. The Subcarpathian Rus becomes a part of the Ukraine.

BIBLIOGRAPHY

Abraham Levy & Sebastian Burckhardt, *The Moon Was My Witness: The Jewish Boy Who Sabotaged the S.S. Commander's Motorcycle* (2015)

Abram L. Sachar, *The Redemption of the Unwanted: From the Liberation of the Death Camps to the Founding of Israel* (St. Martin's/Marek, 1983)

Aharon Golub (with Bennett W. Golub), *Kaddishel: A Life Reborn* (Devora Publishing Company, 2005)

Al Zelczer, *Eight Pieces of Silk: What I Could Not Tell My Children* (Zelczer Publishing, 2013)

Albert Einstein, *The World as I See It* (Philosophical Library, 1949)

Albert Lazar & Steve Chadde, *Innocents Condemned to Death: Chronicles of Survival* (Uncommon Valor Press, 2014)

Alexander Baron, *Rainbows Among the Ruins: One Man's Epic Journey* (Lulu.com, 2011)

Allis Radosh & Ronald Radosh, *A Safe Haven: Harry Truman and the Founding of Israel,* (Harper Perennial, 2010)

Bibliography

Anna Scanlon, *Unravelled* (Key Imprints, 2014)

Andrew Fodor, *The Survivor's Song: Unarmed Soldiers—Budapest to Stalingrad and Back* (CreateSpace 2012)

Anna Berger, *Munkács: A Jewish World That Was*, (thesis submitted in fulfillment of the requirements for the degree of Master of Arts, Department of Hebrew, Biblical and Jewish Studies, The University of Sydney, July 2009)

Aranka Siegal, *Upon the Head of the Goat: A Childhood in Hungary 1939–1944* (Square Fish, 2003)

Arthur Hertzberg, *Being Jewish in America: The Modern Experience* (Schocken Books, 1979)

Ben Lesser, *Living a Life that Matters: From Nazi Nightmare to American Dream* (Abbott Press, 2012)

Ben Shepard, *After Daybreak: The Liberation of Bergen-Belsen, 1945* (Schocken Books, 2005)

Ben Shepard, *The Long Road Home: The Aftermath of the Second World War* (Alfred A. Knopf, 2011)

Benedictus de Spinoza, *The Philosophy of Spinoza* (edited by Joseph Ratner) (The Modern Library, 1954)

Bernice Eisenstein, *I Was a Child of Holocaust Survivors* (Riverhead Books, 2006)

Bill Cotter & Bill Young, *Images of America: The 1964–1965 New York World's Fair: Creation and Legacy* (Arcadia Publishing, 2014)

Bill Kertes, *A Survivor's Story; Enduring and Overcoming the Horrors of the Holocaust* (2011)

Budapest Holocaust Memorial Center web site at http://old.hdke.hu/index.php

Cecil D. Eby, *Hungary at War: Civilians and Soldiers in World War II* (Pennsylvania State University Press, 1998)

Charles Farkas, *Vanished by the Danube: Peace, War, Revolution, and Flight to the West* (State University of New York Press, Albany, 2013)

Charles River Editors, *The Munich Agreement of 1938: The History of the Peace Pact that Failed to Prevent World War II* (2015)

Clouded Sky: Poems by Miklós Radnóti (translated by Steven Polgar, Stephen Berg, and S. J. Marks, The Sheep Meadow Press, 1972)

Collected memories of the Holocaust, at www.museumoffamilyhistory.com (Brad Kleinmann)

Dalia Ofer, *Escaping the Holocaust: Illegal Immigration to the Land of Israel, 1939–1944* (Oxford University Press, 1990)

David. S. Ariel, *What Do Jews Believe: The Spiritual Foundations of Judaism* (Jill Grinberg Literary Management, 2014)

David Cesarani, *Becoming Eichmann: Rethinking the Life, Crimes, and Trial of a "Desk Murderer"* (Da Capo Press, 2004)

David Clay Large, *Between Two Fires: Europe's Path in the 1930s* (W.W. Norton & Company, 1990)

David Ellery, *RMS Queen Mary: 101 Questions and Answers About the Great Transatlantic Liner* (Casemate Publishing, 2006)

David Halberstam, *The Fifties* (Ballantine Books, 1994)

David Hartman & Charlie Buckholtz, *The God Who Hates Lies: Confronting & Rethinking Jewish Tradition* (Jewish Lights Publishing, 2011)

David R. Hawkins, *Power vs. Force: The Hidden Determinants of Human Behavior* (Veritas Publishing, 2013)

David Laskin, *The Family: Three Journeys Into the Heart of the Twentieth Century* (Penguin Group, 2013)

Deborah S. Cornelius, *Hungary in World War II: Caught in the Cauldron* (Fordham University Press, 2011)

Deborah E. Lipstadt, *The Eichmann Trial* (Schocken Books, 2011)

Earl F. Ziemke, *The German Defeat in the East* (Pickle Partners Publishing, 2013)

Early Judaism: A Comprehensive Overview, edited by John J. Collins and Daniel C. Harlow (William B. Eerdmans Publishing, 2010)

Edith Hahn Beer & Susan Dworkin, *The Nazi Officer's Wife: How One Jewish Woman Survived the Holocaust* (Harper Perennial, 2012)

Elaine Kálmán Naves, *Journey to Vaja* (McGill-Queen's University Press, 1996)

Elaine Kálmán Naves, *Shoshanna's Story: A Mother, A Daughter, and the Shadows of History* (University of Nebraska Press, 2003)

Elizabeth Stewart & Ashley Ekins, *War Wounds: Medicine and the Trauma of Conflict* (Exisle Publishing, 2011)

Elizabeth Urbahn, *Shadows in the Lake* (2013)

Encyclopedia Britannica (1911 ed.)

Eoin Dempsey, *Finding Rebecca* (Lake Union Publishing, 2014)

Epiphanius Wilson, *Hebrew Literature* (Colonial Press, 1901)

Erika Elinson, *And I Knew It Not* (Sweet-Art, 2008)

Ernő Szép, *The Smell of Humans: A Memoir of the Holocaust in Hungary* (Central European University Press, 1984)

Eugen Schoenfeld, *Faith & Conflict: Reflections on Christian Faith's Impact on the Rise of the Holocaust* (2001)

Eugene L. Pogany, *In My Brother's Image: Twin Brothers Separated by Faith After the Holocaust* (Penguin Books, 2000)

Eugene Weinstock, *Beyond the Last Path: A Buchenwald Survivor's Story* (Uncommon Valor Press, 2014)

Ezra Mendelsohn, *The Jews of East Central Europe Between the World Wars* (Indiana University Press, 1983)

Ferenc Váradi, *1944 a Leap Year* (P/V Enterprises Inc., 2008)

Flint Whitlock, *The Beasts of Buchenwald: Karl & Ilse Koch, Human-Skin Lampshades, and the War-Crimes Trial of the Century* (Cable Publishing, 2011)

Fred Tessler, *Lost in War* (CreateSpace, 2014)

G.S. Johnston, *The Skin of Water* (2012)

Gabriella Kovacs & Oliver R. Shead, *Georgina: My Mother's Story* (Lightning Source, 2013)

George Eber, *Pinball Games: Arts of Survival in the Nazi and Communist Eras* (Trafford Publishing, 2010)

George Kaczender, *Notebook of an Incurable Romantic* (Red Cat Tales, 2013)

George Konrád, *A Guest in my Own Country: A Hungarian Life* (Other Press, 2002)

Gustav Schonfeld, *Absence of Closure*, (2008)

Guy Walters, *Berlin Games* (HarperCollins Publishers, 2009)

Hannah Trager, *Picture of Jewish Home-Life Fifty Years Ago* (2012)

Harald Waitzbauer, *Over the Mountain—to the Promised Land* (at http://www.alpinepeacecrossing.org/o/104.pdf)

Harry Weinberg, *Against the Tide* (Shengold Publishers, 1989)

Helen Colin, *My Dream of Freedom* (SkipJack Publishing, 2013)

Helen Epstein, *Children of the Holocaust: Conversations with Sons and Daughters of Survivors* (Penguin Books, 1979)

Helen Szablya, *My Only Choice: Hungary 1942–1956* (CreateSpace2013)

Henry Orenstein, *I Shall Live: Surviving the Holocaust Against All Odds* (Beaufort Books, 2010)

Herman Dicker, *Piety and Perseverance* (Sepher-Hermon Press, 1981)

Igor Lukes, *Czechoslovakia between Stalin and Hitler: The Diplomacy of Edvard Benes in the 1930s* (Oxford University Press, 1996)

Imre Kertész, *Fatelessness* (Northwestern University Press, 1992)

In the Catskills: A Century of the Jewish Experience in "The Mountains," Phil Brown editor (Columbia University Press, 2002)

Israel Abrahams, *Judaism* (originally published in 1907)

Jack Riemer, *Jewish Insights on Death and Mourning* (Schocken Books, 2012)

Jack Sacco, *Where the Birds Never Sing: The True Story of the 92nd Signal Battalion and the Liberation of Dachau* (HarperCollins Publishers, 2003)

James Frank, *Beginnings* (ZAP Studio, 2013)

James Steele, *Queen Mary* (Phaidon Press, 2001)

Jean M. Peck, *At the Fire's Center: A Story of Love and Holocaust Survival* (University of Illinois Press, 1998)

Jeffrey S. Gurock, *Jews in Gotham: New York Jews in a Changing City, 1920–2010 (City of Promises: a History of the Jews of New York)* (NYU Press, 2013)

Jeffrey Shandler, *While America Watches: Televising the Holocaust* (Oxford University Press, 1999)

Jewish Virtual Library at http://www.jewishvirtuallibrary.org

John Lukacs, *Budapest 1900: A Historical Portrait of a City and its Culture* (Grove Press, 1988)

John Toland, *The Last 100 Days: The Tumultuous and Controversial Story of the Final Days of World War II in Europe* (Random House, 1966)

Joint Distribution Committee Information Service Letter (File No. 74.01, September 24, 1920)

Joseph Rothschild, *East Central Europe Between the Two World Wars* (University of Washington Press, 1974)

Joseph B. Schechtman, *The Life and Times of Vladimir Jabotinsky: Fighter and Prophet, The Last Years* (Eshel Books, 1961)

Julie Orringer, *The Invisible Bridge* (Vintage Books, 2010)

Julie Salamon, *The Net of Dreams: A Family's Search for a Rightful Place* (Random House, 1996)

Katherine Griesz, *From the Danube to the Hudson* (Create Space, 2012)

Kati Marton, *Wallenberg: The Incredible True Story of the Man Who Saved Thousands of Jews* (Arcade Publishing, 1982)

Kaufmann Kohler, *Jewish Theology* (The Macmillan Company, 1918)

Keith Lowe, *Savage Continent: Europe in the Aftermath of World War II* (St. Martin's Press, 2012)

Kenneth Macksey, *The Partisan of Europe in the Second World War*, (Stein and Day Publishers, 1975)

Kinga Frojimovics, Géza Komoróczy, Viktória Pusztai, and Andrea Strbik, *Jewish Budapest: Monuments, Rites, History* (Central European University Press, 1999)

Kleinmann Family Foundation, "Munkács Ghetto—Jews Alone" available at http://www.kffeducation.org/joomla/Brad-kleinmanns-memoir/one/Munkács-ghetto-jews-alone.html

Krisztián Ungváry, *The Siege of Budapest: One Hundred Days in World War II* (Yale University Press, 2002)

Lawrence L. Langer, *Holocaust Testimonies: The Ruins of Memory* (Yale University Press, 1991)

Leonard Dinnerstein, *America and the Survivors of the Holocaust* (Columbia University Press, 1982)

Leslie Maitland, *Crossing the Borders of Time: A True Story of War, Exile, and Love Reclaimed* (Other Press, 2012)

Levi Cooper, *Legislation for Education: The Munkács Regulations Enacted by Rabbi Tsevi Elimelekh of Dynów*

Life Reborn: Jewish Displaced Persons 1945-1951 (edited with an introduction by Menachem Z. Rosensaft, 2001)

Linda Pressman, *Looking Up: A Memoir of Sisters, Survivors, and Skokie* (CreateSpace, 2012)

Livia Bitton-Jackson, *I Have Lived a Thousand Years: Growing Up in the Holocaust* (Simon Pulse, 1997)

Lola Taubman, *My Story* (2012)

Lucy Lipiner, *Long Journey Home: A Young Girl's Memoir of Surviving the Holocaust* (Usher Publishing, 2013)

Madelaine D. Lang, *Diary of a Young Jewish Girl: World War II Hungary 1941–1946* (CreateSpace, 2012)

Madeline Albright, *Prague Winter: A Personal Story of Remembrance and War, 1937–1948* (Harper Collins, 2012)

Magda Herzberger, *Survival* (2005)

Marianne Szegedy-Maszák, *I Kiss Your Hand Many Times: Hearts, Souls and Wars in Hungary* (Spiegel & Grau, 2013)

Marilyn Mayes Kaltenborn, *An Unconventional Childhood: Growing Up in the Catskill Mountains During the 1950s and 1960s* (The Troy Book Makers, 2013)

Mark Wyman, *DPs: Europe's Displaced Persons, 1945–1951* (Cornell University Press, 1989)

Marta Fuchs, *Legacy of Rescue: A Daughter's Tribute* (Családnak Press, 2011)

Martin Gilbert, *The Second World War* (Henry Holt & Co., 1989)

Martin Greenfield and Wynton Hall, *Measure of a Man: From Auschwitz Survivor to Presidents' Tailor* (Regnery Publishing, 2014)

Maurice McLoughlin, *The Herring: The Holocaust Childhood in Slave Labour of Andras Herskovitz* (Boston Cloud Press, 2013)

Mel Meckler, *Betrayal in Budapest* (2012)

Mel Mermelstein, *By Bread Alone* (Auschwitz Study Foundation, 1979)

Michael Benanav, *The Luck of the Jews: An Incredible Story of Loss, Love, and Survival in the Holocaust* (2014)

Michael Coogan, *The Old Testament: A Very Short Introduction* (Oxford University Press, 2008)

Michael Korda, *Journey to a Revolution* (HarperCollins, 2006)

Michael Lipiner, *Magyar, Stars and Stripes: A Journey from Hungary through the Holocaust and to New York* (iUniverse, Inc., 2005)

Morris Beckman, *The Jewish Brigade: An Army with Two Masters 1944–1945* (The History Press, 2010)

Moshe Goldstein, *Journey to Jerusalem: The Historic Visit of the Minchas Eluzar of Munkács to the Saba Kadisha* (Mesorah Publications, Ltd., 2009)

Moshe Y. Herczl, *Christianity and the Holocaust of Hungarian Jewry* (New York University Press, 1993)

Moyshe Rekhtman (with Phil Shpilberg), *Here My Home Once Stood* (Fourth Generation Publishing, 2008)

Naomi Litvin, *We Never Lost Hope: A Holocaust Memoir and Love Story* (2008)

Neal Bascomb, *Hunting Eichmann: How a Band of Survivors and a Young Spy Agency Chased Down the World's Most Notorious Nazi* (Mariner Books, 2010)

Nicholas Best, *Five Days That Shocked The World: Eyewitness Accounts from Europe at the End of World War II* (Thomas Dunne Books, 2012)

Nigel Thomas & Laszlo Szabo, *The Royal Hungarian Army in World War II (Men-at-Arms)* (Osprey Publishing, 2012)

Pearl Fichman, *Before Memories Fade* (2011)

Peter Hart, *The Somme: The Darkest Hour on the Western Front* (Pegasus Books, 2009)

Peter Tegel, *From a Faraway Country* (Conrad Press, 2013)

Philip Yancy, *Where Is God When It Hurts?* (Zondervan, 1997)

Prit Buttar, *Battleground Prussia: The Assault on Germany's Eastern Front 1944–45* (Osprey Publishing, 2012)

Rabbi Samuel Freilich, *The Coldest Winter* (Holocaust Library, 1988)

Rabbi Yitzchak Kasnett, *The World That Was: Hungary/Romania: A Study of the Life and Torah Consciousness of Jews in the Cities and Villages of Transylvania, The Carpathian Mountains, and Budapest* (The Living Memorial c/o Hebrew Academy of Cleveland, 1999)

Rani Drew, *The Dog's Tale: A Life in the Buda Hills* (Whyte Tracks, 2010)

Raz Segal, *Days of Ruin: The Jews of Munkács During the Holocaust* (Yad Vashem, 2013)

Raz Segal, *Becoming Bystanders: Carpatho-Ruthenians, Jews, and the Politics of Narcissism in Subcarpathian Rus* (Holocaust Studies: A Journal of Culture and History, Vol. 16, No. 1-2, Summer/Autumn 2010)

Rebecca Boehling & Uta Larkey, *Life and Loss in the Shadow of the Holocaust: A Jewish Family's Untold Story* (Cambridge University Press, 2011)

Recollections of the Holocaust at www.degob.com (the staff of the Hungarian Jewish relief organization, National Committee for Attending Deportees (DEGOB) recorded the personal stories of approximately 5,000 Hungarian Holocaust survivors in 1945–46)

Roberta Dietzen, *Gypsy Music Street* (2013)

Rod Israeli, *Living with Dreams: The Days and Nights of Ági Israeli* (2014)

Rodger Kamenetz, *The Jew in the Lotus* (HarperCollins, 2009)

Ruth R. Wisse, *If I Am Not for Myself...The Liberal Betrayal of the Jews* (The Free Press, 1992)

Ruth R. Wisse, *Jews and Power* (Schocken Books, 2007)

Sándor Márai, *Memoir of Hungary: 1944–1948* (Corvina Books Ltd., 1996)

Sara Tuvel Bernstein, *The Seamstress: A Memoir of Survival* (Berkley Books, 1997)

Shari Ryan & Emma Fuchs, *My Kaleidoscope* (Booktrope, 2014)

Shari Vester, *Degrees of Courage* (Mill City Press, 2013)

Stefan Kanfer, *A Summer World: The Attempt to Build a Jewish Eden in the Catskills, From the Days of the Ghetto to the Rise and Decline of the Borscht Belt* (Farrar Straus Giroux, 1989)

Stephen Nasser (with Sherry Rosenthal), *My Brother's Voice: How a Young Hungarian Boy Survived the Holocaust* (Stephens Press, 2003)

Steven Kleiman, *The History of MIS-Y: U.S. Strategic Interrogation During the War (World War II)* (Penny Hill Press, 2006)

Steven J. Zaloga, *Liberation of Paris: Patton's Race for the Seine* (Osprey Publishing Ltd., 2008)

Sune Persson, *Escape From the Third Reich: The Harrowing True Story of the Largest Rescue Effort Inside Nazi Germany* (Skyhorse Publishing, 2002)

Susan Cernyak-Spatz, *Protective Custody: Prisoner 34042* (N and S Publishers, 2005)

Susanna Kokkonen, *The Jewish Refugees in Postwar Italy, 1945–1951: The Way to Eretz Israel* (Lap Lambert Academic Publishing, December 29, 2011)

T. Zane Reeves, *Shoes Along the Danube: Based on a True Story* (Eloquent Books, 2011)

Talking With Angels: A Document from Hungary (transcribed by Gitta Mallasz) (Daimon Verlag, 1988)

The Buchenwald Report, translated Budapest David A. Hackett (prepared in April–May 1945 by a special intelligence team from the Psychological Warfare Division, SHAEF) (Westview Press, 1995)

The Nazis' Last Victims: The Holocaust in Hungary, Randolph L. Braham and Scott Miller, editors (Wayne State University Press, 1998) (published in association with the United States Holocaust Memorial Museum)

The Wartime System of Labor Service in Hungary: Varieties of Experiences, Randolph L. Braham, editor (Holocaust Studies Series, Columbia University Press, 1995)

The Zionist Idea: A Historical Analysis and Reader, Arthur Hertzberg, editor (Atheneum, 1959)

Tom Segev, *One Palestine, Complete: Jews and Arabs Under the British Mandate* (Henry Holt & Company LLC, 1999)

United States Holocaust Memorial Museum, Holocaust Encyclopedia, Jewish Community of Munkács: An Overview, at http://www.ushmm.org

Valdemar Langlet, *Reign of Terror: The Budapest Memoir of Valdemar Langlet 1944–1945* (Frontline Books, 2012) (first published in 1946)

Vera Herman Goodkin, *In Sunshine and In Shadow: We Remember Them* (ComteQ Publishing, 2006)

Victor Frankl, *Man's Search for Meaning* (Beacon Press, 1959)

Victor Sebestyen, *Twelve Days: The Story of the 1956 Hungarian Revolution* (Vintage Books, 2006)

William B. Helmreich, *Against All Odds: Holocaust Survivors and the Successful Lives They Made in America* (Transaction Publishers, 1996)

William Shirer, *Berlin Diary: The Journal of a Foreign Correspondent 1934–1949* (Alfred A. Knopf, 1941)

Winston Churchill, *The Gathering Storm* (Houghton Mifflin Company, 1948)

Yad Vashem: A Jewish Community in the Carpathian Mountains – The Story of Munkács, at http://www1.yadvashem.org.

Yad Vashem: Holocaust Survivor Testimonies: Munkács Under Hungarian Rule, at http://www.youtube.com.

Yehoshue Perle, *Everyday Jews: Scenes From a Vanished Life* (The New Yiddish Library, 2013)

Yeshayahu A. Jelinek, *The Carpathian Diaspora* (Columbia University Press, 2007)

Zoltán Vági, László Csősz, & Gábor Kádár, *The Holocaust in Hungary: Evolution of a Genocide (Documenting Life and Destruction: Holocaust Sources in Context)* (AltaMira Press 2013)

Zsuzsanna Ozsváth, *When the Danube Ran Red* (Syracuse University Press 2010)

www.ingramcontent.com/pod-product-compliance
Lightning Source LLC
Chambersburg PA
CBHW060906300426
44112CB00011B/1368